THE NORTON/GROVE
HANDBOOKS IN MUSIC
PERFORMANCE
PRACTICE
MUSIC BEFORE 1600

THE NORTON/GROVE
HANDBOOKS IN MUSIC

PERFORMANCE PRACTICE

MUSIC BEFORE 1600

Edited by HOWARD MAYER BROWN and STANLEY SADIE

W. W. NORTON & COMPANY

NEW YORK   LONDON

Parts of this material first published in
The New Grove Dictionary of Music and Musicians®,
edited by Stanley Sadie, 1980

The New Grove and *The New Grove Dictionary of Music and Musicians*
are registered trademarks of Macmillan Publishers Limited, London

First published in the UK 1989 by
THE MACMILLAN PRESS LTD
Houndmills, Basingstoke, Hampshire RG21 2XS
and London
Companies and representatives throughout the world

British Library Cataloguing in Publication Data
Performance practice. — (The New Grove handbooks in
musicology).
1. Western music. Performance, 1450–
I. Brown, Howard Mayer, 1930 — II. Sadie, Stanley,
1930 — III. The new grove dictionary of music and
musicians
780'.903
ISBN 0–333–47404–X (hardback)

First American edition 1990

All rights reserved.

W. W. Norton & Company, Ltd.,
500 Fifth Avenue, New York NY 10110
W. W. Norton & Company, Ltd.,
37 Great Russell Street, London WC1B 3NU

ISBN 0-393-02807-0

Typeset by Footnote Graphics,
Warminster, Wiltshire

Printed in Great Britain

1 2 3 4 5 6 7 8 9 0

Contents

Illustration Acknowledgments

We are grateful to the following for permission to reproduce illustrative material. (Every effort has been made to contact copyright holders; we apologise to anyone who may have been omitted): Bibliothèque Royale Albert Ier, Brussels (p.8); Biblioteca Medicea Laurenziana, Florence (p.16); Patrimonio Nacionale, Madrid (p.19); Instituto centrale per il catologo e documentazione, Rome (p.20) photo MAS, Barcelona (p.26); Universitätsbibliothek, Heidelberg (cover, p.30); photo Lauros Giraudon, Paris (p.40); British Library, London (p.43); Rijkmuseum Meermanno-Westreenianum, The Hague (p.91); Nationale Forschungs- und Gedekstätten der klassischen deutschen Literatur, Weimar (p.172); Pinacoteca nazionale, Ferrara (p.174); Koninklijke Bibliotheek, The Hague (p.202); Österreichische Nationalbibliothek, Vienna (p.156, p.205, p.258); National Portrait Gallery, London (p.230); Kunsthistorisches Museum, Vienna (p.228).

Abbreviations

AcM	Acta musicologica	LSJ	The Lute Society Journal
AMf	Archiv für Musikforschung	MB	Musica Britannica
AMw	Archiv für Musikwissenschaft	MD	Musica Disciplina
AnM	Anuario musical	Mf	Die Musikforschung
AnMc	Analecta musicologica	MGG	Die Musik in Geschichte und
AnnM	Annales musicologiques		Gegenwart
BrownI	H. M. Brown: Instrumental	MGH	Monumenta Germaniae
	Music Printed before 1600:		Historica
	a Bibliography (Cambridge,	ML	Music and Letters
	Mass., 2/1967)	MME	Monumentos de la música
CEKM	Corpus of Early Keyboard		española
	Music	MMg	Monatschefte für
CHM	Collectanea historiae		Musikgeschichte
	musicae	MQ	The Musical Quarterly
CMc	Current Musicology	MRM	Monuments of Renaissance
CMM	Corpus mensurabilis		Music
	musicae	MSD	Musicological Studies and
CS	E. de Coussemaker:		Documents, ed. A.
	Scriptorum de musica medii		Carapetyan (Rome 1951–)
	aevi nova series (Paris,	MT	The Musical Times
	1864–76/R1963)	MTS	Music Theory Spectrum
CSM	Corpus scriptorum de	MusA	Music Analysis
	musica	NOHM	The New Oxford History of
DJbM	Deutsches Jahrbuch der		Music, ed. E. Wellesz, J. A.
	Musikwissenschaft		Westrup and G. Abraham
EDM	Das Erbe deutscher Musik		(London, 1954–)
EM	Early Music	PalMus	Paléographie musicale
EMH	Early Music History		(Solesmes, 1889–)
GfMKB	Gesellschaft für	PAMS	Papers of the American
	Musikforschung		Musicological Society
	Kongressbericht	PÄMw	Publikationen älterer
Grove 6	The New Grove Dictionary of		praktischer und
	Music and Musicians		theoretischer Musikwerke
GroveMI	The New Grove Dictionary of	PL	Patrologiae cursus
	Musical Instruments		completus, i: Series latina,
GS	M. Gerbert: Scriptores		ed. J.-P. Migne (Paris,
	ecclesiastici de musica sacra		1844–64)
	(St Blasien, 1784/R1963)	PMFC	Polyphonic Music of the
GSJ	The Galpin Society Journal		Fourteenth Century
HMT	Handwörterbuch der	PRMA	Proceedings of the Royal
	musikalischen Terminologie		Musical Association
IMSCR	International Musicological	RBM	Revue belge de musicologie
	Society Congress Report	RdM	Revue de musicologie
JAMS	Journal of the American	RIM	Rivista italiana di
	Musicological Society		musicologia
JM	Journal of Musicology	RISM	Répertoire international des
JPMMS	Journal of the Plainsong and		sources musicales
	Mediaeval Music Society	RMARC	R[oyal] M[usical]
JRMA	Journal of the Royal Musical		A[ssociation] Research
	Association		Chronicle
JVgGSA	Journal of the Viola da	RMFC	Recherches sur la musique
	Gamba Society of America		française classique

Abbreviations

RMI	Rivista musicale italiana	*TVNM*	*Tijdschrift van de Vereniging*
RRMR	Recent Researches in Music		*voor Nederlandse*
	of the Renaissance		*muziekgeschiedenis*
RQ	*Renaissance Quarterly*	*VMw*	*Vierteljahrsschrift für*
SIMG	*Sammelbande der*		*Musikwissenschaft*
	Internationalen Musik-	WE	Wellesley Edition
	Gesellschaft	*ZMw*	*Zeitschrift für*
SATF	*Société des Anciens Textes*		*Musikwissenschaft*
	Français		

Preface

'Early music', that is, music composed more than 40 years ago (to paraphrase Johannes Tinctoris, the 15th-century theorist who claimed no music written more than 40 years before was worth hearing), has been cultivated at various times and places in the history of the West. Most of the manuscripts containing the songs of the troubadours, for example, were copied out long after the music was composed. The Squarcialupi Codex prepared in the 15th century, some time after the death of Francesco Landini, was intended to celebrate the achievements of the musicians of Florence, evidently as a kind of historical record. By the second half of the 16th century, a number of musicians regularly performed music at least 50 years old. Sacred vocal music often stayed in the repertories of church and cathedral choirs for more than a hundred years. And in the late 18th and early 19th centuries, groups such as the Academy of Ancient Music and the Concert of Ancient Music in London organized performances centred partly around early English church music and partly around the music of Corelli, Handel and Purcell.

On the other hand, the idea that 'early music' should be performed 'authentically' – that is, in a way as close to the composers' original conception as it is possible to come – seems to have been new in the 20th century. Only since the first decades of the present century have scholars and performers alike studied systematically the way music was performed in the past. The discipline of performance (or performing) practice (*Aufführungspraxis*) was born partly through the efforts of German academics who founded the first Collegia musica in universities to perform the old music they studied, and partly through the single-handed efforts in England of Arnold Dolmetsch, the great polymath who believed deeply in the artistic achievement of the old composers and therefore built instruments and learned to play them by studying the treatises of the 17th and 18th centuries. Dolmetsch's book, *The Interpretation of the Music of the Seventeenth and Eighteenth Centuries Revealed by Contemporary Evidence* (London, 1915; new edition with an introduction by R. Alec Harman, Seattle and London, 1969), along with the more comprehensive surveys of past times, such as Robert Haas, *Aufführungspraxis* (Potsdam, 1931; repr. 1949), and Arnold Schering, *Aufführungspraxis alter Musik* (Leipzig, 1931) thus were the pioneering works that first set out the premises and assumptions with which we still operate and which first explained to present-day scholars and musicians how music was performed in earlier times.

In the last quarter of the 20th century, questions of performance practice, like so many other areas of scholarly inquiry that seemed much simpler 50 years ago, have grown ever more complicated. Performing musicians, for example, continue to expand their repertories backwards in time, and today there are many more groups specializing in ever earlier medieval repertories and many more medieval compositions heard in concert halls, churches and university recital rooms than anyone could have imagined 50 years ago.

Most recently, performers have begun to be interested in learning to perform the music of the late 18th and early 19th centuries 'authentically', that is, with instruments and playing techniques no longer in common use, and with the sort of balance of forces and arrangements of musicians familiar to the audiences who first heard the music. This new initiative to perform standard concert repertory in a way close to that envisaged by the composers will surely teach us something important about the sound of Mozart's, Beethoven's and Schubert's music, but it also raises new questions about the propriety of authenticity as an ideal, and about the nature of the discipline of performance practice. The nature of the discipline will change more and more as scholars come to realize that the advent of recordings has changed radically the way we can know about how music sounded in the past.

In short, the study of performance practice has become too extensive and too complicated for any one person to master the entire field. Two works attempt a comprehensive bibliography of studies on performance practice: M. Vinquist and N. Zaslaw, *Performance Practice: a Bibliography* (New York, 1971; supplements in *Current Musicology*, no.12 (1971), 129–49, and no.15 (1973), 126–36), and R. Jackson, *Performance Practice, Medieval to Contemporary: a Bibliographic Guide* (New York, 1987; annual supplements in *Performance Practice Review*). At the same time, it has scarcely yet established itself as a discipline within musicology, partly because relatively few academic scholars have engaged themselves directly with such questions, partly because the cooperation between scholars, performers and instrument makers necessary to debate meaningfully central issues is often difficult to organize, and partly because many scholars still mistrust studies that do not deal with the analysis and criticism of the great works by the great composers, or with philological or social issues that seem to them more central to our main concerns with the great issues of history.

The idea for this handbook of performance practice came about, then, from an awareness that the boundaries of the discipline of performance practice needed to be defined more clearly, and that no one person could do that satisfactorily. In preparing the book, we have kept in mind that we have hoped to address both scholars and performers, although each group has different preoccupations and asks different sorts of question. The purely scholarly problem of finding out how music sounded in the past, for example, differs significantly from the aesthetic and practical questions that arise from the decision to offer earlier repertories to modern audiences.

In a sense, scholars and performers need opposite emphases: performers should learn that there are no simple right answers to most of their most pressing questions, however necessary it may be for them to find a single solution appropriate for a particular performance, and scholars that only through the study of performing traditions can certain kinds of questions regarding the nature of the written evidence be illuminated and that answers to certain of their questions can be reached with enough patient work, if sometimes by means of fairly circumstantial arguments. Both groups need to be reminded of their mutual dependence. We shall never really understand a repertory of music until we have learned how it sounds in performance, but good performances and 'understanding' alike depend heavily on archival, literary, iconographical, analytical and purely philological studies.

This handbook hopes to make clear the traditional areas of research into performance practice while at the same time raising new questions for study. Rather than providing performers with easy, prescriptive answers to complicated questions, the handbook aims to help them ask the right questions and give them some guidance as to how and where answers might be arrived at. We have tried to be suggestive rather than prescriptive, concentrating more on what we do not know than on what we do. The handbook aims, in short, at being comprehensive in the kinds of questions it offers to be answered, but without suggesting any single answer as correct. In that sense, we have conceived it as an attempt to bring up to date the best and most provocative essay on the central issues of performance practice yet published, Thurston Dart's *The Interpretation of Music* (London, 1954).

As in every other scholarly field, certain kinds of question dealing with performance practice are still very much open to debate, and it would be disingenuous to propose answers that are not yet clear. Dialogue is an essential part of the scholarly process. We have tried not to obscure matters under current debate, even at the expense of allowing some contradictory statements to stand from essay to essay. We have tried, too, to bring the discipline of performance practice up to date, by asking what its tasks are in the study of late 19th-century and 20th-century music. As far as we know, this is the first book to attempt an overview of performance practice for these later periods, a field of inquiry still very much in the process of being developed.

Although this book is issued in the *New Grove* handbook series, no part of it is derived from or based on material in *The New Grove Dictionary*; the entire text was expressly commissioned and written in the form in which it now appears.

H.M.B., S.S.

Chicago and London, 1989

PART ONE

The Middle Ages

CHAPTER I

Introduction

HOWARD M. BROWN

The study of the way medieval music was performed centres on two principal questions: (1) its sonorities, and (2) the relationship of the written notes to the actual sounds the first listeners heard. Although we shall probably never be certain of the precise sonorities of much medieval music, we can reconstruct some aspects of medieval sound more or less accurately through a careful study of the evidence. We can be fairly certain that we know, for example, the size of some singing groups, how many men and boys normally took part in the performance of plainchant or polyphony in particular cathedrals, monastic establishments and princely chapels, and even how the voice ranges were distributed – how many basses, how many tenors and how many boys or falsettists sang.[1]

Other aspects of medieval sonority we may never know for certain. It is difficult to imagine how we can ever find out how medieval singers sounded: whether they normally sang with what we would call loud or soft, heavy or light voices, whether they normally used head or chest tones or some combination of the two, whether or not they used vibrato, and what precisely writers on music meant when they referred to a voice as 'high and clear' or 'sweet'.[2]

Still other aspects of medieval sonority can only be reconstructed by interpreting the available evidence in ways that are unlikely to secure complete agreement among scholars or performers. No consensus has yet emerged, or is likely to emerge, for example, about the question of whether or not instruments accompanied singers in the performance of secular music. Some scholars deeply involved with the study of the songs of the troubadours and trouvères, for example, would deny that instruments could have been used to accompany this repertory, although present-day performing groups quite regularly accompany medieval monophonic secular song with instruments to play drones, preludes and interludes, and to double the voices heterophonically.[3] More recently, some scholars have argued that instruments seldom or never accompanied secular polyphony in the 14th or 15th centuries.[4] Their work has shown that performances of medieval secular polyphony by unaccompanied voices were much more common than we have hitherto supposed, but it is less clear whether instruments were excluded from this repertory altogether. Whatever the merits of the arguments on both sides, the principal point to be made here is that such crucial questions of performance practice are still under debate, and the questions are not likely to be resolved quickly or easily. We can only hope that this handbook presents the present state of the controversy in a fair and balanced manner.

3

Much of the scholarly debate in coming years will centre on the ways we should interpret evidence that is by its nature highly ambiguous, and on questions regarding the sort of evidence we should use to formulate our hypotheses. As in every other scholarly endeavour, we should construct theses that fit as many of the known pieces of evidence as possible. To this end, we need to draw in all the kinds of information we can get, since all classes of evidence can surely contribute to our attempts to gain a three-dimensional view (admittedly always slightly fictional and coloured by our own preoccupations) of past societies. Literary and iconographical sources, as well as archival records and the musical manuscripts themselves, must all be called upon for what they can tell us about the Middle Ages. Since they are all products of the same society, all these kinds of evidence should complement and not contradict one another, and the best hypotheses will be those that take most into account and are best able to reconcile apparent contradictions.

Even the formulation of the second central question facing students of performance practice – the relationship of the written notes to actual sounds – reveals the limitations and biases of the discipline, for it makes clear that we are forced to deal with only a part of medieval music: that which has survived in written form. The rest has been irretrievably lost. We must ask of the surviving sources, then, not only whether or not the written version reflects an absolutely fixed intention of the composer, but also how the surviving repertories relate to that music heard in the 12th, 13th and 14th centuries but no longer available to us, either because the manuscripts that contained it have been lost, or because it was a kind of music that was never written down. The study of performance practice must, then, take account of repertories that can no longer be reproduced, and ask how they were performed.[5]

The greater part of the study of medieval performance practice must, of course, continue to deal with notated music. To what extent should manuscript evidence be taken as a literal guide to what was sounded? Did all scribes (or some scribes) indicate precisely the notes to which particular syllables should be sung?[6] Were medieval singers allowed to ornament the notes on the page, or were they expected, or required, to ornament them?[7] How many accidentals and of what kinds were singers and instrumentalists expected to add to the written notes?[8] Did the notation suggest, or require, a single 'correct' rhythm for the performance of plainchant in some churches or monastic establishments, or for the performance of some kinds of secular monophonic music?[9] Did the notation incorporate precise indications of how fast the music should be performed, or what exactly the relationship was between music in one mensuration and music in another?[10] These are but some of the questions that face students of medieval performance practice. Some of them can and will be answered by careful consideration of the surviving evidence by scholars and performers.

There are some aspects of the relationship between notes and sound, however, that we shall probably never know. Precisely how singers and instrumentalists phrased in the 12th, 13th and 14th centuries, whether they had anything like our conception of 'shaping a phrase', for example, whether or not they tolerated or even encouraged slight changes of tempo for

4

expressive or formal reasons, whether they cultivated tempo rubato, how music was articulated then, whether they prized a 'singing' legato or preferred a more detached style of playing and whether or not they valued changes of articulation; these are all questions that appear to be beyond our knowledge. We can never know just what the musicians of the distant past thought about all those details of performing that seem to us so important in bringing the written notes alive.[11]

In putting forward any hypotheses or conclusions about the performance of medieval music we need to keep firmly in mind the particular repertory to which our research applies, lest we distort the past by applying limited results too broadly, a fault that earlier scholars have not always avoided.[12] Indeed, the association of particular repertories with particular methods of performance will, I think, be seen to be one of the important directions the study of performance practice takes in the near future, since it is becoming increasingly clear that quite different questions need to be asked about various repertories. Obviously, for example, questions about how to perform plainchant – the central repertory of sacred music throughout the Middle Ages as well as the Renaissance – will necessarily involve discussion of rhythm. But there are many repertories of medieval music that seem to us to pose no problems (or at least far fewer problems) concerning their rhythm. And with chant, as with every other repertory, we must not expect to learn that it was performed in exactly the same way in every century, in every country, in every city, or even within every church establishment within a given city.[13] Similarly, there will be different answers to the question of how to perform medieval music for all the various repertories of polyphony that grew up in western Europe from the 10th century on. The organum sung at Notre Dame in Paris might well have been associated with conventions of performance quite different from those of St Martial in Limoges, or those of the singers of organum at a slightly later date or in a different place.[14]

If it is important to take account of differences of time and place in the performance of plainchant and organum, it is even more important to consider variant performing conventions of monophonic songs in the vernacular, the central repertory of medieval secular music. Settings of poetry in *langue d'oc* surely had very different conventions of performance from settings of poetry in *langue d'oïl*, and both repertories must have been performed differently from secular songs in English, Spanish, German and Italian.[15] Moreover, it is crucial in considering the performance of monophonic secular music in the Middle Ages to separate and identify clearly the various genres of secular monophonic music. The courtly secular song of the troubadours and trouvères almost certainly should be considered apart from the sorts of *caroles*, dancing songs, that are mentioned, for example, in the *Roman de la Rose*, and they, in turn, were probably sung and/or played differently from lyric or narrative *lais*, refrains, such dancing songs as rondeaux and various other kinds of monophonic song.[16]

The sorts of songs that were sung by, or sung for, aristocrats and members of the *haute bourgeoisie* need to be distinguished from songs of simple citizens, songs of workers and peasants, and the songs and dances that made up the repertory of the professional musicians, not only the itinerant minstrels but also those in the permanent employ of princes or communes.[17] The audience for both sorts of minstrels included members of various classes of society. An especially characteristic part of the repertory of some minstrels consisted of the long narrative songs they sang in courts as well as on street corners in cities throughout western Europe. And they may have developed relatively early in the history of western European music an autonomous instrumental music, almost entirely unwritten and probably largely improvised. Indeed, a large part of their repertory may have consisted of partly improvised songs and dances, a circumstance that makes close study of minstrels' music impossible today.[18]

Finally, polyphony makes up the most important surviving repertory of secular music in the 13th and 14th centuries, but we should not forget that secular polyphony was a relatively late development in the history of Western music, and may well have been the special preserve of a small group of intellectuals and aesthetes.[19] Presumably, some of the motets and other pieces for state occasions were performed publicly in the 14th century, but the truth is that we know relatively little about the occasions when 13th-century motets were performed.[20] The great blossoming of polyphonic settings of vernacular poems that took place in the 14th century both in Italy and in France – the great achievement of the bureaucrat and intellectual Guillaume de Machaut in France, and of a whole circle of musicians (some of them 'professional' and others not) such as Jacopo da Bologna and Francesco Landini in Italy – must at least in part have been inspired by a rise in the standard of general musical culture that encouraged some aristocrats, well-born music lovers, and intellectual clerics to cultivate for themselves a repertory of polyphonic courtly love songs.[21]

Such consideration of the social uses of music, and of the classes of people for whom particular repertories were intended – a sociology of medieval music, as it were – should form an important part of every investigation of the way music was performed in the distant past.[22] Such questions are even crucial to our understanding of the performance of sacred music, for it is important to know whether a particular chant or piece of sacred polyphony was performed only in monastic establishments, collegiate churches and cathedrals, or in every parish of a particular country at a particular time. Moreover, we cannot assume that every piece of sacred music was inevitably a part of the regular cycle of Masses and Offices performed in larger church establishments year in and year out, for many of the most interesting musical compositions prove to have been designed for some extra- or para-liturgical occasion: votive Masses, wedding services, coronations, funerals, dedications of a church, sacred services associated with some secular body such as a confraternity, or for use during processions or for mystery plays.[23] Different sets of conventions will surely have governed the performance of music within the church walls and without.

We can assume, I think, that much, and perhaps most, of the secular music that survives – both monophonic and polyphonic – was intended for performance in upper-class society, not only at courts but also in the houses of the greater bourgeoisie, if only because much of the lower-class music would never have been written down, certainly not normally into the great anthologies and elegant presentation manuscripts that make up the greater part of the surviving musical artefacts from the 13th and 14th centuries.[24]

We are probably correct to emphasize the fact that upper-class music was not performed at formal concerts of a sort we are used to from the 19th and 20th centuries. Medieval people did not go to great temples of music to sit quietly while professionals performed. But on the other hand, we need to argue against the false idea that all secular music in the Middle Ages was played and sung by amateurs in informal contexts. To be sure, there is reason to believe that much upper-class music was performed by aristocrats and courtiers themselves, with or without the assistance of professionals, for their own enjoyment in informal gatherings in gardens, palace halls and the chambers of great houses. [25] But we should also remember that probably the most regular venue for secular music-making in the Middle Ages was the dining room or banqueting hall, when professional musicians performed after mealtimes in more or less formal presentations. [26] Some of their repertory may well have been that music special to minstrels – unwritten songs and dances and the recitation of long declaimed narratives – but minstrels are also likely to have included among their 'concert' pieces some formal, composed, 'written' music of the sort we study in the manuscripts.

Much of the music of lower-class society in the Middle Ages – the music associated with itinerant minstrels, the *laude* of the common citizens, and the sort of music performed in taverns, fields and city streets – is largely inaccessible to us today. To be sure, sizeable fragments of the *lauda* repertory survive, some few 'popular' songs were incorporated into the art music of the 13th and 14th centuries, and here and there in the great anthologies of composed polyphony a scribe has jotted down a song, a dance or an instrumental piece associated with that part of society that was not normally literate in music. [27] But by and large we shall always remain ignorant of the music played and sung by the poorer segments of society, even though we need to keep their musical activities always in mind when studying the performance conventions of the Middle Ages, lest we misread the surviving evidence and conclude that polyphony or courtly or sacred monophony was performed in a way documented by archives, literary descriptions and pictures which may be referring to an entirely different – and now lost – kind of music.

The central problem in studying the way the music of the distant past was performed concerns the paucity of sources of information. In the first place, medieval man was generally disinclined to write about the particular and the everyday. The learned discourse of the Middle Ages was normally about higher things: *musica theorica* as a part of the university curriculum, for example, or *musica practica* as an exposition of what we today would call the 'theory of music'. It is only very rarely that a 13th- or 14th-century writer on music deigns to include information about instruments, or about the way music was performed. A list of the most important medieval treatises that instruct us about performance practice is given at the end of this handbook, but the list is largely restricted (for practical reasons) to treatises that mention musical instruments. [28] Some of the information appears in otherwise rather conventional treatises, as passing remarks or addenda. Jerome of Moravia, for example, added to his *Tractatus de musica*, written in Paris about 1300 to instruct inexperienced Dominicans in the theory and practice of chant, a few remarks explaining the tuning of the medieval fiddle, the

7

Music at a 14th-century banquet: detail of a page from 'Le roman de Marques', c1330. The Emperor Mark is shown dining in the company of two young ladies, as his sister enters on the left; they are entertained by a fiddle player who sings (Brussels, Bibliothèque royale, MS 9433, f.60)

earliest and most detailed such explanation we have, and he writes in passing about the way plainchant should be ornamented. Other treatises that offer useful information about performance stand slightly outside the main tradition of music theory, and seem to be the products of unusually individualistic musicians. Johannes de Grocheo, for example, claims to give an account of music in Paris during the 13th century in a treatise of striking originality, and the anonymous author of the Berkeley Treatise, writing about 1375, includes details about instruments in a treatise that departs in many ways from tradition.[29] These and the other treatises listed at the end of this volume are precious witnesses, but there are so few of them that they are exceedingly difficult to interpret, for it is impossible to know the extent to which they reveal common practice as opposed to a personal and idiosyncratic view of the world.

Introduction

In the absence of extensive theoretical discussion of practical issues, the scholar must turn to other kinds of evidence: archival, literary, iconographical, and even anthropological or ethnomusicological. Some performers – and a few scholars – appear to have based their views of the way medieval music was performed (or perhaps of the way it should be performed) on musical practices in non-Western cultures and in Western societies with a living oral tradition.[30] The strengths and weaknesses of this point of view have not been widely debated, since no reasoned explanation and defence has been published, its adherents presumably believing in the force of an orally transmitted theory. Apparently, followers of this anthropological and non-historical approach to medieval performance practice base their practices on the supposition (doubtless partly true) that the way one society deals with an orally transmitted and essentially monophonic repertory (that is, a repertory unknown to the urban high culture of the West) has much to teach students of other societies. This view of performance practice has not been widely accepted in the scholarly community, perhaps just because it has not been stated in writing, although it finds considerable support among performers of medieval music.

Each of the other sources of information about performance practice – archival, liturgical, literary and iconographical – offers valuable clues about musical practices in the Middle Ages, but each has pitfalls and limitations. Archival documentation, unfortunately not as copious for the Middle Ages as for later periods, has the virtue that it is factual and much of it may even have been true. But archives instruct us chiefly about those institutions whose pay records reveal details about the organization of real life.[31] Many of the questions we have to ask, however, about the performance of music – and especially about the performance of secular music – deal with situations outside an institutional framework. The archives can tell us much, but they cannot tell us everything we want to know.

Certain kinds of liturgical books, and especially ordinaries, customaries and ceremonials, offer another source of information about the way sacred music was performed.[32] Although the systematic study of such sources has hardly begun, liturgical books are likely to reveal much new information about the occasions when singers took part in particular services, how many and who they were, where they stood, how they sang and so on. Service books are factual, and they are even more apt to be true than archives, but they have the limitation, of course, that they refer only to local events in particular religious establishments.

Literary evidence is equally useful to historians of performance, and likewise limited in its applications, although in a completely different way from archival documentation. Many authors of works of imaginative literature – romances, novels, and lyric and narrative poetry of various kinds – mention music and musical practices, often in situations outside an institutional framework, and in contexts that tell us much about private life in the Middle Ages.[33] But before we can trust conclusions drawn from fictional accounts, we must first establish the relationship between the author's imagination and reality. Was the author attempting to describe the musical life of his own time, or was he evoking some more or less distant past that may never actually have existed? Was he presenting a view derived from

9

personal observation or from some purely literary tradition? Was he offering a more or less accurate account of what he thought possible and real, or was he exaggerating for effect? We must, in short, first study literary sources for themselves, before we can use them as documentary evidence. Even passages dealing with music in non-fictional non-musical works – encyclopedias, chronicles, histories and treatises of one kind or another – cannot always be relied on to give us the literal truth, for sometimes they, too, merely borrow from some older tradition.[34] And even when we can believe authors of literary works, we do not always know what they mean. They do not always make clear, for example, whether verbs such as 'to say' (*dicere*) and 'to sing' (*cantare*) mean speaking, declaiming, singing or even singing with instruments,[35] and they do not always refer to particular instruments in an unambiguous way.[36] We cannot always demonstrate precisely what the author of a literary work intended to signify by a particular word or term.

Iconography has limitations similar in scope to those of the other classes of evidence. Pictures can enlighten us about details of musical practice that would not otherwise be clear from verbal descriptions, but we cannot always be certain we know what a picture means, let alone to what repertory of written or unwritten music its imagery applies. As with literature, individual pictures must first be studied for themselves, and some effort made to determine the extent to which they may have some allegorical, symbolic or otherwise non-realistic 'meaning'.[37] And scholars need to consider the sources from which the artist derived his image, whether a biblical account, a patristic commentary, some work of imaginative literature or merely an older fixed artistic tradition.[38] Even after a scholar claims to understand the meaning of a picture, he must take pains to demonstrate why he thinks the evidence applies to some particular repertory.

In short, scholars studying the performance practices of the distant past must cast their nets wide, learning from wherever they can and gradually forming a composite picture of the nature of life in the Middle Ages from as large a pool of information as they can gather. In this sense, the study of performance conventions differs from many other kinds of musical studies, for a close reading of a single text can be highly misleading, unless we can relate it to others like it and offer some hypothesis about the nature of the conventional procedures of the time. For we must remember that (unlike students of musical style or compositional process) we are less concerned to study closely the extraordinary exception that dazzles and delights us than we are to discover the typical, the conventional and the average.

It is a truism that musical notes on paper (or parchment) do not constitute music at all, but only the record of a music that was once performed and can be performed again. Ultimately, we cannot know precisely how music in the 12th, 13th and 14th centuries actually sounded. But there is an enormous amount of evidence still to be studied, and we must make the attempt to find out as much as we possibly can about the performance of medieval music simply so that we can understand it better, and lest we misinterpret its meaning. And we must keep in mind the fact that the effort of bringing those sounds back to life in the 20th century poses totally different kinds of questions and problems from the task of discovering how the music was first performed.

Introduction

Notes

[1] The question of the size and composition of medieval choirs has hardly been studied. For an excellent example of what we can learn from such studies, see R. Bowers, 'The Performing Ensemble for English Church Polyphony, *c*1320–*c*1390', in *Performance Practice: New York 1981*, 161–92.

[2] For an overview of medieval ideas about singing, see F. Müller-Heuser, *Vox humana: ein Beitrag zur Untersuchung der Stimmästhetik des Mittelalters* (Regensburg, 1963). For a more recent view about singing in the Middle Ages, see B. Thornton, 'Vokale und Gesangstechnik: das Stimmideal der aquitanischen Polyphonie', *Basler Jb für historische Musikpraxis*, iv (1980), 133–50.

[3] H. van der Werf, *The Chansons of the Troubadours and Trouvères: a Study of the Melodies and their Relation to the Poems* (Utrecht, 1972), 19–21, denies the use of instruments to accompany songs of the troubadours and trouvères. His ideas have been expanded in the most eloquent case yet made for unaccompanied performance of this repertory, in C. Page, *Voices and Instruments of the Middle Ages* (London, 1987). I. Parker, 'The Performance of Troubadour and Trouvère Songs', *EM*, v (1977), 185–208, cites a number of literary references mentioning instrumental participation in the performance of secular music, although whether they can be applied to the repertory of the troubadours or trouvères remains an open question.

[4] The question is raised in D. Fallows, 'Specific Information on the Ensembles for Composed Polyphony, 1400–1474', in *Performance Practice: New York 1981*, 132–44. Daniel Leech-Wilkinson in his review in *EM*, x (1982), 557–9 of the recording of Dufay's complete secular music by the Medieval Ensemble of London strongly rejects the use of instruments in the performance of 15th-century secular music. Christopher Page, who is the scholar chiefly responsible for this challenge to traditional views, has thus far not made the sort of sweeping generalizations found in the writings of the other two; see for example Page, 'Machaut's "Pupil" Deschamps on the Performance of Music', *EM*, v (1977), 484–91, and Page, 'The Performance of Songs in Late Medieval France', *EM*, x (1982), 441–50. Page can be credited with reminding us that unaccompanied performances were much more frequent than we had been accustomed to think.

[5] Nino Pirrotta has provided the best accounts of the unwritten tradition; see for example his essay 'Novelty and Renewal in Italy: 1300–1600', in *Studien zur Tradition in der Musik: Kurt von Fischer zum 60. Geburtstag* (Munich, 1973), 49–63, and various of the essays in his *Music and Culture in Italy from the Middle Ages to the Baroque* (Cambridge, Mass., 1984). On the relationship between written notes and performance, see among other studies W. Arlt, 'Musik, Schrift und Interpretation: Zwei Studien zum Umgang mit Aufzeichnungen ein- und mehrstimmiger Musik aus dem 14. und 15. Jahrhundert', *Basler Jb für historische Musikpraxis*, iv (1980), 91–132. The distinction between music in the two traditions is very complex and to some extent unreal, since much of the music in the 'written tradition' circulated orally long before being gathered into manuscripts, and some of the music from the 'unwritten tradition' appears in written sources.

[6] See for example L. M. Earp, *Scribal Practice, Manuscript Production and the Transmission of Music in Late Medieval France: the Manuscripts of Guillaume de Machaut* (diss., Princeton U., 1983), 219–26, who argues strongly that editors and performers should follow the scribes exactly. Earp does not point out, however, that doing so creates a disjunction between the phrase structure of the music and the formal elements of the poetry. The propriety of following the scribes literally seems to me to be a topic that badly needs extensive discussion.

[7] Aside from such relatively brief and carefully delimited studies as S. Corbin, 'Note sur l'ornementation dans le plain-chant grégorien', in *IMSCR*, viii *New York 1961*, 428–39, I know of no scholarly works devoted exclusively to the question of ornamentation in music written before 1400, a subject that clearly needs systematic investigation. The best starting-place for work on the subject is, therefore, E. Ferand, *Die Improvisation in der Musik* (Zurich, 1938), and the collection of examples edited by Ferand, *Die Improvisation in Beispielen aus neun Jahrhunderten abendländischer Musik* (Cologne, 1956).

[8] On the addition of accidentals in music before 1400, see A. Hughes, *Manuscript Accidentals: Ficta in Focus, 1350–1450*, MSD, xxvii (1972); M. Bent, 'Musica Recta and Musica Ficta', *MD*, xxvi (1972), 73–100; and Chapter VI.

[9] David Hiley summarizes current views on the rhythm of chant in Chapter III. The question of whether the songs of the troubadours and trouvères were sung in modal or partly modal rhythm, or in a more freely declamatory rhythm, is summarized by van der Werf, *Chansons of the*

11

Troubadours and Trouvères, chap.3, who strongly supports non-metrical transcriptions. See for example his *The Extant Troubadour Melodies* (Rochester, New York, 1984), as opposed to the modal transcriptions offered in *Chanter m'estuet: Songs of the Trouvères*, ed. S. N. Rosenberg and H. Tischler (Bloomington, 1981). For more detailed discussion of these issues, see also E. Jammers, *Aufzeichnungsweisen der einstimmigen ausserliturgischen Musik des Mittelalters*, Palaeographie der Musik, i/4 (Cologne, 1975).

[10] The two most recent extensive studies that deal with questions of tempo and proportion in medieval music are S. Gullo, *Das Tempo in der Musik des XIII. und XIV. Jahrhunderts* (Berne, 1964), and J. A. Bank, *Tactus, Tempo, and Notation in Mensural Music from the 13th to the 17th Century* (Amsterdam, 1972). See also Chapter VII.

[11] On this point, and on the relationship between what we think of as 'musicality' and authenticity, see among other studies M. Morrow, 'Musical Performance and Authenticity', *EM*, vi (1978), 233–46; R. Taruskin, 'The Musicologist and the Performer', in *Musicology in the 1980s*, ed. D. K. Holoman and C. V. Palisca (New York, 1982), 101–18; Taruskin, 'The Limits of Authenticity', *EM*, xii (1984), 1–10; and the essays in N. Kenyon, ed., *Authenticity and Early Music* (Oxford, 1988).

[12] I think of even such important pioneering works as F. W. Galpin, *Old English Instruments of Music, their History and Character* (London, 1910, rev. 4/1965 by T. Dart) and H. Panum, *The Stringed Instruments of the Middle Ages*, trans. and rev. by J. Pulver (London, 1939/R1971).

[13] Scholars are only just beginning to study local repertories and variants of chant in the later Middle Ages; they have hardly yet begun to think about local performing practices. For two recent works on local dialects of chant, see for example J. M. Borders, *The Cathedral of Verona as a Musical Center in the Middle Ages: its History, Manuscripts, and Liturgical Practice* (diss., U. of Chicago, 1983), and A. Walters, *Music and Liturgy at the Abbey of Saint-Denis, 567–1567: a Survey of the Primary Sources* (diss., Yale U., 1984).

[14] On the performance of organum in Paris, see E. Roesner, 'The Performance of Parisian Organum', *EM*, vii (1979), 174–89. On the performance of clausulae, see H. Tischler, 'How were Notre Dame Clausulae Performed?', *ML*, l (1969), 273–7. Performance traditions in other times and places have not, as yet, been studied.

[15] For introductory surveys of musical settings of medieval lyric poetry in the vernacular, see such standard texts as J. A. Westrup, 'Medieval Song', in *NOHM*, ii (1954), 220–69; P. Dronke, *The Medieval Lyric* (London, 1968); R. H. Hoppin, *Medieval Music* (New York, 1978), chaps.11–13; and the more specialized studies listed in A. Hughes, *Medieval Music: the Sixth Liberal Art* (Toronto, 1974, rev. 2/1980), pp. 144–78. The most recent exploration of this subject can be found in J. Stevens, *Words and Music in the Middle Ages* (Cambridge, 1986).

[16] The purely formalistic approach to the problem of genre reflected in earlier studies, such as F. Gennrich's monumental *Grundriss einer Formenlehre des mittelalterlichen Liedes* (Halle, 1932/R1970), is not very helpful in considering questions of performance practice. However, there are illuminating studies of particular genres, such as *Lais et descorts français du XIIIe siècle*, ed. A. Jeanroy, L. Brandin and P. Aubry (Paris, 1901/R1970), and J. Maillard, *Evolution et esthétique du lai lyrique* (Paris, 1963), for example. There needs to be more concentrated scholarly discussion of the question of genres as a whole before we can interpret dependably various sorts of evidence (musical, literary, archival and iconographical). Page, *Voices and Instruments*, offers us a good start in this direction.

[17] On medieval minstrels, see for example E. Faral, *Les jongleurs en France au moyen âge* (Paris, 1910, 2/1964); W. Salmen, *Der fahrende Musiker im europäischen Mittelalter* (Kassel, 1960); R. Rastall, 'Minstrelsy, Church and Clergy in Medieval England', PRMA, xcvii (1970–71), 83–98; and Rastall, 'The Minstrels of the English Royal Households', *RMARC*, iv (1964), 1–41. For an attempt to understand the variety of kinds of minstrels in the 15th century and their repertories, see H. M. Brown, 'Minstrels and their Repertory in Fifteenth-century France' (forthcoming).

[18] On *chansons de geste* and other French epics, see F. Gennrich, *Der musikalische Vortrag der altfranzösischen chansons de geste* (Halle, 1923); J. Chailley, 'Autour de la chanson de geste', *AcM*, xxvii (1955), 1–19; and J. van der Veen, 'Les aspects musicaux des chansons de geste', *Neophilologus*, xli (1957), 82–100. On Italian *cantari*, see E. Levi, *I cantari leggendari del popolo italiano nel secolo XIV e XV* (Turin, 1914), and V. Branca, *Il cantare trecentesco e il Boccaccio del Filostrato e del Teseida* (Florence, 1936).

[19] A point made, among other places, throughout Pirrotta, *Music and Culture in Italy*.

[20] Fragments of information about the performance of 13th- and 14th-century motets are scattered among the studies, mostly bibliographical or stylistic, listed in Hughes, *Medieval Music*, pp. 186–213. The best introduction to the 13th-century motet is probably still that in

Polyphonies du XIIIe siècle, ed. Y. Rokseth (Paris, 1935–9); see also the more recent edition of the Montpellier Codex, *The Montpellier Codex*, ed. H. Tischler (Madison, Wisc., 1978–85).

[21] For information about the cultural and intellectual preoccupations in France during Machaut's time, and in Florence during Landini's time, see *Machaut's World: Science and Art in the Fourteenth Century*, ed. M. P. Cosman and B. Chandler (New York, 1978); M. P. Long, *Musical Tastes in Fourteenth-century Italy: Notational Styles, Scholarly Traditions, and Historical Circumstances* (diss., Princeton U., 1981); and Long, 'Francesco Landini and the Florentine Cultural Elite', *EMH*, iii (1983), 83–99.

[22] P. Gülke, *Mönche, Bürger, Minnesänger* (Vienna, 1975), is an interesting recent attempt at a sociology of medieval music. The series of textbooks on the history of music commissioned by the Società Italiana di Musicologia integrates music with political and cultural history; see G. Cattin, *Il Medioevo I*, Storia della Musica, i/2 (Turin, 1979; Eng. trans., 1984), and F. A. Gallo, *Il Medioevo II*, Storia della Musica, ii (Turin, 1977; Eng. trans., 1985).

[23] Like so many other aspects of the study of the performance of medieval music, the occasions when sacred music was performed have never been studied as a whole, although relevant information is scattered throughout the musicological literature. F. Ll. Harrison, *Music in Medieval Britain* (London, 1958, 2/1963), is quite exceptional in taking so much account of the subject. My ideas have mostly been formed by studies of individual pieces or groups of pieces, such as P. M. Lefferts, 'Two English Motets on Simon de Montfort', *EMH*, i (1981), 203–25, and S. K. Rankin, 'The Mary Magdalene Scene in the *Visitatio Sepulchri* Ceremonies', *EMH*, i (1981), 227–55. P. Petrobelli, 'Some Dates for Bartolino da Padova', in *Studies in Music History: Essays for Oliver Strunk* (Princeton, 1968), 85–112, offers provocative facts and hypotheses about the circumstances of commissioning and the social status of one 14th-century Italian composer, albeit in the context of secular not sacred music.

[24] There appear to be some exceptions to this general rule. The various instrumental pieces in *GB-Lbl* Add. 29987, for example, have been associated with the minstrels' repertory in H. M. Brown, 'St. Augustine, Lady Music and the Gittern in Fourteenth-century Italy', *MD*, xxxviii (1984), 25–65, among other places. But these pieces may also have been performed by minstrels in great houses.

[25] The occasions and venues of performance in the Middle Ages have hardly been studied. Scholars wishing to pursue the question of performances by aristocrats and courtiers themselves (with or without the assistance of professionals) will certainly need to start with the seminal article of H. Besseler, 'Umgangsmusik und Darbietungsmusik im 16. Jahrhundert', *AMw*, xvi (1959), 21–43.

[26] Some idea of the typical venues for the performance of medieval music can be gained from the iconographical evidence provided in E. A. Bowles, *Musical Performance in the Late Middle Ages* (Geneva, 1983).

[27] See n.24 above. The *lauda* repertory has been the best studied, initially in F. Liuzzi, *La lauda e i primordi della melodia italiana* (Rome, 1934), and most recently in Sister M. C. Barr, *The Laude Francescane and the Disciplinati of Thirteenth Century Umbria and Tuscany: a Critical Study of the Cortona Codex 91* (diss., Catholic U. of America, 1965), and in *Laude Cortonesi dal secolo XIII al XV*, ed. G. Varanini, L. Banfi and A. C. Burgio (Florence, 1981), which contains all the *lauda* texts.

[28] Information about the performance of medieval music is scattered widely throughout various kinds of sources, making the presentation of such a list of primary sources very difficult. Many of the treatises that begin with the division of music into its constituent parts, for example, include a remark or two of potential practical interest in the section on *musica instrumentalis*.

[29] For editions, translations and commentaries on the treatises of Jerome of Moravia and Johannes de Grocheo, and on the Berkeley Treatise, see the list of medieval treatises at the end of this volume. Page, *Voices and Instruments*, 196–201, deals with Grocheo's theory of genres in an unusually enlightening way.

[30] The best introduction to the reasoning and attitudes of those scholars and performers influenced by the music of non-Western cultures and societies with living oral traditions can be found in the essays by T. Binkley, H. H. Touma, J. Kuckertz and others in *Basler Jb für historische Musikpraxis*, i (1977).

[31] For exemplary collections of archival documents about particular places, see for example C. Wright, *Music at the Court of Burgundy, 1364–1419: a Documentary History* (Henryville, Ottawa, and Binningen, 1979), and A. Tomasello, *Music and Ritual at Papal Avignon: 1309–1403* (Ann Arbor, 1983).

[32] For examples of what can be learnt from a study of ordinaries, see K. von Fischer, 'Die Rolle

der Mehrstimmigkeit am Dome von Siena zu Beginn des 13. Jahrhunderts', *AMw*, xviii (1961), 167–82, and Fischer, 'Das Kantorenamt am Dome von Siena zu Beginn des 13. Jahrhunderts', in *Festschrift Karl Gustav Fellerer* (Regensburg, 1962), 155–60. A partial bibliography of surviving ordinaries can be found in *Le graduel romain, ii: Les sources* (Solesmes, 1957), 189–96. For two recent studies of chant that include information about performance derived from ordinaries, see n.13 above.

[33] Recent examples of studies that show what can be learned about music and about the performance of music from literary works include I. F. Finlay, 'Musical Instruments in Gotfrid von Strassburg's "Tristan und Isolde" ', *GSJ*, v (1952), 39–43; J. W. McKinnon, 'Musical Instruments in Medieval Psalm Commentaries and Psalters', *JAMS*, xxi (1968), 3–20; H. M. Brown, 'Fantasia on a Theme by Boccaccio', *EM*, v (1977), 324–39; M. V. Fowler, *Musical Interpolations in Thirteenth- and Fourteenth-century French Narratives* (diss., Yale U., 1979); and H. Kästner, *Harfe und Schwert: Der höfische Spielmann bei Gottfried von Strassburg* (Tübingen, 1981).

[34] Recent examples of studies that show what can be learned about music and the performance of music from non-fictional works include G. Vecchi, 'Educazione musicale, scuola e società nell'opera didascalica di Francesco da Barberino', *Quadrivium*, vii (1966), 5–29, and C. Page, 'German Musicians and their Instruments: a 14th-century Account by Konrad of Megenberg', *EM*, x (1982), 192–200.

[35] For a discussion of one aspect of the problem of verb forms and their intended meaning, see U. Mehler, *Dicere und cantare: Zur musikalischen Terminologie und Aufführungspraxis des mittelalterlichen geistlichen Dramas in Deutschland* (Regensburg, 1981).

[36] To take but one example, biblical terms for instruments, such as 'cithara', 'psalterio', 'chorus' and so on, are used sometimes in a general and sometimes in a technical way by medieval writers, and their meanings change from time to time and from place to place. On this point, see for example H. M. Brown, 'The Trecento Psaltery' (forthcoming).

[37] For an amplification of this point, see J. W. McKinnon, 'Iconography', in *Musicology in the 1980s*, ed. Holoman and Palisca (New York, 1982), 79–93; McKinnon, 'Fifteenth-century Northern Book Painting and the *A Capella* Question: an Essay in Iconographic Method', in *Performance Practice: New York 1981*, 1–17; and T. Seebass, 'Prospettive dell' iconografia musicale: Considerazioni di un medievalista', *RIM*, xviii (1983), 67–86.

[38] Recent examples of studies that show what can be learned about music and the performance of music from pictures include T. Seebass, *Musikdarstellung und Psalterillustration im früheren Mittelalter* (Berne, 1973); J. W. McKinnon, 'Representations of the Mass in Medieval and Renaissance Art', *JAMS*, xxxi (1978), 21–52; R. Hammerstein, *Tanz und Musik des Todes: die mittelalterlichen Totentänze und ihr Nachleben* (Berne and Munich, 1980); Hammerstein's earlier books; and the essays in the new yearbook for musical iconography, *Imago musicae*.

CHAPTER II

Instruments

HOWARD M. BROWN

The study of musical instruments as an aspect of performance practice is still in its infancy. To be sure, several excellent surveys of musical instruments in the Middle Ages and the Renaissance have recently been written,[1] and a number of fine and painstaking studies of the forms of particular instruments, their nomenclature, their structural details, their fittings and their playing techniques have been published, and discussion continues about these problems among builders, museum curators, performers and scholars. Much of this work has appeared in the several excellent journals devoted wholly or in part to research into musical instruments, such as the *Galpin Society Journal*, *Early Music* and more recently the *Journal of the American Musical Instrument Society* and the *Basler Jahrbuch für historische Musikpraxis*.[2]

To form plausible hypotheses, or to reach defensible conclusions, about the way musical instruments were actually used in the Middle Ages, however, we need (a) to know which instruments existed at particular times and places, (b) to write a chronicle of events in the history of instruments, explaining when each was invented or introduced into the major European countries, (c) to describe the character and playing technique of each instrument and how they changed from country to country and from century to century (or even from decade to decade if that is possible), and (d) to analyse the conventions of performance in order to discover how the use of instruments differed from country to country, and which repertories of written and unwritten music were regularly associated with instruments and which were not.

Simple lists of the instruments known to each country in every century can be very helpful as a starting point for studying the musical practices of the Middle Ages. It is useful, for example, to compare and contrast the instruments of 14th-century Italy with those of France. We can acquire a general impression of 14th-century Italian instruments by making a conflated list of those pictured on Landini's tombstone, those that adorn the border of his portrait in the Squarcialupi Codex (see illustration over), those he is said by Villani to have played, the list of instruments named in the early 14th-century courtly poem *L'intelligenza*, and those shown in paintings depicting crowds of musical angels praising or entertaining Christ or the Virgin.[3] These pieces of evidence, which complement rather than contradict each other, strongly suggest that (*a*) the fiddle was the principal bowed string instrument in the trecento, (*b*) the gittern, the lute, the psaltery, and later in the century the harp were the principal plucked strings, (*c*) the portative

15

Francesco Landini playing the organetto, with Lady Music and various instruments as marginalia: folio from the 'Squarcialupi Codex', early 15th century (Florence, Biblioteca Medicea-Laurenziana 87, f.121v)

organ was the principal keyboard instrument, and (*d*) 'double recorders' plus loud instruments – trumpets, shawms and bagpipes – were the principal winds.[4] Transverse flutes, for example, are never depicted in trecento art; the flutes occasionally mentioned in literary sources may well refer to 'double recorders'.[5] Comparison with similar French poems and pictures, such as the crowds of French musical angels, and the several long lists of instruments in Machaut's works and in the poem *Les échecs amoureux*, presumably show the contrast between Italian and French musical practice at the time.[6] The French evidence confirms the idea that some instruments, such as the fiddle, were common in both countries, and that other instruments were common in one but not in the other. Incurved trapezoidal psalteries (the so-called 'pig-snout psalteries') and recorders, for example, are found in pictures much earlier in France than in Italy. Some instruments appear to be virtually unknown in one or the other country if the pictures are to be believed. Thus, in addition to the transverse flute, the citole as well as such 'ancient' instruments as the lyre and the *organistrum* seem never to be depicted in Italian pictures,[7] and the double recorder appears to be quite rare in French manuscript illumination.

A particularly interesting and difficult instance of the importance of making and studying simple lists concerns the manuscripts of the *Cantigas de Santa Maria*, assembled by King Alfonso the Wise (or by the royal scribes) and illuminated in Spain during the 13th and 14th centuries (see illustration, p. 19).[8] These Spanish illuminations depict an unusually varied collection of instruments, quite unlike the instrumentaria of the French or Italian sources and much more rich. They have been drawn upon by many present-day musicians to justify the use of one or another instrument, and especially the long-necked lute, and other instruments derived from north Africa and the eastern Mediterranean countries. The *Cantigas* illuminations, however, are difficult to interpret. Scholars do not agree about whether or not they are intended to depict the *Cantigas* actually being performed. The pictures show Spanish as well as Moorish and Jewish musicians, and it is by no means clear which repertories each of them is supposed to be performing, or whether they all played and sang the same kinds of music. It is improbable that Spanish pictures illustrate the common ways that French or Italian music was performed in the 13th and 14th centuries, and it is not even clear that Moorish instruments can have been heard everywhere in Spain; it is debatable, surely, whether or not the evidence of the *Cantigas* can be applied to the performance of music in Catalonia, or the counties of Foix and Narbonne near the Spanish border, let alone Paris, London or Florence. A detailed study of the *Cantigas* illuminations that would help to answer some of these questions seems to me to be an urgent desideratum for students of medieval musical instruments.

Doubtless people in all times and places have invented new things and refined the old. Students of musical instruments need to be reminded of that fact, and concentrate some of their attention on what was new at any given time or place. After having established which instruments were known in a particular country at a particular time, they should write simple chronicles of events to explain when particular instruments were invented, or when they were introduced into each of the major European countries. Which instruments were widely adopted after they were introduced, which were not, and why? What unspoken need on the part of musicians did successful new instruments meet? How were both new and old instruments changed after they had been in use for a while? Although older scholars wrote about the introduction of instruments into Europe in the early Middle Ages (often using more imagination than hard evidence to support their conclusions),[9] relatively little attention has been given to such questions in the recent past. It is therefore impossible to offer dependable brief summaries of what was new in the 12th, the 13th and the 14th centuries, the period that needs to be studied by performers more carefully than the early Middle Ages, if only because various repertories of music survive from then.

Some excellent studies have been written that offer guidelines for how to proceed. Werner Bachmann, for example, has written on the introduction of bowing into western Europe.[10] But we need similar studies on other instruments as well (and on other aspects of the fiddle). Is it possible, for example, that the lute was introduced into Europe, or at least into France and Italy, only in the 13th century? Dante appears to have been the first writer to have used the word 'liuto' (or 'leuto'), and the instrument seems not to be mentioned in French literature until the very late 13th century or to be depicted in paintings before that time.[11] While the harp was common in France during the 12th and 13th centuries, it seems not to have been introduced into Italy until the 14th century,[12] the recorder does not appear in Italian paintings until the very end of the 14th century,[13] and various kinds of evidence, both written and pictorial, suggest that stringed keyboard instruments – virginals or clavichords – were invented about the end of the 14th century.[14] The transverse flute seems to have been reintroduced into Europe after ancient times by way of the Germanic countries and then, in the 13th century, it moved down the Rhine and into England and France; it appears to have been completely unknown, for example, in 14th-century Italy.[15]

In order to write a comprehensive history of medieval instruments – to explain satisfactorily the origins of the most important instruments and their migrations across Europe and to be able to show the sequence of events that led the instrumentarium of one century to differ so radically from that of the next – scholars will need first to study carefully the history of each individual instrument or instrumental type, showing how its form and playing technique changed and offering as much information as they can assemble about the repertories of music each played. Werner Bachmann's study mentioned above, for example, is excellent, but we must nevertheless redouble our efforts to write the history of the medieval fiddle in more detail. We need to know how the instrument changed its shape and function from decade to decade and from country to country, how both flat and rounded bridges were used (and when, why, and with which repertories), and we must offer some hypotheses to explain the presence, in a number of pictures, of what looks like a second bridge between the bow and the fingerboard.[16] We must test Johannes de Grocheo's assertion that the fiddle could and did play every conceivable kind of composition that existed in the 13th century.[17] Pictures will help us a great deal in explaining how the instrument changed its shape and playing technique. We can see, for instance, how the fiddle changed from

King Alfonso the Wise supervising the clerical and secular scribes compiling cantigas, while musicians with fiddles and gitterns stand to left and right: folio from the 'Cantigas de Santa María', c1260 (El Escorial, Real Monasterio de S Lorenzo, b.I.r, f.292)

Choir of angels playing instruments that existed in 14th-century Italy, including (back row) tambourine (left), lute (centre) and gittern (right); (front row, left to right) portative organ, fiddle, psaltery, harp-psaltery and portative organ: mid-14th-century painted panel (probably a fragment of an altarpiece) by Paolo da Venezia, in the Museo di Palazzo Venezia, Rome

a rather tubby oval instrument to a much more slender instrument with incurved sides in the course of the 14th century in Italy,[18] and we seem to be able to see how much more frequently rounded bridges appear on the slenderer instruments, just possibly because they were more often used than the tubby oval instruments to play single lines. The earlier oval shape may have been more closely associated with flat bridges because such instruments were only required to perform drones or simple melodies with drone accompaniments.[19] And we need similarly detailed explanations (many of them doubtless difficult or impossible to give with assurance because of the ambiguity of the evidence) about each of the most important instrumental types. Scholars should concentrate more than they have on explaining what instruments looked like and how they were played in 12th-century France, 13th-century England, 14th-century Germany and so on, in an effort to connect instruments more closely with real cultural milieux, and in order to help answer the question of greatest importance to present-day performers, that is, which repertories of written or unwritten music are appropriate for each instrument.

The repertory of troubadour and trouvère music offers a good example of the need to differentiate genres of music, and the difficulty of interpreting evidence. There have been passing remarks in the musicological literature about the applicability of instruments to these repertories, and the first full-scale study of the question has recently appeared.[20] But we still need to take into account, among other things, such information as that supplied in the 13th-century romance *Guiron le Courtois*.[21] The author of the romance tells us that Tristan's father Meliadus was the first person ever to write a *lai* to be sung to the harp; and literary and pictorial sources tell us that both Tristan and Isolde sang to the harp, alone and together.[22] But wherever one of these *lais* appears in a narrative it is almost always a strophic song, that is, a so-called narrative *lai*.[23] It is clear from *Guiron le Courtois* and from the Tristan stories, then, that from an early period the harp accompanied a particular repertory, although we cannot be certain the extent to which that evidence can be made to apply to repertories other than the strophic *lai*. But in fact the romance does offer us further information, for when King Meliadus's knight comes to the court of King Arthur in Camelot to sing Meliadus's *lai* to the harp before the Queen of Scotland, he interrupts one of the queen's ladies, who has been singing to the harp a song by the 'chevalier de Nogalles', a poet or composer whose works have evidently not survived him.[24] Given that he is noble is it not possible, or even probable, that the 'chevalier de Nogalles' was a troubadour, and that the Queen of Scotland's lady is thus seen to be singing a troubadour song while accompanying herself on the harp? Clearly many more such examples would need to be collected and analysed before we could come to any definitive solution.

A few passages in theoretical treatises give random information about performance that we need to take very seriously indeed, since technical writing by musicians constitutes the best source of information we have. Thus, Johannes de Grocheo, describing the musical life of 13th-century Paris, claims that a good fiddle player performs every *cantus* and *cantilena* and, indeed, every musical form.[25] 'Every musical form' presumably encompasses written and unwritten monophony as well as polyphony. If we do not

21

take Johannes literally, it seems to me, we should feel compelled to explain away his unambiguous remark in some convincing fashion. But in fact, we need many more detailed studies of each bit of evidence – theoretical, archival, literary and iconographic – before we can be at all clear about which instruments accompanied the various kinds of monophony and polyphony in the 12th, 13th and 14th centuries, and how performing conventions differed between England, Spain, France, Germany and Italy.

In short, the study of musical instruments as an aspect of performance practice should place less emphasis on their forms and structures – although these are certainly questions that cannot be ignored – than on their geographical and chronological spread, and on their relationship with individual repertories of music, both those that have survived and those that have been lost. It is not easy to find in the musicological literature discussions of the sorts of instruments in common use, say, in 12th-century France, 13th-century England or 14th-century Italy, let alone studies that investigate the instruments appropriate for Landini's music, say, as opposed to other kinds of music written in 14th-century Italy, or to the music of Guillaume de Machaut.[26] And yet, these more detailed questions are precisely those that performers ought to be thinking about as hard as they can.

It should be obvious that even though a particular instrument can be shown to have existed at a certain period, it does not necessarily follow that it was used to play all repertories. Pictures from every country in the 13th and 14th centuries, for instance, show countless shepherds playing instruments that resemble either shawms or recorders,[27] but it does not follow that shawms and recorders were used then, or should be used now, in perfor-mances of organum, 13th-century motets, or courtly monophonic or polyphonic songs. We must learn to ask more detailed and searching questions about instruments and their uses than we have asked in the past, an exercise that is not always easy or straightforward, because so much of the evidence is fugitive or fragmentary. Questions about the participation of instruments in the performance of particular repertories can scarcely ever be answered simply or unambiguously, or in a way that applies to every surviving composition.

In the introduction to this section, I have suggested that the chief obstacle in understanding the performing conventions of the Middle Ages comes about because there is so little concrete evidence, and because the sources on which we must base our conclusions – archival, literary and iconographical – offer either ambiguous information, or only partial answers to the sorts of questions we have to ask. Pictures, for example, are unlikely to reflect social reality very directly before the 14th century.[28] The musical manuscripts themselves do not, of course, give us precise information about whether or not instruments were intended to take part; scholars seem long since to have reached a consensus in agreeing that the absence of text does not necessarily imply the absence of singers and the presence of instruments, although, like all such questions, debate should and does continue about this question.[29] Even in those rare instances where music that is almost certainly instrumental in character appears in medieval manuscripts, they do not indicate the nature of the instrument or instruments for which the music was intended.[30]

Most important, almost no instruments survive from before about 1500, and those few that do are mostly quite atypical, like the children's whistle flutes found in Russian earthworks, the elaborately decorated gitterns (or whatever they are) presumably intended as ceremonial gifts for some elegant occasion, the folk-like rebec/fiddle originally owned by a 15th-century Bolognese saint and so on.[31] Moreover, there are two special problems in depending on written evidence to study the way instruments were used in the Middle Ages. In the first place, we can never be certain we know what writers mean by a particular word. Biblical or ancient terms, such as 'cithara', 'lyra' and 'psalterium', for example, were translated in a variety of ways in the Middle Ages,[32] and it is not always possible to identify the precise shade of meaning intended when, for example, a poet includes instruments called 'leuto', 'chitarre', 'ceterare', 'ribebe', 'viuola' and 'gighe' together in the same list of instruments.[33] Similarly, there is a problem in using pay records to tell us about instrumental conventions, since they do not always supply information about the kinds of occasions when certain genres of music were normally played, and especially not those private, social occasions which probably constituted the principal forum for the perform- ance of the surviving secular music from the Middle Ages.

As a part of his comprehensive definition of music, which comprised *musica mundana* (the mathematical basis of the external world) and *musica humana* (the harmony of the soul and the body), Boethius in the late 5th century included as well *musica instrumentalis*, the ordered sounds that we today define as music. Like music as a whole, Boethius divided *musica instrumentalis* into three classes: sounds produced by strings, by winds (including voices) and by percussion.[34] This classification scheme, still more or less closely followed to the present day, would seem to be the most convenient in summarizing the chief characteristics of each of the principal instrumental types of the Middle Ages.

Of the bowed string instruments, the fiddle (*vielle* or *viola*) surely takes pride of place among the instruments of the 12th, 13th and 14th centuries, if only because of Johannes de Grocheo's claim that it was apt for all musical forms. Indeed, fiddles in various forms, sizes and contexts feature so prominently in all sorts of reports about the Middle Ages – iconographical, literary and archival – that it is virtually impossible to summarize their characteristics briefly. There is no other medieval instrument that calls more urgently for detailed study, so that we can begin to know how the fiddle of Machaut's time differed from that used in Spain and Germany in the 12th century, in 13th-century Paris, in the circles of the troubadours and the Minnesänger and so on. What we define as 'fiddle' (it was called by many different names in the Middle Ages) is an instrument with a more or less flat back and separate sides, but its body outline differed radically at various times and places. Some were spade shaped, some were oval or even rectangular, and many of those shown in pictures have incurved sides.[35]

The most important questions performers need to ask about fiddles, however, involve neither their nomenclature nor their body outline, but rather more detailed issues that affect how they were played and how they sounded: the nature of the bridge and the fingerboard, the number and tuning of the strings, the presence or absence of frets, and possible playing positions and playing techniques.[36] Such questions are not easy to answer clearly and simply because iconographical and literary sources offer so much contradictory information. In any case, it is a characteristic of all instruments in the Middle Ages that they tend not to be standardized but differ one from another much more than in later periods. We can find pictures or literary descriptions that support various conclusions about the shapes, fittings and playing techniques of fiddles. They do not seem to have been built in two, three or four conventional sizes, so far as we can tell. They could be strung with a varying number of strings, from two to six, although four or five seem to have been most common for most sorts of instruments during much of our period. We can suppose that many fiddles were strung with gut strings, but there is also reason to believe that other sorts of materials were used from time to time. No solution has yet been proposed to explain the enigma that fiddles of approximately the same size sometimes seem to have radically different string lengths, depending on the position of the bridge or string holder. It would almost appear that both were freely movable, at least on some fiddles at certain periods. Some fiddles had fingerboards and others did not. Some had drone strings off the fingerboard and others did not. Some had frets and others did not. Some were played under the chin or across the chest, while others seem to have been played upright, in viola da gamba position.

Individual works of art can never supply all of the information we need to know about an instrument, since we are searching for conventional usages and normal everyday procedures. It is only from a collection of the information to be found in a number of pictures that we can be certain that bridges on some fiddles in the Middle Ages were rounded enough to allow the player access to single strings, while bridges on other fiddles were flat (some were even incorporated into the string holder), suggesting that the latter types played mostly drones, chords, or single melodies with accompaniments.[37] The diversity of musical functions that these differences imply is suggested, too, by the three different tunings Jerome of Moravia gave for fiddles (ex.1), two more appropriate for drone instruments and one

Ex.1 The three tunings for the fiddle given by Jerome of Moravia

better for playing single melodic lines (although he does not explicitly say so).[38]

Similar problems of diversity (and a lack of specialized scholarly studies) hamper our abilities to generalize about other instruments. Many of the ambiguities and contradictions that surround the history of the rebec also cloud our knowledge of the fiddle. Its most common name, 'rebec', 'rebab' or some variant (a few scholars would claim we should make a distinction between the two), strongly suggests that the instruments came from Arabic lands, but the term 'lira' was also used to describe a similar instrument, which we can most simply define as a string instrument with a vaulted back and with no clear demarcation of neck from body.[39] We should probably make two sorts of finer distinctions about types of rebecs, and on the one hand distinguish between those that have no separate fingerboard and those whose fingerboard is a raised part of the soundboard, and on the other hand between those with the shape of a squat pear and long relatively slender instruments. It must be admitted, however, that no one has yet explained how these differences might be correlated with more important musical or historical questions, in order to help us learn what affected the sounds of the instruments, their musical function, or the repertory they were intended to play.

Like fiddles, rebecs can be seen to have had diverse characteristics. Some had frets and others did not. Some were played under the chin or across the chest, and others were played in an upright position like a viola da gamba. Rebecs appear to have had varying numbers of strings, but most in our period seem to have had but two or three. Again, Jerome of Moravia gives us our most precise information in explaining that the two strings of rebecs were tuned a fifth apart,[40] but even this information offers a puzzle, for he claims that the rebec is tuned to low *gamma-ut* (*G*) and its fifth *D sol re* (*d*), improbably low pitches for instruments with so short a string length. It may be that Jerome unwittingly offers the best evidence we have that instruments played at whatever pitch they could, but the lowest pitch was called *gamma-ut*, no matter where it sounded.

For much of its early history, the rebec may have been an instrument especially closely associated with minstrels, and thus appropriate for playing whatever music was included in their repertory.[41] In the absence of detailed studies of the repertories of minstrels or for the rebec, however, we cannot yet make such generalizations confidently. While it seems clear that by the 15th century the rebec in much of western Europe was associated mostly with lower-class music, we must also keep in mind that Johannes Tinctoris in the last quarter of the 15th century praised the instrument (along with the fiddle) as his favourite, more apt for private spiritual enjoyment than for public celebration,[42] and in the 16th century Hans Gerle published German lieder in arrangements for quartets of rebecs.[43]

A third bowed string, the bowed lyre (that is, the crowd or in Welsh 'crwth'), must also be considered one of the principal medieval instruments, even though it was probably seldom or never involved in performances of much of the medieval music we study. It seems to have had a life mostly in Great Britain in the 11th and 12th centuries (although it lived on as a traditional instrument even into the 18th century).[44] In the earlier Middle Ages, too, iconographical and literary evidence makes clear that some version of the ancient lyre (called variously by such names as 'lyre', 'cithara', 'rotte' or even 'harp') continued to be known in western Europe. Lyres generally lacked the fingerboard found on the crowd and they were sometimes bowed and sometimes plucked (we must always keep in mind the possibility that the same or similar instruments could be either plucked or bowed in the Middle Ages). But with the lyre as with the crowd, it is not yet clear the extent to which such instruments were involved with the performance

25

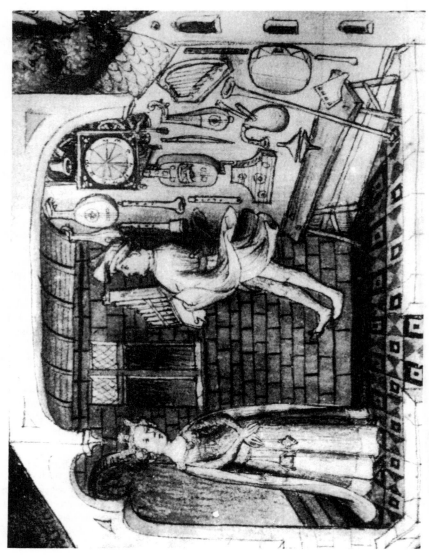

Illustration from a 14th-century manuscript of the 'Roman de la rose': showing (centre) portative organ; (hanging, top row, left to right) gittern and lute; (middle row) bombarde, shawm, recorder, hurdy-gurdy, rebec with bow, and harp; (bottom row) psaltery, bagpipe, trumpet and tabor with tabor pipe (above) and stick (below); and (on bench) cymbals and panpipe

of the music that survives. Some pictures may include lyres for purely symbolic reasons, for example, rather than because they reflect current musical practice.[45]

A serious terminological problem complicates the task of studying the principal plucked string instruments of the Middle Ages. Written sources give various names – 'mandora', 'gittern', 'citole', 'morache', 'guiterre latine', 'guitarra moresca' and 'quitarra saracenica' among others – but we can never be certain we know to which instruments they refer. Probably most of these terms refer to one of two sorts of instrumental types: either gitterns or citoles, although we cannot yet rule out the possibility completely that the long-necked lute (and perhaps other Arabic instruments as well) had a wider distribution in western Europe than their appearance in the *Cantigas de Santa Maria* and a few other arguably peripheral sources might suggest. Although the gittern with its vaulted back looks like a small lute (or a plucked rebec), it does in fact seem to have lived a life of its own during the Middle Ages. Most of those shown in pictures were strung with three or four double courses, supplied with frets, and almost always played (mostly by minstrels) with a plectrum. The citole, on the other hand, resembles a guitar, with a flat back and sides (many are shown in pictures with a body outline rather like a holly leaf). It, too, commonly had three or four strings or courses, whether or not it was fretted, and the minstrels who mostly seem to have played it almost invariably used a plectrum. The citole was probably cultivated much more in northern than in southern Europe. It is never to be seen, for example, in Italian pictures from the 13th or 14th centuries.[46]

The lute, which became the principal plucked string instrument of the Renaissance, is not to be seen as often in medieval pictures as the gittern or the citole, and indeed, the lute may not have been introduced widely into France and Italy until the 13th century, about the same time that it appeared in the Spanish *Cantigas* illuminations. From the contexts in which it is shown in trecento art, it may well be that its musical function, at least in Italy, was often to play tenors or other relatively slow-moving parts, suggesting that it only gradually came to be the instrument of virtuoso soloists, as it was during the Renaissance.[47] But the early history of the lute remains to be written; only a careful scrutiny of the available evidence will confirm the suspicion that its widespread use in western Europe dates from later than we have previously thought.

Unlike fiddles, rebecs, gitterns and citoles, some instruments have one string for each pitch: most notably in the Middle Ages harps and psalteries. Like the fiddle, the harp seems to have been widely used, and especially in northern Europe and Spain. And like the fiddle (and indeed every other medieval instrument), the harp is seen in pictures and described in written sources in a number of different ways.[48] Harps were apparently built in a variety of sizes and shapes, and fitted with various numbers of strings; many presumably had but 10 to 12, a number sufficient to play single lines, whereas others – including the harp that Machaut used as his ideal in his *Dit de la harpe*[49] – had as many as 25, enough to play in any range, or even more than one melodic line at a time. One principal difficulty in playing the harp – and also the psaltery and every other sort of instrument with only one string to a pitch if the stringing is diatonic – involves the problem of chromatic

27

notes; apparently harpists needed to set the chromatic pitches for any given piece before they began to play, unless there was some technique that we do not know about for raising strings a semitone or for retuning quickly during the performance of a composition. Some harps were supplied with brays, hooks against which the strings rattled to produce a buzzing noise, but it is not at all clear how widespread brays were, or whether they were used in some countries but not in others. Again like fiddles, harps seem to have been the instruments most likely to accompany vocal performances of 'art music' throughout much of the Middle Ages. We can be certain that harpists accompanied the performances of strophic narrative *lais*, and they very probably played for a wide variety of other songs as well.[50]

The study of the musical uses of the psaltery presents many of the same problems as that of the harp. The first difficulty involves knowing what to call the various shapes in which the psaltery traditionally appears. The simple demi-trapezoid was probably called 'canon', a word evidently derived from the Arabic 'qanun', and the commonly seen half trapezoid was therefore quite logically the 'demi-canon' (or in Italian 'mezzo canone').[51] Those instruments were more common in medieval Italy than in France, where the pig-snout psaltery (the *psalterium* proper) was much more often seen.[52] Like harps, psalteries seem to have been supplied with varying numbers of strings (indeed, psalteries often seem to have been strung with double or triple courses). They might be played with one or both hands, and with one or two plectra (or with none). While the question must remain open pending further study, some psalteries may have played monophonic music exclusively while others on occasion also played polyphony. Psalteries struck with hammers – that is, dulcimers – did not come into widespread use in western Europe until the 15th century.[53]

The invention of keyboards and their gradual refinement constitute one of the great technological developments in instrument building of western Europe in the Middle Ages. While keyboards of a sort were applied to organs quite early on, they may not have functioned well enough before the 13th century actually to have been used in regular performances.[54] Certainly the small portative organ, held by the musician who presumably played on it single melodic lines, seems not to have appeared in Europe before the 13th century, by which time a truly efficient keyboard had been devised. By the end of the 14th century, large stationary organs had been installed in many churches in western Europe. And by the end of the 14th century, keyboards had been applied as well to stringed instruments to produce the clavichord, the virginals and eventually the harpsichord.[55]

Keyboards were applied as well to fiddles, though rarely in the Middle Ages, and also to the large *organistrum*, and to its smaller relative, the hurdy-gurdy.[56] Present-day musicians are inclined to associate the hurdy-gurdy exclusively with peasants and beggars, but in the 13th and 14th centuries it probably also played its part in the repertory of minstrels, possibly even in the performance of some courtly music of the period. The large *organistrum*, on the other hand, and the monochord, are more likely to have been instruments used merely for demonstrations of the tonal system or to give pitches to singers than as 'real' musical instruments with a repertory of their own.[57]

28

The distinction between loud and soft instruments – between *instruments hauts et bas* – is especially useful in differentiating among the various medieval winds.[58] Trumpets, shawms and bagpipes appear to have been the principal loud wind instruments. Long straight trumpets (with or without kettledrums) were commonly heard at ceremonial occasions – to accompany a ruler (or even the members of a city council), to embellish ceremonies like coronations and weddings (even middle-class weddings), to announce a herald, or to usher in a guest – everywhere in western Europe during the Middle Ages. It may be that they played only on the first few overtones, and thus made relatively low-pitched sounds rather than the brilliant high-pitched flourishes we associate with fanfares today. And we should not rule out the possibility that some trumpets performed as well rather more specifically musical functions, playing cantus firmi, for example, in polyphonic dances, accompanied by shawms and possibly even kettledrums.[59]

Shawms and shawm-like instruments as well as bagpipes are often to be seen in the hands of shepherds in medieval illuminations, but there is evidence that they played a role as well in city and court life in the Middle Ages. Certainly by the 14th century shawms of various kinds – some with cup-like bells and others without – played dance music and perhaps other kinds of polyphony either in groups of two or three, or joined by bagpipes, or even conceivably trumpets.[60] One sort of shawm may even have been a soft instrument, and therefore possibly even appropriate for use in chamber music, if Bara Boydell's conjectures about the nature of the mysterious *douçaine* are correct.[61]

In general, however, these loud winds – trumpets, shawms and bagpipes[62] – probably did not participate in the performance of either monophonic or polyphonic songs of the sort largely preserved in the musical sources for most of our period (although we cannot entirely rule out the possibility that they sometimes performed compositions in the courtly written tradition, as certainly happened with shawm bands in later centuries). The principal part of their repertory probably consisted of improvised (or semi-improvised) polyphony based on cantus firmi, of dances or one sort or another, and for the trumpets of musical formulas appropriate to various ceremonial occasions.

Players of soft wind instruments – recorders, 'double recorders' and various other sorts of whistle flutes as well as transverse flutes and *douçaines* – are also unlikely to have performed regularly all of the sorts of music that have come down to us in manuscript. Medieval artists more often depicted recorders in the hands of shepherds or members of the lower classes rather than courtly or learned musicians, or even minstrels. Surprisingly, the subject has not been much investigated by modern scholars, perhaps just because there is so little evidence on which to base any argument.[63] Surely, the relationship of the transverse flute to the surviving repertory constitutes an exception, for whereas such instruments are never depicted in Italian pictures before the 16th century, and relatively seldom in French pictures before the 15th century, they do appear in the illuminated copies of the Minnesänger repertory (see illustration, p. 30), and the conclusion is inescapable that they did take part in the performance of courtly music in Germany and perhaps in France as early as the 14th century, and possibly earlier.[64]

29

Minnesingers playing transverse flute and fiddle: miniature, 'Der Kanzler', from the Manesse MS, early 14th century (Heidelberg, Universitätsbibliothek, pal.germ.848.f.423v)

Neither pictorial nor written evidence from the Middle Ages indicates the presence of a wide variety of types of percussion instruments in real performances, except for a few standard situations: nakers (kettledrums) normally played with trumpets; small tabors accompanied three-holed pipes, and both instruments were played by a single musician; tambourines were used to accompany singing and dancing; the occasional drum enlivened a charivari or other rowdy celebration (as in the famous illustration from the *Roman de Fauvel*); and so on.[65] No medieval evidence known to me, however, suggests the sorts of elaborate drum parts – often with several drums at different pitches – sometimes heard in present-day performances of medieval music. Like monochords and *organistra*, bells – and especially struck bells hung on a frame – can be seen in a number of medieval illuminations.[66] Such sets of bells were almost certainly used for demonstrations of the tonal system (to show the derivations of pitches), but it is not yet absolutely clear that they also actually played written or unwritten compositions, sacred or secular, in musical ensembles.

It should be obvious that this summary of the principal musical instruments of the Middle Ages is no more than a bare sketch, subject to radical change after detailed studies have been made of particular instruments, and especially of their relationship to the surviving and to the lost repertories of the music heard during the Middle Ages. My sketch, moreover, only touches on those instruments especially widespread across western Europe during the 12th, 13th and 14th centuries; it leaves out instruments about which little is known, those that can be found only in a single region, and those that we know about from only one or two sources.

It would seem, then, that the principal instruments of the period that might have been used for the performance of 'art music' – of the monophonic and polyphonic music that is preserved in the manuscripts we study – were mainly strings: fiddle, rebec, gittern, citole, lute, harp and psaltery, plus a few others, such as portative organ and possibly hurdy-gurdy, and, by the late 14th century, conceivably virginals as well. Of the wind instruments, only the transverse flute and the recorder might possibly have been involved in performances of such music, but the use of the flute appears to have been limited to Germany and in the 14th century France, and the evidence is not yet in about the recorder.

So far as we now know, the novelties of the 12th and 13th centuries that had the most consequences for later music include the invention of efficient keyboards for hurdy-gurdies and organs, and just possibly the introduction of the lute into most of western Europe. In the 14th century, keyboards came to be applied to other stringed instruments, to produce the clavichord and the virginals, and large church organs became widespread. Along with these new instruments and major inventions, the nature of older instruments changed, as the harp spread over all of western Europe, the northern pig-snout psaltery penetrated into Italy, and instrumental types derived from the ancient world, such as lyres, disappeared altogether or became a 'traditional' or folk instrument. If my sketch has done nothing else, it should have demonstrated how much we need more detailed studies to show where, how and why particular instruments were cultivated in particular times and places, and what their connection was with the surviving musical repertories

31

that present-day musicians wish to perform. We are still at the very beginning of the study of the use of instruments in medieval performances. There are many questions we have for far too long neglected or ignored to which performers urgently need answers.

Notes

[1] See for example J. Montagu, *The World of Medieval and Renaissance Musical Instruments* (Newton Abbot, 1976); D. Munrow, *Instruments of the Middle Ages and Renaissance* (London, 1976); and M. Remnant, *Musical Instruments of the West* (London, 1978). *GroveMI* includes entries for all the instruments mentioned in this chapter.

[2] In addition, *FoMRHI Quarterly*, an informal bulletin of the Fellowship of Makers and Researchers of Historical Instruments, regularly publishes valuable information about various aspects of musical instruments, mostly relating to problems of primary interest to makers, conservators and curators of museums.

[3] Landini's tombstone (with portative organ, fiddle and lute) is pictured, among other places, in *La musica: enciclopedia storica*, i, 196. Landini's portrait in the Squarcialupi Codex – with portative organ, fiddle, lute, gittern, harp, psaltery, recorders (!) and shawms – is reproduced, among other places, in *MGG*, viii, pl.3. The instruments which Landini played, according to Villani, are enumerated in Filippo Villani, *Liber de civitatis florentiae famosis civibus*, ed. G. C. Galletti (Florence, 1847), 34–5, in Latin, and, in a shorter version in Italian, in *Croniche di Giovanni, Matteo e Filippo Villani*, ii (Trieste, 1858), 449. The anonymous 13th- or early 14th-century poem *L'intelligenza* has most recently been published in a modern edition in *Poemetti del duecento: Il tesoretto, Il fiore, L'intelligenza*, ed. G. Petronio (Turin, 2/1967); the passage describing instruments is also in *Poeti minori del trecento*, ed. N. Sapegno (Milan, 1952), 650–51, and in *La cronaca fiorentina . . . e L'intelligenza*, ed. D. Carbone (Florence, 1871), 196–7. On the instruments seen in pictures with crowds of angels, see H. M. Brown, 'Trecento Angels and the Instruments they Play', in *Modern Musical Scholarship*, ed. E. Olleson (Stocksfield, 1980), 112–40. All trecento pictures with musical subject matter will eventually be published in Brown, 'A Corpus of Trecento Pictures with Musical Subject Matter', *Imago musicae*, i (1985), 189–243 (Instalment 1), and following volumes.

[4] This point is expanded in Brown, 'Trecento Angels'.

[5] Immanuel Romano's bizarre rhymed account of life at the opulent court of Can Grande della Scala, printed, among other places, in *Rimatori comico-realistici del Due e Trecento*, ed. M. Vitale (Turin, 1956), ii, 103–12, mentions 'flatui' [*sic*], but it is of course unclear whether Immanuel intended to refer to double recorders, the stubby pipe and tabor seen in some of Giotto's paintings, transverse flutes never depicted by trecento painters, or some other sort of instrument entirely. The word 'flaiollo' that Dante uses (in *Paradiso*, xx) for flute seems to me likely to mean a pipe of the sort used with a tabor; on the word, and the fact that some commentators do not believe it refers to a musical instrument, see *Enciclopedia Dantesca*, ii (1970), 943.

[6] On the lists of instruments in Machaut's works, see among other studies J. Godwin, ' "Mains divers acors": Some Instrument Collections of the Ars Nova Period', *EM*, v (1977), 148–59. The instruments in *Les échecs amoureux* are listed and discussed in H. Abert, 'Die Musikästhetik der Echecs amoureux', *SIMG*, vi (1904–5), 346–55. For other French lists of instruments in literary and pictorial sources, see F. Brücker, *Die Blasinstrumente in der altfranzösischen Literatur* (Giessen, 1926); F. Dick, *Bezeichnungen für Saiten- und Schlaginstrumente in der altfranzösischen Literatur* (Giessen, 1932); G. Foster, *The Iconology of Musical Instruments and Musical Performance in Thirteenth-century French Manuscript Illuminations* (diss., City U. of New York, 1977); and M. V. Fowler, *Musical Interpolations in Thirteenth- and Fourteenth-century French Narratives* (diss., Yale U., 1979).

[7] See the index of instruments in Brown, 'Corpus', *Imago musicae*, ii (1986), 189–90, for a characteristic sampling of the instruments shown in 14th-century Italian pictures. See Foster, *The Iconology of Musical Instruments*, 65–103, for an overview of the instruments shown in 13th-century French illuminations. M. B. Owens, *Musical Subject Matter in the Illumination of Books of Hours from Fifteenth-century France and Flanders* (diss., U. of Chicago, 1987) confirms the scarcity of double recorders in later French miniatures.

[8] The *Cantigas* are reproduced in facsimile in *La música de las cantigas de Santa María del Rey Alfonso el Sabio*, ed. H. Anglès (Barcelona, 1943–64). On the instruments in the *Cantigas*, see

also J. Ribera, *La música de las cantigas* (Madrid, 1922). On the instruments mentioned in medieval Spanish literature, see also D. Devoto, 'La énumeracion de instrumentos musicales en la poesia medieval castellana', in *Miscelanea en homenaje a Mons. Higinio Anglès* (Barcelona, 1958–61), i, 211–22. For the latest studies on music at the court of King Alfonso the Wise, see the essays in *Revista de musicología*, x (1987).

[9] I think of such statements as that in Hortense Panum's excellent *The Stringed Instruments of the Middle Ages*, trans. and rev. by J. Pulver (London, 1939/*R*1971), 86–90, where the Crusades are invoked as the conduit for the introduction of many more instruments into western Europe than can be documented.

[10] W. Bachmann, *The Origins of Bowing and the Development of Bowed Instruments up to the Thirteenth Century*, trans. N. Deane (London, 1969).

[11] In *Paradiso*, xiv. On this passage, see K. Meyer-Baer, 'Music in Dante's *Divina commedia*', in *Aspects of Medieval and Renaissance Music: a Birthday Offering to Gustave Reese* (New York, 1966), 620–21.

[12] On the introduction of the harp into Italy, see H. M. Brown, 'The Trecento Harp', in *Performance Practice: New York 1981*, 35–73.

[13] For a sampling of the few depictions of recorders in late trecento art, see the index of instruments in Brown, 'Corpus', *Imago musicae*, ii (1986), 189–90.

[14] On early keyboard instruments, see E. A. Bowles, 'On the Origin of the Keyboard Mechanism in the Late Middle Ages', *Technology and Culture*, vii (1966), 152–62, and also E. M. Ripin, 'Towards an Identification of the Chekker', *GSJ*, xxviii (1975), 11–25; C. Page, 'The Myth of the Chekker', *EM*, vii (1979), 482–9; and W. Barry, 'Henri Arnaut de Zwolle's *Clavicordium* and the Origin of the Chekker', *JAMIS*, xi (1985), 5–13.

[15] For a summary of the early history of the flute, see H. M. Brown, 'Flute', *GroveMI*.

[16] For some examples of fiddles with second 'bridges' in 14th-century Italy, see Brown, 'Corpus', *Imago musicae*, i (1985), nos.77, 80 and 81. There are many other examples in trecento art, and in other repertories of pictures as well. On second bridges on English instruments of the Middle Ages, see M. Remnant, *English Bowed Instruments from Anglo-Saxon to Tudor Times* (Oxford, 1986), chap.2, 'The Ingredients of Bowed Instruments'. For an example of such a fiddle from 16th-century France, see J. Dugot, 'L'iconographie musicale du buffet des orgues de l'église St. Pierre–St. Paul de Gonesse', paper read at the conference 'De l'image à l'objet: La méthode critique en iconographie musicale', sponsored by the Centre d'Iconographie musicale et d'Organologie in Paris, 4–7 Sept 1985, and to be published in the conference proceedings.

[17] See n.25 below.

[18] Florentine depictions of the feast of Herod furnish a convenient point of comparison for the change in the shapes of fiddles during the course of the 14th century. Compare for example the oval fiddle in Giotto's *Feast of Herod*, painted in the 1320s (Brown, 'Corpus', *Imago musicae*, ii (1985), no.172), with the much slenderer instruments shown in Agnolo Gaddi's and Niccolo di Pietro Gerini's versions of the same scene, painted in 1387 and 1388 (Brown, 'Corpus', *Imago musicae*, i (1985), nos.129 and 155).

[19] The statement by P. Holman in *MT*, cxxvi (1985), 452, that bowed instruments did not have arched bridges much before the 1480s is contradicted not only by iconographical evidence but also (at least by implication) by Jerome of Moravia, writing about 1300. For a characteristic sample of the sorts of 13th- and 14th-century pictures that show fiddles with arched bridges, see Remnant, *English Bowed Instruments*, chap.2, 'The Ingredients of Bowed Instruments', and H. M. Brown, 'The Trecento Fiddle' (forthcoming). Jerome of Moravia implies the presence of an arched bridge, or at least of the possibility of playing the middle strings of a fiddle separately, in his second tuning which he describes as 'necessary for secular songs and for all others – especially irregular ones – which frequently wish to run through the whole hand'; see the translation of Jerome's remarks on instruments in C. Page, 'Jerome of Moravia on the *Rubeba* and *Viella*', *GSJ*, xxxii (1979), 77–98. Whether or not Page is correct in assuming that Jerome's second tuning (which is re-entrant but does not call for any off-board drone) requires one double course tuned in octaves, the theorist seems clearly to imply the possibility of playing single notes on the middle strings.

[20] C. Page, *Voices and Instruments of the Middle Ages* (London, 1987). See also Chapter I n.3.

[21] For the author, date and complicated bibliographical history of the romance, see R. Lathuillère, *Guiron le courtois: étude de la tradition manuscrite et analyse critique* (Geneva, 1966). The episode involving Meliadus and the *lai* is summarized there on p.218 and in E. Löseth, *Le roman en prose de Tristan, le roman de Palamède et la compilation de Rusticien de Pise* (Paris, 1891), 444–5.

[22] For a brief discussion of the association of Tristan and Isolde with the harp, see Lathuillère, *Guiron le courtois*, 11–26, and Brown, 'The Trecento Harp', 38, where references to other studies may be found.

[23] On the so-called narrative *lai*, normally strophic, see J. Maillard, *Evolution et esthétique du lai lyrique des origines à la fin du XIVe siècle* (Paris, 1963).

[24] On Nogalles, which I take to be Novaille or Sauver-les-Nauvailles, see U. Günther, 'Eine Ballade auf Mathieu de Foix', *MD*, xix (1965), 69. Given that the story deals with King Arthur's court, the knight may, however, be from north Wales.

[25] See E. Rohloff, *Der Musiktraktat des Johannes de Grocheo* (Leipzig, 1943), 52: 'Bonus autem artifex in viella omnem cantum et cantilenam et omnem formam musicalem generaliter introducit', translated by Albert Seay in Johannes de Grocheo, *Concerning Music* (Colorado Springs, 1967), 19, as: 'A good performer on the vielle uses normally every cantus and cantilena and every musical form'.

[26] There are, however, a few studies that concentrate on questions of performance – including the appropriate instrumentarium – in particular times and places. Besides the studies cited in notes 3 and 6 above, see also F. Gennrich, 'Zur Musikinstrumentenkunde der Machaut-Zeit', *ZMw*, ix (1926–7), 513–17; E. A. Bowles, 'Instruments at the Court of Burgundy (1363–1467)', *GSJ*, vi (1953), 41–51; G. Reaney, 'Voices and Instruments in the Music of Guillaume de Machaut', *RBM*, x (1956), 3–17; Reaney, 'The Part Played by Instruments in the Music of Guillaume de Machaut', *Studi musicali*, vi (1977), 3–19; F. Ll. Harrison, 'Tradition and Innovation in Instrumental Usage 1100–1450', in *Aspects of Medieval and Renaissance Music: a Birthday Offering to Gustave Reese* (New York, 1966), 319–35; R. Rastall, 'Some English Consort-groupings of the Late Middle Ages', *ML*, lv (1974), 179–202; and most recently, Remnant, *English Bowed Instruments*.

There are also a few studies of instruments used for particular kinds of occasion, most notably the series of articles by E. A. Bowles, 'Musical Instruments at the Medieval Banquet', *RBM*, xii (1958), 41–51; 'Musical Instruments in Civic Progressions during the Middle Ages', *AcM*, xxxiii (1961), 147–61; 'Musical Instruments in the Medieval Corpus Christi Procession', *JAMS*, xvii (1964), 251–60; and 'Were Musical Instruments Used in the Liturgical Service during the Middle Ages?', *GSJ*, x (1957), 40–56.

[27] For a selection of 14th-century Italian shepherds playing instruments, see Brown, 'Corpus', ii, p.191. For a short list of northern European medieval shepherds playing instruments, see L. M. C. Randall, *Images in the Margins of Gothic Manuscripts* (Berkeley and Los Angeles, 1966), 130–31, 213. Among the desiderata of students of performing practice and musical iconography are bibliographical studies that can isolate quickly and easily such groups associated with music as shepherds, minstrels, church singers and so on.

[28] On this point, see among other studies E. Winternitz, *Musical Instruments and their Symbolism in Western Art* (New Haven and London, 1979), chap.1, 'The Visual Arts as a Source for the Historian of Music', and chap.2, 'The Knowledge of Musical Instruments as an Aid to the Art Historian'. It seems likely that a significant change in the meaning of pictures of music-making occurred in the 14th century, when artists began to depict the world around them to a much greater extent than they had ever done before.

For an extreme example of the unreality of pan-European pictures of musical instruments in the Middle Ages, see for example the so-called instruments of St Jerome, described and discussed in R. Hammerstein, 'Instrumenta Hieronymi', *AMw*, xvi (1959), 117–34, and H. Avenary, 'Hieronymus' Epistel über die Musikinstrumente und ihre altöstlichen Quellen', *AnM*, xvi (1961), 55–80.

[29] See Chapter V for Christopher Page's forceful presentation of the argument that instruments seldom or never took part in the performance of polyphony in the later Middle Ages, and that textless lines were therefore normally sung.

[30] For a brief overview of medieval instrumental music, see H. M. Brown, 'Instrumentalmusik', *MGG*, suppl., 775–810.

[31] On the instruments in Russian earthworks, see F. Crane, *Extant Medieval Musical Instruments: a Provisional Catalogue by Types* (Iowa City, 1972), pp.xiii–xiv and *passim*. On what I have called elaborate gitterns, see Crane, p.15 (for the British Museum instrument) and p.16 (for the instrument in New York, Metropolitan Museum of Art, called a fiddle by Crane). On the British Museum instrument, see also M. Remnant and R. Marks, 'A Medieval "Gittern" ', in *Music and Civilisation*, The British Museum Yearbook, iv (London, 1980), 83–134. On the New York instrument, see also E. Winternitz, *Musical Instruments of the Western World* (New York, n.d.), 47–51. On the fiddle (or rebec) of St Caterina de'Vigri, see M. Tiella, *La 'Violeta' de S. Caterina de'Vigri (sec. XV) nel Convento del Corpus Domini, Bologna* (Florence, 1974).

[32] On biblical terms see among other studies C. Page, 'Biblical Instruments in Medieval Manuscripts', *EM*, v (1977), 299–309.

[33] These instruments, among others, are cited in the anonymous early 14th-century poem *L'intelligenza* as being among those appropriate for a court; for modern editions of the poem, see n.3 above.

[34] On the various classification schemes for musical instruments in use in the Middle Ages, including Boethius', see E. Hickmann, *Musica instrumentalis: Studien zur Klassifikation des Musikinstrumentariums im Mittelalter* (Baden-Baden, 1971). For an alternative system, derived from St Augustine, and virtually ignored by Hickmann, see H. M. Brown, 'St. Augustine, Lady Music, and the Gittern in Fourteenth-century Italy', *MD*, xxxviii (1984), 25–65. On the modern classification system for instruments, see E. M. von Hornbostel and C. Sachs, 'Classification of Musical Instruments', trans. A. Baines and K. P. Wachsmann, *GSJ*, xiv (1961), 3–29.

[35] On medieval string instruments in general, see Panum, *Stringed Instruments of the Middle Ages*; Bachmann, *The Origins of Bowing*; and Remnant, *English Bowed Instruments*. See also D. Droysen, 'Die Darstellungen von Saiteninstrumenten in der mittelalterlichen Buchmalerei und ihre Bedeutung für die Instrumentenkunde', in *GfMKB, Kassel 1962*, 302–5; C. Page, 'An Aspect of Medieval Fiddle Construction', *EM*, ii (1974), 166–7; M. Remnant, 'The Diversity of Medieval Fiddles', *EM*, iii (1975), 47–51; L. Wright, 'Sculptures of Medieval Fiddles at Gargilesse', *GSJ*, xxxii (1979), 66–76; J. Wiltshire, 'Medieval Fiddles at Hardham', *GSJ*, xxxiv (1981), 142–6; and B. Ravenel, 'Rebec und Fiedel: Ikonographie und Spielweise', *Basler Jb für historische Musikpraxis*, viii (1984), 105–30.

[36] Some of these questions are dealt with in the studies cited in n.35 above. See also M. Remnant, 'The Use of Frets on Rebecs and Medieval Fiddles', *GSJ*, xxi (1968), 146–51. A full-scale study of the fiddle, its playing technique and its repertory from the 14th century on urgently needs to be made.

[37] See n.19 above.

[38] On Jerome's three tunings for the fiddle, see C. Page, 'Jerome of Moravia on the *Rubeba* and *Viella*'.

[39] On the rebec, and especially on the names for it, see M. A. Downie, *The Rebec: an Orthographic and Iconographic Study* (diss., West Virginia U., 1981); and the study by Ravenel cited in n.35 above.

[40] See Page, 'Jerome of Moravia on the *Rubeba* and *Viella*'.

[41] This statement echoes M. Remnant, 'Rebec', *Grove6*, xv, 636. Like virtually every general statement about musical instruments in the Middle Ages, however, it may prove after further study to be over-simple or even inaccurate.

[42] See K. Weinmann, *Johannes Tinctoris (1445–1511) und sein unbekannter Traktat 'De inventione et usu musicae'* (Tutzing, 1961), 45–6, and A. Baines, 'Fifteenth-century Instruments in Tinctoris's *De inventione et usu musicae*', *GSJ*, iii (1950), 24–5: 'The viola and the rebec are my ... chosen instruments, those that induce piety and stir my heart most ardently to the contemplation of heavenly joys. For these reasons I would rather reserve them solely for sacred music and the secret consolation of the soul, than have them sometimes used for profane occasions and public festivities'.

[43] Gerle's two pieces for quartets of *Kleingeigen* are printed in his *Musica Teusch* (Nuremberg, 1532), ff. J1–J2, described in H. M. Brown, *Instrumental Music Printed Before 1600* (Cambridge, Mass., 1965), 41.

[44] On the crowd, see O. Andersson, *The Bowed Harp*, ed. K. Schlessinger (London, 1930); M. Remnant, 'Rebec, Fiddle and Crowd in England', *PRMA*, xcv (1968–9), 15–28; Remnant, 'Rebec, Fiddle and Crowd: some Further Observations', *PRMA*, xcvi (1969–70), 149–50; J. M. Bevil, *The Welsh Crwth: its History and its Genealogy* (diss., North Texas State U., 1973); and J. Rimmer, 'Crwth', *GroveMI*.

[45] On the symbolism of musical instruments in medieval art, see for example H. Steger. *David Rex et Propheta* (Nuremberg, 1961); R. Hammerstein, *Die Musik der Engel* (Munich, 1962); and T. Seebass, *Musikdarstellung und Psalterillustration im früheren Mittelalter* (Berne, 1973).

[46] On the gittern and the citole, see M. Remnant, 'The Gittern in English Mediaeval Art', *GSJ*, xviii (1965), 104–9; and especially L. Wright, 'The Medieval Gittern and Citole: a Case of Mistaken Identity', *GSJ*, xxx (1977), 8–42.

[47] The lute in the 13th and 14th centuries has not been the subject of separate study. C. Page, 'French Lute Tablature in the 14th Century', *EM*, viii (1980), 488–92, offers a speculation that is probably not well founded. Information about the instrument in the Middle Ages, its playing

technique and its repertory, is thus limited to the information given in the more general studies cited in the notes (and see especially notes 1 and 35 above).

[48] On the harp in the Middle Ages, see H. Adolf, 'The Ass and the Harp', *Speculum*, xxv (1950), 49–57; J. Rimmer, 'The Morphology of the Irish Harp', *GSJ*, xvii (1964), 39–49; Rimmer, 'The Morphology of the Triple Harp', *GSJ*, xviii (1965), 90–103; H. J. Zingel, *König Davids Harfe in der abendländischen Kunst* (Cologne, 1968); D. Droysen, 'Zum Problem der Klassifizierung von Harfendarstellungen in der Buchmalerei des frühen und hohen Mittelalters', *Jb des staatlichen Instituts für Musikforschung* (Berlin, 1969); J. Rimmer, *The Irish Harp* (Cork, 1969); R. Rensch, 'The Development of the Medieval Harp: a Re-examination of the Evidence of the Utrecht Psalter and its Progeny', *Gesta*, xi/2 (1972), 27–36; and Brown, 'The Trecento Harp'.

[49] Machaut's *Dit de la harpe* is published in a modern edition in K. Young, 'The *Dit de la harpe* of Guillaume de Machaut', in *Essays in Honor of Albert Feuillerat* (New Haven, 1943), 1–20. See also Jean Molinet's religious poem *Petit traictiet de la harpe*, in *Les faictz et dictz de Jean Molinet*, ed. N. Dupire (Paris, 1937), ii, 439–42.

[50] See notes 21–3 above.

[51] On the various kinds of psalteries and the terminology appropriate for each, see H. M. Brown, 'The Trecento Psaltery' (forthcoming).

[52] See Foster, *The Iconology of Musical Instruments*, 98.

[53] According to D. Kettlewell, 'Dulcimer', *Grove6*, v, 701.

[54] On medieval organs, see J. Perrot, *The Organ from its Invention in the Hellenistic Period to the End of the Thirteenth Century*, trans. N. Deane (London, 1971); H. Hickmann, *Das Portativ* (Kassel, 1972); P. Williams, *A New History of the Organ* (London, 1980); and the bibliography cited in P. Williams, 'Organ', *GroveMI*, ii, 914–16.

[55] For studies of stringed keyboard instruments at the end of the 14th century, see n.14 above.

[56] On the hurdy-gurdy, see M. Bröcker, *Die Drehleier: ihr Bau und ihre Geschichte* (Düsseldorf, 1973); and C. Page, 'The Medieval *Organistrum* and *Symphonia*', *GSJ*, xxxv (1982), 37–44, and xxxvi (1983), 71–87.

[57] On the monochord, see C. Adkins, *The Theory and Practice of the Monochord* (diss., U. of Iowa, 1963); C. Adkins, 'Monochord', *GroveMI*; and T. J. Mathiesen, 'An Annotated Translation of Euclid's Division of a Monochord', *JMT*, xix (1975), 236–58.

[58] On the distinction between *haut* and *bas* instruments, see E. A. Bowles, 'Haut and Bas: the Grouping of Musical Instruments in the Middle Ages', *MD*, viii (1954), 115–40.

[59] On 'brass' instruments in the Middle Ages, see E. A. Bowles, 'Unterscheidung der Instrumente Buisine, Cor, Trompe und Trompette', *AMw*, xviii (1961), 52–72, and A. Baines, *Brass Instruments: their History and Development* (London, 1976).

[60] For much information on 14th-century reed instruments, see B. Boydell, *The Crumhorn and other Renaissance Windcap Instruments* (Buren, 1982). On shawms and shawm-like instruments, see also A. Baines, *Woodwind Instruments and their History* (London, 1957, 3/1967); H. Becker, *Zur Entwicklungsgeschichte der antiken und mittelalterlichen Rohrblattinstrumente* (Hamburg, 1966); and Baines, 'Shawm', *GroveMI*.

[61] See Boydell, *Crumhorn*, 404–18, who identifies the *douçaine* or *dolzaina* as shawms with cup-shaped bells. The principal difficulty with his ingenious suggestion is that such instruments are normally shown in late medieval pictures playing alongside shawms without such bells, as regular members of loud wind bands. See for example Brown, 'Corpus', *Imago musicae*, i (1985), no.31, and the shawm band illustrating the concept 'dance' in the *Tacuinum sanitatis*, illustrated in J. von Schlosser, 'Ein veronesisches Bilderbuch und die höfische Kunst des XIV. Jahrhunderts', *Jb der kunsthistorischen Sammlungen des allerhöchsten Kaiserhauses*, xvi (1895), pl.xxii.

[62] On bagpipes, see A. Baines, *Bagpipes* (Oxford, 1960).

[63] The present state of knowledge about medieval recorders is reflected, for example, in the brief overview given in E. Hunt, *The Recorder and its Music* (London, 1962, rev., enlarged 2/1977), 1–10. For two surviving 14th-century recorders, see R. Weber, 'Recorder Finds from the Middle Ages, and Results of their Reconstruction', *GSJ*, xxix (1976), 35–41.

[64] See n.15 above.

[65] On percussion instruments, see J. Blades, *Percussion Instruments and their History* (London, 1970, rev. 3/1984).

[66] On bells, see J. Smits van Waesberghe, *Cymbala: Bells in the Middle Ages*, MSD, i (1951).

CHAPTER III

Chant

DAVID HILEY

The performance of plainchant has given rise to much controversy. Plain-chant is the sacred music of the church, a part of Christian ritual worship, and questions about the 'right' way to sing it often touch upon deeply held religious beliefs. If a performance tradition be altered, perhaps as a result of religious reform, or if two different practices come into conflict, then not only musical but also religious principles may be felt to be at stake. Plainchant was not intended to stand alone as some sort of isolated artistic phenomenon. Although many listen to it for pleasure, it was conceived as but one element in liturgical ceremonies, adding solemnity and splendour to the daily and yearly celebration of the liturgy. If we are to consider performance practice in chant we should really begin with the liturgy which is its reason for existing in the first place. After that the discussion may move to matters of musical technique: rhythm, expression and so on.

Because chant was sung universally (at least, wherever there were competent singers) much of the detail of performance practice was at first not recorded; it was a matter of custom and tradition. In this respect chant shared the condition of many other elements of religious worship. One of the things which seems most surprising when one first embarks upon the study of liturgical practice is how slowly its various elements were codified. From the early centuries (4th–5th centuries onwards) we know of collections of prayers and lessons, but almost no collections of chant texts survive – except, of course, for the ubiquitous Book of Psalms. Only from the end of the 8th century, during the great movement to raise standards of literacy and liturgical practice known as the 'Carolingian Renaissance', do we have complete copies of the texts to be chanted through the year. And several more decades passed before the music was codified. As to those additional details of ceremonial which have a bearing on musical performance – who shall sing which chants, and where – some information is found in books of ceremonial from the 7th or 8th century onwards. Yet not until the 13th century does a general need to codify all details of worship seem to have been felt. Only from that time do we begin to get books such as those serving the Salisbury liturgy, the Paris liturgy and the Dominican friars, which set out all the spoken and sung material with rubrics instructing those present in their various roles. And these rubrics are concerned not with technical musical matters such as tempo, dynamic and voice production, but simply the personnel responsible for individual items, liturgical movements and vestments, etc. In these circumstances we cannot hope to find information about all those aspects of early chant performance which interest us.

For further information about musical matters a close study of the notation of chant books is therefore essential, and although there is often a disconcerting lack of uniformity in the manuscript sources with regard to some of the detail essential for a better understanding of rhythmic and expressive elements in performance, much of importance is revealed there. The writings of medieval teachers and theorists are also sometimes useful although their main concerns usually lie with the modality of chants and musical rudiments such as consonance and species of scale segments, not with musical performance.

Most performances of Latin plainchant this century have used editions, and have followed performance practices, which are the results of the plainchant revival of the late 19th and 20th centuries, associated principally with the work of the Benedictines of the French monastery of Solesmes. Ample information is available about this version of the chant repertory and about the Solesmes manner of performance (typically, that of the period when Dom Joseph Gajard was choirmaster, 1914–71; in recent years, Solesmes performance has changed in consequence of further research into the notation of early chant sources). Books on the 'method' abound, as do gramophone recordings of the choir of Solesmes. To many, this is *the* way to sing chant. But the historical evidence on which the Solesmes restoration was based was no more complete than the material at our disposal today. In many respects the restorers had to present an unequivocal model where, from a strictly scholarly point of view, no certainty was possible. Although based on the best scholarship of the time, the editions were for practical use and had to take into account the needs of non-scholarly choirs. A clear, firm lead had to be given into territory where even 'pure' scholars, less painstaking than the monks, might fear to tread. It was a remarkable step towards scholarly reconstruction of 'authentic' performance, but it was not the ultimate answer. It is a disservice to the achievements of the Solesmes monks and other scholars of the time to hold up their work as infallible (though it was characteristic of its period to proclaim it as such). What follows will therefore try to give an idea of the sort of evidence that exists for the performance of chant, from the earliest times up to the 19th century, and will place the restoration itself in a historical context.

The liturgical context

The liturgical 'setting' of chant is the most difficult, not to say bewildering, aspect of chant performance for the non-specialist. Let us imagine that we need to perform some 13th-century polyphony in something like an 'authentic' liturgical context. How is the liturgy to be reconstructed? It might be a good first step to gain the interest of a priest of the present-day Roman Church, for the liturgy contains a multitude of details of ritual that are rarely known even to a specialist in medieval church music. Since the reforms of the Second Vatican Council, however, many priests are no longer familiar with the old practice, which had far more in common with the 13th century than it does with modern ritual. There are, of course, many pre-conciliar manuals, such as Fortescue's *The Ceremonies of the Roman Rite Described*,[1] which will serve as a guide. They will help with the general framework and character of the service, though not with the peculiarities which were a feature of the worship of every individual medieval church.

A proper reconstruction of a 13th-century service will therefore require consultation of 13th-century service books. Since the pace of change in medieval ritual was extremely slow, it is often satisfactory to consult 14th- or 15th-century books, if those of the right date are not available. On the other hand, for the period before the 13th century, books containing information about liturgical actions and vestments are rare, and it is usually necessary to proceed by intelligent guesswork, using books of a later date which may be expected to reproduce something approximating to the liturgical use in question. There are often problems in this, however, for liturgical reform may have intervened to place a curtain between the earlier and the later practice. For example we are well provided with service books from Paris from the 13th century onwards, but for the previous century – say, the period when Léonin may have been assembling the local repertory of organum for the Cathedral of Notre Dame – we know nothing precisely of the Parisian liturgy. And while we may expect much in the later books to reproduce earlier practice, we must also take account of the fact that at the turn of the century the Bishop of Paris, Odo of Sully, instituted a number of liturgical reforms (the best known are those affecting the 'Feast of Fools', and the ordinances permitting the singing of *organum quadruplum*). It is therefore a sensitive matter to determine how much of the liturgy of Léonin's time was affected.

Comparatively little research into the history of medieval ritual has been accomplished. There is no easy access even to such essential information as what medieval books survive from a particular church, and what information about liturgical practice they contain.[2] A concrete example may serve to illustrate something of the character of medieval ritual and the part which chant plays in it. Processionals (that is, books containing texts, music and rubric for ritual processions) according to the liturgical customs of Salisbury Cathedral have survived in moderate numbers from medieval Britain. They show that on some of the principal feast-days of the church year the main musical item to be sung in procession was a responsory: a multipartite composition with main section (or respond), verse, prose and doxology (*Gloria patri et filio*, etc). While most sections are in the same relatively ornate musical style, the prose is syllabic, written according to the principle of one syllable per note of music. Each line of the prose is to be sung first by a special group of singers, then repeated without text, that is, vocalized usually to the vowel 'A', by the full choir. From the way in which the prose is worked into the ceremony, it is clear that it is a rather special item, employed only in 11 processions in the year, and always delegated to a special group of singers who are to pause as they sing their versicles, or sing them at a special place in the church, often the choir step (at the east end of the choir stalls).

It might be thought that such a composition, the jewel, as it were, in the crowning musical item of the procession, would be designed with a very specific aural effect in mind. Yet when one peruses the instructions for performance it is clear that ritual considerations take precedence over purely musical ones. For the Christmas procession the prose is sung by 'three clerks of the highest form' (referring to the place in the choir stalls); for St Stephen's

Clerics singing around a lectern: miniature from a 14th-century psalter (Amiens, Bibliothèque Municipale, MS 124, f.98)

Day all the deacons together sing it; for St John's Day all the priests; for Holy Innocents' Day all the boys; for St Thomas of Canterbury 'all who wish' may sing the prose. For the rest of the year it is the three clerks of the highest form who sing the prose, which is what we should expect since these are presumably the most experienced singers. But for those special days of the Christmas season the clerks give way to deacons (St Stephen was a deacon), priests, boys (Herod's slaughter of the innocent children is being commemorated),[3] and then any who may want to join in. At least at Salisbury it was not the custom to dance during the performance.[4]

In fact any service book contains numerous examples of the deployment of different singers, according to the occasion, to sing compositions that are essentially identical in style. This is not to say that it does not matter who sings them, but that the choice of performers will usually be dictated by ritual considerations.

Two further points may be made about the prose, which reflect upon other types of chant. Firstly, the *Gloria patri* is usually sung during the responsory only if the feast-day falls upon a Sunday. On Sunday the full order will therefore be: respond, verse, respond repeated (usually shortened) with the prose inserted near the end, *Gloria patri*, respond again (shortened). On the less solemn occasion: respond, verse, respond (shortened) with prose. It may seem odd that the omission of large sections of the composition should cause no apparent damage to the musical structure, but this is a commonplace procedure. Secondly, although several hundred of these proses have survived, scattered through hundreds of medieval manuscripts,[5] very rarely are we told how they should be performed, that is, who exactly shall sing them, and whether some such *alternatim* scheme as we know for the Salisbury liturgy should be employed. Only recently has a proper search been made of medieval books to establish what may have been normal (and Salisbury does indeed seem to have been normal), and this has had to rely on the evidence of books of the 13th century and later.[6]

The prose is admittedly a special case, a festal ornament of the liturgy. About many other chants – the introit, gradual of Mass and so on – we are better informed from earlier centuries. But as already stated much work remains to be done before we can be sure what to expect in many details of the ritual setting and performance of chant (the sequence is an outstanding case); and for very many churches and periods we shall inevitably never know the answers to all our questions.[7]

Liturgical 'drama'

The vast majority of so-called 'liturgical dramas' would seem to be ceremonies directly comparable with the little ritual described above. They are an integral part of the liturgy of a particular feast-day, performed in a normal liturgical setting, that is, in church and in liturgical vestments. This is true, for instance, for all the very many ceremonies grouped under the *Visitatio sepulchri* umbrella. In all except convents of nuns, the Marys would be represented by men. They would be robed in ecclesiastical vestments such as copes, not women's weeds. Most of the music to be sung resembles 'normal' plainchant (except where incursions by the courtly planctus genre are made, typically in representations of Rachel's lament over the slaughtered innocents). There is little evidence that the singing would have differed in manner from normal chant performance, though there appears to be a greater occurrence of the directions 'alta voce', 'modesta voce' and 'submissa voce' ('in a loud/moderate/soft voice') which we know from chant manuscripts, and sometimes other 'psychological' directions are given.

A different manner of performance may have been required, however, for those ceremonies whose place in the liturgy is doubtful, or marginal, or even out of the question. It is not easy to envisage the liturgical context of, for example, one of the earliest verse-dramas, the *Sponsus* ceremony of the Paris Bibliothèque Nationale manuscript lat.1139. Its repeated use of a limited number of melodies foreshadows the similar compositional technique of the cycle of St Nicholas plays in the so-called 'Fleury Playbook' (Orléans, Bibliothèque Municipale 201), and here too no obvious liturgical setting suggests itself: the links are rather with the art of the singer of tales, the court minstrel; and non-liturgical performance (though perhaps a pious environment) may be envisaged. Elsewhere in the Fleury Playbook are expansive treatments of biblical themes, and here too there may be indications of a move away from purely liturgical ritual – or, perhaps better stated, a fusion of non-liturgical drama with liturgical ritual. An example of this type of composition is the Herod play (one of whose versions, from Bilsen, has rubrics in hexameters; how adequately might these portray the enactment of the play?). 'Herod, seeing the prophecy [of Christ's birth], and being filled with rage, shall throw down the book; but his son, hearing the noise, shall go to soothe his father . . .'; and later Herod and his son notice the Star and threaten it with their swords.[8]

The borderline between liturgical and non-liturgical is not always easy to discern of course, and there is an urgent need to define terms and identify more precisely the possible circumstances of original performance for many liturgical dramas. Is the apparent move towards greater 'realism' a real trend of the 12th and 13th centuries, or simply a reflection of an increasing readiness to spell out performance rubrics? How clear was the demarcation between liturgical and non-liturgical performance? There exist remarkable directions for the Matins service at Epiphany from Padua in the 13th century, where 'Herod' and attendants invade, as it were, the Divine Office, hurling spears at the choir and striking them with bladders; Herod also reads the ninth lesson 'with excessive rage' (it is a discourse on the unbelief of the Jews, alone of all creation). In the face of such licence – not unusual in the Christmas season, as witness the many descriptions of the buffoonery associated with the 'Feast of Fools' – it is inevitably difficult to gauge accurately the mode and milieu of 'dramatic' ceremonies.[9]

Rhythm and expression: documentary evidence

Before discussing some of the notational evidence of rhythm and expressive detail in early chant manuscripts, I shall survey rapidly the information which can be gleaned from theoretical and other writings. They rarely help us, it must be admitted, for although practically all of the medieval writers on music were practising musicians, and some (for example Aurelian of Réôme and Regino of Prüm) expressly state that they are writing in order to improve the musical knowledge of singers, they do not concern themselves with the most intimate details of performance practice: voice production, dynamics and rhythm. There is a certain amount of additional information in such remarks as those of John the Deacon and Adhémar of Chabannes, who refer to difficulties that northerners had in reproducing the subtleties and flexible vocal technique of southern singers. These are colourful, but not very informative.[10] Yet they may suggest that what is indicated in early notation is only a partial musical record. We know from Hucbald, among others, that early neumes indicated not just 'straight' sounds but also 'the slowness or speed of the melody, and where the sound demands a tremulous voice', in other words, rhythmic and expressive detail.[11] No medieval writer,

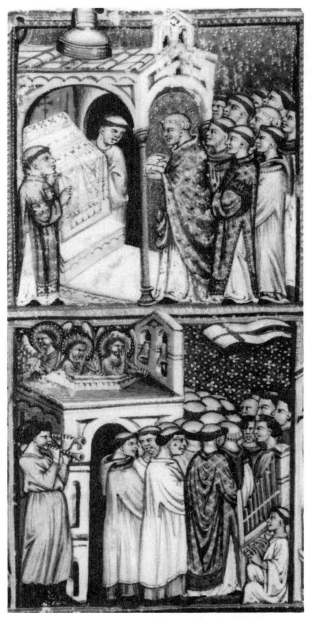

A group of clerics gathered before the altar (top) and a procession (bottom) including two buisine (or shawm) players and a cleric playing a positive organ: detail from the frontispiece of Gulielmus Durandus's 'Rationale divinorum officorum', late 14th century (London, British Library, Add.31.032 f.1)

43

however, has provided us with a 'Neumenkunde' or a 'Nombre musical grégorien'. Their 'aesthetic' prescriptions seem all too often rather irrelevant to actual singing technique, as for example those of the anonymous *Musica enchiriadis*: 'In peaceful subjects let the notes be peaceful, happy in joyous matters, grieving in sad ones; let cruel words or deeds be expressed with harsh sounds – sudden, loud and swift – shaped according to the nature of events and the emotions'.[12]

Even such a writer as the late medieval Conrad von Zabern, who was specifically concerned with singing standards, generalizes tantalizingly in many matters.[13] At least he confirms that chant proceeds in equal note values, something already clear from earlier writers. But it is no surprise to read his recommendations on good ensemble, good tuning and the avoidance of 'coarseness' of various kinds (such as nasal singing and the intrusion of 'h' sounds in groups of repeated notes).[14] More interesting are his observations that chants should be pitched in a middle register; this is common sense, but then he also says that two successive chants should use compatible pitches, to avoid tonal hiatus. Conrad also advises that the tempo of chants should reflect the solemnity of the day: the more important the feast, the slower the singing. More than one medieval writer, incidentally, refers to melodies being 'slowed towards the end' (*Commemoratio brevis*).[15]

The most informative of all medieval writers on refinements of vocal delivery is Jerome of Moravia, a Dominican writing towards the end of the 13th century in Paris. He is one of those who state that most notes of chant are equal in length, to which rule he gives five exceptions. The long notes are: (1) the first note of a chant if its pitch is also the final of the piece; (2) the *plica longa* (a liquescent neume); (3) the penultimate note of a phrase; (4) the final note of a phrase, its length depending on the importance of the break in the music; (5) the second note of a note group, as long as it has not already been made long through rules (1) to (4).[16] Here Jerome is giving simple precepts of 'musical diction', as it were, following the pattern of writers on oratory. But he goes on to describe various types of vibrato, slow and accelerating, through an upper semitone or whole tone. They may only be used on the long notes mentioned earlier, and Jerome specifies when they are appropriate. His use of the terms 'flores' and 'flos harmonicus' (also 'nota procellaris') has occasioned speculation about a possible connection with 13th-century Parisian polyphony. Jerome then mentions further details of performance practice peculiar, so he says, to French singers, including the use of various grace notes (*reverberatio, nota mediata*).

The performance of chant in equal note lengths from the 13th century onwards is well supported by contemporary statements. By contrast there has been much discussion of the possibility of differentiated note lengths in the preceding period. The writings of medieval theorists have been scanned with particular assiduity for support for the notion that chant in the early centuries was performed according to a mensural rhythmic system whose note lengths were in proportional ratios (such as quaver:crotchet = 1:2; or quaver:crotchet:dotted-crotchet = 1:2:3).

It is true that proportion was a subject visited by almost every medieval writer on music (principally as a consequence of the exhaustive discussion of proportions in the writings of Boethius and other writers of late antiquity).

Yet its relevance to what we understand as 'rhythm' is tenuous. Proportions are mostly adduced in connection with the harmonic relationships between pitches and consonances, either successive or simultaneous. One branch of musical theory, it is true, uses proportions in a rhythmic sense: that which the Middle Ages knew from Augustine's *De musica*, among other works. Here metrical Latin poetry is analysed to show that the long and short syllable quantities form proportions: 1:2, 2:3, 3:4 and so on; and that these can combine in sets to form other proportions at a higher level.[17]

It appears to be in this sense that rhythm is understood in the controversial 15th chapter of Guido of Arezzo's *Micrologus*.[18] It is not that the notes themselves will have proportional lengths, but that the sounds will fall into groups which can be understood in a proportional relationship. Guido posits a fourfold hierarchy of notes and note groups, to which he gives both a musical name and one borrowed from the discipline of grammar:

1. the single note – *phtongus* = 'sound' (cf letter);
2. note or group of notes – *syllaba* = 'syllable' (syllable);
3. syllable or group of syllables – *neuma* = 'neume' (foot);
4. neume or group of neumes – *distinctio*, or phrase, after which will come a 'suitable place to breathe' (distinction, verse).

Guido frequently makes analogies between music and quantitative poetry, saying for example that 'it is good to beat time to a song as though by metrical feet', and 'I speak of chants as metrical because we often sing in such a way that we appear almost to scan verses by feet'. When Guido refers to particular metrical feet, however, it is always in connection with the 'neume' mentioned above: that is, the sub-phrase in music rather than the 'syllable', and not the 'neume' as we more commonly understand it (*virga, pes, torculus*, etc).

Only at one critical point does Guido seem to come near suggesting that individual sounds may be longer or shorter in a proportional ratio. First he speaks of a 'hold on the last note' (*tenor*, or *mora*), which will be very small at the end of a (musical) 'syllable', longer at the end of a 'neume', and longest at the end of a phrase. Shortly after this, Guido mentions a 'short hold' (*morula*), twice as long or as short as other sounds, or a 'variable hold' (*morula tremula*). Then he proceeds to recommend that 'neumes ... be arranged to correspond to each other' (that is, display some sort of proportional ratio) 'with respect either to the number of notes or the relationship of the holds'. While it seems reasonably clear that the discussion of 'neumes' need not imply long and short individual notes, the 'holds' may indeed do so, at least on the last notes of the various musical units. Yet these are hardly solid grounds for positing a system of proportional time values in chant. Like Jerome at a later date, Guido is giving guidance on proper musical diction, so that the structure of the chant, in a hierarchy of verses, sections and phrases, may be clear to the hearer.

Some earlier theoretical writings, loosely known as the 'Enchiriadis group' of treatises,[19] also refer to the presence of long and short values in a 2:1 ratio. The *Commemoratio brevis*, for example, recommends that 'All notes which are long must correspond rhythmically with those which are not long through their proper inherent durations ... for the longer values consist of the shorter, and the shorter subsist in the longer, and in such a fashion that one has always twice the duration of the other, neither more nor less'.[20]

It is not easy to assess the significance of these remarks and, not surprisingly, they have been used to support differing interpretations.[21] The question also arises: how representative are they of musical practices in their day? It is interesting that the area from which the Enchiriadis treatises appear to come, possibly the archdiocese of Cologne in the 10th century, seems not to have used a 'rhythmic' musical notation. And the same is true of the Italy of Guido's time (early 11th century). Conversely, the areas from which we have 'rhythmic' notations, St Gall and Laon, do not seem to have left us corroborative theoretical writings.

Rhythm and expression: notational evidence

There is no space here to give more than the briefest sketch of the enormous quantity of research which has been conducted into the detail of some early neumatic chant notations. One focus of the research has been a group of manuscripts written at, or within the cultural ambit of, the monastery of St Gall: principally the manuscripts St Gall 359 and 339 (both from St Gall), Einsiedeln 121 (probably from Einsiedeln) and Bamberg Lit.6 (from St Emmeram at Regensburg). Several other sources, mostly tropers, from St Gall, St Emmeram and Reichenau, have so far not been as thoroughly investigated. These sources use what for convenience is called St Gall notation. A different type of neumatic notation equally thoroughly studied is that of Laon 239, probably from Laon. These sources exhibit more clearly than any others a number of intricate notational details which are usually interpreted as indicating lengthening or stressing of certain notes, more rapid delivery of others, and occasionally dynamics.[22] In St Gall notation these effects are usually achieved:

1. by placing so-called 'significative letters' by the neumes, such as *c = celeriter* (quickly); *t = tenete* or *trahere* (hold or drag out);
2. by adding little straight bars (episemas) to the neumes, to indicate lengthening or stressing;
3. by modifying the normal neume shape, for example by using an angular *pes* (two-note ascending neume), written like a schoolroom tick or check, rather than a rounded *pes*. Related to this procedure is the distinction commonly made between *punctum* (a dot) and *tractulus* (a short horizontal stroke), both indicating a note of relatively low pitch, but shorter/longer or unstressed/stressed respectively. The *tractulus* may even acquire episemas itself, at both ends in rare instances! The relative significance of dot and dash appears to vary from manuscript to manuscript; see ex.1.

In the Laon manuscript the significative letters *t* and *a = augete* (increase) are common; among others used are *c*, and *n = naturaliter* or *non [tenete]*. It also makes a distinction between signs for a relatively low note, using both a

Ex.1 St Gall Neumes

    'normal' pes (= *𝄞•*) ✓

    'longer'   ✓

    forms of punctum and tractulus • — ⊣ ⊢⊣

dot (*punctum*) and a hook or sickle shape (*tractulus* or *uncinus*). The notator is particularly adept at indicating relatively faster or more deliberate delivery by splitting note groups which could be written with a single stroke of the pen; see ex.2. This sort of distinction (and the *punctum/tractulus* one) is also to be found in other neumatic sources. Much sensitive research into the

Ex.2   Laon neumes

'normal' pes (= 𝄢) ∫   flexa (= •̃) ⌐

'longer'   ∫   ᵣ
                          ᵣ

significance of note groupings and separations (*coupures*) has been carried out in recent years by Cardine and his disciples.

Ex.3, a short passage from the introit *Vocem iocunditatis*, shows some of the niceties of notation described above. The pitches are those of the modern *Graduale*. Underneath are copied the neumes of manuscripts Laon 239 and

Ex.3   Introit *Vocem iocunditatis*

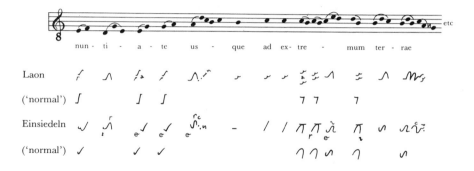

Einsiedeln 121. Where these sources use a 'longer' form of any neume, I have put underneath the 'normal' or 'shorter' form. What is striking is the degree of unanimity these two sources display in their choice of 'longer' neumes at certain points, although in origin they are widely separated geographically, and use quite different types of neumes. It is this agreement which has led scholars to believe that there was in the 9th to 10th centuries a widely understood manner of performance, including rhythmic and expressive elements.

What we have referred to as 'long' may sometimes have meant singing more deliberately or emphatically. Such 'expression', or a special voice production, is clearly indicated in some of the other significative letters used (in particular profusion in Einsiedeln 121), for example:[23]

f – *cum fragore seu frendore feriatur* (with a harsh or percussive attack)
g – *in gutture gradatim* (by degrees in the throat)
k – *clange* (ringing tone)
p – *pressionem* (driving forward)
r – *rectitudinem vel rasuram . . . crispationis* (straight or forthright, without vibrato)

47

The interpretation and application of these is not, of course, without difficulties, but they are certainly suggestive of a considerable range of vocal effect.

The late Middle Ages to the present

If it be right to interpret the pronouncements of theorists or the indications of early neumatic notations as evidence for 'unequal' notes, there seems little doubt that such a tradition must have largely died out by the 13th century. It is at this period that the term 'cantus planus' is used for plainchant, for example by Jerome of Moravia: 'All plain, ecclesiastical chant has notes which are first and foremost equal ones' ('primo et principaliter aequales'); and in the middle of the century Johannes de Garlandia distinguishes mensurable polyphony from 'plana musica, quae immensurabilis dicitur'.[24] At the same time, a small number of chants, in sources from the 13th century onwards, are to be found in mensural notation. These are almost exclusively chants with texts in regular accentual verse, such as sequences (of the 'second epoch' style associated with the name of Adam of St Victor). There are examples not only in major sources of polyphony, such as the Las Huelgas manuscript but also in straightforward chant sources, such as the 14th-century missal of Cambrai, the Paris Bibliothèque National manuscript lat.17311, which among 25 sequences notates just one, *Veni sancte spiritus*, mensurally;[25] see ex.4. (Cf the discussion of this sequence in other contexts in Chapter XIII below.)

Ex.4 F-Pn lat. 17311, f.153r

Ve - ni san - cte spi - ri- tus   et   e- mit- te   ce   - li- tus

It might be argued that, since the rhythm of the texts lends itself to such a rendition, other sequences of this type might well have been performed mensurally but left in traditional chant notation because of the simplicity of the music. The problem here is exactly that of interpreting the notation of any musical setting of accentual verse, from the versus and conductus of 12th-century sources onwards. A mensural interpretation is commonly applied, for example, to the music of the *Play of Daniel*, whose text is almost entirely in regular accentual verse. Moreover, the repertories of vernacular, secular monody (discussed in Chapter IV below), and polyphonic settings of Latin verse, Parisian conductus of the 13th century (Chapter V), raise similar issues. Although the evidence differs between one of these repertories and another, very similar decisions have to be made in each case. The best solutions are probably those that allow something of the nature of the text to be audible, while not imposing an unnecessarily rigid mensural scheme. With music in predominantly syllabic style the verse structure of the text will be clear even in a non-mensural performance, and there are numerous other compositions (particularly among the Aquitanian and Parisian monophonic versus/conductus) where the music is so elaborate as to obscure the text entirely. In neither case will mensural rendition serve any obvious need.

Few mensurally notated chants ever gained any wide currency. One exception, however, was a melody for the Credo found in many 16th-century sources, particularly the printed graduals of Francis of Bruges, printed in Venice from 1499 onward.[26] But more innovations were to occur.[27] In the spirit of reform that followed the Council of Trent, not only were new versions of the melodies prepared, but their publication made use of mensural note shapes. The influential *Directorium chori* (1582) of the papal chaplain Giovanni Guidetti made use of the following:

lozenge	◆	½
square	■	1
square plus arc	▮	1½
square plus dotted arc (fermata)	▮	2

The so-called Medicean edition of 1614–15 was published without an explanation of its note shapes, but appears to have been mensurally conceived, with the same system as in later editions of Guidetti:

lozenge (*semibrevis*)	◆	½
square (*brevis*)	■	1
square with tail (*longa*)	◗	1½

This remained the most common system, down to the end of the 19th century, though others are found which even use modern minims, crotchets and quavers. A system prevalent in France was that described by La Feillée and other 18th-century writers, using:

long with point	■■·	12
long	■■	8
large square with tail	◗	6
large square	■	4
small square with tail	◗	3
small square	▪	2
large lozenge	◆	1
small lozenge	·	½

However not only did the chant (which was often quite new, non-traditional chant) use this variegated metrical vocabulary, and varied tempos, but skilled singers were also expected to employ a rich fund of vocal ornaments, *cadence* (or *tremblement*), *demi-cadence* (*brillant* or *cadence coulée*), *port-de-voix* and *son filé* (with dynamic 'bulge'), upon an instrumental bass accompaniment.[28]

The tempo of chant singing by the 16th century appears to have been generally slow, or at least was felt to be slow. This may have been one reason for the drastic pruning which many chants suffered at the hands of the reformers (not the first time that the repertory had been thus treated, however, since the Cistercian order of monks used a simplified version of many melodies from the 12th century on). Chant sung slowly also invites ornamentation.

The organ accompaniment of chant became increasingly noticeable during the 17th to 19th centuries. The organ was frequently used in the late Middle Ages and Renaissance in alternation with chant (in such parallel-verse chants as hymns, sequences and canticles) – often, one feels, as a 'poor church's substitute' for choral polyphony. The continuous support of chant with organ harmonies is evidence of a more radical change of taste. Complete published graduals and antiphoners with organ accompaniment are known from 18th-century Germany, and manuscripts of accompaniments by, among others, Michael Haydn also survive. Interestingly, organ accompaniment survived the restorations of the early 20th century, for it is a useful aid to less expert choirs, and when skilfully done has undoubtedly enhanced the religious experience of many.[29]

Vocal improvisation on chant (as opposed to the addition of ornaments) was a widespread phenomenon. Within this category of embellishment could be included the simple addition of parallel lines, as in ancient parallel organum, or later English faburden. Up to the highly sophisticated creations of Notre Dame polyphony, all polyphony is of a type which might be improvised: the Winchester organum, employing techniques described by Guido of Arezzo; the types of contrary motion discant, from the 11th century down to 14th–15th century English discant; and later types of improvising 'super librum', vocally or at the organ. One interesting efflorescence was in 18th-century France, embodied in the technique called 'chant sur le livre' (also 'descant' or 'fleuretis').[30] This was improvised counterpoint, adding a new melodic line to chants performed in rigid measure and slow tempo, sung loudly by bass voices with reinforcement by bassoon or serpent – not so far removed in spirit, perhaps, from the 12th-century manner of improvising a florid organal voice to a cantus firmus.

Whatever the standard and manner of performance in the establishments with virtuoso singers, it seems that by the 19th century the general level of chant singing was poor. In France the reign of the serpent was a long one![31] There was little uniformity in the editions used – even when, in the 19th century, the tide of religious opinion swung back in favour of Roman practice. Since the old practices and editions are now little known, it is easy to underestimate the immensity of the revolution in chant performance of the late 19th and early 20th centuries, symbolized, in different ways, by the declaration of Pope Pius X, *Tra la sollecitudini*, of 22 November 1903, the Vatican *Kyriale* and *Graduale* of 1905 and 1908 respectively, and the congress to mark the 1300th anniversary of the death of St Gregory, in 1904, where choirs singing restored chant, and scholars and churchmen speaking about it, were recorded by the Gramophone Company and can therefore still be heard.[32]

The restoration of the pitches of the melodies as they might have been sung in the early Middle Ages was accepted relatively rapidly. Although the editions produced were practical, not critical (and were produced for the Roman liturgy of the early 20th century, not a medieval one), most of what is in them can be supported from the readings of medieval sources. In rhythmic matters, however, much dispute ensued. Most of the reformers were agreed that the notes of plainchant were basically equal in length. But not all agreed with the influential method evolved by Dom André Mocquereau at Solesmes and the rhythmic details indicated in Solesmes chant books, where dots and bars were used to indicate the lengthening and stressing of certain notes.[33] Mocquereau based his performance decisions, of course, on the evidence of the early St Gall and Laon sources mentioned above, and, as with the pitches, most of what one finds in the Solesmes chant books (the *Liber usualis* is the best known) can be supported from those sources. While refinements have been made to Mocquereau's recommendations (for example the middle note of the neume known as the 'salicus' is no longer thought to bear any stress), principally through the work of Cardine and his students, modern Solesmes practice is clearly derived from the older method. Longer and shorter notes do not form any regular metrical pattern, there is ample use of crescendo and diminuendo to reinforce the perceived shape of the melody, the general tempo is an easily flowing one, and voice production is natural and unforced, as one would expect for those who receive no special musical training. For the latter characteristics there is, of course, no clear medieval evidence, and it has been pointed out that the musical aesthetic which gave rise to them was as much late 19th-century French Romantic as medieval. The Solesmes methods are, however, superbly adapted to the needs of choirs at many levels of expertise; they can be used satisfactorily by less expert bodies, and will give excellent results in the hands of the best singers.

Not all, however, either early in the century or today, have agreed on a basically non-metrical approach. A persistent body of opinion – neither as united in belief nor as productive in scholarly work as their opponents – has argued for the use of some system of proportional note values, often worked into regular metrical schemes such as duple or quadruple time.[34] And several performance groups have recently experimented with a radical rhythmic interpretation in which 'longs' become very long, taking on extra structural significance, and 'shorts' are performed as ornaments.

Ex.5 shows the start of the *Magnificat* antiphon *Magnum haereditatis* first with the neumes of the St Gall manuscript 390–391, written *c*1000 (*a*), then as in the Solesmes *Antiphonale monasticum* of 1935 (*b*), which uses bars corresponding to the episemas of the St Gall manuscript. The next line gives the mensural interpretation of Dechevrens (*c*).[35] Finally, an early 19th-century version, that of the Cologne *Antiphonale* of 1846 (*d*), shows considerable differences in the notes given, and uses a notation with two rhythmic values, long (with tail) and short (without); it will be noticed that the shorts are used for unaccented syllables and anticipating notes.

To the present writer, the difficulties of reconciling the evidence of the early sources with a proportional scheme seem insurmountable, and it must also be said that the manuscripts with the most sophisticated notations are local products, not necessarily indicative of universal practice. Nevertheless, the general agreement in matters of note grouping between sources widely separated in time and place of origin is often remarkable, particularly for sources of Mass chants, and this tends to support the notion that there was indeed a widely agreed manner of performing chant in the early centuries.

The degree to which uniformity of practice – to which we are so accustomed in the 20th-century church – was prevalent in earlier times will

Ex.5 *Magnificat* antiphon *Magnum Haereditatis*

5(a) St Gall, Stiftsbibliothek, 390–391, pp.69–70 (*Paleiographie Musicale*, II/1); (b) *Liber Usualis Missae et Officii* ... (Paris, etc., 1964); (c) Antoine Dechevrens: *Composition musicale et composition littéraire à propos du chant* (Paris 1910), ii. pp.69–70; (d) *Antiphonarium Coloniense* (Cologne, 1846), pp.82–3.

nevertheless remain difficult to estimate. One may also question, as Helmut Hucke has done,[36] whether the performance of chants of different function and musical style was necessarily identical in manner. There is clearly still room for further research and experiment. The present age is less inclined than its predecessors to accept any one approach as definitive, and, if responsibly undertaken, further work can only aid our understanding of the problems involved.[37] Although reservations were expressed above about the use of proportional measure in chant, the matter can hardly be said to have been debated in sufficient depth or with sufficient objectivity. Recent fresh thought on the nature and role of early chant sources and notation in general seems likely to inspire new views on interpretation. Above all, the enormous appetite displayed at the present day for the music of past centuries seems destined to ensure closer investigation of chant repertories and performance. The riches of the medieval chant repertory have scarcely been tapped, certainly not by the restoration work of the beginning of the century, which served a contemporary liturgy. With greater knowledge of the full variety and depth of the liturgical experience of former times will come a better understanding of performance. This, if anything, will compensate for the sparsity of documentary evidence about early chant performance practice.

Notes

[1] A. Fortescue, *The Ceremonies of the Roman Rite Described* (London, 1917, with many subsequent edns. and revs.). This is a manual of parish practice, and one must look elsewhere for monastic ritual, episcopal functions and so on (see the bibliography in Fortescue). There is no simple vade-mecum for the uninitiated, who are frequently confused by the complexity of

liturgical books, their way of organizing a very large body of material, some of it 'everyday' and some of it 'special', proper to only one day in the year.

[2] See the items listed in the bibliography by J. Emerson, 'Sources, MS, §II, 2: Western plainchant', *Grove6*, xvii, 611. Among the more important are the catalogues of liturgical sources in English libraries outside London and Oxford by W. H. Frere; V. Leroquais's catalogues of liturgical manuscripts in French libraries; the Solesmes catalogue of graduals and noted missals entitled *Les sources*; and Heinrich Husmann's *RISM* volume describing sources of tropes and sequences.

[3] I have described here what is found in the processional *GB-Ob* Rawl.lit.d.4, from the 14th century, a manuscript following the Salisbury liturgy but with some adaptation for Dublin use. Salisbury use has been better served than most by editions and facsimiles. See F. Ll. Harrison, *Music in Medieval Britain* (London, 1958, 2/1963); Harrison, 'Sarum, Use of', *MGG*; M. Berry, 'Sarum rite, music of the', *Grove6*.

[4] The remarkable evidence of this is found in a 14th-century liturgical book of Sens Cathedral, the precentor's dance occupying the position in a processional responsory equivalent to that of the prose. See J. Chailley, 'Un document nouveau sur la danse ecclésiastique', *AcM*, ii (1949), 18–24, with facsimile.

[5] See H. Hofmann-Brandt, *Die Tropen zu den Responsorien des Offiziums* (Kassel, 1973). This is one of several Erlangen catalogues of chant genres traced through a very large number of manuscript sources. The source lists given in them are in themselves useful bibliographical tools for tracing books of various liturgical uses.

[6] T. F. Kelly, 'Melisma and Prosula: the Performance of Responsory Tropes', in *Liturgische Tropen*, ed. G. Silagi (Munich, 1985).

[7] Editions and facsimiles of liturgical books are an obvious prerequisite for further study. Apart from the facsimiles of chant books in the series Paléographie Musicale, Monumenta Musicae Sacrae and so on, mention should be made of the large number of texts edited for the Henry Bradshaw Society, the series Corpus Consuetudinarium Monasticarum and Studi e Testi. For bibliography see R. W. Pfaff, *Medieval Latin Liturgy: a Select Bibliography* (Toronto, 1982).

[8] A large majority of known texts were edited by K. Young, *The Drama of the Medieval Church* (Oxford, 1933). There is an edition of the Fleury Herod play with music and translation in W. T. Marrocco and N. Sandon, *Medieval Music* (London, 1977). This volume also contains an edition of Mass on Easter Day, complete with rubrics and other non-musical material, following the Salisbury liturgy. Such complete reconstructions, rather than editions simply of the musical items, are highly desirable for non-liturgists.

[9] The Padua text is edited in Young, *The Drama*, i, 99–100. A most important and enlightened discussion of the liturgical and dramatic significance of these ceremonies, and the problems of interpretation, is in the article by J. Stevens, 'Medieval drama, §II: Liturgical drama', in *Grove6*. See also Stevens, 'Music in Some Early Medieval Plays', *Studies in the Arts*, ed. F. Warner (Oxford, 1968), 21.

[10] Johannes Hymmonides, or John the Deacon, was writing *c*880. The passage in questions occurs in a biography of St Gregory: see *PL*, 75:90. Adhémar of Chabannes' account is much later, written in the 11th century, but also refers to the introduction of Roman chant in the Frankish kingdom under Charlemagne. It may not be wholly independent of John. Editions by J. Chavanon (1897), 81f, and in *MGH, Scriptores*, iv, 170f.

[11] Hucbald was writing probably in the early years of the 10th century. Translation from W. Babb, *Hucbald, Guido and John on Music* (New Haven and London, 1978), 37.

[12] On the other hand, this is regarded as an 'elegant formulation of the medieval aesthetic of the affections' in J. Dyer, 'Singing with Proper Refinement', *EM*, vi (1978), 211. Dyer's discussion centres on the treatise *De modo bene cantandi* of 1474 by Conrad von Zabern, and is in fact one of the few available scholarly discussions of many of the practical matters mentioned here.

[13] Dyer, 'Singing with Proper Refinement', provides an excellent introduction, synopsis and part translation of Conrad's treatise.

[14] On medieval voice production see F. Müller-Häuser, *Vox humana: ein Beitrag zur Untersuchung der Stimmästhetik des Mittelalters* (Regensburg, 1963).

[15] The passage in the early 10th-century *Commemoratio brevis* is edited and translated in T. Bailey, *Commemoratio brevis de tonis et psalmis modulandis* (Ottawa, 1979), 102–3. See also Guido of Arezzo's remarks in *Micrologus* (*c*1030), translated in Babb, *Hucbald, Guido and John*, 72.

[16] *Hieronymus de Moravia O.P. Tractatus de Musica*, ed. S. M. Cserba (Regensburg, 1935), pp.LXIIff, 181ff.

[17] See the outline of these ideas presented by R. L. Crocker, 'Musica Rhythmica and Musica Metrica in Antique and Medieval Theory', *JMT*, ii (1958), 2–23.

[18] The chapter is translated by Crocker, 'Musica Rhythmica', and also in Babb, *Hucbald, Guido and John*.

[19] The main three treatises in this group are *Musica enchiriadis*, *Scolica enchiriadis* and *Commemoratio brevis*, all recently edited by H. Schmid, *Musica et Scolica enchiriadis una cum aliquibus tractatulis adiunctis* (Munich, 1981).

[20] Translation and edition in Bailey, *Commemoratio brevis*. Guido appears to have known the *Scolica* at least. For further discussion of the passage in *Micrologus* and commentary on it by Aribo, see *Aribonis De musica*, ed. J. Smits van Waesberghe, CSM, ii (1951), pp.XVIff.

[21] The best-known 'mensuralist' view is J. W. A. Vollaerts's, *Rhythmic Proportions in Early Medieval Ecclesiastical Chant* (Leiden, 1958, 2/1960).

[22] The easiest way to appreciate the variety of neumes used in these sources is via E. Cardine, *Gregorian Semiology* (Solesmes, 1982), a work which had appeared previously in both Italian and French versions. This presents useful tables of the range of neumes used, and discusses their significance neume by neume. It is, in fact, the tip of an iceberg of research carried out under Cardine's direction, or perhaps, better stated, its foundation; see N. Albarosa, 'The Pontificio Istituto di Musica Sacra in Rome and Semiological School of Dom Eugene Cardine', *JPMMS*, vi (1983), 26–33. All the manuscripts mentioned above except *D-BAs* Lit.6 are available in facsimile in the series Paléographie Musicale.

[23] A list, traditionally supposed to come from Notker of St Gall, of the late 9th century, is given on p.132 of the article by S. Corbin, 'Neumatic notations', *Grove6*.

[24] F. Reimer, *Johannes de Garlandia: De mensurabili musica* (Wiesbaden, 1971), i, 35.

[25] *F.Pn* lat.17311, f.253r. A zealous pursuivant of mensurally notated sequences has been B. Gillingham, 'British Library MS Egerton 945: Further Evidence for a Mensural Interpretation of Sequences', *ML*, lxi (1980), 50–59.

[26] Facsimile in F. Tack, *Gregorian Chant* (Cologne, 1960), 50.

[27] This area of chant history is generally neglected. An excellent survey is given by J. Emerson, 'Plainchant, §II: Western', *Grove6*, xiv, especially 825–7. A useful series of facsimiles is to be found in Tack, *Gregorian Chant*.

[28] See D. Fuller, 'Plainchant musical', *Grove6*.

[29] On organ accompaniment, see the numerous works given in Emerson's bibliography, *Grove6*, xiv, 843–4.

[30] See J. Prim, 'Chant sur le livre in French Churches in the 18th Century', *JAMS*, xiv (1961), 37–49.

[31] As Jacques Chailley testifies in his introduction to the centennial reprint of J. Pothier, *Les mélodies grégoriennes* (Paris, 1980).

[32] *The Gregorian Congress of 1904*, Discant Recordings, DIS 1–2.

[33] Joseph Pothier, the most senior scholar of the restoration team, preferred to regard the rhythmic indications of the manuscripts as of local significance, and therefore the Solesmes rhythmic signs were not included in Vatican editions.

[34] Among those supporting proportional rhythm are Peter Wagner and Ewald Jammers. The best-known expression of a 'mensuralist' point of view is Vollaerts's book, cited above; see also G. Murray, *Gregorian Chant According to the Manuscripts* (London, 1963). Vollaerts's book, which was published posthumously, elicited a critical reply from E. Cardine, *Is Gregorian Chant Measured Music?* (Solesmes, 1964; trans. from the Fr. version in *Etudes grégoriennes*, vi, 1963), which is not easy to use unless one knows Vollaerts's work intimately. There is a balanced survey of contrasting theories by B. Stäblein, 'Thèses équalistes et mensuralistes', in *Encyclopédie des musiques sacrées*, ed. J. Porte (Paris, 1969), ii, 80–98. For bibliography see also D. Hiley, 'Notation, §III', *Grove6*, xiii, 354.

[35] A. Dechevrens, *Composition musicale et composition littéraire à propos du chant grégorien* (Paris, 1910), ii, 69.

[36] H. Hucke, 'Zum Problem des Rhythmus im Gregorianischen Gesang', *IMSCR*, vii *Cologne 1958*, 141–3.

[37] This view is well expressed by L. W. Brunner, 'The Performance of Plainchant: Some Preliminary Observations of the New Era', *EM*, x (1982), 317–28. Many of the topics considered here are also discussed in Brunner's article.

CHAPTER IV

Secular Monophony

WULF ARLT

The study of the performance of medieval secular monophony concerns music of a period of over five centuries: from the secular texts to be found among the oldest notated manuscript sources of the late 9th and the 10th centuries to the earliest of the large song manuscripts of the German-speaking area, dating from the 14th and 15th centuries. The material includes the lyrics of clerks and of itinerant singers and also instrumental music, both for the dance and as formal performance. It embraces the declamation of epic poetry and the various forms of the courtly lyric in the widest sense of the word, from the beginnings of European courtly song with the troubadours and trouvères to German lyric *Sprüche*, the monophonic ballate of the trecento, the lais and virelais of Guillaume de Machaut, and indeed the lieder of Oswald von Wolkenstein. Finally, it has become an established practice to include under the heading of secular monophony both sung poetry in the vernacular on religious subjects and songs on the fringes of liturgy; the contrafacta from the *Miracles de Nostre-Dame* of Gautier de Coincy, the Spanish *Cantigas de Santa Maria*, the Italian *laude*, the German flagellant songs (*Geisslerlieder*) and the vernacular songs of the Monk of Salzburg, as well as Latin cantiones.[1]

This material can be classified according to date of origin (that of the manuscript sources and of their content), linguistic area and function; in addition the most important factors for the would-be interpreter are the differences of transmission. These relate to the kind of notation and especially the role of the written music.

With respect to the notation, music in neumes occupies a special position. Depending on the nature of the written record they provide various types of information about the structure of the melody and even about the manner of performance. There are only a few pieces from the early period where it is possible to determine the sequence of intervals from the manuscript source itself. Nevertheless, even neumatic notation enables us to reconstruct a whole series of melodies in such cases as that of the Latin songs of the 13th-century *Carmina burana*.[2]

At the opposite extreme are those late sources in a codified mensural notation with relatively unambiguous directions even for rhythms, such as exist in the case of Machaut. More common, admittedly, are those manuscripts from the late 13th century onwards, in which the signs indicating duration were used pragmatically: the alternative possibilities are not discussed in the theoretical texts and often leave the interpreter considerable room for choice. The majority of the songs – notably the melodies for the texts of the troubadours and trouvères and those of German Minnesang – have come down to us in sources which offer no indication as to the duration of the notes.

As the above implies, the question of rhythm comes to the fore at an early stage when the interpretation of secular monophony is under discussion. A number of plausible suggestions – and a large number of absurd ones – have been made for solving the problem. The debate has shown above all, and with absolute clarity, that (*a*) there can be no generally applicable answers in this area, and (*b*) the question of rhythm cannot be approached in isolation from a large number of other aspects. These concern, in particular, both where and when a version was formulated and where and when that formulation was written down and performed, the function of the songs and of the manuscripts, the various languages, the poetic forms, and the structure of the melody. The *vers* of an early troubadour of the early 12th century was formulated, both poetically and musically, on terms different from those affecting an old French song, written or performed in Paris in the 13th century, where modal rhythm was prevalent, or a German *Spruch* melody of the 14th century. The demands in respect of the performance style of a song for dancing differed from those presented by a complex *sirventes* on a wide-ranging subject, let alone a long epic poem. There are songs where the declamation of the texts clearly points to regular duple or triple rhythms, or sometimes to freer groupings, which correspond to particular traits of the melodic structure. There are others where the musical formulation points to a manner of performance which resists notation in proportional durational values.

It can be assumed that there must have been a variety of solutions in practice, if only because many songs were transmitted for more than a century and were therefore performed in accordance with different premises as time went by, quite apart from the fact that some melodies could serve for more than one text. To that extent the multiplicity of rhythmic formulations found, for example, in the pragmatic, mensural notation of the *cantigas* – from modal rhythms to the greatest variety of duple and triple groupings, or to a recitational manner of performance – probably conveys what is in essence a wholly adequate picture of the performance of a body of material which was 'edited' in the second half of the 13th century. And as long as one takes into account the characteristics of the repertory and the circumstances in which it came into existence, every such source offers a more sensible means of approach to the questions of rhythmic reading than those modern editions which force the melodies of the trouvères and even of German Minnesang – rigorously and without exception – into the rhythmic patterns of modal Parisian polyphony.[3]

The nature of the question of rhythmic interpretation has changed over the last 20 years, not least because of the experience gained and conclusions drawn from expert practical experiment. A systematic consideration of the specific problems involved in performing secular monophony, seeking ways to build a bridge from the notated page to actual sounds, has revealed the usefulness of other kinds of evidence, such as traditional practices in singing songs. As a result, examples of many possible rhythmic usages came to light which have been considered within the confines of academic questioning only briefly, and then been vaguely assigned to a realm of 'free' rhythm. Aspects have also come to the fore which prove to be more relevant in many respects to the resulting sound, to the delivery of the text and therefore to the discussion of questions of performance practice than that which was reflected in the musical notation. These aspects range from aesthetic premises, to the process of communicating unfamiliar texts or the consequences of a specialized vocal technique, to the role of instruments, as testified by pictorial sources, verbal accounts and above all the verse texts themselves.

This brings us back to the role of written musical sources and a consideration of the many and various reasons why secular monophony might be taken down and recorded in written form. Analysis of this aspect creates the prospect of a first methodic step towards bridging the gap between the known facts and artistic intuition, taking into account the special problems of this remote region of a historical practice.[4] Until the late Middle Ages music (outside the theoretical texts and didactic expositions) was notated exclusively as one aspect of the delivery of a text, monophonically or polyphonically as the case might be, in the narrowest sense. Instrumental performance did not come within the scope of written notation. The earliest surviving written example of a monophonic instrumental piece, dating from the late 13th century, bears all the marks of an exception. How this example, and the few instrumental pieces of the 14th and early 15th centuries, can contribute to the reconstruction of what was in principal a notationless practice is discussed in the last section of this essay. How instruments contributed to the performance of monophonic songs and epic texts is not recorded in any of the written musical sources.

The melodies notated with text reflect various different reasons for writing music down. Only exceptionally do we come across a musical text that corresponds to the preconceptions and expectations of modern practice. Its terms can be illustrated with a simple model (see Model A). Here the

MODEL A

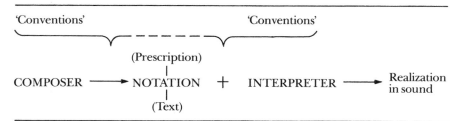

notation gives the interpreter directions (prescriptive advice). It conveys to him the essential factors of the course the music should follow, in so far as he is familiar with the conventions (of the script, the style etc) which are a prerequisite of satisfactory reading of the signs. The text is definitive, because it goes back to a process of composition that reckons with the possibilities of a specific notation, rests on corresponding conventions of reading and leads to a version worked out in writing: to a text with which the work will be disseminated and which simultaneously is intended as the basis for a performance. In the secular monophonic repertory the most outstanding example of this is in the 14th-century French manuscripts using mensural notation which contain the works of Machaut, but there are other examples in the songs of Jehannot de Lescurel and in the one monophonic virelai of the Ivrea Codex.[5] In these sources the musical text can be interpreted entirely in the light of modern practice – in so far as the original notation (within the realm of the possible) is read in the light of the conventions to which the signs relating to rhythm refer.

However, the number of sources of secular monophony that conform to the above model is very small. The qualifications begin at the very point when the move into script called for the services of a scribe as intermediary, because the singer-poet was ignorant of the notation of either music or letters. And even in the case of Oswald von Wolkenstein, whose songs have survived in manuscripts he probably supervised, the transmission raises at the very least the question of how familiar he was with various methods of notating rhythm. If here, at least, the collection of the works in impressive codices leads us into the author's immediate circle of influence, in the case of most songs there is a considerable gap in time between their original conceptions and the surviving sources. There are many cases in which the style of the notation already gives an indication that we are dealing with a collection assembled in the service of a special interest, which has plainly been subjected to an editorial hand, as for example in the case of the Latin songs of the *Roman de Fauvel*.

But the model is most fundamentally open to question in the following cases: written sources which rest at least in part on an oral tradition; musical texts where it is uncertain to what extent they were intended as directions for performance; and a performing situation in which the notated document played no role. That applies to large areas of European courtly song and governs the specific problems of a performance of secular monophony.

Undoubtedly texts were transmitted in written form as well as orally even as early as the 12th century among the troubadours. Bernart de Ventadorn refers to the practice in one of his songs, and there is indirect evidence of it in the emphasis Jaufre de Rudel gives to his statement that he is sending a *vers* 'without a piece of parchment' (*Senes breu de perguamina / tramet lo vers*).[6] The melody could be transmitted in writing at the same time as the text. However, in the case of secular monophony there are no surviving exemplars either of such 'song-sheets' or of individual *libelli* such as served in the liturgical field for the collection and transmission of notated repertories, and which are known to have existed in the case of polyphony too.[7] The determining factors are these: (*a*) the form in which texts and above all melodies have survived in manuscripts from no earlier than the late 13th and the 14th centuries bears many of the signs of an oral tradition; (*b*) French and German courtly song alike survives almost exclusively in codices, that is to say collections of texts (and melodies) made at some later date; and (*c*) performance normally corresponded to the current state of notationless practice. This explains the fragmentary nature of the information yielded by the musical sources, as well as the fact that the various formulations of a melody transmitted in more than one source sometimes differ to a very marked degree.

Scholars and performers have attempted to close the gap between the state of the source material and the conditions of a performance by recourse to a text which offers the information necessary for an interpretation in the sense of modern practice. The primary step is to establish the rhythmic scheme in proportional values, but often an instrumental arrangement is also worked out to a greater or lesser degree. Editing, however, leads to exactly the opposite of what was intended, for working out a piece in writing in this way has the effect of distorting the area in which the interpreter should have the freedom to decide for himself, since it is in that freedom that the performer's specific contribution and opportunities in this kind of music reside.

It is more profitable to compare other fields where free performance within the limits of known conventions was the norm as late as the Classical period. This applies above all to the rediscovery of practices once taken for granted: diminution, playing from a figured bass or the 'wilful alterations' of the 18th century. This has demonstrated the absurdity of working things out in written form for expert performances or even for didactic purposes, and has revealed to interpreters some fascinating possibilities for their own artistic contribution. It has opened our eyes to stylistic differentiation according to date, place and genre, according to instrumental or vocal premises, and last but not least according to personal interests and capabilities. And it has placed on record how strongly the interpretation and transmission of the music in question depends on the recognition and adequate realization of the possibilities of notationless practice.

The experience gained from long and intensive consideration of these late forms of freedom in performance can, in principle, be directly transposed to the broad realm of notationless practices of earlier times that has reappeared within the sights of performance practice today. However, the documentary record of earlier procedures is very variable. Relatively few problems arise with the polyphonic performance of liturgical melodies following a model, or where soloistic improvisation requires *ad hoc* decision-making, since in these cases there survive works of theory and actual examples. Manuscript sources allow the working out by deduction, at least, of other procedures, such as the adaptation of monophonic melodies and polyphonic textures, in the secular as well as the sacred quarter. But a critical point is reached when even this recourse is lacking for a notationless practice which is known to have existed. For then – unless the consideration of history is given up altogether – the only possibility is to take the step of 'reconstructing' conventions on the basis of indirect evidence, comparison with other areas, and consideration of traditional practices. The clarification of these conditions for the extreme case of instrumental performances represents the position in modern practice that is directly opposite to that of Model A; see Model B.[8] In this instance working-out in writing is renounced, even for reciprocal orientation, to be replaced by the establishment of conventions to be worked out in practice. This process looks in the first instance to the surviving music of the period and to everything that pictorial material and verbal texts can offer in the way of indirect information. Confrontation with the instrument mediates between historical knowledge and practical experience, not least in the question of sensitivity towards the conditions set by the instrument: with the tension between the demands it makes and the possibilities it offers. The

59

MODEL B

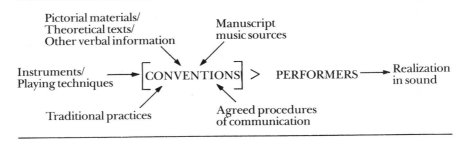

encounter with traditional music indicates possible ways of making the leap from the indirect evidence to the solution of the practical problems, and the agreed procedures of communication come into force wherever more than one performer is involved.

Insights into the various reasons why pieces were written down, into the consequences of an oral tradition, and into the realm of notationless practices are seen to reinforce the experience gained from the performance of the secular music of the Middle Ages. As a result there exist today new premises which represent quite an advance on the first, and in many respects naive, steps taken in the field of performance, and also on the approach of academic research which for a long time concentrated one-sidedly on decipherment and general conclusions. These new premises have considerably enlarged the field of questions and criteria. One specific task to be tackled is that of 'reconstructing' a performance situation on the terms of a notationless practice. In this, differentiation according to time and place, function and genre, language-area and the many other conditions affecting a realization has a decisive role to play. For just as a performance in the Middle Ages was affected by the different circumstances obtaining on different occasions, so today there is a special random factor introduced by deciding to 'locate' the realization in a fictive context and, in doing so, to take into account above all the very different social and cultural preconditions which were linked with various degrees of musical knowledge and experience. Anyone who could read and write, until well into the 13th century, was generally familiar with, and trained in, liturgical music, from plainchant to polyphony in all its various forms. The itinerant singer and minstrel could be exposed to a wide variety of impressions, up to and including encounters with other cultures on the crusades or in circumstances such as those of 13th-century Spain, where races, languages and, surely, musics met at close quarters.[9]

Thus general conclusions have been replaced by the opportunity and the challenge of being precise about place, time and context. Precision involves many choices, even in the interpretation of the same song in varying contexts and circumstances. But it also can serve as a guard against wilfulness and last but not least it encourages critical assessment.

All these circumstances make the performance of secular monophony, in particular, an extraordinarily demanding undertaking. If there is to be a serious confrontation with the music, even the preparation demands extensive knowledge in the fields of history, linguistic and source studies, palaeography and analysis, as well as a wide-ranging familiarity with the music in the context of other areas of the culture of an age. In every respect it leads to problems for which we have not yet found solutions. A high degree of specialization is necessary, too, if interpretation aspires to the musical qualities of a living performance on the basis of a notationless practice rather than using conventions which are distorted in advance by written preparation. The following sections explore individual questions of detail, the extent to which answers to them can be expected from the sources, and what courses have proved helpful, or problematic, in the search. Reference will be made to some of the central aspects of performance and preparation for performance, beginning with song and then going on to instrumental music *per se*.

Songs

The performance of songs must begin with an analysis of what survives. This lays the foundation for 'locating' the performance in a 'context', and for all the other necessary decisions, up to and including those concerning rhythm and the role of instruments. Two related questions need to be tackled first, one about the music–text relationship, and the other about the character of the surviving material, and in particular its position in the wide spectrum of possibilities ranging from an *ad hoc* written version corresponding to a notationless practice or a notationless transmission at one extreme, to composition worked out in writing at the other.

An edition can be used only if it sets out the facts concerning the transmission of both text and music without omissions or misinformation, and as completely as is necessary for analysis. That is rarely the case, however. In the case of European courtly song, for example, the question about the music–text relationship requires both to come from the same source (not a text reconstructed from several different versions, with the melody from one manuscript, let alone one in a 'purged' version from which all the information about transmission has been expunged). Since, in the case of songs which survive in several different sources, a decisive stage in surveying both the transmission and the individual versions is the comparison of the melodies, an edition which reproduces only one version is useless.

In the case of those sources where rhythms are only partly indicated and all those with pragmatic mensuration, it is essential to reveal how much room there is for interpretational manoeuvre by juxtaposing the original note values with the transcription. It goes without saying that scarcely any editions make clear the state of the sources with regard to aspects that seem secondary at first glance, such as punctuation of the text, vertical strokes of division and other means of grouping. And since even Hendrik van der Werf's and Gerald A. Bond's edition of troubadour melodies, which helpfully prints melody and text versions side by side, limits itself to first strophes,[10] it is almost always necessary to go back to the sources when preparing performances.

In the case of the performance of songs, the issues outlined in the first part of this chapter are at best acknowledged by musicologists to exist, without having led to any substantial further investigation. There has been scarcely any critical evaluation of the multifarious experience gained by those performers who have crossed the divide from the page to actual sound.[11] In the case of the music of the 17th and 18th centuries, the canon of aspects relevant to performance practice has long since been expanded to take account of the structure of the music, of the reconstruction of the conventions to which the written signs conform, and above all of distinctions according to dates, styles and genres; but musicological work on the performance of medieval song still confines itself to general discussion of rhythm, vocal and instrumental forces and related details such as accidentals and ornamentation. Individual observations leave no room for doubt that, in the case of medieval song as well, criteria for a well-founded 'reading' can be obtained from the surviving sources, the musical structure and the music–text relationship, if the performers are sensitive to variations of style. We do not yet have the systematic preliminary studies necessary for a comprehensive presentation and for general answers. Quite apart from the fact that examples are still regularly found even of pertinent questions which are doomed from the start because they are approached from outmoded premises. Some examples include taking it for granted that the music–text relationship in Provençal or old French song is confined as a matter of principle to the formal aspects of the strophe; reducing the question of rhythm to the choice between a 'free' delivery which cannot be defined more precisely, and a regular pattern in triple values; or interpreting pragmatic mensural directions according to the requirements and criteria of a systematic method of notation, something which remained an exception until well into the 14th century, even in manuscripts of polyphonic music.

THE MANUSCRIPT SOURCES In most cases, it is not difficult to decipher the poetic and musical text of medieval monophonic song. But the questions surrounding the meaning of what has been written are all the more numerous and fundamental, especially when the manuscript is decisive only about the pitches, as is the case with most sources of Provençal and old French song. The questions begin with the function of individual signs such as *plicae*, accidentals and additional marks, and they bear upon the distinction between variants and actual mistakes, and not least the manuscript's position in the transmission of the song. Rhythmic differentiation always presents problems, except in those few cases where a systematic mensural notation has been used. In all other cases it is possible that a regular pattern lies behind the pragmatic indications, but it may not. In addition to triple metres the possibility of duple metres must also be allowed for and so must the possibility that the signs indicate longer and shorter notes in a freer style of delivery, quite apart from latitude at the start, the finish and between lines. Finally it must be remembered that the musical signs only supplement the information given in the manuscript about the structure and even the expressive content of the poetry. Allowance must be made for the possibilities (*a*) that the notator and the text-scribe were often separate people working in different places, (*b*) that the music was written down later, (*c*) that emendations were made in the notation, and (*d*) that a new melody may even have been substituted for one previously notated.[12]

There are many cases where it would be possible to use a reproduction of the original in analysis, and even as the basis for the step to realization in sound. On the other hand transcription offers the opportunity to assess the state of the source. At the same time it can prepare the most important analytical questions by showing the division of the text by lines, and by indicating longer musical repeats, by juxtaposition if necesssary.

The most important consideration when transcribing an original source is not to lose any of the information. For that it is helpful, when the text is being laid out in lines, to use additional signs to mark the line-changes of the manuscript, and to retain the original orthography (with obvious abbreviations deciphered) and punctuation. When transcription of the music does not adopt the clefs and note signs of the source, the use of unambiguously equivalent signs is crucial in decipherment. Retention of the original signs – a principle that is defended on occasion with dogmatic obstinacy – can lead to a restriction of critical consideration of the information transmitted, especially in the case of more complex notations.[13] Copying is useful above all in acquiring an understanding of the formation and grouping of the signs. But there is absolutely no reason to copy painstakingly every variation in the forms of the 'Messine' neumes of a particular chansonnier, if all its information with respect to denomination, grouping and, where appropriate, modification of the notes can be given unambiguously with stemless note heads, slurs and other signs as appropriate. On the other hand it is sensible, even in the case of clear square notation, to retain the grouping, even down to such details as the distinction between ligatures and appositions (for example: ♩♩ with a double slur as ♫, as distinct from ♪ as ♫). The fact that the significance of liquescence is still found to be important in song manuscripts is not necessarily an argument in favour of fixing a second note on a specific pitch in an edition (i.e. ♪ preferable to ♫ etc).[14]

The primary aid to ascertaining the meaning of individual signs is the study of the writing habits of an individual notator. But allowance must also be made for the possible consequences of different exemplars, especially such as can be deduced from concordances and repertory studies, including the study of clusters in the transmission.[15]

Sometimes the analysis of a single manuscript is enough to reveal errors beyond reasonable doubt, especially if there is a series of symptomatic mistakes arising from the copy of one model. Some examples include the unwarranted transposition of a segment by a third (when a change of clef in the model was overlooked at the start of a new system); the omission (or repetition) of a note which can have been compensated for in various ways (interpolation and abbreviation, distribution of the notes of a ligature over several syllables or alternatively the contraction of notes to one ligature etc).

Earlier research, in the work published by Friedrich Gennrich and his school, produced useful catalogues of possible mistakes and their causes.[16] However, the assumption that something is a mistake must always be supported by internal evidence. And in that respect earlier research proceeded from premises which now appear problematic. These premises began with the assumption of the invariable existence of a model reading, and went on, via the reconstruction of 'authentic' versions of melodies, to conceptions of form in which segments were always repeated identically.[17] These concepts are challenged by the growing recognition of the influence and particular nature of an 'oral tradition'.[18] Different versions can result from the fact that while poetic and musical strategies were clear, their exact formulation could vary. This scope may be comparatively small, or it may play a greater role in some segments of the music than others, or it may lead to such substantial differences that the boundary between two formulations, which came into existence quite independently of each other, becomes fluid. Each of these possibilities can be observed in manuscripts of secular monophony.

Of course there are instances of inadvertent error in the written versions emanating from an oral tradition – even when the notator makes his individual decisions in his role 'as singer'. On the other hand analysis of the written versions coming from sources bearing the hallmarks of an oral tradition offers the specific opportunity for performance to disclose the range of the formulation's scope for variation, and the conventions on which it is based. That can be done by comparing several versions of the same song, but it can also be accomplished in the case of comparable different songs, taking into account the characteristics of specific sections of the transmission (the content of individual sources, or parts of them, the pieces copied by one scribe, or of reconstructed exemplars), and also sections determined by specific styles, genres and individual singer-poets. And when – as is surprisingly often the case – both the scope for variation and the underlying concepts and ground-rules of the formulation of one song can be discerned with sufficient clarity, then it is certainly possible to formulate one's own version as the basis for a performance.

The crux for performance lies in the fact that in every case – even when a melody has survived in only one form – it demands a fundamental decision about the character and function of a written version and, following from that, about the weight it should carry for a performance. Just how little use general assumptions are for this purpose is shown by the fact that among the written examples of music for texts by the earliest troubadours there are melodies which clearly aspire to be taken as definitive formulations. At the same time it is precisely the earliest written versions of Provençal texts with musical notation, dating from *c*1100, that convey a substantial insight into the *ad hoc* formulation of a melody on the basis of a model – though admittedly, and perhaps not fortuitously, the texts in these cases are religious ones.[19] Significantly, in those instances where several strophes are written down, in Latin songs of the early 12th century, constancy and variation can be seen side by side.[20] Examples exist in every area of song of cases where something that appears at first sight to be an error, or at least a problematic form of notation, proves on closer inspection to be a plausible formulation, justifiable for purely musical reasons or perhaps for the sake of the delivery of the text. On the other hand, even the comprehensive parallel edition of the melodies of individual trouvères purges only some of the obvious mistakes.[21] For both of these reasons, performance requires detailed prior analysis and comprehensive understanding of what has been written. In this the music–text relationship plays a key role.

MUSIC AND TEXT It has long been recognized that the relationship between music and text forms an excellent starting point for the interpretation of secular song. The scale of what is thus addressed is less widely understood. Studies of the connection between musical and verbal formulations – even where the scope of the enquiry has not been further limited by the blanket assumption of a modal rhythmic interpretation – commonly confine themselves to the correspondence between the strophic structure and the form of the musical segment. In many respects this is in accordance with the general thesis that other aspects did not play any role or came to bear only in performance.[22] This assumption ignores the fact that the 12th and 13th centuries – especially the 12th – offer examples of the music–text relationship in a wide variety of different forms, in the Latin and the vernacular song alike.[23]

In every case the relationship of text and music was integral to the structure of the stanza. In this respect, however, the widest conceivable scope for variety remained. The music, by its melodic structure, with its formal relationships and articulations, can impose its own accents, avoid cadences at the ends of poetic lines, bridge caesuras, and thus realize an aesthetic concept which offered a wholly plausible resolution, in the tension between musical and verbal forms, for the *discours* of a strophic song of any length.[24] On the other hand, the music can equally well heed the *données* of the text and adopt them in minute detail in its own formulation: from syntax through word-play to expressive content. There are many instances in manuscripts of a close correspondence between a song's textual and musical formulations. Ex.1 is from a song by Bernart de Ventadorn.[25] 'G' emphasizes the

Ex.1

articulation of the line of verse at the caesura after 4, by the repetition of the descending fourth *g–d* and the following turn to *f* at 6–8. In both lines the caesura matches the syntactical articulation, which puts a stress on the following syllables ('lai enves' and 'qe ia' respectively) owing to its position in the line. 'R' does not use repetition as a means of articulation, places a stress on 'there' by the transposition at 5–7 ('en lay'), and ties together what comes next – if one accepts the fact that 7–8 are transposed and continued at 9–10. The difference between the versions is illustrated by translation: 'Indeed they have lost me, *there in Ventadorn*' in G, compared with 'Indeed they have lost me *there*, in Ventadorn' in R. The difference in the text of line 3 in the two versions corresponds to this altered emphasis, with R emphasizing the explicit 'I' ('que ieu'): '*I* have no reason ever to return there'. And this kind of subtle differentiation between versions, from Marcabru onwards, corresponds to clear differences in the music–text relationship determined by genres, stylistic areas and not least by the personal hands of individual poet-musicians.[26]

This example demonstrates the importance for the live performance of a song of studying and understanding the text down to the smallest details in the expressive content, while paying the closest attention to the differences in manuscripts with notation: from syntax, through the role played in the verse structures by the use of caesuras, rhymes and particular characteristics of the language, to expressive content and the literary context.[27] The next step concerns the relationship between the musical and the verbal formulation. And tying up the analytical results of that with the observations about the character and the place of origin of the manuscript(s) in a song's transmission is generally already enough to produce a series of fundamental premises to help determine the next stage in interpretation.

Further analytical questions arise from the fact that the melody of a strophic song is notated only once as a rule. No problem exists in adapting the melody to each succeeding strophe when these all correspond to the first not only in their formal disposition but also in their expressive and syntactical articulation. 'Musical' texts of this kind are more common than appears at first sight.[28] Examples of the diametrically opposite case are presented by the relatively small number of songs in which strophes even differ from each other in construction.[29] The Latin song offers a number of telling examples which confirm, at least for the 12th century, that the musical formulation might vary between strophes. And in the conductus *Da laudis, homo, nova cantica*, which is particularly informative about the music–text relationship, the Latin song gives an example of an artistic melody being reformulated for the sake of the different articulation of one line of verse.[30]

Similarly in the case of vernacular song – quite apart from such liberties in performance as are to be expected with an oral tradition – we must reckon with the widest variety of forms of adaptation: from the adaptation of a melody in accordance with variations in strophic structure to modifications made on the basis of expressive and syntactic details of the text. The scope for variation in performance is as wide as that of the differences in melodic construction and the characteristics of one individual formulation. We cannot even exclude the possibility that in the *discours* of a longer song it affected the *finalis*. That is particularly likely in those Provençal songs in which the melody, having reached the end of the first strophe, leads back to the beginning with a surprising *finalis*, as in ex.2, by Jaufre Rudel.[31] For the close here is on *c*, which leads back to the beginning and strengthens the tension between *ouvert* and *clos* at the end of the first lines. This is all the more surprising because the striking intonation on the words 'mais lo mieu chant comens aisi' emphasizes the Dorian character of the melody as it centres first on *a* and then on *d*. Is there any reason why a singer, coming to the end of his performance, should not have modified the last melisma to a Dorian concluding formula to mark the fact that it was the end of the song and not just of a strophe? On the other hand Latin song, again, gives examples of invariance in the musical formulation in spite of textual variations. And the first comprehensive collection of melodies from the German-speaking area, in

Ex.2

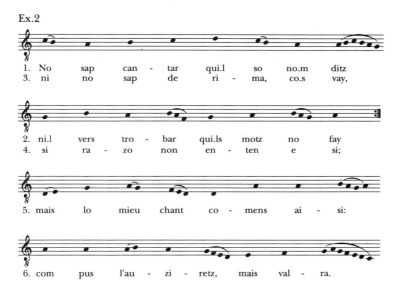

1. No   sap   can - tar   qui.l   so   no.m   ditz
3. ni   no   sap   de   ri - ma,   co.s   vay,

2. ni.l   vers   tro - bar   qui.ls   motz   no   fay
4. si   ra - zo   non   en - ten   e   si;

5. mais   lo   mieu   chant   co - mens   ai - si:

6. com   pus   l'au - zi - retz,   mais   val - ra.

the 14th-century Jena manuscript, offers a whole series of *Spruch* melodies which are so constructed as to permit varying articulation in performance.

Finally the text comprises an important point of departure for the presentation of a song. It consists in the first instance of the unique sound-character of that text in that language, which comes to the fore when the singer makes appropriate use of the various possibilities for sound production and resonance.[32] But more important, in the case of the strophic song, is the singer's exploitation of all the levels of a text's expressive content: from the various aspects of the *discours*, through individual details, to the 'message' of the whole. This calls for an approach which has broken free of the idea of a presentation of different sets of words to the same melody (in accordance with modern practice) and shapes the musical delivery of the text afresh from one strophe to the next (guided by the knowledge of the earlier holistic relationship of music and text).

'LOCATING' THE PERFORMANCE The location of a performance in a specific context also bears directly upon the decisions that must be taken by a performer, and the greater the distance between the first formulation of a song and the surviving sources, the greater the importance is. 'Distance' here is to be understood as both temporal and geographical, but it also relates to the character of the written evidence. Before a performance can be 'located', the surviving version(s) must have been analysed, in order to settle fundamental matters about its/their position in the transmission: from deciding such matters as whether a text originally in Provençal, for example, has been translated into French,[33] to understanding the consequences editing may have had on the musical elements.

The decision about the (fictive) 'location' for the performance is closely connected with a decision about (an equally fictive) time. For example, should a Provençal song of the early 12th century be interpreted in the context of its date of origin and the musical conditions of the time – which would include the background of the Latin song, the transmission of which, since c1100, offers a wide variety of footholds for interpretation? Or should it be placed in a historical situation where the new modal thinking and the mensural alternatives of the 13th century have already made a mark? Locating the performance requires decisions to have been made about the education and the interests of the putative people involved, from clerics at one extreme to itinerant minstrels and singers at the other. The choice of instruments and of models for the performance will also depend on the 'location', and the outcome will be that one and the same song, if its fictive location is the mid-13th-century Spanish court of Alfonso el Sabio, where Christian, Judaic and Islamic cultures met and mingled, will receive a wholly different interpretation from that projected for, say, an episcopal court in northern France at exactly the same date. Choice of location will affect many other decisions about the performance and the position it is to occupy in the broad spectrum between singing before a large audience and singing privately for one's own satisfaction; the widest possible range of sources must be drawn upon, including the numerous depictions of musical occasions in literature.

Locating the performance therefore provides a decisive chance to give it a historic footing and to differentiate accordingly. Doing so demands, admittedly, a consideration of historical factors which leads far beyond the narrow frontiers of any one musical specialization.

QUESTIONS OF RHYTHM – STRUCTURE AND ORNAMENTATION The question of rhythm serves as a focal point, bringing together the separate aspects and the specific requirements for a performance of secular monophony. It calls for analysis of the written record and of what was actually being recorded, with fundamental decisions on the character and values of the notation, the relationship between music and text in the song concerned, and the location of the performance.

The situation is comparatively simple for the few mensurally conceived songs set down in systematic notation. Here, the lack of a second structural voice allows rhythmic liberties not only at the beginnings and ends of verses or sections, but also in the arrangement and combination of metric groups, and not least in the relationship between duration and stress.

In the case of a manuscript with partial rhythmic clarification or a pragmatic mensural notation, the interpretation begins with the reconstruction of the conventions to which differentiation in the notational symbols can refer: a distinction between relatively shorter or longer notes, proportional values in duple or triple metre, or an even more strongly determined rhythmic model (along the lines of the *modi* in triple metre or indeed the 'quatre prolacions' of the 14th century).

In all other cases an analysis of the piece and its transmission combined with decisions concerning the location of the performance determines whether realization starts out primarily from declamation of the text, from the *données* of the melody, or from the rhythmic structure (the latter applies particularly to the realm of dance music), and how it mediates between these three aspects. Thus the question of rhythm shifts from the realization of a simple model to a multifaceted process. By trial and error, that process reveals aspects of the transmitted material because of the demands and conditions for an integral musical performance. This procedure calls for constant analysis of the results and provides a specific opportunity for the understanding of the actual notation and of its musical content. As experience has shown, the main difficulty involved concerns the reaction to the individual aspects of the text within the framework of an established rhythmic interpretation, especially in the case of long poems with changing messages.

From the beginnings of the new concept of song as it emerged in the early 12th century very different possibilities of rhythmic performance have to be taken into account; evidence for this is found in Latin vocal music, with its relationship between the comparatively few melodies of secular texts which can be clearly reconstructed and the large body of liturgical songs with staff notation. Here the great variety of musical formulations – from the syllabic to the melismatic, with transitional stages between them – precludes any general approach and solutions. At the same time, the subtle and ever-changing relationship between music and text offers indications for all kinds of different approach to interpretation.

The range of musical formulation is not so wide for the new art of song in its Provençal aspect. The variety both in the melodic style and in the relationship between music and text in the four songs by Marcabru which survive with music in the late manuscripts of the 13th and early 14th centuries is all the more remarkable.[34] They provide a good example of three different approaches to rhythmic interpretation. The crusade song, *Pax in nomine domini*, has an expansive narrative melody, which in the connection of parts, details of form, and the relationship between music and language, suggests a performance of this *vers* based on the declamation of the text. On the other hand the *canso*, *Bel m'es quan sunt li fruit madur*, has a musically complex and close-knit strophe, with many connections between the two parts and their verses. Consideration of these factors leads to an interpretation which is much more strongly influenced by the character of the melody, with phrases freely rendered regardless of any fixed proportional values. Finally, the *pastorela*, *L'autrier just'una sebissa*, has the simplest of these three melodies. Its formulation allows many different solutions, ranging from a rapid declamation with approximately equal syllabic values to a proportional alternation of long and short values. It may be no coincidence that in the late manuscript in which it survives, this particular song is notated with a regular alternation between breve and long, although of course this detail tells us nothing about performance in Marcabru's own time, the first half of the 12th century.[35]

The stylistic variety found here highlights the absurdity of any attempt at generalization concerning the question of rhythm. This is even more true for the later history of secular song, with its differences between stylistic levels, genres, individual poet-composers, geographical areas – from the Iberian peninsula to the east of Europe, from England to southern Italy – and not least between languages. The reading of a stressed Latin verse differs from that of a syllable-counting Old French verse or from a German verse based on four stresses (*Vierhebigkeit*) comprising different numbers of syllables.[36]

Further rhythmic phenomena were explored in the modal procedures of musicians working at Notre Dame in Paris. An alternation between longer and shorter values in the proportion of 2:1 must have been in existence for some time. In the performance of regularly stressed Latin verse this alternation arises naturally from prolongation of the stressed (or indeed unstressed) syllable. Compositions dating from the end of the 12th century onwards, however, exhibit new features in the consistent creation of more complex patterns, but in particular the development of a specific melodic language on the basis of these set rhythmic procedures.

In this respect, then, it is appropriate to speak of modal rhythm in monophonic song – and to work with the criteria of the rhythmic modes – only when the melodic formulation of a song and the relationship between music and text reflect a modal conception. This, however, occurs relatively rarely in vernacular song. On the other hand we have to take into account the fact that new solutions to the question of performing songs from an older tradition arose in the context of modal rhythm. Symptomatically, we find various solutions in the numerous interconnections between monophonic song and modal polyphony. In some instances of the use of pre-existent monophonic material in a polyphonic context an identical rhythm is preserved, but in others free use is made of the borrowed material.

On the basis of these premises, mensural indications in 13th-century manuscripts are particularly interesting: good examples are found in the *Chansonnier Cangé*.[37] They are of no use as an argument for a general discussion of 'modal' interpretation of trouvère songs. But they offer an excellent chance of studying the wide variety of possible solutions for the rhythmic performance of a substantial contemporary repertory. For this, however, it is necessary to take the pragmatic features (in the use of diverse notational signs) into account, rather than to attempt to accommodate the music to a codified notational system. There are indications of a wide range of rhythmic procedures, based on (*a*) syllabic values of equal or of different lengths, (*b*) duple or triple metres with changes in groupings (and freedom at the beginning of verses and in the way they are linked), (*c*) characteristic modal rhythms and their free use, and (*d*) even pieces whose notation indicates approximately equal basic note values. Until now, however, there has been no systematic investigation of *Cangé* and other pragmatic notations, their implied conventions, their connection with melodic formulations and the relationship between music and text.

Finally, even the mensurally conceived monophonic songs of such composers as Jehannot de Lescurel and Guillaume de Machaut, recorded by means of the new notational techniques of the years around 1300 and of the Ars Nova, indirectly offer helpful indications for the rhythmic interpretation of chansons from an older tradition. Thus, in his virelai *Comment qu'a moy lontaine*, Machaut takes up the melody of the anonymous *chanson de toile*, *Belle Doette as fenestres se siet*. It is striking that in this quotation Machaut does not follow the patterns of declamation found in his early virelais in *tempus imperfectum* with *prolatio maior*. This indicates a performance of the chanson with approximately equal notes and extensions.[38]

The contribution made by Lescurel's ballades and rondeaux to the interpretation of older songs goes a great deal further.[39] In the first instance it can be observed that in several of his songs the melody allows us to infer an ornamented sequence of notes. Thus, in the ballade shown in ex.3, the same basic melody is differently ornamented in lines 1 and 3 and verses 2 and 4 (the transcription gives one of the possible interpretations for the groups of three short values).

Ex. 3

The basic sequence of notes here corresponds, as in other songs, to the melodic language of the trouvère chanson, which would have been transmitted as shown in the transcription by the superscript signs of square notation. The groups of shorter notes indicate some latitude of formulation in performance. They correspond to those found in other contexts: in the melodic 'variants' of song transmission, in organal melismas and in melismatic parts of monophonic songs, in variants of motet voices transmitted in multiple versions, in the ornamentation of *contrapunctus diminutus* and so on. Moreover, a facet of performance or *pronuntiatio* is represented in this ballade by the rapid note repetitions of the 'florificatio vocis' (Garlandia).[40] Characteristically, the integration of these specific aspects of performance into composition – based on notational techniques that had been developed in polyphony – occurs on the rhythmic level, which is subsequently described in theoretical terms as 'prolatio'.

The foregoing observations demonstrate how aspects of an unwritten practice were integrated into written composition. In retrospect this integration constitutes a reference-point for our reconstruction of conventions of

Ex. 4

A - mours   que   vous ai   mef - fait   ...

A - mours   douce   et de - si - re - e   ...

A - mours   que   vous ai   mef - fait ...

A - mours   douce   et de - si - re - e   ...

performance practice. This also applies to the rhythmic values of text declamation. As in the older pragmatic notations, syllables of equal length are found, as well as songs in duple and triple metre. In addition we find expansion and contraction of individual syllables (particularly at the beginnings and ends of verses) and even, interestingly, in the performance of the same basic melody. Thus, in ex. 4, the beginning of the song *Amours que vous ai meffait* has the sequence of notes from the beginning of the refrain 'Amours douce et desiree' in longer declamatory values. Finally, the different basic values of the declamation indicate not only different tempos but also a freer declamation, connected with the content of the text. Thus *Gracieusette/La tres douce Gillette*, a cheerful greeting in mock-flirtatious tone, is declaimed in semibreves throughout. And in the second part of the lament *Amours que vous ai meffait* there is an abrupt change from declamation in longs to declamation in semibreves where the text refers to that unfortunate hour that gave rise to such a miserable life (with similar comments in parallel passages in other verses sung to the same melody).

With regard to ornamentation, there are two possible interpretations. The first concerns the interpretation of neumatic groups in realizing melodies recorded without rhythmic differentiation. The second involves the reconstruction of an ad hoc practice in the free adaptation of what has been recorded in notation. Each piece has to be individually assessed. But one must also consider the possibility that even if a melody is notated in neumatic groups, notes of equal length may have been implied.

INSTRUMENTAL PARTICIPATION There is no doubt that instruments could be used in the performance of songs, as pictorial representations and narrative texts show. However, purely vocal monophonic performance was more usual. Here again, interpretation calls for an analysis of the transmitted material and for a decision concerning the location of the performance. Thus an exemplary survey and interpretation of the information on song performance that has come down to us in poetic texts and didactic writing, as well as in commentaries on the psalms and in sermons from the 12th to the early

14th centuries, reveals the existence of different practices depending on the place and time of performance, on its social function and in particular on the stylistic level of the poetry.[41]

Most mention of instrumental participation is found in the context of low-style genres, such as dance songs and pastourelles, which differ in linguistic style and in musical formulation from the more complex high-style genres, such as the *vers* of the early troubadours and the *gran chan* of the late trouvères. String instruments in particular are mentioned under many different names: fiddle and rebec, harp and psaltery, lute and gittern, and the hurdy-gurdy. As a rule only one or two instruments would appear to have been involved in the performance of a song.

In looking at the role of the instrument in song performance we have to take account of a broad spectrum of possibilities, ranging from performance of a melody in unison or octaves (with or without variation) to alternation between instrument and voice, and diverse types of accompaniment such as instrumental preludes, interludes and postludes. The musical realization depends primarily on the character and capabilities of the instrument. The simplest accompaniments, also found in polyphonic notation, are bourdon and parallels, particularly parallel fifths, differentiated according to the structure of the melody.

Other factors in the musical execution depend on locating the performance in a historical situation and the knowledge and education of the performer. This will have an effect on the use of the various practices of two-part performance as reflected, for instance, in Aquitanian polyphony of the 12th century, on the practice of simple two-part music in 'peripheral' sources and fields of later periods, and, not least, on the use of codified techniques, from fifthing (*quintoier*) to the new sonority of the contrapunctus in the early 14th century. Here again, the interconnections between song and polyphony offer useful models when examined closely. Thus the 'basis' of the motet *Onques n'ami tant com je fui amée*, identified in some manuscripts as 'Sancte Germane', appears to be a free part accompanying that song by Richard de Fournival.[42]

On the other hand, there are no similar clues to the three aspects, now taken for granted, of the purely instrumental parts of the song performance (prelude, interlude and postlude), though comparison with many different forms of traditional folklore suggests the existence of such practices in the Middle Ages. Their inclusion and structure has been based on general considerations and suggestions from other musical fields, in particular the so-called 'Andalusian' practice.[43] This is an extreme case of the 'reconstruction' of notationless practice which can be based on various different aspects concerning the social function, the instruments involved and the character of the song. For purposes of critical consideration, however, the main factor is to examine the findings in the light of the implicit transfer of aesthetic assumptions from later periods.

Instrumental Music

With purely instrumental music, we are concerned with the reconstruction of notationless practice as illustrated in Model B above. Concerning the musical material, the reconstruction can be effected in two ways: by the connection with vocal music and through the evidence of the few documentary records that survive from the 13th and 14th centuries reflecting specific forms of instrumental practice.

The fact that one realm of instrumental practice was associated with the performance of song melodies is shown by relevant descriptions in poetry and the evidence of other texts.[44] As a counterpart, we have the account of how Raimbaut de Vaqueiras composed his 'estampida' *Kalenda maya* at the court of the Marquis of Monferrat, basing it on the instrumental performance of two minstrels from northern France ('dos joglars de Franza'), an account that closes with the comment: 'Aquesta stampida fu facta a las notas de la stampida qe·l joglars fasion en las violas'.[45] The interaction of vocal and instrumental practice ensures that the notated melodies, and in particular the principles on which they are moulded, can be used as guidelines. As clerics are also known to have played instrumental music, the same applies to the reception of various forms of polyphony. On the other hand, we have to take into account the characteristics of instrumental performance for the adaptation as well as the formulation of a melody. These concern the specific features of an instrument, the potential of expert techniques of playing and not least the experience of a qualified or virtuoso musician.

The earliest documentary records of notationless instrumental practice also indicate a broad spectrum of styles.[46] We find the integration of instrumental playing in three modal discants in a miscellany dating from the beginning of the second half of the 13th century, in the British Library (Harl. 978, ff. 8v–9). Rather later is an instrumental piece recorded in a manuscript in the Bodleian Library, Oxford (Douce 139, f. 5v). The addition of several monophonic *danses* and *estampies* to ff. 5 and 103v–4v of the *Chansonnier du Roi* (Bibliothèque Nationale, fr.844) must have been made at the beginning of the 14th century. Definitely later are the *estampies* and motet intabulations for a keyboard instrument in the Robertsbridge Codex (British Library, Add.28500, ff. 43–4v). The sparse body of monophonic music is supplemented, in particular, by the *istampite* of the period around 1400 in a manuscript in the British Library (Add.29987, ff. 55v–8 and 59v–63v).

Each of these documentary records offers an exposition of instrumental practice on the basis of particular styllistic contexts and through the medium of writing. The kind of cultural background that determined even the working-out of a comparatively simple *danse* is clearly evident in the way that the scribe, recording the first four *estampies royales* in the *Chansonnier du Roi*, uses the sign ⧧ for *mi* (i.e. a modification of the ♯). The former sign is used in other sources and in theoretical writing of the late Middle Ages to differentiate between tones of various sizes. The working-out of an 'instrumental' piece is immediately apparent in the second oldest source, that mentioned above in the Bodleian Library. Here corrections show in detail how the notator changed his mind, thus formulating a piece with an obvious aesthetic concept in mind, including the polyphonic conclusion.

The analysis of this piece as a reflection of instrumental practice allows us to infer certain techniques and principles of performance. These form a useful tool for the reconstruction of instrumental practice. On the other hand, the extant sources also show a wide latitude of formulation associated with different historical and stylistic circumstances. That latitude demonstrates how important the location of the performance is in this context. It is one of the pre-conditions for the integration of further reflections of instrumental music as they have come down to us, for instance the sections of a *danse* or *estampie* included in the tenors of motets of the period around 1300, their origin being indicated in such descriptions as 'Chose Tassin' or 'Chose Loyset'.

A determining factor in the arrangement and in particular the specific tonal disposition of instrumental performances is the aesthetic of repetition, which can be deduced from the sources. It is based mainly on the fact that the various units always find their way back to the same endings. The return can be effected in all kinds of ways: as a surprise or as a natural consequence of the use of the material; in new sections of the same length before the semi-conclusion (*ouvert*) or the final one (*clos*), or in longer sections; in completely new formulations or in such a way that the new section leads back to an earlier one – up to the repetition of the music from systematic extension of the preceding material around a new beginning. The fact that the new section leads back to the close of the first is expected by the form. The particularity of the art lies in its process of variation, whereby the new element in the first performance of a unit leading to an *ouvert* is familiar in the repetition, and becomes the starting point for further extensions. One of the *estampies* in the Robertsbridge Codex refers to this kind of artful play in its designation as 'Retrove' ('Found again!' or 'Find it again!'). It shows us in detail the specific potential of this art form, so characteristic of the music of the Middle Ages.[47]

*

The fact that the clues to the realization of monophonic music of the Middle Ages are far fewer than those that exist for polyphony or plainsong makes performance a considerable challenge. The danger is all the greater that a solution, once found, will be adopted uncritically and imitated as a model. A striking example of this is the influence of various interpretational models provided by the 'Early Music Quartet' over the last 20 years. Such an attitude, however, means relinquishing the specific opportunity of a dialogue with the past and declining to see the multifarious and specific tasks still awaiting attention in the interpretation of medieval monophonic music.

Notes

[1] Especially well-documented introductions to the sources are to be found in D. Fallows, 'Sources, §III: Secular monophony', *Grove6* (by language), and E. Jammers, *Aufzeichnungsweisen der einstimmigen ausserliturgischen Musik des Mittelalters*, Paläographie der Musik, i/4 (Cologne, 1975), 2–15 (by method of notation).
[2] See W. Lipphardt, 'Unbekannte Weisen zu den Carmina Burana', *AMw*, xii (1955), 122–42; Lipphardt, 'Einige unbekannte Weisen zu den Carmina Burana aus der zweiten Hälfte des 12. Jahrhunderts', in *Festschrift Heinrich Besseler zum 60. Geburtstag* (Leipzig, 1961), 101–25.
[3] Higinio Anglés published one of the sources of *cantigas* in facsimile, and the entire repertory in transcription. In the latter he placed the original notation above the transcriptions, which gives a useful insight into the spectrum of choice and decision in the interpretation of such a repertory: *La música de las cantigas de Santa Maria del Rey Alfonso el Sabio* (Barcelona, 1943–64). An example of a more recent, rigorously modal transcription is offered in S. N. Rosenberg and H.

Tischler, *Chanter m'estuet: Songs of the Trouvères* (London and Boston, 1981); see also the detailed review of that work by Hendrik van der Werf, *JAMS*, xxxv (1982), 539–54.

[4] For discussions of the conceptual questions addressed, and their consequences, see W. Arlt, ' "Vom Umgang mit theoretischen Quellen zur Aufführungspraxis" oder "Warum die Begegnung nicht stattfand" ', in *GfMKB, Bayreuth 1981*, 221–32; and L. Dreyfus, 'Early Music Defended Against its Devotees: a Theory of Historical Performance in the 20th Century', *MQ*, lix (1984), 297–322.

[5] In the case of Machaut the role of the script is also confirmed by statements in the *Voir dit* which were first elucidated by Friedrich Ludwig (*Guillaume de Machaut: Musikalische Werke*, ii, Leipzig, 1928/*R*1968, 54*–8*); on that and on its consequences for the sources, see S. J. Williams, 'An Author's Role in 14th-century Book Production: Guillaume de Machaut's "Livre ou je met toutes mes choses" ', *Romania*, xc (1969), 433–54; and L. W. Earp, *Scribal Practice, Manuscript Production and the Transmission of Music in Late Medieval France: the Manuscripts of Guillaume de Machaut* (diss., Princeton U., 1983) (with detailed bibliographical references). On the connection between structure and notation in the case of Lescurel and on the virelai of the Ivrea Codex, see W. Arlt, 'Aspekte der Chronologie und des Stilwandels im französischen Lied des 14. Jahrhunderts', *Aktuelle Fragen der musikbezogenen Mittelalterforschung* (Winterthur, 1982), 209–27, 271–3.

[6] For discussions of this and other similar statements see F. Gennrich, 'Die Repertoire-Theorie', *Zeitschrift für französische Sprache und Literatur*, lxvi (1956), 96–9; and D. Rieger, 'Audition et lecture dans le domaine de la poésie troubadouresque: quelques réflexions sur la philologie provençale de demain', *Revue des langues romanes*, lxxxvii (1983), 75–80.

[7] See M. Huglo, 'Codicologie et musicologie', in *Miscellanea codicologica F. Masai dicata* (Ghent, 1979), 71–82, and 'Les "libelli" de tropes et les premiers tropaires-prosaires', in *Pax et sapientia: Studies in Text and Music of Liturgical Tropes and Sequences*, ed. R. Jacobsson (Stockholm, 1986), 13–22; the observations of Sarah Fuller in 'The Myth of "St. Martial" Polyphony: a Study of the Sources', *MD*, xxxiii (1979), 5–26; and the analysis of a 14th-century codex in W. Arlt and M. Stauffacher, *Engelberg Stiftsbibliothek Codex 314* (Winterthur, 1986), 41–61.

[8] For a more detailed exposition, see W. Arlt, 'The "Reconstruction" of Instrumental Music: the Interpretation of the Earliest Practical Sources', in *Performance Practice: New York 1981*, 75–81.

[9] The overlapping between different areas was already demonstrated by Edmond Faral in his early but still standard study, *Les jongleurs en France en moyen âge* (Paris, 1910); see also D. Hoffmann-Axthelm, 'Instrumentensymbolik und Aufführungspraxis: zum Verhältnis von Symbolik und Realität in der mittelalterlichen Musikanschauung', *Basler Jb für historische Musikpraxis*, iv (1980), 9–78 (especially 42–9), and the appended bibliography of performance practice of medieval music, 79–89; W. Hartung, *Die Spielleute: eine Randgruppe in der Gesellschaft des Mittelalters* (Wiesbaden, 1982).

[10] H. van der Werf, *The Extant Troubadour Melodies: Transcriptions and Essays for Performers and Scholars* (Rochester, NY, 1984).

[11] See the general remarks and the analysis of a monophonic example in W. Arlt, 'Musik, Schrift und Interpretation: Zwei Studien zum Umgang mit Aufzeichnungen ein- und mehrstimmiger Musik aus dem 14. und 15. Jahrhundert', *Basler Jb für historische Musikpraxis*, iv (1980), 91–114.

[12] One example of the extensive substitution of a melody was disclosed by Elisabeth Aubrey in one of the few musico-historical analyses of a song codex to include detailed observations on the palaeographical findings and a consideration of the codicological evidence: *A Study of the Origins, History and Notation of the Troubadour Chansonnier Paris, Bibliothèque Nationale, f. fr. 22543* (diss., U. of Maryland, 1982), 122–4.

[13] For a history and critique of this view see W. Arlt, *Aspekte der musikalischen Paläographie*, Paläographie der Musik, i/1, 20–5.

[14] On liquescence in song codices and other 13th-century sources see D. Hiley, 'The Plica and Liquescence', in *Gordon Athol Anderson (1929–81) in Memoriam* (Henryville, 1984), 379–91.

[15] Observations on this subject are to be found in studies of individual MSS such as Elisabeth Aubrey's work on troubadours (see above, n.12) and Johann Schubert's on trouvères, *Die Trouvèrehandschrift R. Die Handschrift Paris, Bibl. nat. fr. 1591* (diss., U. of Frankfurt am Main, 1963).

[16] See F. Gennrich, *Die autochthone Melodie: Übungsmaterial zur musikalischen Textkritik* (Langen, 1963), and, especially, W. Bittinger, *Studien zur musikalischen Textkritik des mittelalterlichen Liedes* (Würzburg, 1953).

[17] Pragmatic investigation of the formal concepts underlying the monophonic song of the 12th and 13th centuries has long been hindered by the dominance exercised by Friedrich Gennrich's *Grundriss einer Formenlehre des mittelalterlichen Liedes als Grundlage einer musikalischen Formenlehre des Liedes* (Halle, 1932/*R*1970). The systematic premises of the book are governed by 19th-century ideas of 'Form(en)lehre', and in particular its backward projection of the *forme-fixe* theory; its unquestioning equation of formal derivations with historical developments has distorted recognition of the formal variety and originality of earlier songs.

[18] In the case of medieval monophonic music, it was above all Leo Treitler who drew attention to the particular character and consequences of a notationless transmission and the traces that it also left on written sources; see his contribution to the round-table discussion ' "Peripherie" und "Zentrum" in der Geschichte der ein- und mehrstimmigen Musik des 12. bis 14. Jahrhunderts', in *GfMKB, Berlin 1974*, 58–74, and his 'Transmission and the Study of Music History', in *IMSCR*, xii *Berkeley 1977*, 202–11.

[19] The reference is to the Provençal songs in the manuscript *F-Pn* lat.1139, and in particular to *O Maria deu maire*; see W. Arlt, 'Zur Interpretation zweier Lieder: *A madre de Deus* und *Reis glorios*', *Basler Jb für historische Musikpraxis*, i (1977), 124–6, with emendations in x (1986), 39, n.24.

[20] See, for example '*Nova cantica*: Grundsätzliches und Spezielles zur Interpretation musikalischer Texte des Mittelalters', *Basler Jb für historische Musikpraxis*, x (1986), 26–52.

[21] As an example of an error not corrected in an edition, I would cite one already discussed by Gennrich: the transposition by a third at the end of the third line of a song by Blondel de Nesle (*Quant je plus sui*) in the trouvère MS R; see H. van der Werf, *Trouvère-Melodien I*, Monumenta Monodica Medii Aevi, xi (Kassel, 1977), 64.

[22] Among the more recent, symptomatic examples of the categorical exclusion, for analytical purposes, of all aspects of a text's expressive content I would cite K. Schlager, 'Annäherung an ein Troubadour-Lied. "Tant m'abellis l'amoros pessamens" von Folquet de Marseille', in *Analysen: Beiträge zu einer Problemgeschichte des Komponierens: Festschrift für Hans Heinrich Eggebrecht zum 65. Geburtstag* (Stuttgart, 1984), 1–13, and H. van der Werf, *The Extant Troubadour Melodies*, 62, but the latter at least allows a more extensive connection between music and text in performance.

[23] John Stevens, too, has recently emphasized this in his comprehensive survey *Words and Music in the Middle Ages* (Cambridge, 1986). Stevens concerns himself with a far broader spectrum of questions than the works cited, but, in my view, he nevertheless allows himself to be influenced by too restrictive a framework of criteria in his detailed analytical comments, especially on the song, and by the search for general answers in his conclusions. For clarification of my own position I refer, for the Latin song, to my study on the *Nova cantica* (see above, n.20) and, for the vernacular song, to my paper 'Musica e testo nel canto francese: dai primi trovatori al mutamento stilistico intorno al 1300', and to the discussion which followed it, both in the conference report *La musica nel tempo di Dante: Ravenna 1986*, (Milan, 1988), 175–97, 306–21.

[24] See T. Karp, 'Interrelationships between Poetic and Musical Form in *Trouvère* Song', in *A Musical Offering: Essays in Honor of Martin Bernstein* (New York, 1977), 137–61; L. Gushee, 'Analytical Method and Compositional Process in Some 13th and 14th-century Music', *Aktuelle Fragen der musikbezogenen Mittelalterforschung*, 169–80.

[25] See the article from which this example was taken: N. Gossen, 'Musik und Text in Liedern des Trobadors Bernart de Ventadorn', *Schweizer Jb für Musikwissenschaft*, iv–v *1984–5* (1988), 9–40 (20–23 for the discussion of *Be m'an perdut*). 'G' = *I-Ma* R71, f.14r; 'R' = *F-Pn* fr.22543, f.57r – here transposed down a fifth for the purpose of comparison.

[26] On Marcabru, see Arlt, 'Musica e testo', 182–8.

[27] The importance of a context of other poems for the understanding of, in particular, vernacular songs has been demonstrated by Jörn Gruber in *Die Dialektik des Trobar: Untersuchungen zur Struktur und Entwicklung des occitanischen und französischen Minnesangs des 12. Jahrhunderts* (Tübingen, 1983).

[28] One example is Folquet's *Tan m'abellis*, which has been discussed under various aspects. It displays a striking cadential turn in mid-line. See Schlager, 'Annäherung'; Arlt, 'Musica e testo', 190; Gossen, 'Musik und Text', 16–20.

[29] Some significant examples are discussed by J. H. Marshall in 'Textual Transmission and Complex Musico-metrical Form in the Old French Lyric', in *Medieval French Textual Studies in Memory of T. B. W. Reid* (London, 1984), 119–48.

[30] See Arlt, '*Nova cantica*'.

[31] From Van der Werf, *The Extant Troubadour Melodies*, 220.

[32] See the discussion of this subject, with conclusions based on practical experience, by A. von Ramm, 'Style in Early Music Singing', *EM*, viii (1980), 17–20.

[33] See M. and M. Raupach, *Französisierte Trobadorlyrik: zur Überlieferung provenzalischer Lieder in französischen Handschriften* (Tübingen, 1979).

[34] For details see the comments in Arlt, 'Musica e testo', 182–8 (see n.23).

[35] There is a transcription of these notations in Hendrik van der Werf's edition, *The Extant Troubadour Melodies*, 226* (see n.10).

[36] In this context the work of Ewald Jammers provides particularly helpful suggestions, especially the introduction to *Ausgewählte Melodien des Minnesangs* (Tübingen, 1963) and his contribution to the *Aufzeichnungsweisen der einstimmigen ausserliturgischen Musik des Mittelalters* (see n.1).

[37] Paris, Bibliothèque Nationale, fr.846, in the facsimile edited by Jean Beck (Paris and Philadelphia, 1927), as *Corpus cantilenarum medii aevii*, i.1.

[38] For details see Arlt, 'Aspekte der Chronologie', 268–271 (see note 5), with a comparative version of the melodies on 269.

[39] The following comments are based on a fuller study: 'Zu den Liedern des Jehannot de Lescurel', in Arlt, 'Aspekte der Chronologie', 209–27; the examples are also taken from p. 218 and p. 222 of this study, where they are discussed at greater length.

[40] Erich Reimer, ed., *Johannes de Garlandia: De mensurabili musica*, i (Wiesbaden, 1972), 95. 14–15 (Beihefte zum Archiv für Musikwissenschaft, x).

[41] Christopher Page, *Voices and Instruments of the Middle Ages: Instrumental Practice and Songs in France 1100–1300* (London, 1987), with a comprehensive bibliography. The material, observations and reflections in this book form the point of departure for any study of the aspects briefly set out below.

[42] Compare the editions by Friedrich Gennrich, 'Trouvère-Lieder und Motettenrepertoire', *Zeitschrift für Musikwissenschaft*, ix (1926–7), 17–20, and Hans Tischler, *The Earliest Motets (to ca. 1270)*, ii (New Haven and London, 1982), 1019–23.

[43] See Thomas Binkley's account of the work of the Early Music Quartet, which has also moulded recent practice in this respect: 'Zur Aufführungspraxis der einstimmigen Musik des Mittelalters: ein Werkstattbericht', *Basler Jb für historische Musikpraxis*, i (1977), 19–76.

[44] Page cites and discusses much evidence in *Voices and Instruments in the Middle Ages*.

[45] The *Razo*, from Jean Boutière and Alexandre Herman Schutz, *Biographies des troubadours* (Paris, 1964), 565.

[46] The two oldest are discussed in my article, 'The "Reconstruction" of instrumental music' (see n.8). A list of the other sources to the end of the 14th century may be found in the complementary text, 'Instrumentalmusik im Mittelalter: Fragen der Rekonstruktion einer schriftlosen Praxis', *Basler Jb für historische Musikpraxis*, vii (1984). Both contain information about editions, literature and further considerations.

[47] See the observations ' "Wiedergefunden?": zum kunstvollen Spiel mit dem Formablauf in einer Estampie des Robertsbridge-Kodex' in the appendix to my contribution to 'Instrumentalmusik im Mittelalter' (57–64).

CHAPTER V

Polyphony before 1400

CHRISTOPHER PAGE

In the Middle Ages trained singers regarded performance as the naked body of musical art: as a natural thing, but a shameful one, which writers on *musica* should discreetly ignore. Far better for writers on music to dwell upon the measurement of intervals, for example, or upon the proportions of mensural notation, for these were subjects which allowed them to hold their heads high in the company of the mathematicians and astronomers whom they claimed as fellows. However, the men who compiled the Latin *musica* treatises were often teachers with a wealth of practical knowledge, and although they associated serious authorship with the art of covering that knowledge in a mantle of Latin, the garment sometimes slips and details of performance practice come into view. These details, together with the musical manuscripts themselves, provide most of our solid information about performance practice in medieval polyphony before 1400.[1]

The range of music generalized by the words 'medieval polyphony' is vast. It includes the motets, conductus and organa of the Parisian school; the insular polyphony of 13th- and 14th-century England; a handful of polyphonic songs from Germany; the motets, rondeaux, virelais and ballades of the Ars Nova and the extraordinarily florid repertory of ballate, madrigals and cacce from 14th-century Italy. Each repertory presents special problems and it is beyond the scope of this survey to discuss them individually; I intend to consider a few fundamental questions of performance which, in one way or another, bear upon them all: tuning, rhythm (in the contexts of certain Ars Antiqua genres), vocal timbre, ornamentation (where appropriate) and instrumentation.

In the Romanesque and Gothic centuries musicians regarded polyphony as an advanced technique for producing musical beauty by accurate measurement,[2] and to judge by the writings of theorists they approached it with an enthralled but objective curiosity as a contemporary astronomer might contemplate the working of his astrolabe. There were two things to be measured: the duration of notes and the distance between them, and the *musica* treatises imply an intense awareness of each interval in a piece of polyphony as a separately calibrated step. Indeed, there is reason to believe that medieval singers were exceptionally interested in tuning as a means of colouring and dramatizing musical effects in polyphonic music. Their delight in scrupulous intonation is sufficiently evident from the central position allotted to the perfect consonances of fifth, octave and twelfth in medieval polyphony, for these intervals must be sung with a very high degree of accuracy. (The leeway which a performer enjoys in the placing of imperfect consonances such as a third, major or minor, is much wider.) Throughout the period covered by this chapter composers explored the contrast between perfect consonances and imperfect ones with unflagging excitement; the stillness of fifths, octaves and twelfths, and the almost fierce beauty of imperfect consonances which could be widened (as we shall see) to the point where they became disturbing dissonances – these were the raw materials of composition for musicians of the Ars Antiqua and Ars Nova. For performers, fidelity to this counterbalance of intervals was the first task, and from infancy their ears were trained to catch subtle differences of pitch. They had barely emerged from boyhood, for example, before they were taught to distinguish two different kinds of semitone, the major and the minor; it is chastening for modern musicians to reflect that the difference between these two intervals is only 24 cents, approximately a quarter of a tempered semitone.[3]

Almost without exception, the theorists of the 13th and 14th centuries teach Pythagorean intonation.[4] In this system the seven naturals, A, B, C, D, E, F, G, and B♭, are established in steps of pure fifths and octaves. Expressed in the convenient form of cents (one-hundredths of a tempered semitone), and contrasted with the intervals offered by equal temperament, the Pythagorean tones prove to be large (204 cents rather than 200), as do the major thirds (408 not 400) and major sixths (906 not 900). The minor thirds are comparatively narrow (at 294 cents rather than 300) and so are the semitone steps which medieval polyphony exploits (the diatonic semitone, 90 cents not 100). For an illustration of the artistic importance attaching to the contrast between 'wide' imperfect intervals and pure perfect ones we need look no further than the basic cadences of medieval French polyphony (ex.1a–c; we shall come to a distinctively Italian form in a moment). These

Ex.1

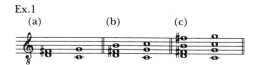

figures establish an exceptionally strong contrast between 'dissonant' imperfect intervals and consonant perfect ones. In ex.1a and b, for instance, Pythagorean intonation demands wide major thirds and sixths that strain to reach the perfect consonance just beyond them (an effect that is intensified when the third is doubled at the octave, as in ex.1c).

A tuning system can only be a guideline for performance, and by the later 13th century there is evidence that French musicians sometimes modified the intervals of the Pythagorean system. 'Not every minor semitone is equal to every other minor semitone' says one 13th-century theologian who must often have heard polyphony at Paris where he studied; 'indeed, one minor semitone may be greater than another'.[5] This airy disregard for the prescriptions of the theorists (who acknowledge only one size for the minor semitone) sounds like performers' talk, and there are many passages in Ars Antiqua motets, for example, that gain incisiveness in performance from wide thirds and correspondingly narrow semitone steps (ex.2). In a performance taking Pythagorean intonation as its starting point, the major thirds with which the

Ex.2

triplum and tenor begin will be wide, perhaps considerably so, giving melodic incisiveness (to the triplum especially) and lending a dissonant, leading quality to the sixth between triplum and motetus on the third beat.

The early 14th century brings remarkable evidence of such tuning practices as these. In his *Lucidarium*, written in 1317/18, Marchetto da Padova recommends a basic semitone step of 82 cents, smaller than a Pythagorean minor semitone and 18 cents short of the equal-tempered semitone.[6] These discrepancies are dwarfed, however, by Marchetto's ruling on cadential figures such as those shown in ex.1*a–c*. He proposes that imperfect intervals in movements such as these should be 'striving' (*tendendo*) towards the perfect ones, and to convey this impression he advises semitone steps that amount to only 41 cents, less than a quarter of a tone![7] Performed in this way the major thirds and sixths in ex.1*a–c* are almost unbelievably wide; none the less, they prove beyond doubt that Marchetto, singer and teacher of choristers at the Cathedral of Padua, required imperfect consonances to be widened in certain cadential positions beyond all modern expectations.

It may be significant that Marchetto was an Italian, for the two-part textures of trecento polyphony invite a creative approach to tuning. A characteristic figure of trecento counterpoint will serve as an illustration; it may be called the 'convergence cadence' since it occurs when the tenor rises through a fifth to converge on a unison with the voice above (ex.3). There is

Ex.3

considerable melodic tension in this movement for it usually requires three consecutive steps of a tone (whence the *ficta* note in the example) and produces a surge of colour in the harmony; note the diminished interval established by the *c′♯*, preceded by a fourth and a seventh. It calls for a widened major third so that the *c′♯* before the convergence may be almost startlingly 'colourful', emphasizing the transparency of the unison which is to follow. In ex.4 the abrupt variation between *f′* and *f′♯*, common in the two-

81

Ex.4

part repertory of the trecento, invites the performer to point the contrast by raising the f'♯ even further than Pythagorean intonation requires, especially as it forms a major sixth with the tenor and is about to resolve in circumstances where Marchetto recommends a very wide interval. Such raising helps to colour many passages where major thirds or sixths are prolonged to produce a tension eventually released into the top part which springs forward as soon as it may (ex.5).

Ex.5

French music calls for similar techniques. In Guillaume de Machaut's rondeau *Rose, liz*, for instance (ex.6), a major third is held for two bars in the

Ex.6

tenor and contratenor while the cantus part flirts with the resolution to come. The *f♯* in the contratenor will stand a good deal of raising here and the singer of the cantus should respond by raising his *b* s until they form a perfect fourth with it. In effect, these bars prolong and adorn a standard cadence (ex.1c) and it has been suggested that such movements are the quintessence of 14th-century musical style in France.[8] This interpretation becomes all the more persuasive in the light of the tuning practices that we have been considering. Wide and imperfect intervals straining towards the nearest perfect ones – this is one way in which 14th-century polyphony expresses the erotic desire explored in the texts of so many rondeaux, virelais and ballades.

English music responds to a different kind of tuning, principally because of its singular treatment of thirds and sixths. For French and Italian musicians conspicuous triads were usually tense and unstable sonorities, as we would expect them to be in music performed in Pythagorean intonation.[9] However, English composers use triads as building blocks and lay them side by side to create sonorities rarely heard in French or Italian music (ex.7). This suggests

Ex.7

that insular musicians may have mollified their thirds to produce more relaxed and sonorous triads, and Walter of Odington reports that Pythagorean thirds are not consonances from the mathematical point of view but can be made consonant in performance by 'the voices of men [which], through their subtlety, draw them into a sweet and thoroughly consonant mixture'.[10] To judge by the context of this remark Walter is referring to nominally pure thirds (giving 386 cents for the major and 316 for the minor).

The role of creative tuning in medieval music brings other aspects of performance into focus. It is widely held that polyphonic pieces, both sacred and secular, were performed with one voice to a part, at least until the mid-15th century,[11] and the artistic significance of this disposition may now be seen more clearly; the kind of tuning-awareness that we have been describing is possible only when singers go directly to the centre of the note, unhindered by doubling of any kind. (Doubling, whether vocal or instrumental, introduces slight discrepancies of intonation that blur the centre of each pitch.) The same may be said for vibrato, a more or less rapid fluctuation of pitch; although vibrato appears to have been employed as an ornament in the two-part organum of the Parisian tradition,[12] it is a studied inaccuracy of tuning, and it is inconceivable that medieval performers used it as anything more than an ornament.

Pronunciation and diction are of cardinal importance here. In every language there are dark vowels and bright vowels, and the dark ones must often be sung slightly sharp to avoid giving an impression of being more than slightly flat. (The radical vowel in British English 'father' is an example of a dark vowel; it accounts for the flatness which is often heard when performers of plainchant sing the final note of a melisma on the word 'Alleluya'.) Until a singer knows where each vowel belongs in the mouth and how it should feel (for that, in the final analysis, is how singers tune) it is impossible to attend to tuning in a creative way.[13] This is particularly important in genres where a text is simultaneously declaimed in all parts, as in the polyphonic conductus, for example; the essence of such word-setting is that changes in the harmony of the music are dramatized by abrupt changes in the harmonics of the sound. In the English piece *O sponsa dei electa*, for instance (ex.7), the beauty of the rising triads in bar 9 lies in the way each sonority is distinguished by its own 'field' of harmonics, established by the vowel to which it is sung. Unanimity of pronunciation counts for a great deal in passages such as this, and singers must agree upon the quality of each vowel, its brightness, its place in the mouth – upon everything, in fact, which contributes to its colour. The importance which medieval musicians attached to these considerations is suggested by their use of the verb 'pronuntio', 'to enunciate', in the sense 'to perform', recorded in many music treatises.[14]

Mention of the conductus brings us to the first conventional division of medieval polyphony, the Ars Antiqua. Loosely interpreted, the Ars Antiqua phase embraces all Western polyphony before *c*1300 and includes many tantalizing repertories fraught with problems arising from the rhythmic indeterminacy of the notation in which they are often recorded. Fundamental work is still being done not only on rhythmic questions but also on matters of musical style.[15] The writings of theorists such as Johannes de Garlandia are indispensable here, yet the statements of these authors are often so terse, or so cryptic, that it becomes impossible to secure general agreement about their meaning. This accounts for many current controversies. Good editions of several important treatises (including Garlandia's *De mensurabili musica*)[16] have appeared in recent years and many accepted notions have been questioned as a result. Were the texted sections of conductus always performed in modal rhythm? Should performances of *organum purum* obey the 'law of consonance' that requires notes in the top part to be protracted when they form a perfect consonance with the tenor? These are issues of capital importance to the performer which are still under debate.

Whatever may be uncovered by research in the coming years, modern performers will always be faced with the task of creating a style for Ars Antiqua polyphony themselves in long hours of rehearsal. This is a process in which scholars gradually recede from view like well-wishers on a quay as a ship leaves port. There is an academic consensus, for example, that the

12th-century organa that have repeatedly been linked with the name of the Abbey of St Martial de Limoges were originally performed in some kind of 'free rhythm', and every modern singer of St Martial polyphony must obviously be informed of this before he begins. Yet to perform a piece like *Rex omnia tenens* (ex.8) is to discover that 'free rhythm' in academic parlance usually

Ex.8

means 'not having the regular alternation of strictly measured long and short notes found in modal rhythm'; it is a negative concept, in other words, and therefore it is not particularly useful to the performer. Indeed the modern singer stands alone here and must find answers to fundamental questions by trial and error. Should the upper voice be presented as a decoration of the plainchant tenor, or does the plainchant tenor 'accompany' the top voice? Must the singer on the top contract his notes when he has more than the tenor, or should the tenor prolong his? An enormous range of possibilities, many of them undiscoverable and untestable except through practical experiment, lie within the notion of 'free rhythm'.

The problem of rhythm pervades several major genres of Notre Dame polyphony including the conductus and *organum duplum*. In conductus the rhythm of the melismatic sections can be recovered when scribes employ modal notation for them, but the texted sections could not be recorded in this way and the central Notre Dame sources provide little information about their rhythm. It has long been assumed that these texted passages share the modal rhythms of the melismatic ones[17] and that the accents of the poetry call for these rhythms. According to this familiar argument a line like 'Nóvus míles séquitùr' corresponds to a mode one pattern ♩♩♩♩♩♩♩♩ᵢ. These assumptions have often been questioned, however,[18] and it must be admitted that scansion provides a poor foundation for any theory about conductus rhythm. During the Middle Ages there can never have been a single or correct way of reading Latin accentual poetry; scansions varied according to the reader's degree of conservatism in such matters[19] and were undoubtedly responsive to vernacular stress-patterns. (It is debatable, for example, whether Frenchmen in the 13th century would have distinguished four accents in a line like 'Novus miles sequitur'.) Furthermore it is clear that some details of rhythmic interpretation in conductus were left to the performer's discretion, for in the early layer of the *Discantus positio vulgaris* (Paris, perhaps *c*1225), singers of conductus are advised to interpret ligatures having more than four notes according to any rhythmic pattern they please.[20] When we add the consideration that the polyphonic conductus was cultivated for many years over a

85

wide geographical area it seems clear that the issue of 'conductus rhythm' is a very complex one indeed. Sometimes, and especially in the later 13th century, the texted sections of conductus appear to have been modal; otherwise, to judge by some recent research, each syllable was allotted the value of a perfect long (three beats) and any ligatures appearing over a syllable were divided into that time.[21]

The problem of rhythm and rhythmic style in *organum purum* is more delicate still. In this repertory, one of the most virtuosic cultivated by the Parisian *organistae*, a florid part lies over a plainchant tenor performed in unmeasured notes. Since the 1950s ideas about the performance of *organum purum* have been moving rapidly. Many early music ensembles will have met this repertory for the first time in Waite's controversial book *The Rhythm of Twelfth-century Polyphony* (1954), where modal rhythm is used to transcribe the organum repertory of the *Magnus liber*. The impression given there, one of strict and uncompromising triple movement, is difficult to reconcile with a 12th-century description of organum as music which displays 'a kind of wondrous flexibility',[22] and 13 years after the appearance of Waite's book Reckow concluded that 'the ligature combinations of the organal melismas [have] no modal significance whatever',[23] giving his support to the 'rule of consonance' theory whereby notes in the upper part forming a perfect consonance with the tenor are assumed to have been lengthened. Matters have not been allowed to rest there, however, for Sanders has recently proposed that the passage in Johannes de Garlandia's treatise which seems to enunciate Reckow's 'rule of consonance' should be read as an account of pauses at the ends of phrases and at other breathing places where perfect consonances occur. 'In a word', Sanders concludes, 'the performance [of *organum purum*] is free and evidently quite fast, rather in the manner of cadenzas'.[24] This takes us a long way from the transcriptions published by Waite and it is up to performers to see what they can make of this most challenging music.[25]

The theorists say little about the tempos to be used in the various Ars Antiqua genres, although they do record that hocket pieces should be performed quickly,[26] and the same appears to have been the case with the copula (a section of *organum purum* where a measured upper voice, characterized by melodic sequence, moved over a held tenor note).[27] Beyond this the theorists offer no help. The evidence of notation is also unhelpful – indeed, it is misleading, for while it is true that the tempo 'slowed down' during the 13th century this should be viewed as a notational response to changes in the style of the motet rather than as a sign of changing tastes in performance.[28] This point deserves some elaboration. During the later 13th century composers began to establish a new idiom by intensifying the contrast – endemic in the motet from the very first – between a chattering triplum and a slow-moving tenor. Exx.9 and 10 show patterns characteristic of this new idiom and of the older style from which it grew. The new idiom uses a brisker triplum declamation (relative to the tenor) than the old, and so requires a slightly slower beat because the singer of the triplum must pack more words and notes into each perfection. In performance the distinction between the two styles does not strike the listener as one of tempo, exactly, but rather as a contrast between a faster beat with fewer notes (ex.9) and a slower beat with more notes (ex.10).

Ex.9

Ex.10

It can hardly be doubted that the basic pulse should be strict in all the measured genres of Ars Antiqua polyphony (clausula, motet, conductus, copula, *organum triplum* and *quadruplum*). As mentioned above, medieval singers regarded polyphony as an art of objective measurement and the terms which they associate with it include *recta*, 'correct', *integralis*, 'whole', and *regularis*, 'disciplined'.[29] One theorist of the mid-14th century, for example, records that the tenor parts of motets are best delivered 'in a strict and secure fashion'.[30] This objective approach to pulse, however, did not prevent singers from 'feeling' rests nor from employing devices such as ritardando – to judge by a passage in the later layer of the anonymous *Discantus positio vulgaris* (perhaps of the 1270s) where a pause 'of plainchant type for as long as seems fitting' is recommended when all the parts of a motet phrase together.[31] Another anonymous treatise from the end of the 13th century confirms this practice, adding that 'when three melodies are found harmonizing together and making their rests at the same moment, let there be a double line [in the notation of the] tenor, motetus and triplum to signify that the penultimate notes should be unmeasured'.[32] No doubt these unmeasured pauses were regulated by the singer appointed to control the proceedings, the *rector*, whose task was to signal such rests with his hand, either in the air or upon the surface of the book (ex.11); his intervention would also have been required in penultimate bars where a ritardando was habitually employed – a technique carried over from plainchant.[33]

Ex.11

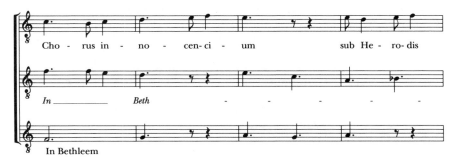

The doubled notes and longs which occur at structural points in polyphonic conductus suggest that performers sometimes 'placed' the final notes at the ends of phrases by protracting them,[34] and it may be that the concerted pauses which followed were sometimes 'of plainchant type' and unmeasured. *Organum purum*, however, was the genre in which such 'felt' and concerted rests came into their own. No doubt singers breathed and phrased independently when they could do so without disrupting the design of the music, but the singers of tenor parts were expected to accompany the duplum to the extent of phrasing with it, punctuating the texture in a way that has barely been attempted by modern musicians who have generally treated organum tenors as drones, using overlapping voices and sometimes – apparently without direct historical justification – an organ.[35]

The degree of ornamentation attempted must have influenced choice of tempo in the 13th century. 'Let anyone who wishes to indulge in practical music beware that he does not exult too much in his voice', says the author of the *Ars contrapuncti secundum Johannem de Muris*, addressing himself to singers determined to show off their skill,[36] and references to liturgical music in the writings of outraged churchmen suggest that polyphony was sung with Romanesque exuberance and Gothic flamboyance in the 12th and 13th centuries.[37] The task of keeping control (at least in improvised polyphony) fell to the *rector*, according to the French theorist Elias of Salomon (*Scientia artis musicae*, 1274): 'let him correct anyone who may embellish his part excessively by whispering a reproach into his ear during performance'.[38] The upper parts of *organum purum* were elaborated with ornaments such as the *longa florata* ('a long bedecked with flowers'), apparently a long held out and decorated with some kind of flourish (vibrato, perhaps), and there were many other kinds of ornament that singers were encouraged to employ.[39] Even motets, which often sound so busy with their colliding texts, were sometimes decorated in performance. An anonymous (and possibly English) theorist of the 14th century emphasizes that a tenor part does not have to be sung exactly as written (*prout figuratur*); a singer is at liberty to make 'beautiful ascents and descents' when he senses that the counterpoint will not be damaged as a result,[40] and if this were an acceptable practice in the performance of a tenor, the *fundamentum totius cantus*, then it is likely that singers of motetus, triplum and quadruplum voices would also have felt free to decorate their lines. The melodic variants which crept into many motets during transmission may be a clue to the nature of this ornamentation (ex.12).[41]

Ex.12

Something more can be learnt from a chapter appended by Jerome of Moravia to Johannes de Garlandia's *De musica mensurabili*. This describes various ways of embellishing (or perhaps composing) triplum and quadruplum parts.[42] The examples given include what appear to be decorations for a single note (ex.13*a*) and for several notes in a descending sequence (ex.13*b*). The flourishes for a single note are downward skips reaching as far as a fifth, while those for several pitches seem to embellish a descent *a–g–f* with passing notes within a third.

Ex.13
(a)   (b)

Some general conclusions may be offered concerning the voice types and timbres used during the 13th and 14th centuries. The improvised organum described by Elias of Salomon in 1274 requires four adult men to double chants at the fifth, octave and twelfth, and when a chant spanning an octave or so is performed in this manner the compass of the organum, from the lowest sounding pitch to the highest, can reach two octaves and a fifth.[43] This is a very generous compass – sufficient for nearly all of Dufay's music, for example – and it implies that both the bass–baritone voice and the male alto voice were cultivated in the 13th century. This seems to be confirmed by Jerome of Moravia's comments on plainchant performance:[44]

> We say in general parlance that there are 'chest voices', 'throat voices' and 'head voices'. We call chest voices those which form their notes in the chest; throat voices are those which form their notes in the throat while head voices form them in the head. The chest voice is good for the *graves*, the throat voice for the *acutae*, and the head voice for the *superacutae*.

The *graves*, *acutae* and *superacutae* are the three divisions of the medieval gamut (G–G, G–g, g–e), spanning between them the kind of compass that

89

Elias of Salomon's improvised organum must often have required. Yet although trained singers could produce the whole gamut between them, most Ars Antiqua polyphony lies within a twelfth – and even this fell within the category of 'discant according to the furthest proportions' according to the theorists.[45] The 100 motets in the Bamberg codex (Lit.115), for example, use on average a compass of about 11 notes, and yet there are many individual voice parts in the Bamberg anthology which span an eleventh. It is therefore clear that these motets usually exploit a compass, from top to bottom, that was considered to be the best working range of one trained voice. Similar figures could probably be produced for the rest of the motet repertory and indeed for other genres such as *organum purum* and conductus. These pieces would therefore appear to have been designed for groups of two, three or four identical singers who could (at a pinch, perhaps) perform any part in the composition. The result would presumably have been a well-blended sound, and it is interesting to note Jerome of Moravia's insistence that head voices, throat voices and chest voices should not be mixed in plainchant performance.[46]

The problem of instrumentation in Ars Antiqua polyphony is a delicate one. An enormous number of compositions, both monophonic and polyphonic, have survived from the 12th and 13th centuries, and amongst these are some which may be regarded as instrumental in the sense that they appear to have been designed exclusively (or primarily) for instrumental execution. There are few of these, however: scarcely more than the *estampies* added to the Manuscrit du Roi (Bibliothèque Nationale, fr.844) in a 14th-century hand.[47] As for the habitually 'textless' parts in motets, the tenors, it was widely held in the days of Jean Beck and Pierre Aubry that these parts were performed by instrumentalists,[48] and in many quarters this view still obtains.[49] Some musicologists have even argued for instrumental involvement in sacred genres such as *organum purum* and the clausulae.[50] Krüger, for example, has attempted to demonstrate that some liturgical polyphony was performed as combined vocal-instrumental music from Carolingian times onwards.[51] His position is in sharp conflict with the Anglo-American view (traceable to Harrison, Bowles and McKinnon among others) that medieval sacred music was generally performed by voices only save on special occasions when there may have been some instrumental involvement.[52]

The arguments which have been advanced in favour of instrumental participation in medieval sacred music before the 15th century are founded upon a mass of misinterpretations.[53] The amount of relevant evidence is much smaller than advocates of Krüger's position acknowledge; most of it is of a literary nature, and once passages which echo biblical language (or explore conventional symbolism) have been set aside, then little of any certain value remains. Two examples may suffice. The Parisian theorist Johannes de Grocheo (*fl c*1300) discusses instruments and instrumental music within the section of his treatise devoted to 'monophonic, civil or laymen's music', a category which includes the trouvère chanson, dance-song, the *chanson de geste* and various instrumental forms.[54] This has been taken to imply that instruments were not involved with the other categories of music which Grocheo distinguishes: liturgical chant and 'composed, measured, rule-bound music' including the motet and polyphonic

Singer and gittern player: from an illustrated copy of Nicholas Oresme's translation of Aristotle's 'Ethics', prepared for Charles V of France in 1376 (The Hague, Meerman Museum, 10-D-1, f.00)

conductus.[55] However, a second illustration points in a different direction. In his discussion of the ways in which *organum purum* may be brought to a close, Anonymous IV remarks that 'some singers finish with a single note either in an octave or a unison or a fifth, but rarely on a fourth, unless it is a string instrument' (*nisi fuerit in instrumento cordarum*).[56] This is a tantalizingly cryptic comment, but we are not at liberty to juggle with the various musical meanings of *instrumentum* here ('pipe-organ', 'monochord', 'the organs that produce the human voice' and so on); Anonymous IV is referring to a string instrument and of that there can be no reasonable doubt. But why should musicians have refrained from ending passages of *organum purum* on a fourth save when an *instrumentum cordarum* was involved? One answer is that Anonymous IV is thinking of a fiddle with octave strings; in this case a final fourth between the fiddle and voice – if the fiddle were above the singer – would also be heard as a fifth below the voice, an acceptable sonority. It is possible to have many reservations about this theory, but Anonymous IV's comment cannot be ignored.

The question of instrumentation in secular polyphony before 1300 is also fraught with uncertainties. Singers of motets and conductus may sometimes have been doubled, but this is only supposition and there seems no good reason why modern performers should thicken the sonorities of Ars Antiqua polyphony in this way, especially as it can hinder singers in their tuning.[57] Doubling aside, it is plausible that motet tenors, mostly of plainchant origin, were performed instrumentally, and modern experience suggests that a combination of voices and harp works well since the clear but broad sound of the harp endows the glib patterns of 13th-century tenor parts with lightness and charm, achieved without loss of clarity in articulation. It is more likely, however, that these tenors were sung in performance, perhaps to the fragment of plainchant text that usually accompanies them in the sources; this would explain why Franco of Cologne describes motet tenors as 'equivalent to a certain text'.[58] Performances in this manner would certainly have highlighted the wit that is inherent in motet form; the composer's resourcefulness in devising two (or three) well-formed melodies to fit patterns made from a pre-existing scrap of plainchant becomes the more evident the more clearly the independent origin of the tenor part is evoked in performance.

The issue of instrumentation brings us to the Ars Nova. In recent years the role of instruments in 14th- (and 15th-)century music has come under fresh scrutiny and seems to dominate current enquiry; accordingly, it will occupy our attention until the end of this chapter. As little as a decade ago, however, it was not an issue at all, for at that time the textless parts of Ars Nova compositions were thought to have been conceived for instruments, whence the 'unvocal' devices (so the argument ran) which are often to be found in them.[59] This matter bears directly upon the sonority of the various Ars Nova repertories but it also raises an important question about musical style: did 14th-century singers regard the untexted parts of motets, rondeaux, virelais and other genres as 'unvocal'?

Pictorial sources, including manuscript paintings and tapestries, are currently being examined for information about instrumental practice (usually with reference to the 15th-century French chanson)[60] and it is undeniable that iconography offers many representations of singers and players. The crippling problem with this material, however, is that it is usually impossible to establish what kind of music is being 'performed in the picture'. The illustration on p.91 shows a case in point. A singer with a rotulus is accompanied by an instrumentalist with a gittern. We might suppose, for instance, that they are performing a two-part secular song such as the ingratiating virelai, *Tres dolz et loyauls amis* (ex.14), the singer

Ex.14

performing the cantus while his associate plucks the tenor. An ensemble of voice and gittern seems well suited to this virelai, but to assume that a piece like *Tres dolz et loyauls amis* is being performed is like assuming that the cake in the picture contains cinnamon. The singer and his associate might equally well be performing a simple monophonic rondeau, the kind of song which was often used for courtly dancing during the 14th century.[61]

Perhaps the best way to broach the question of instrumentation is via the issue of 'vocal' and 'unvocal' writing in 14th-century music. Clearly these are subjective concepts, for modern singers vary in their assessment of what is

93

singable according to their taste, training and experience. The 'unvocal' appearance of some medieval music is deceptive. The triplum of a four-part ballade by Grimace (*fl c*1380), for instance, uses repeated notes and tiny rests which might be said to lend it an 'instrumental' appearance (ex.15*a*), and there are some who would interpret these features as a call for a lute or some other plucked instrument.[62] However, such arguments are not easy to reconcile with the character of the one indisputably vocal part in Grimace's ballade, the cantus; there we find melodic figures which are comparable to those of the triplum, if less flamboyant (ex.15*b*).

Ex.15

Here it is important to consider the secular and sacred repertories together. As we have seen, it is generally believed that sacred polyphony was involved with instruments (whatever the nature of that involvement may have been) only on exceptional occasions; it follows that liturgical polyphony of the kind shown in ex.16 (from a troped Kyrie) was performed with voices on all parts, including the animated contratenor with its 'instrumental' look.

Ex.16

The significance of this is that the piece is very close in style to some contemporary French chansons, and indeed an important number of liturgical works from 14th-century France and Italy borrow their textures from secular music. This strongly suggests that there is nothing inherently 'unvocal' in the mainstream secular styles – at least in 14th-century terms – for pieces resembling secular music in almost every particular except their texts were generally sung in liturgical contexts by voices alone.

Some of the features which modern singers might deem 'unvocal' were regarded by 14th-century musicians as forms of ornamentation: as felicities of style, in other words, and not as encumbrances. A striking illustration is provided by a three-part troped Kyrie in the Apt manuscript (ex.17) whose

Ex.17

contratenor appears in two versions, one more elaborate than the other. The simpler version moves in a plain, almost note-against-note style with the tenor, but the second contratenor is more active. The embellished version (on the upper staff) displays some of the 'unvocal' characteristics found in many secular contratenors: the placing of short rests where strong beats are expected (bars 3, 5 and 27; in the simpler version of the part these beats are supplied); the repeated notes (bars 10 and 16); the willingness to introduce *musica ficta* colours at cadences, however angular the results may be in melodic terms (bars 63–4); the outlining of wide intervals in a short space (bars 58 and 59). These are all standard features of the 14th-century contratenor and their decorative character becomes clear when the bars just cited are compared with the simpler version of the part. Ornamentation of this kind was designed to make the music more animated and its *tactus* more eager, not to make the lines more melodious or florid as in later ornamentation. Musicians of the 14th century who had acquired a taste for this nervous style of embellishment regarded it as a token of advanced musical artistry. Others detested it. The conservative theorist Jacques de Liège, for example, expresses his distaste for this kind of music in words that could almost have been written to describe ex.17. There are some singers, he reports, who:

> discant in a way that is too luxuriant, and multiply superfluous notes [ex.17, bar 10 and *passim*]. Some of them hocket too much [bars 70–75] and excessively break their notes into consonances [bars 33, 36 etc]; they ascend too much [? bars 22, 58 and 66] and split things asunder [*passim*]; they jump about at inopportune moments, they howl, bellow and yelp and bark like dogs.[63]

97

It is one thing to claim that some of the features we consider 'unvocal' in 14th-century music would have been seen in a different light by contemporary singers; it is quite another thing to make this music work in performance today with voices on all parts. What is to be done with the textless tenors and contratenors?

As far as the French secular repertories are concerned there is almost no evidence in the sources that tenors and contratenors were texted.[64] The chansons that do survive with text in more than one part usually disrupt the standard cantus–tenor–contratenor arrangement (and they are usually poly-textual pieces into the bargain). It is possible, of course, that the absence of text for tenor and contratenor parts in the sources is sometimes a shorthand,[65] but while this may be true in a few cases it can hardly apply to the entire 14th-century French repertory. It may also be that singers performing the untexted parts of these chansons were not expected to perform the whole text, but again this cannot be confirmed. Two solutions may be suggested: the untexted parts were performed upon instruments as has generally been assumed, and they were vocalized as they must often have been when liturgical pieces with secular textures were performed in church. No doubt both solutions were adopted by 14th-century musicians.

As far as instrumentation is concerned the secular polyphony of 14th-century Italy presents a slightly less complex problem than contemporary French music. The standard French disposition of cantus–tenor–contratenor rarely appears in the trecento repertory, and when it does it is usually a deliberate Gallicism.[66] In the two-part madrigals and ballate which predominate in the sources of trecento music the usual disposition comprises two texted voices, the lower often less florid than the upper. It is possible that singers were sometimes doubled by instruments, but it is difficult to imagine what these superbly balanced vocal duets would gain from instrumental participation. (From the purely technical point of view it may be remarked that the freedom to widen or narrow intervals, so important in this repertory, is seriously impaired by doubling of any kind.) The caccia presents a different set of possibilities since it usually comprises two texted voices over a textless tenor which may have been performed instrumentally. Vocalization remains a possibility here also.

The three-part music of the trecento often presents a more puzzling state of affairs. A significant number of Landini's three-part works, for example, comprise two texted parts (cantus and tenor) which are supplemented by a textless contratenor. In some cases the contratenor can be underlaid if a few adjustments are made (principally the division of long notes into shorter ones to accommodate syllables),[67] and a 15th-century description of Landini's ballate *Orsù(n), gentili spirti* being sung by two young girls and a man shows that music which may look ill designed for all-vocal performance as it survives may sometimes have been performed in that way: the piece has only one texted part, the cantus.[68]

The task of determining which musical instruments were used in the performance of polyphony before 1400 is more than a matter of establishing what instruments were cultivated by trained musicians; in the first instance the problem is to determine which ones were associated with playing techniques overtaken by musical literacy to the point where written polyphony began to fall within the scope of the instrument, displacing older, improvised repertory. In this connection it is revealing that Jerome of Moravia's advanced fiddle technique, used in Parisian circles *c*1300, appears to be based upon the vocal practice of 'fifthing', a rudimentary method of doubling a melody in fifths (with movements to and from octaves at the beginnings and ends of phrases).[69] As a vocal practice 'fifthing' occupied a low position; it was little more than a preliminary stage in the musical education of a *discantor*. However, as a technique for the fiddle (the leading art-instrument of the 13th century), Jerome regards it as a sophisticated procedure employed by 'the most advanced players'. This might be taken to suggest that the artistic horizons of vocal and instrumental music were quite differently placed *c*1300, and it is undoubtedly the case that musical instruments had some unwritten repertories of their own at this date, largely unrelated to written polyphony (the narrative epics or *chansons de geste* provide an example).

Of all the instruments known to Gothic Europe, it is perhaps the harp which has the outstanding claim to be used where instrumental performance is judged appropriate. In recent years it has gradually emerged that the harp was the chief instrument of the medieval nobility and the first string instrument to be cultivated by known composers (from the late 14th century on) whose works have survived.[70] Although the harp was usually a diatonic instrument throughout the Middle Ages[71] it would have been possible for harpists to tune in one or two *ficta* notes, or, in many cases, to sacrifice the *ficta* in their tenor or contratenor parts altogether without impairing the harmony (always assuming that the performers of the other parts were prepared to make allowances here and there). By *c*1400 we encounter composer–harpists such as Baude Cordier and (a little later) Richard Loqueville; it is likely that these men played the kind of secular polyphonic chansons which they composed. They may have accompanied singers in the performance of such works, playing one (or perhaps two) of the textless parts, or alternatively they may have played instrumental 'intabulations' of vocal originals, perhaps in two parts (tenor and superius), along the lines of the pieces in the Faenza codex.

Notes

[1] For the contribution of archives (relating exclusively to the activities, musical and non-musical, of minstrels and chapel clerks) see R. Rastall, 'Some English Consort-groupings of the Late Middle Ages', *ML*, lv (1974), 179–202; R. Bowers, 'The Performing Ensemble for English Church Polyphony, *c*.1320–*c*.1390', in *Performance Practice: New York 1981*, 161–92. Pictorial sources can reveal a good deal about instruments (their shapes, sizes, string-numbers, techniques of manipulation and so on) and may sometimes shed light upon the social contexts of music (especially ceremonial music). As far as the period covered by this essay is concerned it has yet to be established whether their evidence can be taken further. See G. Foster, *The Iconology of Musical Instruments and Musical Performance in Thirteenth-century French Manuscript Illuminations* (diss., City U. of New York, 1977).
[2] See for example the comments of Marchetto da Padova in *Marcheti de Padua Pomerium*, ed. G. Vecchi, CSM, vi (1961), 184–5.
[3] For an explanation of the acoustics behind the 'dissonant' and unstable character of the Pythagorean major triad see J. Backus, *The Acoustical Foundations of Music* (London, 1970), 116ff, and Ll. S. Lloyd and H. Boyle, *Intervals, Scales and Temperaments* (London, 1978), 14ff. The subject of tuning in medieval music has principally been investigated in terms of keyboard temperaments and therefore with a marked emphasis on the 15th century. See M. Lindley,

'Fifteenth-century Evidence for Meantone Temperament', *PRMA*, cii (1975–6), 37–51, and Lindley, 'Pythagorean Intonation and the Rise of the Triad', *RMARC*, xvi (1980), 4–61. For an attempt to employ Pythagorean tuning in 14th-century music see the recording by Gothic Voices, *The Service of Venus and Mars* (Hyperion A66238), the French items.

[4] For a readily accessible example of classic outline see Odo's essay on the monochord (*GS*, i, 252ff), trans. O. Strunk, *Source Readings in Music History*, i (London, 1981), 105ff.

[5] I cite the printed edition: *B. Aegidii Columnae . . . Quodlibeta* (Louvain, 1646), 139.

[6] For a discussion of this and the following points see J. W. Herlinger, 'Marchetto's Division of the Whole Tone', *JAMS*, xxxiv (1981), 193–216.

[7] ibid, pp.205ff.

[8] D. Leech-Wilkinson, 'Machaut's *Rose Lis* and the Problem of Early Music Analysis', *MusA*, iii (1984), 19.

[9] Examples in Machaut's polyphony, for instance, are legion. In addition to the example from *Rose, lis* just cited see *Dame, de qui toute ma joie* (ballade 42), bars 5–6, 16, 30 etc; *Je sui aussi* (ballade 20), bars 2–3 and 10; *Dame, mon cuer* (rondeau 22), bars 12–13 and 19. The technique is used in its most striking form in the motets, a spectacular example being *Inviolata genitrix/ Felix virgo/Ad te suspiramus*/Contratenor (motet 23), bars 31–3, 38–9, 57–8, 69–70 etc.

[10] *Walteri Odington Summa de Speculatione Musicae*, ed. F. F. Hammond, CSM, xiv (1970), 70–71.

[11] The evidence on this point, however, is far from unanimous. For the literary evidence see the following texts: (*a*) Elias of Salomon's account, completed by 1274, of improvised parallel organum in *GS*, iii, 57ff; each part is sung by one adult male, although Salomon admits that the lowest part may be doubled if there is a danger of it being overpowered by the upper voices. See J. Dyer, 'A Thirteenth-Century Choirmaster: the *Scientia Artis Musicae* of Elias Salomon', *MQ*, lxvi (1980), 83–111. (*b*) The *Summa musicae* (probably *c*1300) where various kinds of polyphony are described, some of them quasi-improvisatory or perhaps completely so; the author seems to allow that parts in some styles may be sung by one singer or more (*GS*, iii, 239ff). (*c*) Jacques de Liège (*Speculum musice*, bk7, chap.3) states 'when there are just two parts [in discantus] there is nothing to prevent there being more [than two] singers performing together, whether on the tenor or on the discantus'. See *Speculum musice*, ed. R. Bragard, SM, iii/7 (1973), 8. (*d*) Eustache Deschamps, Guillaume de Machaut's nephew, mentions 'threefold voices' as the medium best suited to the performance of pieces with tenor and contratenor parts, a remark which I construe as a reference to the performance of three-part secular polyphony one to a part. For text and translation see C. Page, 'Machaut's "Pupil" Deschamps on the Performance of Music', *EM*, v (1977), 484–91. (*e*) All of the fully explicit sources cited by David Fallows ('Specific Information on the Ensembles for Composed Polyphony, 1400–1474', in *Performance Practice: New York 1981*, 133–142) seem to describe secular pieces being performed by as many voices as there are parts. (*f*) A Wycliffite sermon of *c*1380 refers to 'three or four pleasure-seeking wastrels' who perform liturgical polyphony to the stupefaction of the congregation (quoted most recently in Bowers. 'The Performing Ensemble', 177); this presumably refers to three- and four-part music with one voice per part.

Pictorial sources offer little help here since it is rarely possible to be certain what kind of music the performers shown in a picture are supposed to be performing. As far as pictures of liturgical singers are concerned, the usefulness of the material is often vitiated by the influence of the *Cantate Domino* iconography, found in psalters, where the number of clerical singers shown varies considerably. For cases of correspondence between picture and music see for example (*a*) the Gorleston psalter (*GB-Lbm* Add.49622, f.126, East-Anglian, *c*1325), where three singers perform from a roll showing what appears to be three-part polyphony; (*b*) the first folio of the Montpellier Codex (*F-MO* H196), where three clerks stand before a three-part setting of *Deus in adiutorium*. There are also three tonsured singers in the initial to Pérotin's three-part conductus *Salvatoris hodie* in *D-W* 1206 [W$_2$], f.31r. There appear to be four singers, however, before the two-part conductus *Presul nostri* in W$_2$, f.92r. See further C. Wright, *Music and Ceremony at Notre Dame of Paris 500–1550* (Cambridge, 1989), pp.235f. See below, n.33.

[12] E. Roesner, 'The Performance of Parisian Organum', *EM*, vii (1979), 177.

[13] The importance of pronunciation, from the point of view of tone colour, is stressed in E. J. Dobson and F. Ll. Harrison, *Medieval English Songs* (London, 1979), 331. Little has been done to provide singers with the authoritative guides that they need beyond the excellent handbook by J. Alton and B. Jeffery, *Bele buche e bel parleure* (London, 1976). See further C. Page, 'The Performance of Ars Antiqua Motets', *EM*, xvi (1988), 147–64.

[14] See for instance *CS*, iii, 361.

[15] J. Knapp, 'Musical Declamation and Poetic Rhythm in an Early Layer of Notre Dame

Conductus', *JAMS*, xxxii (1979), 383–407; E. Sanders, 'Consonance and Rhythm in the Organum of the Twelfth and Thirteenth Centuries', *JAMS*, xxxiii (1980), 264–86; Sanders, 'Conductus and Modal Rhythm', *JAMS*, xxxviii (1985), 439–69; J. Yudkin, 'The Rhythm of Organum Purum', *JM*, ii (1983), 355–76. On musical styles see for example Yudkin, 'The Anonymous of St. Emmeram and Anonymous IV on the Copula', *MQ*, lxx (1984), 1–22 (with literature there cited), and H. Tischler, 'The Evolution of the *Magnus Liber Organi*', *MQ*, lxx (1984), 163–74.

[16] The principal contributions have been F. Reckow, *Der Musiktraktat des Anonymus 4* (Wiesbaden, 1967), and E. Reimer, *Johannes de Garlandia: De mensurabili musica* (Wiesbaden, 1972).

[17] The arguments which have been advanced in favour of this view are principally (*a*) that some conductus were produced by simply adding words to the melismatic sections of other conductus, presumably taking over their modal rhythms; (*b*) that some texted sections in conductus repeat melodic material which also appears in modal melismatic passages; (*c*) that several sources not usually regarded as 'central' to the Notre Dame tradition contain versions of conductus in which all the material is measured in a way that proves to the satisfaction of some that the texted sections of conductus were performed modally. For further details see G. A. Anderson, 'The Rhythm of *Cum Littera* Sections of Polyphonic Conductus in Mensural Sources', *JAMS*, xxvi (1973), 288–304.

[18] See the articles by Knapp and Sanders listed in n.15 above.

[19] The English Franciscan Roger Bacon (*d* ?1292), who heard polyphonic music in both England and France, reports in his *Opus tertium* that 'whatever has been composed during the last 30 years conflicts with both art and truth because composers do not understand which metrical feet they should work with, nor how many feet, nor with what kind of metre, nor how they should be put together in artistic ways; but, following the hymns of others, and of those who operate in this way, they count syllables in a casual fashion, not observing the law of metre in any respect'. *Fr. Rogeri Bacon Opera . . . Inedita*, ed. J. S. Brewer (London, 1859), 302. This confirms that many musicians lacked the training – or the inclination – to distinguish between long and short syllables in Latin; composers who did not know their quantities would often have been unable to place word accents correctly in Latin verse.

[20] Jerome of Moravia, *Tractatus de musica*, ed. S. M. Cserba (Regensburg, 1935), 190.

[21] See Knapp, 'Musical Declamation', and Sanders, 'Conductus and Modal Rhythm'.

[22] Sanders, 'Consonance and Rhythm', 265.

[23] Reckow, *Anonymus 4*, ii, 45.

[24] Sanders, 'Consonance and Rhythm', 270.

[25] A recent, and outstanding, attempt to make sense of the organal styles of St Martial is *Polyphonie Aquitaine du XII siècle: St Martial de Limoges*, Ensemble Organum de Paris, directed by Marcel Pérès, Harmonia Mundi (France), HMC1134.

[26] For the evidence, and a discussion of related points of interest, see E. Roesner's remarks on performance practice forming the preface to the reprint of *Le Roman de Fauvel*, ed. L. Schrade, PMFC, i (1984), pp.iv–vii.

[27] See E. Roesner, 'Performance of Parisian Organum', 183. Yudkin, 'Anonymous of St Emmeram', 22, points out that the performance characteristics of the copula seem to vary from theorist to theorist; for the evidence that copula was associated with some special vocal quality, see his article, pp.5ff.

[28] For a brief introduction to the notational considerations see *Compositions of the Bamberg Manuscript*, ed. G. A. Anderson, CMM, lxxv (1977), p.xxxiv. On performing tempo see further, Page, 'The Performance of Ars Antiqua Motets'.

[29] See for example *CS*, iii, 110 (*Ars discantus secundum Johannem de Muris*).

[30] Anonymous I, *CS*, iii, 362.

[31] Jerome of Moravia, *Tractatus de musica*, ed. Cserba, 193.

[32] *Compendium musicae mensurabilis artis antiquae*, ed. F. A. Gallo, CSM, xv (1971), 71. For further discussion of this technique, with musical examples, see Page, 'The Performance of Ars Antiqua Motets'.

[33] For the duties of the *rector* see the account given by Elias of Salomon in *GS*, iii, 57ff, discussed in Dyer, 'A Thirteenth-century Choirmaster'. For the hand gestures of singers shown in pictorial sources the article by J. Smits van Waesberghe, 'Singen und Dirigieren der mehrstimmigen Musik im Mittelalter', *Diapason* (Buren, 1976), 165–87, must be read in conjunction with J. W. McKinnon, 'Iconography', in *Musicology in the 1980s*, ed. D. K. Holoman and C. V. Palisca (New York, 1982), 79–93. For the technique of pausing in the penultimate 'bar' of polyphonic pieces in discant style see for example Anonymous I (*CS*, iii, 362), and for the device of drawing out a chant 'slightly near the end' see *Hucbald, Guido and John on Music*, ed. C. V. Palisca (New Haven, 1978), 139 (John).

[34] For indications of such protractions (for the sake of convenience I draw the examples from a single source) see W_2, f.31v 'candida-tur', protraction of the penultimate sonority at the end of a cauda; f.42r 'glori-am', protraction of penultimate sonority at the end of a piece (cf f.110v 'pa-cem', where the protracted sonority is a dissonance of a major second).
[35] See Roesner, 'Performance of Parisian Organum', *passim*.
[36] *CS*, iii, 60.
[37] For some examples see W. Dalglish, 'The Origin of the Hocket', *JAMS*, xxxi (1978), 3–20.
[38] *GS*, iii, 58.
[39] Discussed in Roesner, 'Performance of Parisian Organum'.
[40] *CS*, iii, 362.
[41] Luxurious material is available for the study of these variations. *Polyphonies du XIIIe siècle*, ed. Y. Rokseth (Paris, 1935–9) prints variants on the same staff. See also H. Tischler, *The Earliest Motets (to c1270)* (New Haven, 1982), and *The Style and Evolution of the Earliest Motets (to c1270)* (Henryville, Ottawa and Binningen, 1985), i, *passim*.
A device often used by modern performers, and one which might be loosely classified as a form of ornamentation, is the sequential performance of individual motet voices followed by a 'tutti'. Despite the advocacy of Rokseth (*Polyphonies*, iv, 221), and however plausible it may seem, this practice appears to have no direct sanction from the theorists. The passage which Rokseth cites from Jacques de Liège (*Speculum musice*, bk7, chap.3) appears to be discussing the way in which the notes of individual motet voices may be considered not only in contrapuntal terms (i.e. according their relationship with the tenor) but also in melodic terms, 'separately and successively one after the other, as when anyone sings any motetus, triplum or quadruplum without the tenor and hence complete in itself' (*Speculum musice*, CSM, iii/7, 1973, 9). It is possible of course that 13th-century musicians sometimes wished to produce longer, integrated performances of motets than could be achieved by performing any one motet straight through.
[42] Reimer, *Johannes de Garlandia*, i, 94–6.
[43] For Elias's account of this organum see Dyer, 'A Thirteenth-century Choirmaster'. The music examples on p. 99 are marred by errors in the clefs but are easily corrected.
[44] Jerome of Moravia, *Tractatus de musica*, ed. Cserba, 188.
[45] As in the classification of Anonymous IV (Reckow, *Anonymus 4*, i, 75).
[46] Jerome of Moravia, *Tractatus de musica*, ed. Cserba, 188.
[47] For transcriptions and excellent facsimiles of these see P. Aubry, *Estampies et danses royales* (Paris, 1907).
[48] See for example P. Aubry, *Cent motets du XIIIe siècle* (Paris, 1908), iii, 147–59.
[49] However it is coming under fresh scrutiny, even in that most conservative genre of musicological writing, the preface to a music edition. For a recent example see *Five Anglo-Norman Motets*, ed. M. Everist (Newton Abbot, 1986), 1: 'Performance by single voices alone is most musically convincing and historically accurate'.
[50] See for example M. Bröcker, *Die Drehleier* (Düsseldorf, 1973), i, 259–81 (I have not seen the revised edition of this work), and W. Bachmann, *The Origins of Bowing*, trans. N. Deane (Oxford, 1969), 121–2. I share the view of Roesner ('Performance of Parisian Organum', 188, n.6) that Bröcker's arguments are unconvincing. Some of Bachmann's evidence is also of very dubious value. The passage from Aimery de Peyrac which, according to Bachmann, shows that the cantus firmus was sometimes performed upon a bowed instrument, says nothing of the sort, as may be determined from the source of most modern references to Aimery's text: A. Pirro, *Historie de la musique de la fin du XIVe siècle à la fin du XVIe* (Paris, 1940), 20. The meaning of the passage which Bachmann cites from the treatise of Lambertus (*CS*, i, 253) is also misconstrued. Lambertus is not saying that instrumental music has dared to enter the church; his point is that the art of music has dared to enter the liturgy (consideration of the full structure of Lambertus's remarks makes this clear). Finally, the passages which Bachmann cites from John of Salisbury and Honorius Augustodunensis do not serve his purpose as he imagines. Honorius does indeed say that instruments are used in church, but he refers only to the organ, bells and *cymbala*. John of Salisbury does record that the Fathers encouraged the faithful to use both voices and instruments in the liturgy, but he is referring to the early centuries of the church when the faith was being disseminated, and in his famous harangue against contemporary abuses in liturgical music, which directly follows, he does not mention instruments at all. Bachmann cites Gerbert, *De cantu et musica sacra*, ii, 98 and 100 for both passages; they are better read in PL 194:499–500 (Honorius) and *Ioannis Saresberiensis Episcopi Carnotensis Policratici*, ed. C. I. Webb (Oxford, 1909), i, 41.
Finally, mention must be made of H. Tischler, 'How were Notre Dame Clausulae

Performed?', *ML*, 1 (1960), 273–7. According to Tischler the Castilian poet Juan Ruiz (*Libro de buen amor*, *c*1330) 'refers to the performance of late thirteenth-century motets with the aid of the portative organ' (p.276). The reference proves to be to stanza 1232 of the poem, and none of the three sources of the work provides any indication that singing is involved (which Tischler's phraseology seems intended to imply). The reading of the Salamanca manuscript for example is 'los organos y disen chançones e motete', where the subject of 'disen' is 'organos'. Nor is it certain that Ruiz is thinking of polyphonic music when he refers to 'motete', let alone 'late thirteenth-century motets' as Tischler would have us believe.

[51] W. Krüger, *Die authentische Klangform des primitiven Organum* (Kassel, 1958).

[52] This point needs to be stressed since it is clearly not enough to show that instruments were used 'in church', for there is no reason to doubt that instrumentalists sometimes played at shrines when magnates made offerings, for example, nor that (in the 15th century, at least) the raising of the host was sometimes accompanied by fanfares. It is quite another matter to argue that instrumentalists supplied or doubled lines in the composed polyphony performed by the choir. See Fallows, 'Specific Information', 127, n.42.

[53] Most of these errors arise from selective quotation of texts and indifference to conventional symbolism. On p.49 of Krüger's study, for example, the passage about voices and instruments quoted from Amalarius, beginning 'Igitur cunctis' comes directly from the Vulgate (2 *Par*.5:xiii). The passage beginning 'psalterium, cithara . . .', also from Amalarius, is quoted out of context and is misleading; Amalarius is using a conventional symbolism as the context shows. The passage from Hrabanus Maurus on the same page fares even worse. Hrabanus's meaning (that the combination of voices and instruments mentioned in the Old Testament presages the way in which the church has joined people of many languages into one harmonious faith) is misinterpreted. Examples might easily be multiplied from any page.

[54] For Grocheo's division of music see E. Rohloff, *Die Quellenhandschriften zum Musiktraktat des Johannes de Grocheio* (Leipzig, 1972), 124.

[55] This implication was first seen by L. Gushee, 'Two Central Places: Paris and the French Court in the Early Fourteenth Century', in *GfMKB, Berlin 1974*, 143.

[56] Reckow, *Anonymus 4*, i, 88.

[57] The question of doubling introduces another knotty passage in the theorists. A chapter appended by Jerome of Moravia to Johannes de Garlandia's treatise discusses polyphony in four parts, and records that the range of a quadruplum part is normally much the same as that of a triplum. 'Such a quadruplum', the author comments, 'with three parts associated with it, is called double discant by some, *quia duo invicem nunc cum uno, nunc cum reliquo audientibus tamquam esse[n]t duplex cantus. Percipitur tamen in instrumentis maxime completis*' (*De mensurabili musica*, ed. Reimer, 96–7). I retain the Latin, since it is not clear whether Reimer's text makes sense. In the first sentence the subject of 'esse[n]t' is in doubt, whence Reimer's decision to emend the manuscript (which scarcely improves matters); this sentence also lacks a main verb. 'Percipitur', which begins the next sentence, would do very well as the missing verb, but this leaves the crucial passage referring to instruments without a verb in its turn! Rokseth (*Polyphonies*, iv, 44) construes this passage as a probable reference to instrumental doubling in four-part vocal polyphony, while S. J. Birnbaum, *Johannes de Garlandia: Concerning Music* (Colorado Springs, 1978), 56, interprets it as a reference to wholly instrumental compositions in four parts.

[58] Franco of Cologne, *Ars cantus mensurabilis*, ed. G. Reaney and A. Gilles, CSM, xviii (1974), 69.

[59] See for example G. Reaney, 'Voices and Instruments in the Music of Guillaume de Machaut', *RBM*, x (1956), 8.

[60] For references see Chapter XI.

[61] There are many literary references to these *caroles*. Some of the most arresting appear in Froissart's romance of *Meliador* where the texts of *caroles* danced by courtiers in the story are often inserted into the narrative. Usually they are simple rondeaux with little semantic density. For example:

> *Ou que je soie, doulz amis,*
> *N'aiés ja doubte de moi.*
> Mes coers n'iert ja de vouz partis,
> *Ou que je soie, doulz amis,*
> Je vous seray loyaus toutdis
> Et vous jure par ma foy:
> *Ou que je soie, doulź amis,*
> *N'aiés ja doubte de moi.*

(For this rondeau, and the passage which encloses it, see *Meliador*, ed. A. Longnon, SATF

Et vous jure par ma foy:
Ou que je soie, doulz amis,
N'aiés ja doubte de moi.

(For this rondeau, and the passage which encloses it, see *Meliador*, ed. A. Longnon, SATF (Paris, 1895–9), iii, lines 13294f.) This rondeau, like all of the poems inserted in *Meliador*, is the work of Wenceslas of Bohemia, Duke of Luxembourg (*d* 1383). Some of these lyrics probably had musical settings, for in one instance Froissart expresses his regret that he knows only the poem of one of them, having forgotten the *note* (ibid, i, lines 8463–6). It may be that many (perhaps all) of the rondeaux by Wenceslas were originally composed by him as monophonic dancing songs or *caroles* to enliven courtly festivities.

[62] This school of thought cannot be readily identified by reference to authoritative books and articles. It finds less tangible expression in the teaching and advice given at international summer schools, courses and workshops.

[63] *Speculum musice*, ed. Bragard, 23.

[64] For some of the early 15th-century evidence see G. Reaney, 'Text-underlay in Early Fifteenth-century Musical Manuscripts', in *Essays in Musicology in Honor of Dragan Plamenac* (Pittsburgh, 1969), 245–51.

[65] As it would appear to be, for example, in Guillaume de Machaut's rondeau *Dame, mon cuer* (rondeau 22). As preserved in the major Machaut manuscripts this work has text in the cantus only, yet the equal melodic interest of all parts (with much passing of motifs from one part to another), together with the even distribution of ligatures between all three voices, suggests that this is effectively a triple cantus work.

[66] For examples see *French Secular Compositions of the Fourteenth Century*, ed. W. Apel, CMM, liii (1970–72), no.11 (Bartolino da Padua, *La douce cere*), and no.48 (Francesco Landini, *Adyou, adyou*).

[67] An example is provided by one of Landini's best-known ballate, *Questa fanciull'amor*, edited in *Francesco Landini: Complete Works*, ed. L. Schrade, PMFC, iv (1958), two volumes with notes on performance by Kurt von Fischer (Monaco, 1982), ii, no. 6(97). On the textless contratenors in Landini's three-part ballate see the important remarks in J. Nádas, 'The Structure of MS Panciatichi 26 and the Transmission of Trecento Polyphony', *JAMS*, xxxiv (1981), 422ff.

[68] *Francesco Landini*, no.45 (136). See Fallows, 'Specific Information', 133f, and H. M. Brown, 'The Trecento Harp', in *Performance Practice: New York 1981*, 58–9.

[69] C. Page, *Voices and Instruments of the Middle Ages: Instrumental Practice and Songs in France 1100–1300* (London, 1987), 69–75.

[70] The one composer known to have been a harpist is Richard Loqueville; for the evidence see the review by David Fallows in *JAMS*, xxxiv (1981), 551–2; works in *Early Fifteenth-century Music*, ed. G. Reaney, CMM, xi/3 (1966), 1ff. For the possibility that Baude Cordier may have been a harpist see C. Wright, *Music at the Court of Burgundy 1364–1419: a Documentary History* (Henryville, Ottawa and Binningen, 1979), 132ff. For further information on the late medieval harp and harping see H. M. Brown, 'The Trecento Harp'; Fallows, 'Specific Information' and C. Page, 'The Performance of Songs in Late Medieval France', *EM*, x (1982), 441–50.

[71] Page, *Voices and Instruments*, chap.9 *passim*.

Interlude

CHAPTER VI

Musica ficta

KAROL BERGER

Written and implied accidental inflections

Since the early 11th century European musicians have had at their disposal everything they needed to notate pitches unambiguously. In spite of this, composers of vocal polyphony until the end of the Renaissance, and even beyond, did not think they had to write down every accidental they required. They knew that some accidentals could be left out in notation, since singers would make the appropriate inflections anyway. We learn about the existence of this practice from the infrequent but express statements of theorists, such as the late 14th-century author who writes that 'in general, it is not necessary to notate [accidentals]'.[1] We learn, further, that most musicians wrote some accidentals down and left others out, although there was no agreement on exactly how much to notate. There was a tendency, however, to leave out particularly those accidentals needed to avoid melodic tritones and those inflecting cadential progressions. From the early 16th century on, writers on music advocated with increasing frequency that accidentals should always be written down.

The theorists explain why some accidental inflections were notated while others were not. Since some inflections were implied, as a matter of convention, by the musical context, composers could rely on singers to make them in performance regardless of whether the accidentals were written. To write them out was not necessary, but neither was it prohibited. Since not all contexts implied inflections with equal clarity, one might decide to provide some accidentals even if, strictly speaking, they were redundant. (In the choirbook or partbook formats it was easiest to spot the necessity of an inflection required by a melodic context, and almost as easy to discover one demanded by a cadential formula, but much more difficult to find one stipulated by a vertical relation.)

It is obvious, then, that the realization of implied accidental inflections belonged to the realm of performance practice. But if we are to avoid misconceptions about what medieval and Renaissance musicians did, we need a clear understanding of whether implied accidentals belonged to the domain of the musical text (which, for any given work, had to remain invariable from one performance to another if the work were to retain its identity), or to the domain of performance (which might vary from one realization of the text to another without endangering the identity of the work). The idea that an aspect of a work might be a matter of performance practice yet not belong to what I have defined here as the domain of performance but rather to the domain of musical text may appear bizarre only on the anachronistic assumption that the function of musical notation is to fix an ideal musical text existing independently of specific realizations, a modern attitude which did not become common until the late 18th century. For earlier musicians the function of notation was to provide adequate instruction for performers. This explains their pragmatic attitude that what was implied could be, but did not have to be, written down. Thus the practice of implying rather than specifying some accidental inflections does not necessarily mean that such inflections could not belong to the musical text.

In fact, it appears that the borderline between the domains of musical text and performance cut across the area of implied inflections. Once we have discussed the conventions which governed their use, it will become clear that many inflections belonged to the invariable musical text, since contexts that required them could be realized in only one way. But it will also be seen that the conventions allowed singers in certain situations to choose from among several available solutions. In some contexts musicians might legitimately hesitate whether to inflect or not, in others there might be no question that an inflection was required, but the choice of the specific inflection might be left open. We have evidence, moreover, that singers could occasionally disagree on how to realize the text.[2] Consequently, some implied inflections must be understood as belonging not to the invariable text but to its variable performing realizations.

Thus even though some contexts may have allowed performers to choose from among several acceptable solutions, for the most part we should think about the problem of implied inflections in terms of the intended musical text to be correctly realized by singers reading from a more or less abbreviated notation.[3] This way of seeing the problem will allow us to avoid the false track taken by those scholars who have argued that since implied accidentals were a matter of performance practice 'it is useless to strive for an "authentic" version',[4] and improper even to include them in modern critical editions.[5] Once it is realized that many implied inflections belonged to the domain of musical text, and that, unlike the attitude of early musicians, the modern view of notation requires that the complete text be written down, it becomes clear that the search for the correct realization (or, in some cases, the range of acceptable realizations) of implied inflections is the responsibility of the editor and that the results of this search should be spelled out in a critical edition.

Available accidental inflections

GAMUT From the mid-13th until the end of the 16th century, musicians commonly thought of the total set of steps available to them, their gamut, as divided into two realms, those of 'true' or 'correct music' (*musica vera* or *recta*) on the one side, and 'feigned' or 'false music' (*musica ficta* or *falsa*) on the other.[6] The former was identified with the content of the so-called 'Guidonian' hand, a structure whose principal elements originated in the early 11th-century teaching of Guido of Arezzo but which acquired its fully developed form only in the late 13th century,[7] and the latter with all steps which could not be found within the hand.

The 'hand' (*manus*) consisted of 10 'places' (*loca*) in which steps could be located. The places defined only the order of steps contained in them, but not the intervals between the steps. To identify the places one used 20 'letter names' (*claves*), in ascending order, the Greek letter G (*G* in modern letter notation), seven 'low' (*graves*) letter names from A to G (our *A* to *g*), seven 'high' (*acutae*) ones from a to g (our *a* to *g'*), and five 'highest' (*superacutae*) ones from aa to ee (our *a'* to *e''*).

Intervals between steps located in places were defined by means of the six 'syllables' (*voces*) of the 'hexachord' (*deductio*), in ascending order, *ut, re, mi, fa, sol, la*, which were located in consecutive places of the hand, and which formed an intervallic series consisting of a diatonic semitone surrounded on both sides by two consecutive whole tones. A step of the gamut was identified by means of a letter name and at least one syllable; by locating the syllable within the place, one defined the intervals between the step and the steps surrounding it within the range of the hexachord.

The hand contained seven hexachords beginning, respectively, on *G, c, f, g, c', f'* and *g'*, so that each of its 20 places contained one, two or three syllables. In order to define intervals beyond the range of a hexachord, one made a 'mutation' (*mutatio*) within a single place from a syllable belonging to one hexachord to a syllable belonging to another, interlocking one. Since it was assumed that *ut* of each hexachord had the same pitch as the syllable of the lower hexachord present in the same place, the gamut of *musica vera* consisted, in modern terms, of all the 'white-key' steps from *G* to *e''* plus *b♭* and *b♭'*.

In addition, from the late 15th century on, theorists were increasingly aware of the possibility of extending the range of the gamut,[8] *and in the 16th century there were many who considered a step to be a part of musica vera as* long as its syllable could be found among the syllables of the seven regular hexachords in another octave.[9] In modern terms, they extended the 'true' gamut to include 'white-key' steps beyond *G* and *e''* as well as *B♭*. *This less restrictive view of musica vera*, however, cannot be documented before the 16th century and even then it was not universally shared.

A step of *musica ficta* was produced when a syllable not belonging to any of the seven regular hexachords was located in any of the 20 places. In principle, any syllable could be located in any place. The resulting step could, but did not have to, differ in pitch from a *musica vera* step present in the same place. *Fa* and *mi* located in the same place differed by a chromatic semitone, just as they did in *musica vera* at *b* and *b'*.

While it was possible to have *fa* and *mi* in every place, it was, obviously, redundant to locate *fa* or *mi* more than once in a single place. This meant that the largest conceivable gamut contained 16 different pitches in an octave, in modern terms, the seven 'white-key' steps, plus five flattened 'black-key' steps (B♭, E♭, A♭, D♭, G♭; roman capital letters will be used when the octave of the pitch is of no concern), plus four sharpened 'black-key' steps (F♯, C♯, G♯, D♯). The gamut was fully utilized by *c*1400 in such sources as the Chantilly codex and in Old Hall. In the early 15th century, Prosdocimus de Beldemandis noticed that *mi* was possible on the low *A* and, consequently, introduced one more step, A♯.[10] The resulting gamut of 17 different pitches in an octave remained the largest possible gamut of musical practice through to the end of the Renaissance.[11] From the early 16th century, the possibility of going beyond these limits began to be explored in pieces of clearly experimental character (the earliest of which was most likely Adrian Willaert's celebrated *Quid non ebrietas*, written probably in 1519)[12] and discussed by theorists (initially stimulated by Willaert's puzzle).[13]

A consensus concerning the practical selection of steps considered to be most useful emerged by the mid-15th century.[14] It limited the gamut to 12 different pitches in an octave, in modern terms, seven 'white-key' steps, plus three flattened (B♭, E♭, A♭) and two sharpened (F♯, C♯) 'black-key' ones. The choice was explained by the desire to have *fa* in every place which in *musica vera* contained *mi*, and *mi* in every place which contained *fa*. It is easy to guess that this desire was dictated by one of the conventional uses of *musica ficta* steps, the prohibition of *mi*-against-*fa* discords (see section 3(iii) below); in order to be able always to avoid singing *mi* against *fa*, musicians had to have a gamut which contained *fa* in every place which already included *mi*, and the reverse.

Already in the late 15th century, however, some musicians chose G♯ instead of A♭,[15] and by the second quarter of the 16th century, this became the more common choice.[16] It was dictated by another conventional use of *musica ficta* steps, the use of *mi*-steps as cadential leading notes (see section 3(iv) below); of these, G♯ was the third most commonly used. In short, since the late 15th century, the selection of most commonly employed steps included, in modern terms, three flats and three sharps.

NOTATION In notation, the places were represented by the alternating lines and spaces of the staff. One 'principal letter name' or 'principal clef' (*clavis principalis*) sufficed to identify all the places of the staff, of course. In *musica vera*, an ambiguity as to the desired pitch could arise at only two places, *b* and *b'*, since only these contained syllables differing in pitch; in them, *fa* was a chromatic semitone lower than *mi*. Because of this, two distinct forms of these letter names were used, the 'round *b*' (*b rotundum*, the ancestor of our flat; will be used here) standing for *fa*, and the 'square ♭' (♮ *quadrum*, the ancestor of our natural; its most common graphic variant, ♮ will be used here) standing for *mi*. In the early 14th century, one more sign, usually known as 'diesis' (*diesis*, the ancestor of our sharp; its common graphic variant, ♯, will be used here), was introduced by Marchetto da Padova.[17] Until the end of the Renaissance it was normally considered to have exactly the same meaning as ♮.[18] *Mi* was assumed in the places of *b* and *b'*, so that when *fa* was desired, it had to be either implied or expressly indicated by an additional, 'less principal letter name' or 'less principal clef' (*clavis minus principalis*).[19]

In *musica ficta*, *fa* and *mi* could be located in every place, so that an ambiguity as to the desired pitch could arise anywhere. In any place, a pitch identical with that of a *musica vera* syllable found in the same place was assumed, so that when a pitch differing by a chromatic semitone was wanted, it had to be either implied or expressly indicated by means of the sign of *fa* or *mi*, ♭ or ♮/♯, respectively. In principle, the signs did not have to affect the pitch at the place in which they were located, since they merely indicated the position of the diatonic semitone, *mi–fa*.[20] In practice, however, the signs almost always did flatten or sharpen the pitch in the place in which they were located by a chromatic semitone, just as they did at *b* and *b′*.[21] The only common exception was the location of ♭ (or ♮/♯) in a place which already contained *fa* (or *mi*), in which case the sign merely confirmed that *fa* (or *mi*) was wanted there and did not affect the pitch.[22]

A sign of *fa* or *mi* placed at the beginning of the staff was valid for the duration of the staff. If placed internally, it generally applied only to the note it accompanied.[23] Innumerable examples of signature accidentals an octave apart found in sources through the end of the Renaissance (and beyond) show that such signs were valid in only one octave.

Conventional uses of accidental inflections

SIGNATURES The normal use of the 'less principal clefs' at the beginning of the staff was to transpose a melody without changing its mode, that is to say, it was identical with that of a modern key signature.[24] A signature made a modal transposition possible, since it transposed a system of hexachords. Until the late 15th century this was probably the regular system of seven hexachords, but in the 16th century the system which was transposed was normally seen as consisting of interlocking hexachords alternately a fifth and a fourth apart, that is, hexachords on C and G.[25] In either case, the transposed system of hexachords was considered to represent *musica ficta*,[26] and consequently there is no reason to believe that E♭ under the one-flat signature, or A♭ under the two-flat signature, was ever thought of as belonging to *musica vera*.[27]

The use of different signatures in different voices, a common practice until the early 16th century, continues to puzzle musicologists.[28] Relevant theoretical evidence is unfortunately very scarce, but it is unanimous in suggesting that the function of such differing signatures was to provide an automatic insurance against prohibited vertical imperfect fifths (for this prohibition, see section 3(iii) below).[29] Indeed, it is plausible to suppose that differences between signatures helped to fulfil those conventional functions of internal accidental inflections which involved more than one voice. Since voices were notated separately (either in separate areas of an opening in a choirbook or in separate partbooks) rather than vertically aligned in score, the accidentals that musicians were most likely to miss were the ones needed because of vertical relations arising between voices. One less flat in the signature of an upper voice, or one more flat in the signature of a lower voice, would be used when the fear of a vertical imperfect fifth was greater than the fear of a vertical imperfect octave.[30] Note that since cadences also involve more than one voice (see section 3(iv) below), the central part of Edward E. Lowinsky's hypothesis,[31] the claim that the lack of a flat in the signature of an upper voice automatically provided leading notes at some cadences, is also plausible and can supplement the explanation presented above. But it should be pointed out that there is no theoretical evidence to support Lowinsky's hypothesis and that the need for a leading note was more easily discovered from reading a single part, since cadences involved characteristic melodic-rhythmic formulae.

In order to be able to reconcile our explanation of the function of differing signatures with the knowledge that the function of a signature was to produce a modal transposition, we must realize that the use of differing signatures flourished in the period of 'successive' composition in which complete parts fulfilling different functions were successively added to the voice which defined the mode of the polyphonic whole (usually, but perhaps not always, the tenor)[32] and gradually disappeared with the advent of 'simultaneous' composition which minimized the functional differentiation of individual parts and encouraged musicians to employ mainly the species of fifth and fourth of a single modal pair in all parts. This suggests that, in a work using different signatures, the signature of one voice only was relevant to the modal definition of the whole, while 'conflicting' signatures of other voices automatically provided the inflections required by contrapuntal rules and were relevant at most to the modal definition of individual parts.

THE PROHIBITION OF MELODIC TRITONE, DIMINISHED FIFTH, IMPERFECT OCTAVE AND CHROMATIC SEMITONE The main use of accidental inflections in purely melodic contexts was to avoid the tritone. From the time of Ars Antiqua polyphony through to the end of the Renaissance, the tritone prohibition was discussed by theorists in remarkably similar terms and it is therefore unlikely that the general way of handling the problem evolved significantly, or differed much, from place to place.[33] The diminished fifth began to be commonly prohibited from the late 15th century on.[34] It is uncertain, but seems likely, that the prohibition was followed by earlier musicians as well, and that theorists had omitted to mention it because they felt that discussions of the tritone covered the whole problem adequately. The imperfect octave was regularly prohibited in the 16th century[35] and again we do not know whether the prohibition was practised earlier, though probably it was. The prohibition of the chromatic semitone, on the other hand, is theoretically documented from at least the early 14th century on.[36] What all these prohibitions have in common is that they involve *mi* and *fa* located in places distant by a fourth, fifth, octave or unison. This similarity, plus the fact that exactly the same relations were prohibited when they occurred vertically, is the main reason for thinking that the prohibitions of diminished fifth and imperfect octave were in force long before theorists bothered to discuss them.

The tritone, diminished fifth, imperfect octave and chromatic semitone were prohibited regardless of whether they were ascending or descending, direct or indirect. But the prohibition had several exceptions:

1. A prohibited progression did not offend if anything (a rest, a cadence) which produced a sense of punctuation in the flow of the melody intervened between the notes forming the progression. It is obvious that differences of opinion over what constituted a sufficiently strong musical punctuation could arise. In this, as in all other cases of this sort, we shall have to study the practice followed in a given repertory on the basis of source accidentals and we shall have to remember that some contexts may have admitted alternative solutions.

2. An indirect prohibited progression lost its force if it was filled with many notes. Again, it is clear that musicians could occasionally disagree over how many notes were enough.

3. A prohibited progression was tolerated when it was resolved by a diatonic semitone, up if its last note was *mi* (for instance, *f–. . .–b–c'*), and down if it was *fa* (*b–. . .–f–e*). Many theorists thought that this exception applied only to indirect progressions, but some made it even with direct ones. The prohibition of a direct imperfect octave, however, seems to have been absolute.[37] A direct chromatic semitone (such as *f* to *f♯*), on the other hand, while generally prohibited, could be tolerated if its use was justified by contrapuntal rules and if it was properly resolved to fill the whole tone.[38] An acceptable resolution of a prohibited progression could be delayed by a few notes which, again, might lead to disagreements. On the other hand, a musical punctuation intervening between the last note of the progression and its resolution cancelled the effect of the resolution.

In describing an ascent by step to *b* but not further in the untransposed system, theorists often explained that if one wanted to proceed beyond *a–la* without producing the tritone, one had to make the following step into *fa*.[39] By the early 16th century some musicians began mechanically to follow the rule according to which one always made *fa* when ascending only one step above *la*, whether or not there was *f* before or after,[40] while others continued to remember that one did it only when there was a tritone to be avoided.[41] An examination of relevant source accidentals will show which solution is preferable for a given repertory.

Theoretical evidence is practically unanimous in indicating that one normally avoided an offending progression by changing *mi* into *fa* and not the reverse, that is, using a flat rather than sharp. From comments of those few theorists who addressed the question of what was done when an internal flat introduced to correct a tritone produced a diminished fifth in turn, we may infer that the idea that one internally introduced *fa* could lead to another at a place distant by a fourth or fifth (for instance, *f–. . .–b♭–. . .–e♭*) in a kind of 'chain reaction' was alien to them, since they recommended in such cases that the originally offending tritone be left uncorrected.[42] Thus it is unlikely that normal practice made use of implied flats applied to a chain of descending fifths or ascending fourths, though the existence of such 'chain reactions' can be demonstrated in two early 16th-century experimental pieces.[43]

Theorists consistently point out that the tritone was avoided particularly often in the F modes (tritus) (since it arose there in relation with the final), and fairly often in the D modes (protus). On the other hand, B♭ was uncommon in the E modes (deuterus) (because it produced a diminished fifth with the final there) and particularly rare in the G modes (tetrardus) (where, unlike in other modes, a consistent use of B♭ destroyed the identity of the mode). In addition, it should be remembered that at least since the early 14th century a basic feature of contrapuntal theory and practice was the differentiation of the simple note-against-note consonant counterpoint and the embellishing diminished one, so that it was always possible to reduce a composition to its underlying simple counterpoint. These facts suggest that musicians made distinctions as to the relative structural importance of notes in their music, distinctions based on contrapuntal and, once modal concepts began to be applied to polyphony, also on modal considerations. It is possible that distinctions of this sort were taken into account when one

113

decided whether a given melodic progression had to be corrected or not. For instance, there seems to be no theoretical evidence concerning how tritones embedded in perfect fifths, such as *c'–b–. . .–f* or *e–f–. . .–b*, were handled, but it seems plausible that the treatment of these and similar progressions in which the flattening of *b* produced a conflict with *e* depended on whether the structurally important notes formed the tritone, in which case the tritone would have to be corrected, or the fifth, in which case it could be left alone. More generally, it seems plausible that the more important structurally the notes forming a forbidden progression the more offensive it was found, and that a resolution by means of a note at least equally important to the offending one was more satisfactory than a resolution by means of a structurally less weighty note. Needless to say, instinctive or conscious decisions based on an evaluation of relative structural importance of notes would have to lead occasionally to disagreements.

THE PROHIBITION OF MI-AGAINST-FA DISCORDS From the moment the modern classification of consonances and dissonances emerged *c*1300 until the end of the Renaissance, a common rule of counterpoint prohibited vertical, nonharmonic relations between *mi* and *fa* located in places a perfect consonance apart.[44] Since most treatises presented no more than elementary instruction in simple two-part counterpoint from which the fourth was excluded as a dissonance, the rule most often prohibited expressly *mi* against *fa* on the fifth and octave (and, of course, their octave equivalents) only, that is, it prohibited imperfect fifths and octaves. But since in simple counterpoint for more than two parts the fourth could be used as a consonance provided it had a fifth or third below, it is obvious that, when it was meant to be so used, *mi* against *fa* had to be avoided also on the fourth.[45] The use of accidental inflections to correct all such nonharmonic relations was often said to be 'because of necessity' (*causa necessitatis*).[46]

While theorists inform us of no exceptions to the prohibition of the imperfect octave, the prohibition of the imperfect fifth and fourth had some exceptions:

1. From the late 15th century on, we regularly learn that a vertical nonharmonic relation was tolerated even in simple counterpoint when it was followed by a consonance with at least one, and preferably both, notes forming the relation properly resolved, that is to say, with *mi* going a diatonic semitone up and/or *fa* a diatonic semitone down.[47] The most common instance of the exception was a diminished fifth resolving to a third. The resolution could be delayed by structurally less important notes belonging to diminished counterpoint or by a short rest.[48] The notes of resolution could even be exchanged between the two parts.[49] It is clear that disagreements could occasionally arise as to whether a given relation was properly resolved or not. It is interesting to note that a properly resolved nonharmonic fifth could be preceded or even followed by a perfect one without this being taken as an offence against the prohibition of parallel perfect consonances.[50] The exception allowing properly resolved *mi*-against-*fa* discords is not documented in theoretical literature before the late 15th century, but since the general tendency in the development of counterpoint was toward the increasing restrictions on the use of dissonances, it is unlikely that the *mi*-

against-*fa* prohibition would be followed unconditionally at first and liberalized later. Hence it seems probable that in practice the exception was attached to the prohibition from the beginning.

2. From a mid-16th-century theorist who claimed to describe the teaching of Josquin Desprez we learn that a nonharmonic vertical relation was allowed as a passing discord of short duration (the maximum duration of any dissonant passing note) even if this was not properly resolved.[51] Once again, since earlier practice was more lenient rather than stricter in its handling of dissonances, it seems likely that this exception was followed in practice from the beginning of the prohibition.

Cross relations involving imperfect octaves, fifths and fourths were not discussed in any depth before Zarlino, whose treatment of the problem gives the impression that he was attempting to reform, rather than to describe, current practice.[52] It is possible, but by no means certain, that by the mid-16th century musicians tended to avoid the imperfect octave cross relations. As for the cross relations involving the imperfect fifth and fourth, Zarlino's concern with these seems to reflect the teaching of Willaert, but not the common practice.[53] It may be, however, that the prestige of Zarlino's contrapuntal theory spread this concern more widely among the followers of the 'first practice' in the late 16th century. Recent researches based on practical evidence demonstrated widespread tolerance of nonharmonic cross relations, including the cross relation of the imperfect octave, in late 15th- and 16th-century music.[54] We need more research of this kind to determine when and where musicians began to avoid nonharmonic cross relations, if they ever did, and whether the treatment of the imperfect octave differed from that accorded to the imperfect fifth and fourth.

Theoretical evidence indicates that, when confronted by the necessity of correcting a vertical nonharmonic relation by means of an accidental inflection, musicians did not normally think in terms of which voice to inflect (lower or upper, tenor or counterpoint written against it),[55] but rather in terms of whether to use *fa* or *mi* (flat or sharp). Since the same relations occurring melodically were normally corrected by means of flats, it is not surprising that, from the 1470s on, it seems to have been self-evident to theorists that the usual way to correct a *mi*-against-*fa* discord was to change the *mi* into *fa*.[56] Theorists of the 14th and early 15th centuries, however, appear to have had no clear preference for either *fa* or *mi* in such cases.[57] An examination of source accidentals will be necessary to determine whether the preference for flat solutions in practice antedated the 1470s.

The question of what one did when a correction of a melodic relation produced an undesirable vertical one or the reverse was discussed by Tinctoris who made it clear that one corrected in such cases the vertical nonharmonic relation and not the melodic one.[58] It is particularly noteworthy that it did not even occur to the theorist that one could correct both relations by means of a 'chain reaction' in which the introduction of one accidental would lead to the introduction of another at a place a fourth or fifth apart. We can be confident that Tinctoris described the normal practice in this case and that the practice was followed not only in the late 15th but also in the 16th century, since it was independently confirmed by Giovanni del Lago in 1538.[59] The question of whether vertical considerations took precedence over melodic ones also before the late 15th century requires further investigation.

CADENCES From the moment the modern classification of consonances and dissonances emerged *c*1300 through to the end of the Renaissance theorists universally stipulated that in a progression from an imperfect to a perfect consonance one part should proceed by a diatonic semitone and that one of the steps forming the imperfect consonance might be accidentally inflected if this was necessary to produce the semitone progression.[60] They also made it clear that the progression provided a sense of closure, or punctuation, that is, that it functioned as a cadence. The use of accidental inflections in such contexts was occasionally said to be 'because of beauty' (*causa pulchritudinis*).[61] It is immediately apparent that a consistent application of accidental inflections to all progressions from imperfect to perfect consonances would lead to results which would be unacceptable from the standpoint of rules governing correct usage in early polyphony. Thus we have to be able to distinguish those imperfect-to-perfect progressions which were meant to serve as cadences from those which were not, that is, we have to find additional criteria allowing musicians to recognize a cadence.

The following additional criteria were regularly mentioned by theorists from the late 15th century on:[62]

1. A cadence signifies a certain degree of closure of the whole musical discourse or of its part.

2. It is analogous to a punctuation sign marking the articulation of a verbal text into such units as clauses, sentences and paragraphs, and it may reflect such articulation of the text.

3. The octave (or its equivalent) is an indispensable component of the final harmony in a cadence. In simple counterpoint, a cadence consists of three consecutive harmonies, with one of the two parts which end on the octave following the melodic formula 8–7–8 (= 1–7–1; the consecutive Arabic numerals signify the consecutive steps above the final, 1, of the cadence) and the counterpoint against it involving 1 (or 8) as the final step, 2 or 5 as the penultimate step, and any step which produces a consonance against 8 (or 1) as the antepenultimate step. In diminished counterpoint, the penultimate imperfect consonance is preceded by a dissonant suspension and the cadence may, of course, be further embellished.

4. The final harmony should fall at the beginning of a mensuration unit which under the 'ordinary measure' (*misura commune*: ₵) of the early 16th century seems to have been no smaller than a semibreve. Theorists do not explain what was, for each of the time signatures used, the smallest mensuration unit at the beginning of which it was possible to place the final harmony of a cadence and the matter requires further investigation.

5. A cadence may be 'interrupted', in which case it consists of only the first two harmonies of the regular cadence, with the second one placed in a metrically strong position reserved normally for the final harmony of the regular cadence. A cadence may also be 'evaded', in which case both structural voices behave normally for the first two harmonies, but go (both, or just one of them) to unexpected steps for the final harmony. In either case, the leading note should be inflected if this were necessary

to produce the semitone progression to the final in the corresponding regular cadence.

Unfortunately, cadences began to be described in detail only from the late 15th century on, but since cadences belong to the most conservative stylistic features it may well be that the criteria listed above were in operation long before theorists began to mention them. Before a full history of the cadence is written we have to study the unmistakable (final) cadences in a given repertory, determine whether our criteria apply and whether additional criteria may be derived from such a study, and use the applicable criteria when trying to distinguish the cadential from the non-cadential imperfect-to-perfect progressions within the repertory.

We also have to remember that cadences reflected various degrees of punctuation of the text and were themselves of various strength, perfection or finality, from the most regular and perfect cadential progressions ending on long notes, in metrically strong position, on the final of the mode, to a variety of interrupted and evaded cadences. This suggests that the borderline between cadential and non-cadential imperfect-to-perfect progressions may be somewhat blurred. A progression may exhibit some, but not all, of the characteristic features of a cadence. While some progressions were certainly treated as cadences and others certainly not, there was a grey area in between in which a decision had to be made as to whether a given progression should be treated as a cadence or not and in which alternative solutions might have been acceptable. From the 1520s on we learn that if the final harmony of a cadence contain 3, then the third (or its octave equivalent) between 1 and 3 should be major.[63]

The only context in which musicians may have been confronted with the question of how to inflect a cadential progression, specifically whether to use sharp or flat, was the penultimate cadential harmony containing only 7 and 2, and optionally 4, when 1 had naturally a whole tone below and above, for instance, the penultimate harmony in a cadential progression of $d'-c'-d'$ in the cantus moving against $f-e-d$ in the tenor (and, optionally, $a-g-a$ in the contratenor) when the voices had no signature accidentals. Since the only indispensable steps in such a harmony were 7 and 2 (c' and e in our example), the main decision must have concerned these two steps. Doubling a step in another voice might well have been an indication that it was not meant to be inflected, since an inflection implied a continuation of the melodic movement (*mi* going to *fa*, or *fa* to *mi*), while the prohibition of parallel perfect consonances prevented the proper resolution of one of the inflected notes. Assuming an entirely neutral melodic and vertical context for 7 and 2, that is, a context allowing either solution, theoretical evidence leaves no doubt that the preferred choice for cadences on D and G in the untransposed system was to sharpen 7.[64] The choice was less obvious, however, in cadences on A when the voice which had 2 had no flats in the signature (and in corresponding cadences on D with one flat in the signature, and on G with two flats in the signature).[65]

While it is clear that, at least since the early 15th century, both solutions were acceptable for these cadences,[66] theorists do not explain whether any one solution was preferred in a specific context and, if so, how one made the choice, and practical evidence has not yet been examined with this question in mind. One late 15th-century theorist, Ramos de Pareia, suggests that the disagreement as to which leading note to use in cadences on A resulted from conflicting modal interpretations of such cadences as representing either the irregularly placed protus, in which case the sharp leading note proper to the regular protus on D would be used, or the transposed deuterus, in which case one chose the flat leading note proper to the untransposed deuterus on E.[67] Hence, it is possible that a well-trained musician chose the leading note for a cadence on A depending on the modal context of the cadence. In a piece the tenor of which was notated without a signature and had the final on A, the sharp leading note would be used since A cadences would be understood to represent the protus. But in a piece conceived in another untransposed mode, the treatment of a cadence on A may have depended on whether the cadence was understood to represent a strong shift away from the main tonal centre of the piece, in which case one would choose the sharp leading note forcefully conveying the shift to the protus on A, or just a momentary emphasis on a degree different from the final, in which case one might prefer the weaker flat leading note, especially if the piece was in the tritus or protus in which B♭ was common anyway and, consequently, would not unduly disturb the fundamental mode. The choice would have involved musical decisions difficult, though not impossible, to articulate in the theoretical language of the period, and hence ones that are most likely to have been made instinctively, which would account for conflicting decisions in this area.

If the penultimate cadential harmony contained 4 (in addition to the structural 7 and 2) which went on to 5, and if the 7 had been sharpened, the 4 had to be sharpened as well, provided the context allowed it (that is, most likely, provided the 4 had not been doubled), because of the secondary cadential progression of the major third going to the fifth. That in a cadential progression from a vertical third to a vertical fifth the third should be major, was asserted by theorists from the early 14th through to the late 16th century.[68] Thus we shall have to examine practical evidence to find out whether the secondary leading note (the sharp 4) ever went out of fashion (which is likely, since 16th-century lute intabulations, for instance, seem almost never to use them)[69] and, if so, when and where precisely. A clear indication that a composer, school or generation wanted to avoid the sharpening of the penultimate 4 would be that the 4 regularly goes not to 5 but elsewhere (to 3 or 1), or that it is shunned altogether in favour of 5.

CANON AND IMITATION In addition to the increasingly ubiquitous technique of imitation, early vocal polyphony developed a family of special techniques involving the use of the same *complete* melody more than once in a composition, so that in principle the melody might have been, but in reality did not have to be, notated just once, its repetitions and transformations being directed by a written 'rule' (*canon*). The matter certainly requires further investigation; so far, however, no evidence has been found that imitative or canonic voices were given special treatment when it came to adding inflections because of the *mi*-against-*fa* prohibition or in order to produce cadential leading notes. But both imitative and canonic techniques raise the question of whether accidental inflections were used when the melody was imitated or repeated at a different pitch in order to preserve its original intervals. (That the preservation of exact sizes of original intervals when the melody was imitated or repeated at the same pitch or at the octave was desirable should probably go without saying and there is mid-16th-century evidence for it,[70] but it is unlikely that this desire affected the normal ways in which *mi*-against-*fa* and cadential inflections were made.) Zarlino's 1558 discussion of canon and imitation,[71] by far the most detailed early treatment of these techniques, allows us to conclude that only canons (but almost certainly not imitations) at fourth and fifth above and below were normally (but not always) assumed to reproduce the intervals of their guides exactly, which means that only such canons might have called for accidental inflections in their consequents in order to preserve the exact intervals of their guides. Since no earlier theorist approaches the comprehensiveness of Zarlino's discussion, it is difficult to know for sure how long before his time the above conclusion was valid. But the conclusion is so simple and agrees so well with other aspects of the medieval and Renaissance theory (in particular, with the location of the seven identical hexachords of the regular gamut at places distant by the fourth and fifth), that it can provide a working hypothesis for further study of the problem.

Conventional and unconventional written accidental inflections

Written accidental inflections found in practical sources of early vocal polyphony may be divided into two classes. Some accidentals may have been written down by the composer or by the editor of a given version of the work (I shall refer to both as the 'author' of a given version), or they may have been implied by the author and written down by someone else: a scribe, printer or performer. Other accidentals had to be written down by the author, because there was no possibility of implying them. The class of potentially non-authorial accidentals contains all internal accidentals used for conventional reasons discussed in sections 3(ii)–(v) above and signature accidentals 'conflicting' with the key signature of the mode-defining voice.[72] The class of certainly authorial accidentals comprises all internal accidentals used for unconventional reasons, whether structural or expressive, and the key signature of the mode-defining voice. (Thus, for instance, the flats which endow the celebrated 'miserere' phrase in the second 'Agnus Dei' of Dufay's *Ave regina caelorum* Mass with much of its expressive power would not be supplied by singers had they not been notated, since they serve no known conventional function.)[73]

The division of all source accidentals into two classes proposed here should prove useful to editors and performers. First, a study of the functions of 'conventional' source accidentals in a given repertory will allow them to find out how those situations about which we know that they may have admitted alternative solutions were handled in this particular repertory.[74] Second, the division may help them to distinguish and reconstruct the complete texts of all versions of the work, both authentic (that is, representing the composer's wishes) and inauthentic ones, and, for each version, to reveal and evaluate the relative authority and plausibility of all the alternative realizations implied by the notated text.[75] If the sources differ to a significant degree in 'unconventional' accidentals, they must transmit different versions of the work, since differences in 'unconventional' accidentals could not be obliter-ated in performance.[76] And, within each version of the work, 'unconventional' source accidentals possess a much greater degree of authority than the 'conventional' ones which may have been added in the process of transmis-sion.

Notes

[1] 'Virtualiter licet semper non signentur', *The Berkeley Manuscript*, ed. and trans. O. B. Ellsworth (Lincoln, Nebraska and London, 1984), 44f. For other representative statements, see for example Johannes Legrense, *Ritus canendi vetustissimus et novus*, in *CS*, iv, 360f; Johannes Tinctoris, *Liber de natura et proprietate tonorum*, in *Opera theoretica*, ed. A. Seay, CSM, xxii/1 (1975), 74; Pietro Aaron, *Toscanello in musica* (Venice, 1539/*R*1971), bk2, chap.20, and 'Aggiunta', through to sig.Iiir; Gioseffo Zarlino, *Le istitutioni harmoniche* (Venice, 1558/*R*1965), 222, 237. Aaron's 1529 'Aggiunta' to *Toscanello* contains the fullest known discussion of the problem of implied accidentals extant. For a more extended presentation and discussion, see K. Berger, *Musica ficta: Theories of Accidental Inflections in Vocal Polyphony from Marchetto da Padova to Gioseffo Zarlino* (Cambridge, 1987).

[2] L. Lockwood, 'A Dispute on Accidentals in Sixteenth-century Rome', *AnMc*, no.2 (1965), 24–40.

[3] Aaron's invaluable 'Aggiunta' to *Toscanello* (see n.1 above) could not be construed in any other terms.

[4] C. Dahlhaus, 'Tonsystem und Kontrapunkt um 1500', *Jb des Staatlichen Instituts für Musikforschung* (1969), 14. Dahlhaus's paper represents the most radical attempt to prove that until the second third of the 16th century accidental inflections belonged largely to what I have called here the domain of performance. It is based on the claim that since the theorists of the period formulated their rules using such concepts as 'perfect' or 'imperfect consonance' therefore composers thought in terms of these abstract interval classes and hence were indifferent toward the specific sizes of, say, the fifths that they used. The most fundamental problem with this theory is that thinking in terms of interval classes of this kind does not make one indifferent to the specific sizes of intervals: the concept of 'perfect consonance', when applied to the interval of fifth, suffices to specify the size of this fifth most precisely.

[5] A. Mendel, 'The Purposes and Desirable Characteristics of Text-critical Editions', *Modern Musical Scholarship*, ed. E. Olleson (Stocksfield, 1980), 14–27.

[6] For this distinction see M. Bent, 'Musica Recta and Musica Ficta', *MD*, xxvi (1972), 73–100.

[7] For the origin, development and function of the concepts in terms of which early musicians thought about their gamut and of the signs they used to notate it, see K. Berger, 'The Hand and the Art of Memory', *MD*, xxxv (1981), 87–120, with further literature to be found there.

[8] See for example Bartolomeo Ramos de Pareia, *Musica practica*, ed. J. Wolf (Leipzig, 1901/ *R*1968), 12. By 1533, Stephano Vanneo presented a system of places extending a full octave below and above the customary one, *Recanetum de musica aurea* (Rome, 1533/*R*1969), ff.10r– 11v.

[9] See for example Nicolaus Wollick, *Enchiridion musices* (Paris, 1512), sig.b.iiir; Johannes Cochlaeus, *Tetrachordum musices* (Nuremberg, 1514), sigs.Cr–Cv; Vanneo, *Recanetum*, f.11r– 11v; Heinrich Glarean, *Dodecachordon* (Basle, 1547/*R*1969), 5.

[10] Prosdocimus de Beldemandis, *Libellus monochordi*, in *CS*, iii, 248–58.

[11] For a view that the gamut of vocal polyphony had no limits, see M. Bent, 'Diatonic *Ficta*', *EMH*, iv (1984), 1–50. (I would like to thank Professor Bent for kindly sending me the proofs of her paper before publication.) Bent's hypothesis is based essentially on the idea that, for early musicians, the definition of any step was independent not only of an absolute pitch standard (which is correct), but also of a relative standard established at the beginning of a composition's performance by the singers, so that, for instance, if a melody started with *G* and ended with what for us is *Gb*, early musicians would not think of the two pitches as being different. This, however, neglects the fact that for an early musician a step was identified not by a letter alone, but by a letter combined with a syllable. He would assign the last *G* a syllable from a different hexachord than that of the first *G*, and his choice of the syllable would depend on the syllables and mutations taken since the melody started. This shows that his definition of a step did depend on a standard established at the beginning of the performance of a work.

[12] The best discussion of the work is E. E. Lowinsky, 'Willaert's Chromatic "Duo" Re-examined', *TVNM*, xviii (1956), 1–36. Relevant to the question of dating are the discoveries concerning Willaert's early career in L. Lockwood, 'Josquin at Ferrara: New Documents and Letters', in *Josquin des Prez: New York 1971*, 118ff. The second unmistakably experimental piece of the first half of the 16th century has been explored in Lowinsky, 'Matthaeus Greiter's *Fortuna*: an Experiment in Chromaticism and in Musical Iconography', *MQ*, xlii (1956), 500–519; xliii (1957), 68–85. For other, more debatable, candidates for 'experimental' status, see Lowinsky, 'Music in Titian's *Bacchanal of the Andrians*: Origin and History of the *Canon per Tonos*', in *Titian: his World and his Legacy*, ed. D. Rosand (New York, 1982), 191–282, and H. M. Brown, 'Introduction', *A Florentine Chansonnier from the Time of Lorenzo the Magnificent (Florence, Biblioteca Nazionale Centrale MS Banco Rari 229)*, MRM, vii/1 (1983), 16–22.

[13] Apart from specific references to Willaert's puzzle, the earliest important discussion concerned the problem of whether one can really flatten C or F and sharpen B or E which was a subject of the correspondence between Giovanni Spataro, Pietro Aaron and Giovanni del Lago in 1533, in *I-Rvat* lat.5318, ff.47r–53v, 116r–29v, 165r–6r, 234v.

[14] See for example Anonymous, *[Libellus] Ex Codice Vaticano Lat. 5129*, ed. A. Seay, CSM, ix (1964), 46f; Anonymous XI, *Tractatus de musica plana et mensurabili*, in *CS*, iii, 426–9; Ramos de Pareia, *Musica practica*, 29ff, 35, 40; Vanneo, *Recanetum*, ff.43r–4r; Hermann Finck, *Practica musica* (Wittenberg, 1556/*R*1970), sigs.Biijr–Biijv.

[15] See Ramos de Pareia, *Musica practica*, 101f.

[16] See for example Aaron, *Toscanello*, bk2, chap.40; Aaron, *Lucidario in musica* (Venice, 1545/*R*1969), ff.35v–6v; Zarlino, *Le istitutioni harmoniche*, 138f.

[17] Marchetto needed a new sign, since he supplemented the normal division of the whole tone into the minor (or diatonic) and major (or chromatic) semitones with another division into a 'diesis' which was smaller than the minor semitone and a semitone which was larger than the major one. The sign of diesis marked the interval of diesis between a lower leading note and its resolution. The sign was subsequently adopted, and used indistinguishably from ♮, also by those who did not follow Marchetto's ideas on the division of the whole tone. For Marchetto's division of the whole tone, the invention of the diesis sign and the historical influence of these developments, see especially M. L. Martinez-Göllner, 'Marchettus of Padua and Chromaticism', in *L'ars nova italiana del trecento II: Certaldo 1969*, 187–202; J. W. Herlinger, 'Fractional Divisions of the Whole Tone', *MTS*, iii (1981), 74–83; Herlinger, 'Marchetto's Division of the Whole Tone', *JAMS*, xxxiv (1981), 193–216.

[18] See for example Ugolino of Orvieto, *Declaratio musicae disciplinae*, ed. A. Seay, CSM, vii/3 (1962), 243; Ramos de Pareia, *Musica practica*, 29; Heinrich Faber, *Ad musicam practicam introductio* (Nuremberg, 1550), pt.i, chaps.1 and 3; Zarlino, *Le istitutioni harmoniche*, 170. In the late 15th century, John Hothby wanted to distinguish the functions of ♮ and ♯ and claimed that the former should be used as the sign of *mi* only in the places of ♭ and its octaves, the latter – at all the other places. He was followed in the early 16th century by Giovanni Spataro and Pietro Aaron. This was the first step in the transition from the medieval to modern understanding of these three signs. See Hothby, *La Caliopea legale* in E. de Coussemaker, *Histoire de l'harmonie au moyen âge* (Paris, 1852), 297ff; Spataro, letter to Aaron, Bologna, 27 November 1531, *I-Rvat* lat.5318, ff.228v–9r; Aaron, *Lucidario in musica*, bk1, oppenione 10 and ff.3v–4r.

[19] See for example Jacques de Liège, *Speculum musicae*, ed. R. Bragard, CSM, iii/6 (1973), 138, and Glarean, *Dodecachordon*, 13. For the terminology, see F. Reckow, 'Clavis', in *HMT*.

[20] Thus Ugolino of Orvieto (*Declaratio*, bk2, p.45, ex.121) indicated what for us is *f* by preceding *f* with a ♭ located in the place of *g*.

[21] For unambiguous statements to that effect, see for example Petrus frater dictus Palma ociosa, *Compendium de discantu mensurabili*, in J. Wolf, 'Ein Beitrag zur Diskantlehre des 14. Jahrhunderts', *SIMG*, xv (1913–14), 515; Prosdocimus de Beldemandis, *Contrapunctus*, ed. J. W. Herlinger (Lincoln, Nebraska, and London, 1984), 76; Ramos de Pareia, *Musica practica*, 29; Aaron, *Lucidario in musica*, f.38r–38v.

[22] An example is the frequent use of a redundant flat at *f''* to indicate that the place lies beyond the regular system of 20 places. See E. E. Lowinsky, 'The Function of Conflicting Signatures in Early Polyphonic Music', *MQ*, xxxi (1945), 254ff. Another type of example is the common use of a redundant flat (or sharp) to ensure that a note it accompanies is not sharpened (or flattened) by the singers. A few examples of this type may be found among the cases of 'cautionary signs' collected in D. Harrán, 'New Evidence for Musica Ficta: the Cautionary Sign', *JAMS*, xxix (1976), 77–98. We must distinguish, however, between genuine 'cautionary signs' (the signs of *fa* – or *mi* – used to ensure that the notes they accompany are not made into *mi* – or *fa*) and

Harrán's main type of 'cautionary sign' (the sign of *mi* used to indicate that *fa* is wanted there). The former do indeed occur; the latter would require that the same sign be used in two opposed meanings, a bizarre practice for which I see no convincing evidence. See also Harrán, 'More Evidence for Cautionary Signs', *JAMS*, xxxi (1978), 490–94 as well as comments in *JAMS*, xxxi (1978), 385–95; xxxii (1979), 364–7.

[23] See for example Prosdocimus, *Contrapunctus*, 78f; Ramos de Pareia, *Musica practica*, 39; Giovanni Maria Lanfranco, *Scintille di musica* (Brescia, 1533/*R*1970), 18; Martin Agricola, *Rudimenta musices* (Wittenberg, 1539/*R*1966), chap.2; Sebald Heyden, *De arte canendi, ac vero signorum in cantibus usu* (Nuremberg, 1540/*R*1969), 23f. Tinctoris's claim that an internal sign of *fa* or *mi* retains its force so long as the melody remains within the range of the hexachord around the *fa* or *mi* (*Liber de natura*, 74) probably represents an unsuccessful attempt to reform the current practice, since it was not repeated by other theorists.

[24] See for example Marchetto da Padova, *Lucidarium in arte musicae planae*, in J. W. Herlinger, *The Lucidarium of Marchetto of Padua: a Critical Edition, Translation, and Commentary* (diss., U. of Chicago, 1978), 622; Tinctoris, *Liber de natura*, 98–103; Pietro Aaron, *Trattato della natura et cognitione di tutti gli tuoni di canto figurato non da altrui piu scritti* (Venice, 1525/*R*1969), chaps.4–7; Glarean, *Dodecachordon*, 31, 101f.

[25] The notation without signature was now said to represent the 'hard hand' (*manus dura*), that with one flat in the signature – the 'soft hand' (*manus mollis*) – and that with more than one flat in the signature – the 'feigned hand' (*manus ficta*; the terms 'song' (*cantus*) or 'scale' (*scala*) could be used instead of 'hand'). See, for example, Andreas Ornithoparchus, *Musice active micrologus* (Leipzig, 1517/*R*1977), sigs.Biiir–Biiiv.

[26] In the early 15th century, Ugolino referred to gamuts consisting of the regular system of seven hexachords and the same system transposed as combining steps of *musica vera* and *ficta* (*Declaratio*, bk2, pp.48ff) which shows that he considered a transposed system to represent *musica ficta*, not *vera*. For the 16th century, the same is shown by the very fact that a signature of more than one flat was thought to produce a 'feigned scale' (see the preceding note).

[27] The assumption that a transposed system represented *musica vera* was made in C. Dahlhaus, 'Zur Akzidentiensetzung in den Motetten Josquins des Prez', in *Musik und Verlag: Karl Vötterle zum 65. Geburtstag am 12. April 1968* (Kassel, 1968), 207ff. Elaborate hypotheses were erected on this assumption in M. Bent, 'Musica Recta and Musica Ficta', and A. Hughes, *Manuscript Accidentals: Ficta in Focus 1350–1450*, MSD, xxvii (1972).

[28] For the most important papers on the subject see E. E. Lowinsky, 'The Function of Conflicting Signatures'; R. H. Hoppin, 'Partial Signatures and Musica Ficta in Some Early 15th-century Sources', *JAMS*, vi (1953), 197–215; Lowinsky, 'Conflicting Views on Conflicting Signatures', *JAMS*, vii (1954), 181–204; Hoppin, 'Conflicting Signatures Reviewed', *JAMS*, ix (1956), 97–117.

[29] See John Hothby, *Spetie tenore del contrapunto prima*, in Hothby, *De arte contrapuncti*, ed. G. Reaney, CSM, xxvi (1977), 86; Aaron, *Toscanello*, sig.Iiir; Aaron, *Trattato*, chap.3, sig.br. See also G. Reaney, 'Transposition and "Key" Signatures in Late Medieval Music', *MD*, xxxiii (1979), 31f.

[30] This makes sense of Hoppin's valuable discovery ('Partial Signatures and Musica Ficta') of the frequent correlation between signatures differing by one flat and voice ranges differing by a fifth: vertical imperfect fifths are most likely to occur between parts the ranges of which are a fifth apart.

[31] 'The Function of Conflicting Signatures', 234 and *passim*.

[32] From Tinctoris through to the end of the 16th century most theorists considered the tenor to be the mode-defining part, but it is possible that in some genres, styles or textures another voice could have this role. See especially H. S. Powers, 'Mode', *Grove6*, xii, 400, and B. Meier, 'Die Handschrift Porto 714 als Quelle zur Tonartenlehre des 15. Jahrhunderts', *MD*, vii (1953), 175–97.

[33] The following summary is based on the most substantial discussions of the prohibition in Jacques de Liège, *Speculum musice*, bk6, pp.59, 138f; Pseudo-Tunstede, *Quatuor principalia musicae*, in *CS*, iv, 247f; Tinctoris, *Liber de natura*, 73–6; Ramos de Pareia, *Musica practica*, 37; Nicolaus Burtius, *Florum libellus*, ed. G. Massera (Florence, 1975), 90; Franciscus de Brugis, 'Opusculum', in G. Massera, *La 'mano musicale perfetta' di Francesco de Brugis dalle prefazioni ai corali di L. A. Giunta, Venezia, 1499–1504* (Florence, 1963), 82, 87f; Gonzalo Martínez de Bizcargui, *Arte de canto llano*, ed. A. Seay (Colorado Springs, 1979), 17–20; Aaron, *Toscanello*, 'Aggiunta'; Aaron, *Lucidario in musica*, bk1, oppenioni viii, x and f.13*v*.

[34] For particularly interesting discussions of the prohibition on which the following summary

is based, see Ramos de Pareia, *Musica practica*, 50; Zarlino, *Le istitutioni harmoniche*, 203, 236, 287.

[35] The following summary is based primarily on Nicolaus Wollick, *Opus aureum*, in *Die Musica gregoriana des Nicolaus Wollick*, ed. K. W. Niemöller, Beiträge zur rheinischen Musikgeschichte, xi (Cologne and Krefeld, 1955), 46; Ornithoparchus, *Musice active*, bk1, chaps.7 and 10; Martin Agricola, *Musica choralis deudsch* (Wittenberg, 1533/*R*1969), chap.8; Giovanni del Lago, *Breve introduttione di musica misurata* (Venice, 1540), 40; Aaron, *Lucidario in musica*, f.30r; Zarlino, *Le istitutioni harmoniche*, 236f.

[36] The following summary is based primarily on Jacques de Liège, *Speculum musice*, bk6, p.60; Pseudo-Tunstede, *Quatuor principalia musicae*, CS, iv, 215; Ramos de Pareia, *Musica practica*, 66, 99f; Franciscus de Brugis, 'Opusculum', 74, 78; Ornithoparchus, *Musice active*, bk1, chap.6.

[37] Glarean, *Dodecachordon*, 22.

[38] Marchetto da Padova, *Lucidarium*, 245–57, 430–33; John Hothby, *Tractatus quarundam regularum artis musicae*, *I-Fn* pal.472, f.10r; Ramos de Pareia, *Musica practica*, 66; Franchinus Gaffurius, *Practica musicae* (Milan, 1496), bk1, chap.4; Aaron, *Lucidario in musica*, ff.8v–9r, 30v; Zarlino, *Le istitutioni harmoniche*, 170.

[39] See for example Prosdocimus de Beldemandis, *Tractatus plane musice*, *I-Lg* 359, f.57r–57v.

[40] See for example Cochlaeus, *Tetrachordon musices*, sigs.Fr–Fv, examples; Vanneo, *Recanetum*, f.16r; Nikolaus Listenius, *Musica* (Nuremberg, 1549/*R*1927), chap.5.

[41] See for example Georg Rhau, *Enchiridion utriusque musicae practicae* (Wittenberg, 1538), sig.Ciiijv; Martin Agricola, *Musica choralis deudsch*, chap.4. For a most forceful statement against those who use *fa* above *la* indiscriminately, see Aaron, *Lucidario in musica*, bk1, oppenione viii and f.4v.

[42] See especially the most substantial comment on this matter in Aaron, *Toscanello*, 'Aggiunta'. See also Domingo Marcos Durán, *Lux bella* (Seville, 1492), [p.6]; Durán, *Comento sobre Lux bella* (Salamanca, 1498), [p.59].

[43] See n.12 above. E. E. Lowinsky's hypothesis that a small group of Franco-Flemish motets of mid-16th century conceal a 'secret chromatic art' consisting to a large extent of such 'chain reactions' depends on whether one finds the claim of a similarly experimental (or 'secret') status of the repertory plausible or not. See Lowinsky, *Secret Chromatic Art in the Netherlands Motet* (New York, 1946), and Lowinsky, 'Secret Chromatic Art Re-examined', in *Perspectives in Musicology*, ed. B. S. Brook, E. O. D. Downes and S. V. Solkema (New York, 1972), 91–135.

[44] See for example Philippe de Vitry, *Ars nova*, ed. G. Reaney, A. Gilles and J. Maillard, CSM, viii (1964), 22; Petrus frater dictus Palma ociosa, *Compendium*, 514f; Philippus de Caserta, *Regule contrapuncti*, in N. Wilkins, 'Some Notes on Philipoctus de Caserta (*c*1360?–*c*1435)', *Nottingham Mediaeval Studies*, viii (1964), 96; Prosdocimus de Beldemandis, *Contrapunctus*, 62–5, 78–81; Ugolino of Orvieto, *Declaratio*, bk2, pp.31, 44–7; Tinctoris, *Liber de natura*, 73ff, 81; Ornithoparchus, *Musice active*, bk1, chap.10; Vanneo, *Recanetum*, ff.15r, 74v.

[45] That the prohibition of *mi* against *fa* included the imperfect fourth can be seen clearly, for example, in Zarlino, *Le istitutioni harmoniche*, 169ff.

[46] See for example Philippus de Caserta, *Regule contrapuncti*, 99; Franchinus Gaffurius, *Extractus parvus musice*, ed. F. A. Gallo (Bologna, 1969), 128. For the distinction between *causa necessitatis* and *causa pulchritudinis*, see E. E. Lowinsky, 'Foreword', *Musica nova*, ed. H. C. Slim, MRM, i (1964), pp.v–xxi.

[47] Tinctoris, who disapproves of this exception, informs us that it was the common practice of his time and includes illuminating examples in *Liber de arte contrapuncti*, *Opera theoretica*, bk2, pp.143f. That the exception continued to be practised in the 16th century may be inferred from Giovanni del Lago, letter to Piero de Justinis, Venice, 3 June 1538, *I-Rvat* lat.5318, ff.102v–3r; Aaron, *Lucidario in musica*, ff.6v–7v, 14r; Aaron, *Compendiolo di molti dubbi, segreti et sentenze intorno al canto fermo, et figurato* (Milan, [after 1545]), chap.68; Zarlino, *Le istitutioni harmoniche*, 169f, 180f, 197f, 248f.

[48] See the examples in Tinctoris's text referred to in the preceding note.

[49] This we learn from Zarlino, *Le istitutioni harmoniche*, 180f, who adds that it was also the practice of some of the musicians of the past.

[50] Some theorists add the provision that the discord should last no longer than a part of the 'beat' (*mensura, tactus* or *battuta*). See Ramos de Pareia, *Musica practica*, 65; Gaffurius, *Practica musicae*, sig.ddiv; Spataro, letter to Aaron, Bologna, 27 November 1531, *I-Rvat* lat.5318, f.228r; del Lago, letter to de Justinis, ibid, ff.102v–3r; Aaron, *Lucidario in musica*, f.7v.

[51] Adrianus Petit Coclico, *Compendium musices* (Nuremberg, 1552/*R*1954), sigs.[Iivv]–Mr.

[52] Zarlino, *Le istitutioni harmoniche*, 177–80.

[53] See Jerome Cardan, *De musica*, in *Opera*, x (Lyons, 1663), 106.

[54] See especially J. Haar, 'False Relations and Chromaticism in Sixteenth-century Music', *JAMS*, xxx (1977), 391–418. See also J. van Benthem, 'Fortuna in Focus: Concerning "Conflicting" Progressions in Josquin's *Fortuna dun gran tempo*', *TVNM*, xxx (1980), 1–50; T. Noblitt, 'Chromatic Cross-relations and Editorial *Musica Ficta* in Masses of Obrecht', *TVNM*, xxxii (1982), 30–44; R. Toft, 'Pitch Content and Modal Procedure in Josquin's *Absalon, fili mi*', *TVNM*, xxxiii (1983), 3–27.

[55] Prosdocimus de Beldemandis, writing between 1425 and 1428, appears to have been the only theorist who considered the question in terms of whether it is preferable to inflect the lower or upper voice and even he concluded that one could inflect either the tenor or discant, but if both solutions sounded equally good, it was better to inflect the discant, because a change in the tenor might produce a clash with another voice written against it. *Contrapunctus*, 94f.

[56] See for example Tinctoris, *Liber de natura*, 73f, 81; Burtius, *Florum libellus*, 122; Ghiselin Danckerts, *Trattato sopra una differentia musicale*, *I-Rv* R56, f.407r.

[57] See for example Vitry, *Ars nova*, 22; Petrus frater dictus Palma ociosa, *Compendium*, 514ff; Philippus de Caserta, *Regule contrapuncti*, 98; Prosdocimus de Beldemandis, *Contrapunctus*, 78–81; Ugolino of Orvieto, *Declaratio*, bk2, pp.45f.

[58] Tinctoris, *Liber de natura*, 75f.

[59] Giovanni del Lago, letter to Piero de Justinis, Venice, 3 June 1538, *I-Rvat* lat.5318, f.102r–102v.

[60] See for example Marchetto da Padova, *Lucidarium*, 239, 245ff, 257ff, 261ff, 335ff, 347, 353; Johannes de Muris, *Quilibet affectans*, in *CS*, iii, 59f; Petrus frater dictus Palma ociosa, *Compendium*, 513f; Prosdocimus de Beldemandis, *Contrapunctus*, 80–87; Ugolino of Orvieto, *Declaratio*, bk2, pp.12f, 47f; bk3, p.248; Ramos de Pareia, *Musica practica*, 65ff; Burtius, *Florum libellus*, 118f; Gaffurius, *Practica musicae*, sigs.ddiiv–ddiiir; Aaron, *Toscanello*, bk2, chap.14; Lanfranco, *Scintille di musica*, 116; Zarlino, *Le istitutioni harmoniche*, 156f, 188, 190, 235f.

[61] See for example Gaffurius, *Extractus parvus musice*, 128, 75.

[62] For the sources of the following summary, see especially Johannes Tinctoris, *Terminorum musicae diffinitorium* ([Treviso, 1475]), sig.aiiiir; Hothby, *Tractatus quarundam regularum artis musicae*, f.12r–12v; Gaffurius, *Practica musicae*, sig.ddiijr; *Die Musica figurativa des Melchior Schanppecher*, ed. K. W. Niemöller, Beiträge zur rheinischen Musikgeschichte, ii/50 (Cologne and Krefeld, 1961), 26f; Cochlaeus, *Tetrachordum musices*, sigs.[Eviv]–Fr; Ornithoparchus, *Musice active*, bk4, chaps.4–5; Pietro Aaron, *Libri tres de institutione harmonica* (Bologna, 1516/*R*1971), f.49r–49v; Vanneo, *Recanetum*, ff.75v, 77r, 85v–7v, 93v; Giovanni del Lago, *Breve introduttione di musica misurata* (Venice, 1540), 37, 39f; Vicentino, *L'antica musica ridotta alla moderna practica* (Rome, 1555/*R*1959), ff.51v–2r, 53r–53v, 54v–8v; Zarlino, *Le istitutioni harmoniche*, 191, 193, 221–6, 250f, 320.

[63] See especially Aaron, *Toscanello*, bk2, chap.20 and 'Aggiunta', sigs.Iv–Iiir; Lanfranco, *Scintille di musica*, 126; Vicentino, *L'antica musica*, f.82r.

[64] See for example Prosdocimus de Beldemandis, *Contrapunctus*, 84f; Aaron, *Libri tres*, ff.50r–50v; see also theoretical sources referred to in n.65 below.

[65] On these cadences, see especially Marchetto da Padova, *Lucidarium*, 263, 353; Petrus frater dictus Palma ociosa, *Compendium*, 515; Prosdocimus de Beldemandis, *Tractatus musice speculative contra Marchetum de Padua*, in D. R. Baralli and L. Torri, 'Il "Trattato" di Prosdocimo de' Beldomandi contro Il "Lucidario" di Marchetto da Padova', *RMI*, xx (1913), 750ff; Ugolino of Orvieto, *Declaratio*, bk2, pp.51f; Ramos de Pareia, *Musica practica*, 66f, 101; Anonymous, *Quot sunt concordationes*, in *CS*, iii, 73; Gaffurius, *Practica musicae*, sig.eeiijr; Aaron, *Lucidario in musica*, ff.8v–9r; Lanfranco, *Scintille di musica*, 127; Vanneo, *Recanetum*, f.90r–90v. The Bent–Hughes hypothesis that the flat leading note was the normal choice for cadences on A because of the preference for the *recta b♭ over the ficta g♯* (see n.27 above) ignores the fact that the great majority of theorists from the early 14th to the late 16th century who exemplified the treatment of cadences on A, used the sharp leading note.

[66] This is shown not only by theoretical evidence cited in the preceding note, but also by practical evidence of source accidentals. See especially H. M. Brown, 'Accidentals and Ornamentation in Sixteenth-century Intabulations of Josquin's Motets', in *Josquin des Prez: New York 1971*, 475–522.

[67] See Ramos de Pareia, *Musica practica*, 101.

[68] See the evidence listed in n.60 above.

[69] Private communication from Professor Howard M. Brown.

[70] See, in addition to the evidence referred to in the following note, Lockwood, 'A Dispute on Accidentals', 38f.

[71] Zarlino, *Le istitutioni harmoniche*, 212–20. The theorist's discussion has been thoroughly elucidated in J. Haar, 'Zarlino's Definition of Fugue and Imitation', *JAMS*, xxiv (1971), 226–54.

[72] For evidence that 'conflicting signatures . . . seem to have been added arbitrarily, at the whim of the scribe', see Brown, 'Introduction', 160–67.

[73] *Guillaume Dufay: Opera omnia*, ed. H. Besseler, CMM, i/3 (1951), 119f, bars 72–8.

[74] In his 'Accidentals and Ornamentation in Sixteenth-century Intabulations', Howard Mayer Brown has demonstrated how much may be learned in this respect from a judicious evaluation of lute intabulations of vocal models. We have just as much to learn from accidentals in sources of vocal polyphony. Some fruitful research has already been conducted along these lines (see especially the literature referred to in n.54 above), but much remains to be done.

[75] For the assumptions which should govern editors of early polyphony in matters concerning implied accidentals, see especially L. Lockwood, 'A Sample Problem of *Musica Ficta*: Willaert's *Pater Noster*', in *Studies in Music History: Essays for Oliver Strunk* (Princeton, 1968), 161–82.

[76] In his work on the methodology of relating sources which share concordances, Allan Atlas concluded, in *The Cappella Giulia Chansonnier (Rome, Biblioteca Apostolica Vaticana, C.G.XIII.27)*, Musicological Studies, xxvii/1 (Brooklyn, 1975), 39–48, that source accidentals belong to those 'notational characteristics that do not indicate that the sources that share them are necessarily related, since their nature is such that two or more scribes could very well have happened upon them quite independently of one another' (ibid, p.46). The conclusion should probably be revised to exclude the 'unconventional' source accidentals.

CHAPTER VII

Tempo and Proportions

ALEJANDRO ENRIQUE PLANCHART

Among those aspects of the performance of medieval and Renaissance music that are not irretrievably lost to us, that of tempo is one of the most elusive and difficult to frame. The reasons for this go beyond the absence of concrete information about tempo for most repertories of music composed before 1600, and include the manner in which composers and performers throughout the history of Western music have regarded certain aspects of musical notation. David Fallows is surely right when he begins the article 'Tempo and Expression Marks' in *The New Grove Dictionary* with the remark that these 'are probably the most consistently ignored components of a musical score'.[1] Further, the history of tempo and tempo markings after the Renaissance, which includes not only the period after the invention of the metronome, but also the recent past – when composers have been able to record performances of their own music or to supervise such recordings – provides us with numerous examples of widely different and yet presumably authoritative tempos for a given work. The choice of tempo is often dependent not only upon aspects inherent in the work itself, but upon external circumstances such as the acoustical environment and on such imponderables as the familiarity of the work to performers and audience alike as a cultural artifact.[2] The audience often includes the composer, and composers have been known to change their view of the proper tempo of a work, sometimes quite drastically, over a period of time.[3]

The problems encountered in matters of tempo with the music of the recent past are compounded in the case of medieval and Renaissance music by added factors such as the absence of general indications of tempo in any source and by the source situation for a majority of the works, which survive only in copies far removed in time and place from the point of origin of the works themselves. The few specific mentions of tempo that we have from the Middle Ages and the early Renaissance are found in theoretical treatises that may not always faithfully reflect contemporary performance practice. Also, national differences in compositional style and instrumentarium that can be observed in the music and musical iconography of France and Italy in the 14th century suggest that similar differences may have also obtained in matters of tempo.

If an experienced performer of 18th- and 19th-century music can, even in the absence of tempo indications, derive some clue to a plausible tempo for a work from the notation itself, this is not possible with any of the monophonic repertories of the Middle Ages, where the notation offers us no guide to the tempo of any piece. In the case of polyphonic music, particularly after the advent of rhythmic notation in the 12th century, some aspects of the notation offer a few vague clues to plausible tempos for some repertories, particularly in relation to each other. One thing that can be seen, for example, is the gradual slowing down of note values as composers expanded the rhythmic depth field of music. Thus one can posit that the breve of a Notre Dame motet should move faster than that of a motet by Petrus de Cruce, and that this breve should in turn move faster than that of a late motet by Machaut. Indeed, theorists writing around 1300 confirm the existence of several different tempos,[4] but in the end we still do not know the actual rate of the slowing down nor the actual tempos at which early Notre Dame motets or those by Petrus de Cruce or Machaut were taken.

In this respect attempts have been made in this century to establish an objective foundation by studying the connection between such human phenomena as the pulse rate, the rhythm of breathing and that of relaxed walking, and some scale of tempos that may be used to measure the basic pulse of musics throughout different cultures and ages.[5] These studies are useful and have a measure of historical justification in that Renaissance theorists who discuss *tactus* relate it to the pulse rate and to other physical actions,[6] but all the caveats noted above concerning theoretical citations apply here as well, and the theory of *tactus* itself cannot be traced much further back than the end of the 15th century in the writings of theorists.

Turning now to specific repertories, we have no information on the tempo of chant during the centuries that saw the spread of Gregorian chant throughout the Carolingian empire and the rise of musical notation, but many of the earliest notated manuscripts, dating from the 10th to the early 11th century, have a wealth of signs that affect the duration of certain notes or groups of notes. These signs are not only the so-called 'rhythmic forms' of the neumes, but added traits such as episemata that affect either single notes or groups of notes, and the *litterae significativae* that also modify single notes or entire neumes, in particular the letters 't' (*tarde, tenere, trahere*), 'c' (*cito, celeriter*) and 'm' (*mediocriter*), though this last letter may refer to pitch as well as to duration.[7] These signs, together with the rhythmic forms of the neumes, have been one of the sources of a long and sometimes acrimonious controversy between scholars who contend that Gregorian chant in its earliest tradition made use of different and proportionally related note values, and those who contend that the chant moved in essentially equal note values with very subtle nuances of lengthening and shortening indicated by the signs in the early manuscripts.[8] The controversy is far from over and may never be put entirely to rest. The different theories and their consequences for the performance of chant are described in Chapter III.[9] At this time Eugène Cardine and his students have gathered a large amount of palaeographic evidence in support of an equalist view where the many rhythmic signs in the early manuscripts indicate durational nuances, and where the neumes themselves are an 'iconic notation'[10] with regard to articulation and phrasing,[11] that is, a notation where the physical shape of the neume, its aggregation or desegregation, conveys essential information. If Cardine and other semiologists are correct then the tempo of chant was one that allowed these details to be executed and heard even when sung by the schola and not just by the soloists.

In the later Middle Ages we find considerable evidence for two developments that may be related. One is the relatively early loss of the traditions of
chant performance involving duration nuances. They are already mentioned
as long dead by Aribo, writing $c1070$,[12] and their disappearance may be
deduced from the comments on performance in the *Commemoratio brevis*,
written at the beginning of the 10th century.[13] Apparently the loss of this
tradition led to an equalist performance with a prolongation reserved for
cadential and precadential tones. A second development is the slowing of the
tempo of chant to the point where single notes are the actual carriers of the
pulse. This had already begun in certain repertories as early as the 10th
century if we are to believe the *Commemoratio brevis*, and is confirmed by
numerous descriptions of the chanting of the psalms.[14] It led to the tradition
of *cantus planus* that survived until the Baroque era. Late medieval chant
sources and traditions have not been properly studied for 19th-century
scholars regarded them as corrupt and decadent. Some scholars have
suggested that the tempo of *cantus planus* is probably reflected accurately in
alternatim settings, for keyboard or vocal performance, composed in the 14th
and 15th centuries.[15] Chant manuscripts, from the 14th century on, began
transmitting works, mostly sequences and cantiones but also chants for the
Mass and Office, in mensural notation and showing definite rhythmic
organization. Presumably these *cantus fracti* were sung at the prevailing
tempo for mensural notation at the time and place where the manuscripts
that contain them were copied.[16]

For monophonic secular music of the Middle Ages we have, if anything,
even less information about tempo than we have for chant. The source
situation for almost all these repertories is parlous not just in terms of
rhythmic notation but in terms of any notation at all. A large number of
poems survives without music, and the melodies that we have show
considerable variation from source to source. It appears that the written
documents transmit at best a fragmentary and distant reflection of a number
of oral traditions that lay outside the realm of learned music. Thus it is not
safe to assume that the few and relatively late manuscripts that transmit
some of the melodies with a definite rhythmic organization, usually one
borrowed from polyphonic music, give us anything beyond one possible
approach to these pieces, and probably one unlikely to have been commonly
used in the milieu where the pieces originated. This caveat applies even more
to the use of songs or refrains embedded in polyphonic works as voices of a
conductus or a motet as guides to the possible performance of these songs as
independent pieces. In both cases the rhythmic structure derived from
polyphonic music may be a distortion of the song. In terms of tempo this
means that whatever we may gather about tempo in measured polyphonic
music cannot be uncritically transferred to the monophonic repertories.

As for independent information concerning the tempos in monophonic
music, there are a few pertinent passages in the treatise by Johannes de
Grocheo, written around 1300. Johannes mentions tempos for a few song
categories: *cantus coronatus*, which he calls monophonic conductus (*simplex
conductus*) – though the two works he cites are in fact French songs – which
moves slowly; *rondellus* (rondeau), which is sung slowly like a *cantus
coronatus*; and the *ductia*, which is light and swift in ascent and descent.[17]

Johannes mentions other monophonic song genres but says nothing about their tempo, and he is also exasperatingly ambiguous about what kind of piece a *cantus coronatus* is, though it is clear that it has a slow tempo. Near the end of the treatise, describing the chants of the Mass and the Office, Johannes offers the following comparisons with monophonic songs: the hymn is a solemn (*ornatus*) song in the manner of *cantus coronatus*, the Kyrie is sung slowly in perfect longs in the manner of *cantus coronatus*, the gradual and alleluia are sung in the manner of *stantipes* or of *cantus coronatus*, the sequence is sung in the manner of a *ductia*, the Credo is light in ascent and descent in the manner of a *ductia*, the offertory is composed in the manner of a monophonic conductus and sung in the manner of a *ductia* or *cantus coronatus*, the Sanctus is sung solemnly (*ornate*) and slowly, and the communion is composed like the introit or offertory and sung in the manner of the final phrase of a *ductia* or a *stantipes*.[18] The apparent contradictions in the comparisons led Hendrik van der Werf to call into question the validity of any of Johannes's statements about these genres.[19] But even allowing for inconsistencies and some play on words on the part of Johannes, his comparison between chant and monophonic song makes sense if one is aware of the nature and the state of the chant repertory at this time.

The references to the hymn and communion are probably not to tempo but to the nature of the hymn and to the position of the communion at the end of the Mass. Concerning actual tempos, the Kyrie and Sanctus are sung slowly, the sequence is sung fast and most likely in a patterned rhythm, the Credo moves lightly and perhaps also in a patterned rhythm, the gradual and alleluia are sung slowly or else like a *stantipes* (by implication faster than *cantus coronatus* but slower than *ductia*), and the offertory is sung either slow or fast and in a patterned rhythm. Now it is worth noting that in chant sources contemporary with, or slightly later than, Johannes, (*a*) it is sequences that are most often copied in some manner of quasi-modal rhythm with a pattern of longs and shorts, (*b*) that among Ordinary chants it is the Credos that most often appear in mensural notation and hence with shorter note values, and (*c*) that among the Proper chants it is for the offertory that a large and still unexplored repertory of rhythmic music was written.[20] This leaves the gradual and alleluia unexplained, but it is possible that in Paris around 1300 the manner of singing these chants was affected by a long tradition of organal settings, and then even when sung without polyphony the syllabic sections were sung slowly and the melismatic ones were sung at a faster tempo. It is then possible to posit that for Johannes *stantipes* moved faster than *cantus coronatus* but not as fast as *ductia*. This does not eliminate all ambiguities and problems in Johannes's remarks on monophonic songs, but it shows them to be not entirely arbitrary. A great deal remains to be done in the recovery of late chant and in finding descriptions of performances of medieval song that may tell us something about the rhythm and tempo of its different repertories. Also we must be cautious in assuming that anything written in Paris around 1300 may be useful in dealing with Galician, German or Italian music, or with the very different music of the south of France.

The tempos used in the repertories of early polyphony up to the Notre Dame school of the 12th century are almost completely obscure to us. The *Musica enchiriadis* and related treatises refer to organum as moving slowly (*morose*),[21] and it is reasonable to think that note-against-note polyphony moved at the same tempo as *cantus planus* or slightly slower. But we have no information to guide us on the tempo of the rhythmically free melismas of Aquitanian and Compostelan organa of the 12th century. The situation is different with the earliest layer of music of the Notre Dame school, the two-voice organa of Léonin, since this repertory is specifically discussed by a number of theorists working in Paris in the 13th century. To be sure, they are writing after the event, but they are part of the same cultural milieu as Léonin and his successors; witness the extraordinary excursus into history by Anonymous IV.

The central problem in performing Léonin's organa is not tempo but rhythm, specifically the rhythm of the sections in organum. A number of solutions have been proposed over the years by different scholars,[22] but the most recent scholarship shows that there were three different kinds of rhythmic organization in Léonin's music: (1) organum, a rhythmically unpatterned duplum moving over a held tenor; (2) copula, a rhythmically patterned duplum often set in repeating or sequential melodic phrases, moving over a held tenor; (3) discant, a rhythmically patterned duplum moving over a tenor consisting of ternary longs.[23] The unpatterned duplum of the *clausulae* in pure organum was probably not 'free', but made use, in an unsystematic manner, of the available note values.[24] The singer had the choice of dwelling longer on any note consonant with the tenor, and the ligation of the dupla in the manuscripts seems conceived to offer the singer a structured range of possible choices for melodic and rhythmic points of rest. Semiotic aspects of the notation make it unlikely that a singer trained to read ligatures rhythmically in order to be able to sing the *clausulae* in copula and in discant would, when singing a *clausula* in organum, sing a long note in the middle of a set of *currentes* or in the middle note of a ternary ligature, no matter how consonant with the tenor.[25] But it appears that the relative freedom offered by organum or even copula affected the tempo of the sections so that the *clausulae* in copula, and by implication those in organum, moved faster than *clausulae* in discant. This seems to be the meaning of Franco of Cologne's description of copula as a fast discant.[26]

The slowing down of note values in the 13th century can be observed in the repertory of the large motet collections copied at the end of the century, which have a retrospective character and seem to be organized in roughly chronological layers, such as Montpellier, Bibliothèque de l'Ecole de Méde-cine, MS H 196 [Mo], and Bamberg, Staatsbibliothek, MS lit.115 [Ba]. It is reflected in the writings of theorists; the early layer of *Discantus positio vulgaris*, which shows the state of affairs around 1225, refers to semibreves as notes *ultra mensuram* because they move too fast,[27] though some conducti and numerous early motets (but no discant *clausulae*) show three semibreves to the breve instead of the more usual two.[28] Mentions of semibreves by Johannes de Garlandia are not consistent; he uses that term also to designate the note value later called a *brevis altera*, which indicates that the semibreve had not yet emerged as a completely independent and measurable note value.[29] But by the time Franco of Cologne writes his treatise (c1280), the tempo of note values has slowed down to the point that it is possible to distinguish between major and minor semibreves.[30] Petrus Le Viser, whose

work postdates Franco, is cited by Robert de Handlo as giving three tempos
for the breve: *mos lascivus* that allows two or three semibreves to the breve,
mos mediocris that allows up to five semibreves to the breve, if these are sung
melismatically, and *mos longum* that allows more than five semibreves to the
breve and permits each to have a syllable set to it.[31] It is worth noting that in
Handlo's colloquy Viser describes on his own only the *mos lascivus* and the
mos mediocris, and that his description of the *mos longum* is only implied in
response to a comment by Petrus de Cruce.[32]

The unit of time measurement used by nearly all 13th-century theorists –
later called the *mensura* – is the *tempus*, which is represented in notation by
the *brevis recta*. The speed of the *tempus*, however, is defined only in relative
terms. Franco's definition is the clearest and most influential one: 'Unus
tempus appellatur illud quod est minimum in plenitudine vocis'.[33] The
qualification 'in plenitudine vocis' affects the adjective 'minimum' and
makes it clear that the *tempus* is not the shortest singable value. It is rather a
moderately fast value that serves as the centre of the system (as the *brevis
recta* does in the notation) rather than as one of the extremes. From the
comments of the *Discantus positio vulgaris* we may gather that the speed of
the *tempus* was somewhat faster early in the century, and within a generation
after Franco the *tempus* could be taken at three different speeds depending
upon the notational context and the text underlay. This is all that can be said
with any certainty about the speed of the *tempus* up to this point.

Further slowing down of the *tempus* is documented in the writings of
Jacques de Liège and Philippe de Vitry in the early 14th century. Jacques,
in a polemic against the moderns (by whom he means Johannes de Muris
and Philippe de Vitry), states that they sing the *mensura* so slowly that their
perfect breve equals the perfect long of the ancients (that is, of Franco).[34]
This is confirmed by Philippe de Vitry's *Ars nova*, where *tempus perfectum* is
divided into three categories, *minimum*, *medium* and *maius*. In *tempus
perfectum minimum* the semibreve moves so fast that it cannot be divided
except by semiminims. *Tempus perfectum medium* allows the semibreve to be
divided into two minims, and *tempus perfectum maius* allows division into
three minims.[35] In contrast, *tempus imperfectum* has only two categories,
minimum and *maius*. The first permits the semibreve to be divided into two
minims and the second permits it to be divided into three minims.[36] Thus it
is clear that the two imperfect *tempora* and the *medium* and *maius* perfect
tempora are interrelated and represent the four prolations that the author of
Les règles de la seconde réthorique credits him with inventing.[37] But *tempus
perfectum minimum* is something else; its semibreves can be divided only by
semiminims, that is, they move as fast as the minims of the other four
tempora, and it is this *tempus* that Vitry specifically connects with the
teachings of Franco.[38] Though the author of *Les règles de la seconde réthorique*
claims that Vitry was the inventor of the prolations, the term is not used in
that sense in the *Ars nova* but in a number of treatises derived from his
teachings.[39] The first writer actually to describe the division of a semibreve
into two or three minims as minor or major prolation is Petrus frater dictus
Palma ociosa.[40] Nevertheless, one of the principal implications of the
writings of Vitry and his followers is that the minim has emerged as a note
value in its own right and has become the basic unchanging note value of all

tempora and prolations, that the semiminim exists as a theoretical possibility (it is not used in any of Vitry's surviving compositions) and that the minim of Vitry's time moves as fast as the Franconian semibreve. Once again, we are not told what the duration of this or any other note value is in absolute terms.

The cumulative impression given by theoretical writings and by the notation of the motet collections is that the surface tempo of polyphonic music remained relatively constant, but that note values used to signify this tempo changed. Such a change implies a slowing down of the tempo within each repertory to the point where composers felt the need to introduce a new subdivision and, so to speak, restore the balance. Such a slowing down need not have been a deliberate choice of composer or performer, but rather something akin to the noted slowing down of the tempo in Wagner's operas. There are, of course, mentions of different tempos in connection not with a historical process but with different genres such as Johannes de Grocheo's remarks about the different types of monophonic music. Similarly, Franco of Cologne (as reported by Handlo) and Johannes de Grocheo mention that the hocket is a fast piece.[41] But again, in this case we are also faced with the reworking of three of the best-known hockets in the Bamberg codex which are presented in two manners, *ad longum* and *ad brevem*.

The first recorded attempt to establish the tempo of polyphony by an external point of reference comes from the middle of the 14th century and from an Italian theorist, Johannes Vetulus de Anagnia. The attempt may be a consequence of the development of mechanical clocks in France and Italy in the 13th and 14th centuries, and the pride that the Italian cities took in the new invention.[42] Vetulus is working with the trecento notational system, which has its roots in the theories of Franco but differs in a number of important aspects from the notation of the French Ars Nova.[43] The principal early source is the *Pomerium* of Marchetto da Padova, and one of the ways in which it shows its indebtedness to Franconian doctrine is in the implied equation of the *divisio ternaria* of the breve with the perfect breve of Franco.[44] It would be possible to suggest that the *diviso ternaria* of Vetulus could approximate the tempo of Vitry's *tempus perfectum minimum*.

At the heart of Vetulus's system is the mathematical measurement of time by astronomical and mechanical means. One divides time into years, months, weeks, days, quadrants, hours, points, moments, *unciae* and atoms. The day is divided into four quadrants, each quadrant has six hours, each hour has four points, each point has ten moments, each moment has 12 *unciae* and each *uncia* has 54 atoms.[45] The atom is then $\frac{1}{432}$ of a modern minute, and the *uncia* is therefore 7.5 seconds. Vetulus then states that 'ab ista uncia musicus accipit tempus rectum et perfectum, tamen neque maius neque minus sed mediocriter. . . . Et istud tempus dividitur in tres partes . . . et dicitur tempus perfecte medie quod dicitur tempus breve'.[46] From the context of the treatise it is also clear that the *tempus perfectum medium* is the *tempus* of the *divisio novenaria*. Thus it could appear at first sight that according to Vetulus the breve of the *divisio novenaria* takes one *uncia*, and thus moves at MM8. The *semibrevis maior* moves at MM24 and the *semibrevis minor* at MM72. Already Curt Sachs pointed out that this was surely too slow a tempo for any trecento work using the *divisio novenaria*,[47] but Salvatore Gullo has argued in an ingenious and convincing manner that

Vetulus's text cited above can be construed to mean that the *uncia* is to be divided into three parts, and that the duration of the *tempus perfectum medium* is in fact one third of an *uncia*.[48] This yields the following tempos for the note values in the *divisio novenaria*: breve = MM24, *semibrevis maior* = MM72, *semibrevis minima* = MM216. It is perhaps no coincidence that this interpretation places the note value that is the probable carrier of the *tactus* at a value close to that of the human pulse. This does not remove all difficulties from Vetulus's text, but it suggests that Gullo's reading may indeed be correct.

From his description of the divisions, it is clear that Vetulus has in mind a system where the minim remains constant in all divisions and the other values contract and expand according to the number of minims. The tempos for the note values in each division would then be as shown in Table 1. We must remember that not all Italian theorists favour the minim equivalence used by Vetulus. Most early trecento writers suggest that the perfect breve remains constant in all divisions with the imperfect breve as two thirds of a perfect breve.[49] If we use the *novenaria* as our reference, this yields the tempos for each division as shown in Table 2. A notable aspect of the tempos

TABLE 1

Division	Breve	SB maior	SB minor	SB minima
Duodenaria	18	54	108	216
Novenaria	24	72	—	216
Octonaria	27	54	108	216
Senaria perfecta	36	108	—	216
Senaria imperfecta	36	72	—	216
Quaternaria	54	108	—	216

TABLE 2

A Perfect tempus	Breve	SB maior	SB minor	SB minima
Duodenaria	24	72	144	288
Novenaria	24	72	—	216
Senaria perfecta	24	72	—	144

B. Imperfect tempus	Breve	SB maior	SB minor	SB minima
Octonaria	36	72	144	288
Senaria imperfecta	36	72	—	216
Quaternaria	36	72	—	144

given in Table 2 is that they result in semibreve equivalence among all divisions, something for which there is considerable theoretical evidence in later Italian writers, who seem to have adapted this approach also to the notation that they eventually adopted from France in the 15th century.[50] Vetulus's notion of minim equivalence appears to be a French trait in his thinking, and like Marchetto he appeals to the authority of Franco in a number of places in his treatise. Thus it may be possible in this case to posit a comparable tempo of MM216 for the minim of the central Ars Nova on the authority of Vetulus's writing.[51]

Comparing the tempos given in Tables 1 and 2 with those of some of the performances of 14th-century music given by 20th-century specialists in this repertory, it is interesting to note that the tempos of Table 1 are not greatly different from what one encounters in performances of French Ars Nova music rather than that of the Italian trecento. Performances of trecento works, in terms of tempo, seem too dependent on the vagaries of transcription and the often tacit use of multiple rates of reduction by modern editors of this repertory, but the impression remains that for much of the trecento music Vetulus's scheme of tempos may be still too slow and far too rigid.

The slowing down of the tempo of note values continues in the 15th and 16th centuries, but it is reflected less in the addition of shorter subdivisions – though flagged semiminims are found from about 1420 and *fusae* after 1450 – than in the use of proportions. We have no theoretical writings about tempo for much of the early 15th century, and when theorists begin to concern themselves with it in the second half of the century, their work takes two main forms, a discussion of *tactus* and the explication of notational proportions.

In all discussions of *tactus* it is defined simply as a motion of the hand up and down (*levatio* and *positio*) that is used to establish the basic pulse of the music. As noted above, most theorists relate the *tactus* to the human pulse.[52] In duple time both motions of the hand are equal, but in triple time the *positio* is twice as long as the *levatio*. It appears that the *tactus* was meant to stay constant throughout a composition, though there is also some small amount of evidence that it could vary slightly, and even more evidence that it could change to some degree from work to work.[53] The tempo of the note values, however, is affected drastically depending on which value is connected with the *tactus*; in normal *tempus*, when notes have their full value (*integer valor*), the *tactus* falls on the semibreve, but in *tempus diminutum* the *tactus* falls on the breve.[54] The simplest way of notating *tempus diminutum* was by drawing a line through the mensuration signs, as shown in Table 3.

But from the beginning, these signs carried an ambiguous meaning in certain cases. There is no doubt that in all cases the note values in ₵ moved twice as fast as those in C when these two signs were used simultaneously or

TABLE 3

Integer valor	Tempus diminutum
⊙	⏀
○	⏀
₡	₵
C	₵

successively, creating a simple 1:2 proportion between ₡ and ₵. But in every other case it was possible to have a diminution of the note values by one third. To be sure, composers were far from consistent in their notation, and depending on the context a sign such as Φ may mean diminution by half or by one third when used against ☉. By far the most common difference may be summarized as follows: in simultaneous use, diminution by one half is always the rule, in successive use, when the mensuration changes in all voices, diminution by one third may sometimes obtain.[55]

The relationship between perfect and imperfect time becomes a more ambiguous problem since there is evidence of at least three national traditions, all of which may be found side by side in the music of some of the more peripatetic composers of the 15th century. Of these traditions only the Italian one has been studied in detail.[56] The French tradition implies minim equivalence between all four combinations of *tempus* and *prolatio* and a 1:2 ratio between *integer valor* and *tempus diminutum* at the semibreve level. The Italian tradition, under the influence of trecento notation, gives preference to breve equivalence between the difference mensurations, which leads to a host of complex relationships between them,[57] as well as the use of a number of other symbols such as Ɔ and Ꝺ and numerical ratios to express these relationships. The English tradition is the least well understood; it appears to be closely related to the Italian one but the English were apparently reluctant to use the slash through the mensuration signs, preferring to allow the notational context of the music to make the performer aware of *tempus diminutum*.[58] The desire on the part of musicians to circumvent the minim equivalence of the French Ars Nova notation led, in the last decades of the 15th century, to the use of proportions, which were expressed through the conventional mensuration signs and often used just as the mensuration signs were – that is, as non-cumulative. In the course of the 15th century, mostly on account of the writings of Tinctoris, the use of mensuration signs to indicate proportional relationships was gradually abandoned in favour of the clearer notation by means of fractions.[59] By the middle of the 15th century the mensurations ☉ and ₵ were obsolete and were replaced by different uses of Φ, ₡3 and ○3, but were resurrected as proportional signatures, where a minim in ₵ or ☉ equals a semibreve in ₡ or ○.[60]

Under certain conditions composers sought to have the mensuration signs indicate not *tempus* and *prolatio*, that is, the relation of breve to semibreve and semibreve to minim, but rather *modus* and *tempus*, that is, the relation of long to breve and breve to semibreve. With these signs the *tactus* shifts from the semibreve to the breve. The signs in question are ₡2, ○2, ₡3 and ○3. They were used in combination with *integer valor* mensurations to indicate very fast-moving parts.[61] But the first two of these signs, ₡2 and ○2, appear also as primary mensurations in a number of works composed in the 1440s by Guillaume Dufay.[62] Their meaning in such a context is not immediately apparent, but it seems to be connected with the actual tempo of the music, that is, the signs demand a tempo different from what would be obtained by notating the piece with *integer valor*. The shift in note values and the organization of the *integer valor* and the *modus* notation signs is shown in Table 4 (p.136). A summary of the various proportional meanings of the combinations of signs and figures from *c*1400 to *c*1520 is shown below the table.

TABLE 4

Sign:	C	O	Ȼ	⊙	C2	O2	Ȼ3	⊙3
Long:	—	—	—	—	2B	3B	2B	3B
Breve:	2SB	3SB	2SB	3SB	2SB	2SB	3SB	3SB
Semibreve:	2MI	2MI	3MI	3MI	—	—	—	—

(*a*) Mensuration signs with *integer valor*.
These are the foundation of the proportional system and all other signs will be described in relation to them.

C Organization: (L = 2B), B = 2S, S = 2M.
1. Normally it has minim equivalence with O (this is always the case in simultaneous use).
2. In the early 15th century, C has minim equivalence with Ȼ and ⊙, but this changes around 1450 on account of the special meaning the last two signs acquire.
3. In English pieces, C with motion mainly in breves and semibreves appears to have been intended to produce a proportional shift of 4:3 in relation to O.[63] Some continental composers (for example, Dufay) adopted this practice, but most continental composers and scribes used Ȼ to indicate this relationship (see below). In a few instances they also used C with breve–semibreve motion to indicate a truly slow tempo.[64]

O Organization: (L = 2B), B = 3S, S = 2M.
1. Normally it has minim equivalence with C (this is always the case in simultaneous use).
2. In the early 15th century O has minim equivalence with Ȼ and ⊙ (in the French tradition); this changes around 1450 on account of the special meaning the last two signs acquire.

Ȼ Organization: (L = 2B), B = 2S, S = 3M.
1. In the early 15th century it has minim equivalence with C, O and ⊙ in the French tradition. Some Italian works call for breve equivalence instead.
2. By 1430 it begins to be replaced by Φ, and it is obsolete by 1450. After this time it is used mainly as a sign of augmentation, where a minim in Ȼ equals a semibreve in C or O. Ockeghem and a few other composers use it with both the old and the new meaning, sometimes in the same work.[65]

⊙ Organization: (L = 2B), B = 3S, S = 3M.
1. In the early 15th century it has minim equivalence with C, O and Ȼ in the French tradition. Some Italian works call for breve equivalence instead.
2. By 1430 it begins to be replaced by Φ, and it is obsolete by 1450. After this time it is used mainly as a sign of augmentation, where a minim in ⊙ equals a semibreve in C or O. Ockeghem and a few other composers use it with both the old and the new meaning, sometimes in the same work.

(*b*) Mensuration signs for *tempus diminutum*

Ȼ Organization: same as C.
1. In simultaneous use with O or C it calls for a 2:1 proportion at the minim level. In the early 15th century it also calls for a 2:1 proportion in relation to Ȼ and ⊙.
2. In successive use without overlaps it calls for a 2:1 proportion at the minim level

in relation to C and either the same proportion in relation to O, or else in 3:4 ratio at the semibreve level. The successive relationship O to ₵ is both the most common in works around 1450 and the most vexing in its interpretation. The 3:4 relationship at the semibreve level between O and ₵, used intuitively by many modern specialist performers as a matter of common sense, has for the most part only indirect support in theoretical literature of the time, though it can be considered as a consequence of the Italian tradition of breve equivalence and also as a result of continental adaptation of English mensural practices. Recent studies of the proportional design of a number of works, however, have lent new weight to such an interpretation.[66]

3. By the early 16th century ₵ becomes the normal sign for virtually all music in duple metre.

Ⓞ Organization: same as O.
1. In simultaneous use with O, ₵ and ☉, in the early 15th century it calls for a 2:1 proportion at the minim level.
2. In successive use with O it sometimes calls for diminution by a third of the note values, thus an imperfect breve in O equals a perfect breve in Ⓞ.[67]
3. In the late 15th century and in the early 16th century, the successive use of O, ₵, Ⓞ calls for a 4:3 proportion between O and ₵ (see above), but minim equivalence between ₵ and Ⓞ. Thus for example in the several instances in Josquin's masses where the Kyrie shows the organization O to ₵ to Ⓞ, three semibreves in O equal four in ₵, but then this faster semibreve remains constant when the piece shifts to Ⓞ.[68]

₵ Organization: same as C.
1. Rarely found, indicates a 2:1 proportion in relation to C.
2. In exceptional cases, such as Ockeghem's *Missa prolationum*, it is used as a subsidiary sign to indicate an acceleration of the tempo in C, probably in a 3:2 ratio.[69]

Ⓒ Organization: same as ☉.
1. Indicates a 2:1 proportion in relation to ☉, or in successive use sometimes a diminution by a third.[70]
2. Used exceptionally in the late 15th century (for example Ockeghem, *Missa prolationum*) to indicate an acceleration of the tempo under ☉.

Ɔ Organization: (L = 2B), B = 2S, S = 2M.
1. Indicates a 4:3 proportion at the minim and semibreve levels in relation to O and ☉, its function in successive usage is taken over by ₵ or C with breve–semibreve movement after 1450, but it remains in use as the one mensuration sign capable of indicating such a proportion in simultaneous use.
2. Occasionally used to indicate a 2:1 ratio in relation to C.

Ɖ Organization: same as Ɔ.
1. Extremely rare, it indicates a 4:3 proportion at the minim and semibreve levels in relation to Ⓞ and ☉. Found occasionally in instances of scribal confusion or 'overkill' where Ɔ should be used.[71]

C3 Organization: (L = 2B), B = 2S, S = 2M (or B = 3S, S = 2M).
1. This sign calls for a 3:2 proportion at the minim (or at the semibreve) level in relation to C.
2. In the early 15th century this sign provides for an organization similar to that of C, but as a temporary change in the context of C. In mid-15th-century pieces the sign is used with an organization like that of O (3:2 at the S level) but with a S moving faster than that of O or C. In the later 15th century, when C is an augmentation signature, C3 permits the writing of imperfect *tempus* with major prolation.

O3 Organization: (L = 2B), B = 3S, S = 3M.
1. In the early 15th century this sign calls for a 3:2 proportion at the minim level in relation to O.
2. In the later 15th century, when the sign ☉ is an augmentation sign, O3 permits the writing of perfect *tempus* with major prolation.

₵3. Organization: same as C3.
1. This sign calls for a 3:2 proportion at the minim (or at the semibreve) level in

relation to ₵. In the late 15th century it is used as an opening sign to denote a fast tempo with the organization of Ȼ3.

2. In the 16th century ₵3 becomes the standard manner of notating triple metre within the context of ₵. Depending on context, it is used to indicate a 3:2 or a 3:1 proportion at the semibreve level in relation to ₵.

Ф3. Organization: same as O3.

1. This sign calls for a 3:2 proportion at the minim level in relation to Ф. In the late 15th century it is used as an opening sign to indicate a fast tempo for pieces in perfect *tempus* with major prolation.

(*c*) Signs indicating *modus* and *tempus*

The indication of the *modus*, that is the division of the long into two or three breves, could be done by the length of the long rests: a rest covering three spaces on the staff indicates that longs are perfect (*modus maior*), one covering two indicates that longs are imperfect (*modus minor*). Theorists discuss this at length and offer alternative and more precise notations which are almost universally absent from practical sources.[72] In any case, this manner of indicating the *modus* has no proportional significance in terms of the notation or the tempo. The indication of the modus by a figure in the mensuration sign, however, does affect the tempo of the note values.

C2 Organization: L = 2B, B = 2S, (S = 2M).

1. Shifts the beat to the breve, which moves as fast as a semibreve in C. It is found as a primary mensuration or used against both C and O to notate very fast tempos.

O2 Organization: L = 3B, B = 2S, (S = 2M).

1. Shifts the beat to the breve, which moves as fast as a semibreve in O. Is found both as a primary mensuration or used against both C and O to notate very fast tempos.

Ȼ3 Organization: L = 2B, B = 3S, (S = 2M).

1. Shifts the beat to the breve, which moves as fast as a semibreve in Ȼ (old style) or C3. Rarely found in any of the practical sources.

O3 Organization: L = 3B, B = 3S, (S = 2M).

1. Shifts the beat to the breve, which moves as fast as a semibreve in O (old style) or O3. Rarely found in any of the practical sources.

Ф3/2 Organization: (L = 2B), B = 3S, S = 3M.

1. Found in some practical sources of the 16th century (Rore, *Missa Vivat felix Hercules*) to indicate a 3:2 proportion at the semibreve level following a section in ₵, part of the kind of semiological overkill produced by the decay of the proportional system and of the understanding of the old *tempus perfectum*.[73]

Composers of the 15th century used a number of signs, particularly C and ₵, but after 1450 also O, Ȼ, Ф and ₵ as subsidiary signs without an absolute meaning but rather one that depended entirely in the context created by O, C and ₵ (but rarely Ф).[74]

Apart from the mensuration and proportion indications combining signs and figures, composers used simple figures and fractions to indicate proportions. The one commonly used figure, 3, indicating a shift to triplets at the minim level in O and C as well as in Ф and ₵, has been considered above as part of the discussion of the combined signs: Ф3, O3, C3 and ₵3. When fractions were used, the numerator indicated the new value and the denominator the old one; thus 3/2 means 'three in the time of two'. Usually the note value affected is the semibreve, though upon occasion the minim may be affected. This manner of indicating proportions was overwhelmingly endorsed by the theorists, particularly Tinctoris, but it was used far less frequently by the composers. Finally, proportional shifts expressed in the manner of a written indication, a canon, are common, particularly in the tenors of isorhythmic motets and early cantus firmus masses.

The most common proportional notation throughout the period, however, was the use of 'coloration', that is, changing from the prevailing note-colour of the piece: from void (white) to solid (black), or from solid black to solid red or black void in order to express usually hemiola proportions in any mensuration with triple division, or else triplet notation within duple metres. The most sophisticated use of coloration was that of English composers of the late 14th and early 15th centuries, who used simultaneously black full, black void, red full and red void notation. Their notational practice was not always understood by their contemporaries on the Continent, and in the surviving English repertory in continental manuscripts numerous scribal errors can be traced to imperfect attempts by the continental scribes to render the 'four-colour' English notation into the 'two-colour' notation of the Continent.[75]

The description of the proportions given above is based almost entirely on practical sources. The 15th- and 16th-century theoretical literature on proportions is immense,[76] but much of it has little relevance to practice.[77] In efforts to be thorough, theorists discuss dozens of proportional relationships that are never found in practical sources and time and again quote each other's examples. The most influential treatise was the *Proportionale musices* of Johannes Tinctoris,[78] which was widely read and influenced virtually every theorist writing afterwards. A French-trained musician writing and working in Italy, and a particularly systematic thinker, Tinctoris is suspicious of the use of mensuration signs or *modus* signs to indicate proportions. After a short discussion of what he considers to be the incorrect use of signs by some composers, he dismisses the signs themselves: 'these signs are so frivolous, so wrong and so remote from all appearance of reason'.[79] In addition, Tinctoris takes a strong stand against the Italian tradition of equating semibreves in the different mensurations and proportions, since this inevitably leads to the equation of perfect with imperfect values, and advocates the principle of minim equivalence in all *integer valor* mensurations and of equating only comparable values in proportions.[80] Tinctoris's views were adopted by Gaffurius, but led to a bitter controversy between Gaffurius and other theorists who followed Tinctoris and such theorists as Ramos de Pareia and Spataro, who understood the old Italian tradition and knew well the notational practices of the 15th century. In the end, Tinctoris's view prevailed, largely because he is consistent and systematic, but it must be remembered that in his *Proportionale* he is writing as something of a crusader, and proposing a notational practice and proportional usage not common at the time. Given the number of times that he takes issue with Dufay, Ockeghem and Busnois on their use of proportions, it seems unwise to use him, without any further checking, as a primary authority on 15th-century proportions. Part of Tinctoris's systematic approach to proportions is his preference for numerical ratios over signs in the indication of proportion, a practice found far more often in theoretical works than in practical sources.

German theorists of the 15th century adopted essentially the Italian view of diminution and proportions, albeit with some changes in such matters as diminution by a third,[81] but with Andreas Ornithoparchus[82] and Sebald Heyden[83] the views of Tinctoris found their way into Germany as well. The conflation of different traditions on the part of German theorists makes their writings occasionally ambiguous and contradictory,[84] so it is not always entirely possible to rely upon them even in dealing with proportional problems within the German repertory.

In Italy and France after 1520 the majority of the theorists are, to all intents and purposes, in agreement with Tinctoris, but most of the music written between 1520 and 1600 makes virtually no use of proportional notation, and even the old *tempus perfectum* has virtually disappeared, being replaced by ₵3. This obtains also for the Spanish repertory of the 16th century, which is dependent upon Italian traditions with the exception of the music of the vihuelists. The English theorists, particularly Morley, also transmit essentially the views of Tinctoris and of his Italian followers, but in English practical sources of the late 16th century, notably the several prints of music by William Byrd, a number of archaic mensuration signs, for example ₵, do appear, but the musical context makes it clear that Byrd's ₵ is exactly the same signature as the continental ₵3.

Proportional notation reappears in the early 17th century in the works of the Gabrielis, Monteverdi, Schütz and others, and is discussed extensively by Praetorius in the *Syntagma musicum*.[85] But by the end of the 16th century the old proportional system was not well understood, and signs and figures are often reinterpreted by the theorists and used in idiosyncratic manners by the composers. Perhaps the most common reinterpretation is the use of the figure 3 to indicate not a 3:2 proportion at whatever level the notational context indicates, but rather a true *proportio tripla*, that is, a 3:1 proportion, thus requiring the use of the fraction 3/2 to indicate *sesquialtera*.[86] The decadent proportional system of the 17th century, however, is one of the least well studied or understood aspects of the early Baroque.[87]

Both theorists and practical sources in the 16th century begin to indicate also non-proportional changes of tempo, including ritenutos and accelerandos, by means of added instructions to the performer in the form of the by now familiar Italian terminology or of suitable words in the vernacular of the place of publication. Some theorists also counsel the consideration of the text being sung as one of the determinants of tempo.[88] The earliest use of words to indicate tempos appears in the editions of the Spanish vihuelists, beginning with Luis de Milán, who gives elaborate indications of the tempos for different works;[89] this practice was then followed by a number of other Spanish musicians.[90] Thus at the end of the 16th century we encounter the beginnings of the tradition of tempo indications by means of mostly Italian words that obtains to the end of the 18th century and beyond.

Notes

[1] D. Fallows, 'Tempo and expression marks', *Grove6*, xviii, 677.

[2] See for example R. Taruskin, 'On Letting the Music Speak for Itself: some Reflections on Musicology and Performance', *JM*, i (1982), 339–41.

[3] No studies of the tempos in recordings by such composers as Stravinsky or Hindemith have appeared, but see D. Kämper, 'Zur Frage der Metronombezeichnungen Robert Schumanns', *AMw*, xxi (1964), 140–55; P. Stadlen, 'Beethoven and the Metronome – I', *ML*, xlviii (1967),

330–49; and D. Fallows, 'Tempo and Expression', 678 (about the recorded timings of Wagner's operas in Bayreuth).

[4] Petrus Le Viser, cited by Robert de Handlo in his *Regule*, in *CS*, i, 387–9, mentions three tempos, *mos longus*, *mos mediocris* and *mos lascivus*. Anonymous IV has nine, three each for the slow, middle and fast motions. See F. Reckow, *Der Musiktraktat des Anonymous 4* (Wiesbaden, 1967), i, 83. Other 13th- and 14th-century theorists give also similar sets of tempos.

[5] J. Smits van Waesberghe, *De muzische mens: zijn motoriek* (Amsterdam, 1971).

[6] Bartolomeo Ramos de Pareia, *Musica practica*, ed. J. Wolf (Leipzig, 1901/*R*1968), 83; Franchinus Gaffurius, *Practica musicae* (Milan, 1496/*R*1967), bk2, chap.1; Eng. trans., C. A. Miller, MSD, xx (1968), 70; Giovanni Maria Lanfranco, *Scintille di musica* (Brescia, 1533/ *R*1970), 67; Lodovico Zacconi, *Practica di musica* (Venice, 1592/*R*1967), i, 21.

[7] See J. Froger, 'L'épître de Notker sur les "lettres significatives" ', *Etudes grégoriennes*, v (1962), 23–72.

[8] Mensuralist scholars, proposing a measured and proportionally varied use of rhythmic values in chant, include George Louis Houdard, Hugo Riemann, Antoine Dechevrens, Peter Wagner, Ewald Jammers, J. W. A. Wollaerts and Gregory Murray. There are virtually as many different theories as there are scholars. The equalist view is essentially that of the Benedictines of Solesmes, proposed at first by Joseph Pothier, but subjected to a thorough revision by his student, André Mocquereau, in *Le nombre musical grégorien* (Tournai, 1908–27). A new approach to equalism, closer in some ways to that of Pothier, has been the work of Eugène Cardine in 'Sémiologie grégorienne', *Etudes grégoriennes*, xi (1970), 1–158, available also as a separate monograph in English, *Gregorian Semiology*, trans. R. Fowels (Solesmes, 1982).

[9] See above, p.46ff.

[10] On the concept of iconic notation see L. Treitler, 'The Early History of Music Writing in the West', *JAMS*, xxxv (1982), 238–41.

[11] Cardine, 'Sémiologie'. A number of semiological studies by Cardine's students has appeared in *Etudes grégoriennes* from 1970 on. For a bibliography of Cardine's writings and of theses directed by him to 1980 see *Ut mens concordet voci: Festschrift Eugène Cardine* (St Ottilien, 1980), 488–94.

[12] Aribo, *De musica*, ed. J. Smits van Waesberghe, CSM, ii (1951), 49.29.

[13] *Commemoratio brevis de tonis et psalmis modulandis*, ed. T. Bailey (Ottawa, 1979), 102–7.

[14] See S. J. P. van Dijk, 'Medieval Terminology and Methods of Psalm Singing', *MD*, vi (1952), 7–26.

[15] Mother Thomas More, 'The Performance of Plainsong in the Later Middle Ages and the Sixteenth Century', *PRMA*, xcii (1965–6), 121–34.

[16] Sources for chant in mensural notation have been ignored by modern scholarship and we have no clear view of their distribution. Among them a Moosburg Gradual, *D-Mu* 156; *D-Mbs* Clm9508; *CS-Pnm* Mus.11C7; *CH-SGs* 546; *A-Wn* 15501. These manuscripts contain largely *cantus planus*.

[17] E. Rohloff, *Die Quellenhandschriften zum Musiktraktat des Johannes de Grocheio* (Leipzig, 1972), 130–32.

[18] ibid, 156, 162–6.

[19] H. van der Werf, *The Chansons of the Troubadours and Trouvères* (Utrecht, 1972), 153–5.

[20] The texts of the rhythmic offertories are edited in Analecta Hymnica Medii Aevi, xlix, ed. C. Blume and G. M. Dreves (Leipzig, 1906), 300–342. Most of the sources used by the editors are very late, but some include not only 12th- and 13th-century Parisian chant manuscripts (for example, *F-Pn* lat.13252), but also two central sources of Parisian polyphony, *I-Fl* Plut.29.1 [F] and *DK-W* 677 [W].

[21] *Musica et scholica enchiriadis una cum aliquibus tractatulis adiunctis*, ed. H. Schmid (Munich, 1981), 38, 89, 97.

[22] This is discussed in Chapter V.

[23] The common duplum pattern in copula and discant became later known as the first rhythmic mode, the tenor pattern in discant forms the basis for the fifth rhythmic mode. The most recent studies are F. Reckow, *Die Copula* (Wiesbaden, 1972), and 'Das Organum', *Gattungen der Musik in Einzeldarstellungen*, ed. W. Arlt *et al* (Berne, 1973), 434–79; E. Sanders, 'Consonance and Rhythm in the Organum of the 12th and 13th Centuries', *JAMS*, xxxiii (1980), 264–86; J. Yudkin, 'The *Copula* According to Johannes de Garlandia', *MD*, xxxiv (1980), 67–84; and Yudkin, 'The Rhythm of Organum Purum', *JM*, ii (1983), 355–76.

[24] The system of rhythmic modes appears to be the work of Pérotin. Léonin's patterned rhythms are not yet 'modes' and there is evidence that his rhythmic patterns evolved over a period of

time. We have no redaction of the *Magnus liber* in its earliest notational form, but 'symptoms' of such a form can be perceived in the versions found in the two oldest sources. See E. Sanders, 'Duple Rhythm and Alternate Third Mode in the 13th Century', *JAMS*, xv (1962), 278–82, for evidence of notational transition towards the system of rhythmic modes in the work of Pérotin.
[25] Note that in the earlier redactions of the *Magnus liber* the rhythmic organization is restricted to what later became known as modes one, two, five and six, though they were clearly not thought of as modes by Léonin's generation (see E. Sanders, 'Conductus and Modal Rhythm', *JAMS*, xxxviii (1985), 449–50 and n.14). Of these, mode two – found only in a section in discant – may be the result of a later addition or alteration, mode five is restricted to unpatterned series of longs *ultra mensuram* in the tenors, and mode six is merely an ornamented form of mode one. Thus a late 12th-century singer had as yet no experience of reading a ternary ligature as *brevis, brevis altera, longa*; the middle note of a *ternaria* was always short. Yudkin's view of a continuum of length values in organum, based upon Garlandia's descriptions of consonance values and Anonymous IV's list of irregular modes ('The Rhythm', 374–6), has much to recommend it, but may need some slight modifications to account also for the semiotic impact of the notation itself on the singer.
[26] Franco of Cologne, *Ars cantus mensurabilis*, ed. G. Reaney and A. Gilles, CSM, xviii (1974), 75.
[27] Jerome of Moravia, *Tractatus de musica*, ed. S. M. Cserba (Regensburg, 1935), 190.
[28] Such is the case, for example, with a number of conducti that have seven semibreves forming a single rhythmic unit (usually a cadential pattern). The appearance of groups of three semibreves to the breve may be a direct result of the patterning of discant *clausulae* when words were added to the dupla.
[29] Johannes de Garlandia, *De mensurabili musica*, ed. E. Reimer (Wiesbaden, 1972), i, 46, 51.
[30] Franco, *Ars cantus*, 38–40.
[31] Handlo, *Regule*, CS, i, 388–9.
[32] ibid, i, 389.
[33] Franco, *Ars cantus*, 34.
[34] Jacques de Liège, *Speculum musice*, ed. R. Bragard, CSM, iii (1955–73), bk7, p.36.
[35] Philippe de Vitry, *Ars nova*, ed. G. Reaney, A. Gilles and J. Maillard, CSM, viii (1964), 29–30.
[36] ibid, 30–31.
[37] E. Sanders, 'Philippe de Vitry', *Grove6*, xx, 25.
[38] Vitry, *Ars nova*, 29: 'Minimum tempus posuit Franco'.
[39] ibid, 63, 79–80; Sanders, 'Philippe de Vitry', 24.
[40] Edited in J. Wolf, 'Ein Beitrag zur Diskantlehre des 14. Jahrhunderts', *SIMG*, xv (1913–14), 504–34, especially 517.
[41] Rohloff, *Die Quellenhandschriften*, 144–6; Handlo, *Regule*, CS, i, 388.
[42] Johannes Vetulus de Anagnia, *Liber de musica*, ed. F. Hammond, CSM, xxvii (1977), 18, with further literature on the development of mechanical clocks.
[43] See F. A. Gallo, *La teoria della notazione in Italia dalla fine del XIII secolo all'inizio del XV secolo* (Bologna, 1966).
[44] Marchetto da Padova, *Pomerium*, ed. G. Vecchi, CSM, vi (1961), 57; see also Gallo, *La teoria*, 18–21.
[45] Vetulus, *Liber*, 28.
[46] ibid, 29.
[47] C. Sachs, *Rhythm and Tempo: a Study in Music History* (New York, 1953), 186–8.
[48] S. Gullo, *Das Tempo in der Musik des XIII. und XIV. Jahrhunderts* (Berne, 1964), 70–71.
[49] Marchetto, *Pomerium*, 161.
[50] See A. M. Busse Berger, 'The Relation of Perfect and Imperfect Time in Italian Theory of the Renaissance', *EMH*, v (1985), 1–28.
[51] See Gullo, *Das Tempo*, 76–85.
[52] See n.6 above.
[53] See C. Dahlhaus, 'Zur Theorie des Tactus im 16. Jahrhundert', *AMw*, xvii (1961), 22–39.
[54] The *tactus* was on the imperfect breve in *tempus diminutum*, even when the *tempus* itself was perfect, thus *tactus* in Φ was called *sesquitactus*; see C. Dahlhaus, 'Miszellen zur Musiktheorie des 15. Jahrhunderts', *Jb des Staatlichen Instituts für Musikforschung*, i (1970), 24–6.
[55] See A. E. Planchart, 'The Relative Speed of *Tempora* in the Period of Dufay', *RMARC*, xvii (1981), 35–8 (see pp. 36–41 for a detailed description of examples of both instances).
[56] A. M. Busse Berger, *Mensuration Signs and Proportions in Italian Music Theory from ca. 1400*

to ca. 1600 (diss., Boston U., 1986). This is a very comprehensive and well thought-out work that also covers some of the French tradition.

[57] Busse Berger, 'Relation', 5–18 and Table 1.

[58] C. Hamm, *A Chronology of the Works of Guillaume Dufay Based on a Study of Mensural Practice* (Princeton, 1964), 91–8, called attention to this. See also A. Hughes, 'Mensuration and Proportion in Early 15th Century English Music', *AcM*, xxvii (1965), 48–61.

[59] See A. M. Busse Berger, 'The Early History of the Proportion Signs', *JAMS*, lxi (1988), 403–33.

[60] See R. Taruskin, 'Antoine Busnoys and the *L'homme armé* Tradition', *JAMS*, xxxix (1986), 260–61, where he suggests that this particular use of C and ⊙ is connected with the tradition of the *L'homme armé* masses.

[61] See Taruskin, 'Antoine Busnoys', 169 and 284, for references to their typical use in the works of Busnois, but Taruskin's contention that Busnois is the inventor of some of these signs, for example, ⊙2 is patently untenable; see below, n.62.

[62] Most of the pieces using these signs are settings of the Propers of the Mass first attributed to Dufay by Laurence Feininger in *Auctorum anonymorum missarum propria XVI*, Monumenta Polyphoniae Liturgicae, 2nd ser., i (Rome, 1947). Many of Feininger's attributions of these pieces, though not generally accepted at the time, have been confirmed by new findings. See D. Fallows, 'Dufay and the Mass Proper Cycles of Trent 88', in *I Codici musicali trentini a cento anni dalla loro riscoperta: Atti dal convengo Laurence Feininger*, ed. N. Pirrotta and D. Curti (Trent, 1986), 46–59. The full argument for Dufay's authorship of these works appears in A. E. Planchart, 'Guillaume Du Fay's Benefices and his Relationship to the Court of Burgundy', *EMH*, viii (1988), 117–71. [In this article Professor Planchart argues that the composer's name is correctly spelt 'Du Fay'; for the sake of conformity, however, in the present volume we have uniformly adopted the spelling 'Dufay'.]

[63] Hamm, *A Chronology*, 91–6, first called attention to C with breve–semibreve movement as an English trait.

[64] See Planchart, 'Relative Speed', 40–41.

[65] See Taruskin, 'Antoine Busnoys', 261, n.35.

[66] See Busse Berger, 'The Relation', 12–14, concerning the Italian theoretical tradition; Planchart, 'Relative Speed', 41–2, on the continental interpretation of English mensural practices; and Taruskin, 'Antoine Busnoys', 276–9 and n.37, for a particularly cogent proportional analysis of a work that supports this interpretation as well as references to other analytical literature.

[67] Diminution by a third is based on the discussion of diminution by Johannes de Muris, *Libellus cantus mensurabilis (secundum Johannem de Muris)*, *CS*, iii, 58. Busse Berger, *Mensuration Signs*, 173–5, indicates that Johannes meant in this case diminution by two-thirds, and that his view was understood in this manner by later Italian theorists, while the German theorists (for example, Anonymous XII, *Tractatus de musica*, *CS*, iii, 484) understood it as diminution by a third; this may be a simple misreading of Johannes or it may be a deliberate reinterpretation of his statement. In 15th-century practical sources, however, no works can be found that make use of diminution of any form of *tempus perfectum* by two-thirds. Busse Berger, in a later paper 'The Myth of *diminutio per tertiam partem*' (forthcoming), which she has kindly allowed me to see, questions that it ever had any practical existence, and suggests that it was the figment of the imagination of a few German theorists. But the theorists do mention this relationship and once again, proportional analysis of the duration of works that simply alternate between ○ and ⊕ (for example, Dufay's *Vergene bella*) suggests that some northern composers, even those active in Italy, did use such a relationship in a few of their works.

[68] Planchart, 'Relative Speed', 43, citing an example from Josquin's *Missa Pange lingua*. This usage in Josquin's music is supported by proportional analyses similar to that proposed by Taruskin (see n.63 above). But a generation after Josquin ⊕ is no longer understood. Gombert, in his *Missa Da pacem*, the only piece in his entire output that uses either ○ or ⊕, follows the Josquin Kyrie pattern in the Kyrie, but only as *Augenmusik*, since in the successive movements it is quite clear that he is using ○ and ₵ simply as triple and duple metre without any proportional tempo shift between them.

[69] Planchart, 'Relative Speed', 44–5; see also Taruskin, 'Antoine Busnoys', 285–6, for evidence of use by Busnois.

[70] But see n.64 above.

[71] See, for example, Taruskin, 'Antoine Busnoys', 282, Table 6, and 286.

[72] See W. Frobenius, 'Modus', *HMT*, 1 and 6, and Busse Berger, *Mensuration Signs*, 13–48. The

indication of *modus* by means of rests does appear in a few motet tenors of the late 14th and early 15th centuries.

[73] See n.64 above concerning Gombert's mensural usage. The music of Clemens non Papa has not one instance of O mensuration in it.

[74] See Taruskin, 'Antoine Busnoys', 261, n.14, for examples in the works of Ockeghem, 285–6 for examples in the works of Busnois, and Planchart, 'Tempora', 44–6, for examples in the works of Ockeghem and Dufay where even O and ₵ are treated on occasion as subsidiary signs without absolute value.

[75] See M. Bent, 'Notation, §III, 3', *Grove6*, xiii, 369, for a description of the proportional meanings of coloration in English notation *c*1400.

[76] Busse Berger, *Mensuration Signs*, 287–93, has the most complete bibliography of theoretical sources dealing with proportions.

[77] This was already noted by Thomas Morley; see *A Plain and Easy Introduction to Practical Music* (London, 1597), ed. R. A. Harman (New York, 1952), who gives a very detailed explanation of the proportions, but then pokes fun at the theoretical preoccupation with them (pp.214–15). In the treatise Morley provides one of the few pieces of music that makes use of virtually all the proportions discussed in the treatise, *Christes crosse*.

[78] Johannes Tinctoris, *Proportionale musices*, in *Opera theoretica*, ed. A. Seay, CSM, xxii (1975–8), 2a; A. Seay, 'The *Proportionale musices* of Johannes Tinctoris', *JMT*, i (1957), 22–75.

[79] *Proportionale musices*, 48: 'haec signa adeo frivola, adeo erronea adeoque ab omni rationis appariencia sunt remota'.

[80] ibid, 47.

[81] See n.65 above.

[82] *A Compendium of Musical Practice*, ed. G. Reese and S. Ledbetter (New York, 1973), with a facsimile of Ornithoparchus's treatise of 1517 and John Dowland's translation of 1609.

[83] *De arte canendi* (Nuremberg, 1540/*R*1969); Eng. trans., C. A. Miller, MSD, xxvi (1972).

[84] See A. Mendel, 'Some Ambiguities of the Mensural System', in *Studies in Music History: Essays for Oliver Strunk* (Princeton, 1968), 137–60, particularly 141–8.

[85] Michael Praetorius, *Syntagma musicum* (Wittenberg and Wolfenbüttel, 1614–20/*R*1958–9), iii, 48–79.

[86] ibid, iii, 79.

[87] P. Brainard, 'Zur Deutung der Diminution in der Tactuslehre des Michael Praetorius', *Mf*, xvii (1964), 169–74; C. Dahlhaus, 'Zur Entstehung des modernen Taktsystems im 17. Jahrhundert', *AMw*, xviii (1961), 223–40, and 'Zur Taktlehre des Michael Praetorius', *Mf*, xvii (1964), 162–9; A. Mendel, 'A Brief Note on Triple Proportion in Schütz', *MQ*, xlvi (1960), 67–70.

[88] See C. Dahlhaus, 'Über das Tempo in der Musik des späten 16. Jahrhunderts', *Musica*, xiii (1959), 767ff.

[89] Luis de Milán, *Libro de música de vihuela de mano intitulado El maestro* (Valencia, 1536/*R*1978); also *El maestro*, ed. C. Jacobs (University Park, Penn., 1971).

[90] See C. Jacobs, *Tempo Notation in Renaissance Spain*, MSD, viii (1964).

PART TWO

The Renaissance

CHAPTER VIII

Introduction

HOWARD M. BROWN

Musicians have to make a number of fundamental decisions before they can offer a convincing performance of whatever 15th- or 16th-century composition they choose to play or sing, regardless of whether they use a modern edition, a manuscript or printed book from the Renaissance, or a facsimile or pseudo-facsimile of such a source. If musicians wish to perform a vocal piece, they must first decide how to distribute the words among the notes. They must decide which accidentals to add to those indicated in the original source. They must decide whether all voices of the composition should be sung, only some, or only one – that is, whether the composition should be sung by unaccompanied voices (and if so, with how many to a part and of what sorts), or by a mixture of voices and instruments. If instruments are to be used, they must decide which, and whether or not the composition needs to be arranged for instruments such as the lute which can play all or most of the voices and therefore needs a special score (usually in tablature), since the player cannot easily perform from a set of individual parts. They need to decide whether to write out or improvise ornamentation, and if so, how elaborate the decorations should be, and to which voices they should be applied. They must decide how fast the piece should be performed, and how the sections written in contrasting mensurations should relate to one another. They must decide at what pitch their instruments should be tuned, which temperament they wish to play in and whether or not they want to transpose the written notes in relation to what they normally think of as the correct pitch of their instruments. They must decide whether to play or sing their melodic lines legato, staccato or with some degree of detachment between those two extremes, and they need to decide whether they wish to try to make thin clear sounds without vibrato, or fatter, richer sounds with some vibrato on particular notes, or throughout.

These are the same kinds of decisions that performers in the 15th and 16th centuries had to make. Finding out how such problems were solved at the time the music was written is the chief duty of the scholar of performance practice. One of the tasks of the present-day performer is to decide whether the speculative solutions proposed by scholars are practical and can be reconstructed today, and, if they can, to determine the extent to which they should be applied to performances in the 20th century.[1]

Strictly speaking, the placement of text beneath the notes (text underlay), and the addition of accidentals implied but not written down by composers or scribes (*musica ficta*), are aspects of editorial technique. Ideally, present-day performers should expect that scholars immersed in the stylistic subtleties of whatever repertories of music they study will have expended much thought and energy in considering precisely how the composer intended the words of his compositions to be sung, and which unwritten accidentals he considered essential. But in fact we cannot be certain that composers actually fixed those features of a composition firmly in their minds before sending their compositions out into the world, and there is evidence to suggest that 15th- and 16th-century performers enjoyed a certain freedom to alter details as they thought best. A single 'correct' solution to the problem of which accidentals to add to a particular piece, and precisely how to sing the words – a solution about which all scholars will agree – seems beyond our grasp. In any case, present-day editors do not invariably offer carefully considered and practical solutions, so that performers need to learn about the conventions governing text underlay and *musica ficta* as much as scholars do. They are subjects that intersect the area between the preparation of a modern critical edition and the actual performance of a composition.

The sources that contain polyphony change from the 15th to the 16th century in the amount of detail they offer about the placement of text beneath the musical notes.[2] In general, the earlier the scribe or editor the less information and explicit advice they offer. In spite of the inclination of some scholars to argue that we should follow the scribes as exactly as we can, the truth is that in 15th-century manuscripts, text was not supplied for some voices intended to be sung, and many syllables are not placed directly beneath particular notes. This lack of exact correlation is all the more to be regretted since the highly melismatic melodic style of the 15th century raises fundamental questions about the nature of the relationship in the composer's mind between words and music.[3] We cannot always be certain, for example, which phrases of text belong with which phrases of music, or even about the basic question of which voices should be sung with text. (In Mass settings written out for the cathedral choir of Cambrai, for example, the text was omitted from many of the lower voices, although they must have been sung since no organ was present.)[4] In short, questions of text underlay in 15th-century music significantly affect the way we understand particular compositions, and the compositional style of the time in general. In the 16th century, on the other hand, composers generally wrote a more declamatory and word-oriented kind of music, and scribes and editors generally offer more detail both about the placement of phrases and of particular syllables. Questions about 16th-century text underlay, therefore, generally involve details rather than fundamental issues.

To be sure, there are 15th-century sources that provide quite specific indications of where syllables should be sung. The scribe (or an early performer) has added to some pieces in Oxford, Bodleian Library, MS Canonici misc.213 (and one or two other manuscripts of the period), for example, lines connecting syllables and notes in some pieces, presumably as an aid in remembering how to sing the words correctly.[5] For the most part, however, the musical sources do not offer special help in understanding 15th-century conventions, and there are no clear and unequivocal statements in the 15th-century theoretical literature about text underlay. The earliest theorist to mention the subject, an anonymous author whose remarks appear on a single isolated leaf described by Don Harrán, is somewhat disingenuous

in recommending that performers sing exactly what they see in the manuscript, especially since his own musical examples are unperformable as they
stand.[6]

Some sources of the 16th century show a careful concern on the part of the
editor to indicate precisely where syllables should be sung, which phrases of
text should be repeated and so on; Mary Lewis points out, for example, that
in the late 1540s the Venetian publisher Antonio Gardane began to take
much greater pains than he had before to indicate text underlay exactly,
perhaps under the influence of Gioseffo Zarlino.[7] And several writers on
music in the 16th century gave quite explicit advice on the subject: in 1533,
Giovanni Lanfranco explained to choirboys the principles to follow in
preparing performances;[8] in 1558, Gioseffo Zarlino instructed composers
about what they ought to do to ensure a good fit between words and music;[9]
and in the 1570s, Gaspar Stocker offered a slightly more refined version of
Zarlino's rules, making important and useful distinctions between the
conventions governing music 50 years old and the music of his own time.[10]
All three theorists seem to reflect the opinions of Adrian Willaert, chapel
master at the basilica of St Mark in Venice and probably the most influential
teacher of composition in Italy during the middle years of the 16th century, a
composer whose strict views about text underlay are reflected in his own
music. But we must then ask to what extent Lanfranco, Zarlino and Stocker
reveal a special viewpoint adopted at a single musical centre in the 16th
century, and to what extent they describe a general practice of the time. It
is possible that present-day editors, following these 16th-century theorists,
run the risk of imposing Willaert's solutions, as elegant as they are, on
everyone and ignoring, for example, the idiosyncrasies of other composers
and other practices (such as the conventions governing Latin pronunciation
in various western European countries) which may have been subject to
widespread variation. Even more important, we need to consider carefully
whether Willaert's teachings as reflected in Lanfranco, Zarlino and Stocker
represent a wholly idiosyncratic view, or a refinement and culmination of
commonly held beliefs. If the latter hypothesis is true, we can then
extrapolate backwards in time, supposing that Willaert's rules reflect a set of
conventions already old by the time he began promulgating them to his
students in Venice.

Throughout the Middle Ages and the Renaissance, musicians were
expected to add accidentals not indicated in the written sources when they
performed a composition. These chromatic inflections were made principally
at cadences, where the seventh scale degree was to be raised (or more rarely
the second degree lowered), or to avoid tritones and other awkward intervals,
either melodically or harmonically. In the chapter on *musica ficta* in the
present volume, Karol Berger succinctly sets out the reasons why such a
convention developed, and what the theorists tell us about which accidentals
should be added and where.[11] He raises larger issues that will doubtless
continue to be debated as long as people study and perform these repertories,
for the nature of the convention is not entirely clear. Did the composer have a
single fixed correct solution in mind, or does the fact that the accidentals
were not written down imply that performers were given a certain leeway, so
that various alternative solutions were equally valid? Was *musica ficta* a

single unified convention throughout the later Middle Ages and the Renaissance, or did it change from place to place and from time to time? Certainly, the study of the way 16th-century lutenists added accidentals to intabulated arrangements of vocal music (in which the accidentals are indicated more precisely than in normal staff notation) suggests that there was a lot of room for disagreement then about where and how to add accidentals to a particular piece,[12] and we should doubtless continue our discussions about whether we are right to think of some of these solutions as good and others bad, or whether we should regard them all as equally satisfactory alternative versions. We need to keep in mind, too, that one of the virtues of this unwritten convention is that it did allow performers to take account of the limitations of their instruments, by changing or leaving out the accidentals they could not conveniently play. Moreover, there were doubtless local traditions affecting the way particular groups of musicians were taught to add accidentals, and surely the range of acceptable solutions changed in many ways from the 13th to the end of the 16th century.

Once performers – whether in the 15th, 16th or 20th century – have agreed about how the text can suitably be sung in a particular piece, which accidentals to add and where, they need to decide just who should perform. As with every other aspect of performance practice, the size and disposition of vocal ensembles must have depended on where and when a composition was performed, and what sort of composition it was. In general, men and boys normally sang sacred polyphony in the 15th and 16th centuries, but not every church, princely chapel or monastic establishment made use of boys; in many places men regularly sang the top lines of polyphony, presumably in falsetto.[13] Although women were normally excluded from the musical portions of the liturgy (except, of course, in convents) some ensembles of women – such as those organized by several orphanages in Venice in the 16th century and later – were famous for their skill in sacred music.[14] Many choirs in the cathedrals and princely chapels of Italy seem to have been organized or reorganized in the second half of the 15th century. A systematic survey of the size and disposition of church choirs in western Europe during the 15th and 16th centuries is likely to show that sacred polyphony in the 15th century was normally sung by relatively small groups, often perhaps with only one singer to a part, that choir sizes increased suddenly at the end of the 15th or in the early 16th century (when 15 to 25 singers appear to have constituted a large choir), and that there was a tendency to use more singers on the top and bottom lines than on the inner parts.[15]

It seems safe to say that secular polyphony involving unaccompanied vocal ensembles was normally sung one to a part during the 15th and 16th centuries (although when mixtures of voices and instruments were used, not every part was sung), but the question has not been studied as carefully as the size of sacred ensembles, and certain exceptions (such as the great concerts for special occasions in late 16th-century Ferrara that seem to have involved much larger forces) come immediately to mind.[16] At the other extreme, the existence of such collections as the Verdelot madrigals arranged by Willaert for solo voice and lute remind us that what appears to be music for unaccompanied vocal ensemble was also on occasion performed by one or two soloists with instrumental accompaniment.[17] Already by the 15th century, various individuals, such as Pietrobono in Ferrara, were famous for their virtuosity and skill as solo singers, although it is not entirely clear whether his repertory included the sorts of written compositions that appear in the surviving sources, or whether he, like the other Italian *improvvisatori*, sang mostly an orally transmitted repertory, including long narrative songs.[18] Certainly, more and more virtuoso singers made their claims on the attentions of music lovers as the 16th century wore on, and many of them sang highly ornamented versions of madrigals and other pieces of composed polyphony.[19] Throughout the 15th and 16th centuries, women as well as men regularly took part in the performance of secular polyphony, not only aristocratic ladies and courtiers, but also well-educated courtesans, and doubtless members of the *haute bourgeoisie* (quite aside from those lower-class women who were among the class of minstrels).[20] There may even have been professional women singers at some courts. Certainly the famous singing ladies of Ferrara in the later 16th century, although of good families, seem to have been tolerated there chiefly for their musical abilities, as Anthony Newcomb has shown.[21]

Answers to questions about whether to use men, women or boys in the performance of a particular composition, how many of each and in what combinations, depend partly, of course, on whether or not instruments accompanied the singers or substituted for them on some parts. If instruments did regularly play with singers in some repertories, we need to know which instruments and what parts they normally played. The widely held belief that all instruments except the organ were normally banned from performances of sacred music within the church during the 15th and early 16th centuries will probably hold up under continued scrutiny, even though it may eventually be seen that there were exceptions to the general rule.[22] The possibility that instruments other than the organ occasionally played with princely chapel choirs (as opposed to church or cathedral choirs) needs to be investigated more thoroughly.[23] A wind player, possibly a trombonist, seems regularly to have been assigned to the chapel of the dukes of Savoy in the late 15th century, for example, and he may conceivably have played cantus firmi in sacred music,[24] and some notices about the Burgundian chapel about 1500 mention a cornett player who accompanied the singers.[25] Moreover, instrumental ensembles may sometimes have accompanied singers in church for very special occasions such as coronations and weddings, and just possibly also in side chapels for devotional services sponsored by confraternities of laymen. By the second half of the 16th century, ensembles of instruments, and especially of bands of cornetts and sackbuts, were regularly hired by some churches, and there are even notices from that time of occasional performances involving other instruments as well.[26]

Even if we can determine the presence of instruments in church for special occasions, we need also to determine just what they played. Trumpets at coronations, for example, may have done no more than furnish independent fanfares from time to time, and other groups of instruments, if they ever performed in church, may have limited their participation to purely instrumental pieces rather than accompanying the singers. The Elevation of the Host at Mass, for example, seems to have been an occasion when instrumental music was often played, a tradition that may have existed as early as the

The knight Paris and his friend Edward serenading Vienne, from 'L'histoire du tresvaillant chevalier Paris et de la belle Vienne fille du dauphin' (Antwerp, Gherard Leeu, 1487, f.3): the two men have their mouths closed although the romance describes them as singing and playing

15th century. We know that organists sometimes added more or less elaborate counterpoints to a cantus firmus taken from chant, alternating with choirs singing plainchant or polyphony during liturgical services (so-called *alternatim* performances), but we are much less certain about the extent to which organists ever accompanied singers by doubling their parts.[27]

The recent view that challenges the participation of instruments to accompany secular polyphony in the 15th century derives partly from a rigorous, literal reading of selected bits of difficult, ambiguous evidence.[28] The case of *L'histoire du tresvaillant chevalier Paris et de la belle Vienne* (Antwerp, 1487) can be taken as an example.[29] Paris, playing a lute, is seen in woodcuts illustrating the romance, serenading his beloved Vienne, while his friend Edward sits on a nearby bench with his harp (see illustration above). Paris is said to be singing and playing, a description that recurs a number of times in the romance. One manuscript version of the romance, however, says that 'he sang and then he played' to Vienne, a variant that has been used as proof that neither Paris nor Edward accompanied Paris's singing, although it can just as well be argued that the scribe responsible for the variant distorted the author's meaning and that in any case he did not intend his remark to be taken so literally. Whatever the truth of their claims, those who have been arguing for the unaccompanied vocal performance of secular music do remind us of two important things: in the first place, secular polyphony does in fact seem to have been sung without instruments much

152

more often than we have hitherto supposed, and in the second place, whatever opinion we hold, we must always take pains to offer evidence that is as unambiguous as possible. One real problem in debating the subject of the instrumental accompaniment to secular polyphony – and, indeed, of most questions dealing with performance practice – involves the limitation of basing far-reaching conclusions on the close reading of one or two pieces of evidence, when we in fact should be attempting to illuminate common conventions rather than exceptional procedures.

Moreover, students of performance practice, whatever their views, need to attempt an explanation of just what the instruments that existed then did play. The view that secular music in the 15th century was almost always sung unaccompanied, for example, would be strengthened considerably if it could be shown that instrumentalists never played music of the sort that survives in 15th-century manuscripts, but instead had a special unwritten and largely improvised repertory, or even a lost repertory of compositions conceived and intended specifically for instruments. But such a view cannot be sustained, partly because it is improbable that many of the aristocratic amateurs who played instruments would have deigned to master so merely professional an art as that of improvisation, and partly because it is easy to show that instrumentalists were regularly associated with the performance of written secular polyphony at least from the time of Simone Prudenzani and the Faenza Codex at the very beginning of the 15th century through to the end of the Renaissance.[30] In other words, it is certain that there was no completely separate repertory to which instrumentalists were restricted, no matter how much the more professional among them improvised a kind of music that has now been lost to us, or played compositions specially intended for instruments.

Consider, for example, the repertory of the lutenists of the 16th century.[31] As soon as most of them adopted the technique of playing with their fingers rather than with a plectrum, they could perform all the voices of polyphonic compositions, but they needed special intabulated parts to do so. If the printed music for lute in the 16th century reflects fairly what lutenists played – and by extension what instrumentalists in general played – then we see that the repertory of instrumentalists (or at the very least of lutenists) included motets, chansons, madrigals, lieder, various other kinds of secular music, and even masses, in addition to a relatively small repertory of autonomous instrumental music, that is, every genre known at the time.

The existence of this vast amount of music for lute, and especially of the arrangements of polyphonic music for solo singer and lute, reminds us that much 16th-century music appears to be published in 'neutral' versions that allows musicians considerable freedom to present the music in performance in more than one form. Thus many 16th-century books of music are described on their title pages as 'apt for voices or viols' (or some other similar sentiment);[32] frottole were published in four-part polyphonic versions although they were often sung in three parts or in versions for lute or viol and voice;[33] and the souvenir booklets published to commemorate courtly festivals sometimes include music published for four or more parts, although the descriptions of the occasions make clear that many of the pieces were performed in a variety of ways that would preclude the musicians from actually having used the version incorporated in the volume.[34] It seems clear that in the 16th century, vocal ensembles as well as solo singers were often accompanied by instruments in the performance of a wide variety of kinds of music, even sacred music (notwithstanding the strictures against instruments in church) if the evidence of the lute books is taken into account. Lutes, keyboard instruments, consorts of viols or combinations of diverse instruments may quite regularly have accompanied ensembles of singers performing secular music; the possibility has not in fact been much investigated as a general convention of the time.[35]

Some quite fixed groupings of instruments cultivated repertories of their own, or particular versions of the common repertory. Bands of shawms and sackbuts, for example, played for outdoor or gala occasions, sackbuts and cornetts accompanied church choirs,[36] and the curious mixture of plucked and bowed strings and winds that constitutes the so-called 'English mixed consort' played arrangements of popular tunes and dances for academic and civic audiences alike.[37]

Almost all the intabulations for solo lute of polyphonic music are more or less heavily embellished with passage-work (diminutions or *passaggi*). Some of these ornamented versions contain nothing more than occasional written-out turns and trills, some add virtuoso running passages to four or five sections of a composition, and some construct an elaborate pattern of repeating figuration patterns over the original polyphonic fabric. The fact that so few completely undecorated intabulations exist suggests that no 16th-century lutenist who was proud of his abilities would have thought to play a piece unembellished. The intabulations – special parts prepared for lutenists – instruct us about the techniques of embellishment for one class of instrumentalist.[38] A number of instruction books published in the 16th century, starting with Silvestro di Ganassi's *Fontegara* of 1535, teach us that other kinds of instrumentalists, who did not need special parts in order to perform, were also wont to embellish their melodic lines, with simple graces and occasional more elaborate running figures if they were playing in ensemble, and with highly virtuoso embellishments if they were playing solo (with the accompaniment of a lute or keyboard instrument).[39] Some writers, such as the Neapolitan doctor Giovanni Camillo Maffei, tell us that singers in the Renaissance also embellished their lines.[40] Maffei makes especially clear the different standards for the discreet ornamentation appropriate for ensembles and the sometimes breathtakingly virtuoso embellishments for solo singing.

The evidence of the intabulations and of the writers on performance practice suggests that present-day performers ought to feel as constrained to add *passaggi* (or at least some discreet embellishment) at cadences when they perform 16th-century music as they do when they perform the music of the 17th and 18th centuries. It is less clear that similar sorts of embellishments should be added to 15th-century music, for we do not have so many different kinds of witnesses from the earlier period. We do not know for sure the extent to which embellishing techniques were cultivated either by singers or by instrumentalists then, although a series of organ tablatures from northern Italy and from Germany instruct us about the conventions of one class of performer, and a handful of *giustiniane* offer examples of ornamenting technique for one genre of 15th-century Italian song.[41] Even with 16th-century music, there is a question of taste and propriety to be raised in connection with embellishing techniques. Some and perhaps many 16th-century composers objected to the way virtuoso musicians obscured the character of the compositions they performed with an avalanche of breath-takingly fast notes.[42] If the goal of the present-day performer is to reveal as best he can the intentions of the composer, embellishments should be reduced or eliminated; but if his goal is to reproduce common practices of the time, then he needs to command all the skills of ornamentation taught in the instruction books and found in lute and keyboard intabulations. In truth, such tensions between composers and performers have almost always existed.

In theory at least, there was a single invariable beat that underlay all music in the 15th and 16th centuries. According to the late 15th-century Milanese choirmaster and theorist Franchinus Gaffurius, the *tactus* took the time of the pulse of a quietly breathing man, that is, about 60 beats per minute.[43] In theory, then, composers – at least in the 15th century – who wished faster music had to write with smaller note values, and longer note values signalled slower music. A system of proportions regulated changes of pace from section to section, so that music under ₵ for example, was supposed to be performed twice as fast as music under C, and a 3:2 proportion (called 'sesquialtera') governed most changes from duple to triple mensuration.[44] Whereas the theory is simple and consistent, practice in the 15th and 16th centuries seems not to have been nearly so straightforward. About 1500, for example, ₵ became the principal mensuration sign for much music, and appears to have lost its proportional significance. The *tactus* may well have speeded up or slowed down at certain times and places, for particular genres, or even for individual pieces within any given genre, and there is even some evidence from the second half of the 16th century that musicians established tempos and changed them within a mensuration in certain kinds of compositions depending on the meaning of the words.[45]

It is virtually impossible to know at what pitch level music was played or sung in the 15th and 16th centuries. Some instruments of fixed pitch (such as large church organs and recorders) do, of course, survive from the Renaissance, but they do not always give us clear-cut answers to our questions. In many organs, for example, the pipes have been changed since they were originally built, and with particular recorders we cannot always be certain at what pitch level they were said to play (even if the ravages of time have not changed the pitch at which they originally sounded). In any case, pitch levels seem to have varied from time to time and from place to place.[46] At whatever pitch musicians performed, they observed a different and slightly more complex convention with regard to temperaments than we do today. Choirs (and singers in general) may well have sung more or less the way they do now, that is, with a flexible temperament that approaches just intonation. Keyboard instruments in the 15th and 16th centuries made use of one of a variety of mean-tone temperaments that brought some sonorities into perfect tune while leaving others so bad as to be unusable (equal temperament was not established as a regular practice for keyboards until much later: the 18th century or perhaps even later). And fretted instruments such as the lute, the cittern and the viola da gamba were normally played in a temperament close to equal, even though theorists then could not yet quite justify or explain it and some players of viols and plucked strings attempted to tune their frets unevenly to produce a mean-tone temperament.[47] Some writers in the 16th century acknowledge the imperfections of intonation that result from mixing various classes of instruments – Ercole Bottrigari's *Il desiderio* is chiefly devoted to this subject[48] – but consorts of voices and instruments singing and playing with three different tunings, just, mean-tone and equal, were nevertheless common in the 16th century. Musicians clearly found some way to overcome the problem satisfactorily.

Musicians then also found ways to fit a wide variety of compositions to the capabilities of their instruments by transposing the apparent pitch of written music from one level to another. These transposing conventions have been much less well studied than other aspects of performance practice, but it is important to understand them, for they affected the way musicians went about their performances, and how they thought about what they did.[49] Transposition involves the relationship of a written note to what the pitches on an instrument are called. That is, a lute or viol player plays the string he calls g' whenever he sees a g' on the page. He can, then, imagine the same string to be called d', a fourth lower, so that when he sees g' on the page he will actually play a higher string position, raising the pitch level a fourth. Conventions of transposition developed mostly to allow players to fit music more comfortably on their instruments: when the notes on the page went too high or too low to fit, performers transposed them down or up, and when lutenists or viol players found that they could not get good sonorities in certain 'keys' because of the accidentals (or when the singers they accompanied felt more comfortable at a different pitch level), instrumentalists learned to transpose music so that they had more opportunities to sound open strings on the most important notes of a piece, or so that the physical limitations of particular singers could be accommodated. The practice of transposition was so common and so widespread that some keyboard instruments of the later 16th century appear to have been built in such a way that they transposed automatically.[50]

Once performers of 15th- or 16th-century music have made most of the crucial decisions about how to play or sing a composition – how to sing the words and where to add editorial accidentals, which voices or instruments to use, whether or not to add embellishments, at what tempo to perform and at what pitch and in which temperament – their job has, of course, just begun, for they must then bring the music to life, making innumerable musical decisions about aspects of performance that can probably never be informed by knowledge of what was actually done in the Renaissance. Perhaps we can eventually reach a consensus about how 15th- and 16th-century musicians articulated music: whether they valued a detached style of singing and playing more than what we could call a 'singing' legato (some of the 16th-century instruction books suggest that slurred notes began to be used in the 16th century but were not highly valued).[51] And perhaps we can eventually reach a consensus about the quality of voice singers preferred in the Renaissance, and about how they produced it, although the evidence for this sort of information is much less clear-cut than about other aspects of performance practice, so that it is open to more than one interpretation. We shall probably never know, however, about some of the qualities of performance during the 15th and 16th centuries, for example, whether musicians regularly slowed down at cadences, whether they varied the dynamic level of individual notes or whole phrases, whether they regularly made use of crescendos and diminuendos, whether they accented the goal note of a phrase (and, if so, whether they had a whole variety of kinds of accents to enliven different kinds of music): in short, whether musicians in the Renaissance shaped phrases the way we do, and whether they valued the kinds of phrasings that give us so much pleasure and seem to us to make the music come alive.[52]

Certain questions about performance practice – and especially those dealing with arranging and scoring and those affecting the choice of repertory for particular groups of voices or instruments – can be answered only by considering broader issues about the way music was performed in the 15th and 16th century, that is, questions relating to the structure of society at large, and especially the way musical institutions were organized, how they came into being and how they changed and developed over the course of time. The study of performance practice intersects with cultural or social history whenever it is important to know what music was played at court, in cities or by the peasants in the country, and how performances differed from one social context to another.

The court was the microcosm of the world at large in a musical as well as a more general sense. The courtly musical institutions that grew up in the 15th century duplicated in miniature the practices of the outside world. Most courts seem to have employed three kinds of musicians. King François I's establishment can serve as a paradigm.[53] He hired a group of singers and an organist for his chapel (the *Musique de la chapelle*); instrumentalists for his so-called stable musicians (the *Musique de l'écurie*); and a much more loosely organized group of virtuoso singers and instrumentalists who formed the musicians of his chamber (the *Musique de la chambre*). The chapel singers officiated at Mass and Office hours, and some or all of them may also have sung from time to time at great state occasions. The stable musicians, who consisted of the ceremonial trumpeters and drummers as well as a band of shawms and sackbuts (and in François I's reign the first band of violins as well), played for dances and other gala events. And the chamber musicians performed for the delectation of the king and his courtiers when they were in chambers, and doubtless took part at other times whenever there was reason to wish to hear solo players and singers, or small ensembles.

In the 16th century, the greatest princely chapels numbered 20 to 30 singers. They were among the most skilful and best-educated musicians of the time, and included among their members many of the most distinguished composers. Some courts, but not all, had a special choir for plainchant, and some maintained schools for the training of the choirboys who sang the higher parts. At least one, and sometimes two, organists were usually associated with chapel choirs, although not all establishments allowed even the organ to be sounded within the chapel walls. The pope's choir, the Sistine Chapel, for example, had no organ, nor did some cathedrals, such as that in Cambrai. On the other hand, other instrumentalists can occasionally be associated with princely chapels as early as the late 15th century. As mentioned above, at the court of Savoy a trumpeter (who could conceivably have been a slide trumpeter or even a trombonist) was assigned to the chapel musicians, and he may have played cantus firmi in the performance of sacred vocal music. But princely chapel choirs, and cathedral choirs as well, normally sang unaccompanied (*a cappella*) in the 15th century. It was not until the middle of the 16th century that we begin to find archival notices that reveal the fact that some chapel and cathedral choirs began regularly to hire instrumentalists, and especially players of wind instruments (cornetts and sackbuts). It remains to be seen just when and where the convention of doubling church choirs with instruments began and how long it lasted.[54]

Trumpeters and drummers made up an important part of King François I's stable musicians. They played signals to his troops in battle, announced his ceremonial entries in peacetime, and presumably proclaimed his royal edicts in the streets of Paris; and they enlivened his banquets and made various other purely ceremonial noises whenever such were called for.[55] The stable musicians also included players of shawms and sackbuts, who accompanied formal social dancing and performed for whatever gala occasions required a splendid loud sound. It remains to be seen how the shawm and sackbut band changed and developed in the course of the 16th century, and the extent to which these stable musicians were competent to play soft as well as loud winds, and perhaps even some string instruments as well. Presumably the new band of violins under François, as well as the older group of winds, were capable of improvising dance music, using techniques by then quite different from the earlier 15th-century practice of adding counterpoint over basse danse tenors, the sorts of tenors preserved for us, for example, in the Brussels basse danse manuscript. Both the wind and the string band of François I's court may also have performed arrangements of chansons, motets and other kinds of composed polyphony when the occasion demanded.[56]

The chamber musicians at an elaborate courtly establishment were the least fixed of the musical ensembles, and therefore (since institutional records do not always identify them clearly as a group) the hardest to study.[57] Rulers appear to have kept about their courts a few singers and a few virtuoso instrumentalists, who would perform for the private enjoyment of the prince and his courtiers (and who might even have performed with them informally). Archival notices also record the presence at a number of courts of a pipe and tabor player (usually called merely 'tabourineur' or something similar), who may have played for informal dancing, and conceivably even functioned as a dancing master. Presumably the chamber musicians were hired for their great skill rather than to fill a fixed vacancy, and so the groupings tend to change from court to court and from decade to decade, although for most of our period there was usually a harpist, a fiddle player or an organist among them. Of all the instrumentalists trained through the apprenticeship system rather than through more formal education at a cathedral school, those hired to play in princely chambers had reached the top of their profession, and they were the most socially mobile of all musicians in the Renaissance. A number of chamber musicians in the 15th and 16th centuries were appointed as *valets de chambre* in various courts, and some were even ennobled.

Although the courts obviously differed one from another in their detailed organization, the division of courtly musicians into those associated with the chapel, the stable and the chamber offers a convenient framework within which to consider musical life in the 15th and 16th centuries. The larger courts of emperor, kings and princes must have been a model for the many smaller households of nobles, church prelates, and even some of the wealthiest bourgeoisie, which have scarcely been studied, since few records of them survive. We can get some idea of the character of the music at one of these smaller establishments from the account of Gutierre Diaz de Gamez, who described a visit to the country house of a retired French admiral in the early 15th century, when he was in the service of the Spanish nobleman Don Pero Niño whom he wished to extol as the ideal courtier. Life in the French country house began every morning with Mass celebrated in the admiral's private chapel, after which the ladies of the household rode in the countryside, played games and sang songs. After the main meal in the middle of the day, minstrels (Gamez does not make clear whether these were hired by the admiral on a regular basis or brought in for particular occasions) entertained the guests, by singing and playing music among other things. And the late afternoon and evening was often taken up with dancing. Even in a private noble house, then, occasions for music involved not only the participation of the aristocracy itself, but also opportunities for professionals who would have fulfilled the functions allotted to chapel, stable and chamber musicians in a royal establishment.[58]

The principal musical institutions of towns and cities consisted of the cathedral choir and the town band. Even though cathedral choirs in the late 15th and 16th centuries were surely organized like courtly chapel choirs, we need to keep open the possibility that each had quite distinctive conventions of performance, a possibility that has not been much explored by scholars yet. It is, for example, possible that certain kinds of music (such as Mass cycles based on secular songs) were more appropriate for private chapels than for cathedrals, or that princely chapels regularly made use of instruments earlier than cathedral choirs. On the other hand, it is possible that instruments participated in the devotional or even more strictly liturgical services (such as Salve services after Compline or the celebration of votive Masses) performed at side altars in a church and sponsored by confraternities of lay people. The wind bands hired by town councils were not unlike those employed at courts, save that many of the civic musicians had duties as night watchmen in addition to their obligations to give daily or weekly concerts and serenades to certain town officials on holidays, and to participate in such civic events as annual parades and banquets and the celebration of such notable occurrences as royal births and weddings, national victories and the signing of peace treaties.

The music in towns and cities aside from that provided by the church choir and the town band was apt to be less well organized and hence less capable of being studied systematically. The guilds of minstrels that sprang up in many cities in northern Europe in the 15th century functioned chiefly to regulate the supply of instrumentalists and to supervise the conditions of their employment.[59] We know from guild statutes and from surviving contracts that minstrels formed freelance bands of three or four to play for whatever occasions citizens wished to hire them, mostly, of course, for weddings and other private anniversaries. Some minstrels were more or less regularly attached to such large civic corporations as the Basochiens of Paris, the association of law clerks, and some minstrels organized schools for the education of lay people (as distinct from the schools or annual conferences that the minstrels themselves attended as late as the 15th century). In some cities during the Renaissance, there was surely lively activity among the bourgeoisie in making music at home for private enjoyment, and we may presume that a part of the explanation for the apparent success of the music printing industry in the 16th century is that volumes of printed music were destined for this market of amateur chamber players. Certainly, the prefaces of some of the anthologies and instruction books published in the 16th century and intended to offer music and training in playing a particular instrument explain that the volumes were intended for amateurs.[60] And we know that in Italy, groups of aristocrats formed academies and hired music masters to supervise their private musical education and their performances.

We can never know much about the music of the lower classes in the 15th and 16th centuries, the music sung and played by simple citizens and peasants in town, in the countryside, in taverns and so on, simply because information about the activities of the semi-literate and the illiterate does not survive in great abundance. Writers of imaginative literature make occasional passing remarks about the musical activities of townspeople and peasants, and some pictures show them singing and playing, but there are no great manuscript or printed collections of 'folk music' or 'popular music' in the 15th and 16th centuries, except possibly for the printed collections of song texts (without music) that circulated in France during the Renaissance, the two elegant manuscripts of French popular songs copied in the early 16th century at a time when such tunes began to penetrate 'art music' and therefore became fashionable enough for the more literate segments of society to wish to collect, and for the remnants of popular music incorporated into the polyphonic repertories at various times and places.[61]

It would seem that there were more occasions for the performance of music in the 15th and 16th centuries than there had been in earlier times, although possibly our impression of expanded opportunities comes simply from the fact that so much more information survives from the Renaissance than from the Middle Ages. Polyphonic music was performed not only at the main altar at Mass and Office hours; growing numbers of votive Masses and devotional services began to be offered at side altars, and processions through church and city increased the number of performances church musicians gave each year.[62] Music continued to be an important element at great banquets and intimate meals alike, and both courtiers and members of the *haute bourgeoisie* cultivated the performance of music in private as one of the ideal social accomplishments of ladies and gentlemen.[63] Municipal authorities sponsored concerts by the town band, and even organized great civic celebrations when the cathedral choir and the local wind band collaborated in entertaining citizens.[64] Some Italian courts (such as that of Ferrara with its famous ladies) seem also to have offered regular concerts by their resident virtuosos, or occasional concerts just to show them off.[65] And the reports of the splendid music organized by Adrian Willaert for his rich patrons in Venice make clear that evening entertainments dominated by professional singers and players had become a fixture of social life in late 16th-century Italy.[66]

Information about when, where and how music was performed in the 15th and 16th centuries appears in great abundance in a number of kinds of sources. Archival documentation becomes more copious and more informative in the 15th century than it had been previously, and scholars have made regular use of the archives of various cities and courts not only to discover biographical details about local composers, but also to uncover strategies of patronage and to understand better the nature and organization of musical institutions (and hence the conventions of performance) in the Renaissance. A few of the musical sources themselves instruct us about the reasons why the music was commissioned, and when and even sometimes how it was first performed. I think in the first place of those souvenir booklets of especially important courtly or civic celebrations that report in great detail about the events that took place, including what music was performed and how.[67] But the sorts of information not found either in archives or in the music, that is, detailed descriptions of the way music was performed outside an institutional framework, can also be found in abundance in the later 15th and 16th centuries. Literary evidence – more or less detailed explanations to be found in works of imaginative literature and also chronicles and other non-fictional accounts of the way some kinds of music were actually performed – also becomes more abundant in the 15th and 16th centuries than it had been before, and it is likely to be more useful than earlier information, simply because we know more about the social contexts to which authors refer. Iconographic information is likewise more copious, and more instructive in that pictures from the 15th and 16th centuries often depict real events or idealized versions of what happened in real life, even though in dealing with later pictures we must always take into account the possibility that artists were copying an older artistic tradition rather than painting from real life.

Finally, treatises written by professional musicians for the education of lay people or other professionals appear in far greater numbers in the 16th century than they had before, and many of them deal directly with problems connected with performance. There was a dramatic increase in the number of books, for example, that claim to substitute for a private tutor in offering instruction in a particular instrument. Although it is difficult to know for certain, these instruction books (listed at the end of vol.i of this handbook) must surely signal a dramatic rise in the general musical level of the populace – the extent to which music had increasingly become a desirable social accomplishment – and not merely an indication of improvements in technology signalled by the rise of music printing in the 16th century, which made books more easily available to a much larger segment of the population. In short, there is a mountain of material to study that can enlighten us about the performance of music in the 15th and 16th centuries, and we have by no means exhausted it yet; on the contrary, we have hardly even begun to mine its riches.

The Renaissance

Notes

[1] On the question of authenticity as an important criterion in modern performances of 'early music', see the studies cited in Chapter I n.11.

[2] On this point see among other studies H. M. Brown, *A Florentine Chansonnier from the Time of Lorenzo the Magnificent (Florence, Biblioteca Nazionale Centrale, MS Banco Rari 229)*, MRM, vii (1983), text vol., chap.xv, 'Text Underlay', 168–80, which cites earlier studies. For the view that voices not supplied with text were not meant to be sung, see L. Litterick, 'Performing Franco-Netherlandish Secular Music of the Late Fifteenth Century', *EM*, viii (1980), 474–85.

[3] For a challenge to the idea that the highly melismatic nature of 15th-century music calls into question the relationship of words and music, see D. M. Randel, 'Dufay the Reader', *Studies in the History of Music*, i: *Music and Language* (New York, 1983), 38–78. In my view, Randel does not take sufficient account of the variety of solutions offered by 15th-century scribes, or of the difficulty modern scholars have in reaching an agreement about details of text placement in any one 15th-century composition.

[4] A point made in C. Wright, 'Voices and Instruments in the Art Music of Northern France during the 15th Century: a Conspectus', in *IMSCR*, xii *Berkeley 1977*, 644–6.

[5] The connecting lines in *GB-Ob* Can. misc. 213 are mentioned in passing in *Polyphonia sacra: a Continental Miscellany of the Fifteenth Century*, ed. C. van den Borren (Burnham, 1932, rev. 2/1962), p.iii. They have not, so far as I know, been studied in detail.

[6] See D. Harrán, 'In Pursuit of Origins: the Earliest Writing on Text Underlay (c.1440)', *AcM*, l (1978), 217–40.

[7] See M. S. Lewis, 'Zarlino's Theories of Text Underlay as Illustrated in his Motet Book of 1549', *Notes*, xlii (1985), 239–67.

[8] See Giovanni Maria Lanfranco, *Scintille di musica* (Brescia, 1533/R1970); translated into English with an extensive commentary in B. Lee, *Giovanni Maria Lanfranco's 'Scintille di musica' and its Relation to 16th-century Music Theory* (diss., Cornell U., 1961). On Lanfranco's rules for text underlay, see D. Harrán, 'New Light on the Question of Text Underlay Prior to Zarlino', *AcM*, xlv (1973), 24–56.

[9] Zarlino's well-known rules of text underlay appear in *Le istitutioni harmoniche* (Venice, 1558/R1965), bk4, chap.33. Zarlino's chapter is translated into English in O. Strunk, *Source Readings in Music History* (New York, 1950), 259–61, and in Zarlino, *On the Modes*, trans. V. Cohen (New Haven, 1983); see especially 98–9.

[10] Gaspar Stocker's manuscript treatise, in the Biblioteca Nacional of Madrid, is described and Stocker's rules elucidated in E. E. Lowinsky, 'A Treatise on Text Underlay by a German Disciple of Francisco de Salinas', in *Festschrift Heinrich Besseler* (Leipzig, 1962), 231–51. See also Lowinsky's extensive discussion of text underlay in the first volume of his edition of *The Medici Codex of 1518*, MRM, iii (1968), 90–107, and also D. Harrán, 'Vicentino and his Rules of Text Underlay', *MQ*, lix (1973), 620–32; H. M. Brown, 'Words and Music in Early Sixteenth-century Chansons', in *Quellenstudien zur Musik der Renaissance I: Formen und Probleme der Überlieferung mehrstimmiger Musik im Zeitalter Josquins Desprez*, ed. L. Finscher (Munich, 1981), 97–142; and A. Atlas, 'Paolo Luchini's *Della musica*: a Little-known Source for Text Underlay from the Late Sixteenth Century', *JM*, ii (1983), 62–80, where further recent studies are cited.

[11] See the studies cited in Karol Berger's chapter above. A practical introduction to many of the problems of adding editorial accidentals may be found in N. Routley, 'A Practical Guide to Musica Ficta', *EM*, xiii (1985), 59–71.

[12] On this subject, see especially H. M. Brown, 'Accidentals and Ornamentation in Sixteenth-century Intabulations of Josquin's Motets', in *Josquin des Prez: New York 1971*, 475–522, and Brown, 'La musica ficta dans les mises en tablature d'Albert de Rippe et Adrian le Roy', in *Le luth et sa musique II*, ed. J.-M. Vaccaro (Paris, 1984), 163–82.

[13] On the size and composition of church and chapel choirs in the 15th and early 16th centuries, see F. A. D'Accone, 'The Performance of Sacred Music in Italy during Josquin's Time, c. 1475–1525', in *Josquin des Prez: New York 1971*, 601–18; C. Wright, 'Performance Practices at the Cathedral of Cambrai 1475–1550', *MQ*, lxiv (1978), 295–328, who gives some details about the occasions when only a part of the choir was used; and D. Fallows, 'Specific Information on the Ensembles for Composed Polyphony, 1400–1474', in *Performance Practice: New York 1981*, 109–59.

[14] On the concerts given by the nuns of S Vito in Ferrara in the second half of the 16th century, for example, see Ercole Bottrigari, *Il desiderio or Concerning the Playing Together of Various Musical Instruments*, trans. C. MacClintock, MSD, ix (1962), 57–60.

[15] On these points, see Chapter X.

[16] The large Ferrarese *concerti* for special occasions are described in Bottrigari, *Il desiderio*, 50–54.

[17] The volume with Willaert's arrangements for solo voice and lute of Verdelot's madrigals is described in *BrownI* as 1536[8]. The collection is published in a modern edition as *Intavolatura de li madrigali di Verdelotto de cantare et sonare nel lauto, 1536*, ed. B. Thomas (London, 1980).

[18] On Pietrobono and some few pieces in his repertory, see L. Lockwood, *Music in Renaissance Ferrara 1400–1505* (Oxford, 1984), 96–108, who cites earlier studies of the improvising poet-singers at 15th-century Italian courts.

[19] On virtuoso singers in the late 16th century, and the way they embellished the music they sang, see among other studies H. M. Brown, *Embellishing Sixteenth-century Music* (London, 1976).

[20] On women as musicians during the Middle Ages and the Renaissance, see the essays by Anne Bagnall Yardley, Maria V. Coldwell, Howard Mayer Brown, Anthony Newcomb and Jane Bowers, in *Women Making Music: the Western Art Tradition 1150–1950*, ed. J. Bowers and J. Tick (Urbana and Chicago, 1986).

[21] On the singing ladies of Ferrara, see A. Newcomb, *The Madrigal at Ferrara 1579–1597* (Princeton, 1980).

[22] For the view that instruments other than the organ never played in church in the Middle Ages and the Renaissance, see among other studies J. W. McKinnon, 'Musical Instruments in Medieval Psalm Commentaries and Psalters', *JAMS*, xxi (1968), 3–20, who cites earlier studies, and D'Accone, 'The Performance of Sacred Music'. On the possibility that some 15th-century masses were intended to be performed with instruments, see A. E. Planchart, 'Fifteenth-century Masses: Notes on Performance and Chronology', *Studi musicali*, x (1981), 3–29.

[23] S. Zak, 'Fürstliche und städtische Repräsentation in der Kirche (Zur Verwendung von Instrumenten im Gottesdienst)', *MD*, xxxviii (1984), 231–59, offers a number of notices of occasions when instruments other than the organ were used in connection with various ceremonies in churches.

[24] See M.-T. Bouquet, 'La cappella musicale dei duchi di Savoia dal 1450 al 1500', *RIM*, iii (1968), 236–9, 251.

[25] The archival notice reporting that in 1502 the chapel of Philip the Fair sang a mass with the Spanish royal chapel in Toledo and that 'avoecq lesquelz chantres de Mgr [Philip] jouoit du cornet maistre Augustin' is given in M. Brenet, 'Notes sur l'introduction des instruments dans les églises de France', in *Riemann-Festschrift* (Leipzig, 1909/R1965), 281. For other notices about maistre Augustin and about cornetts in church, see also G. Karstädt, 'Zur Geschichte des Zinkens und seiner Verwendung in der Musik des 16.–18. Jahrhunderts', *AMf*, ii (1937), 415–22.

[26] For a discussion of this point, see Chapters X and XII.

[27] On this point, see Chapter IX nn.11 and 12.

[28] See for example Chapter XI.

[29] The passage is reproduced in 'Der altfranzösische Roman Paris et Vienne', ed. R. Kaltenbacher, *Romanische Forschungen*, xv (1904), 405. For differing interpretations of the two passages, see H. M. Brown, 'Instruments and Voices in the Fifteenth-century Chanson', *Current Thoughts in Musicology*, ed. J. W. Grubbs (Austin, Texas, and London, 1976), 102–3, and C. Page, 'The Performance of Songs in Late Medieval France', *EM*, x (1982), 441–50.

[30] Prudenzani wrote a series of *novelle* framed by descriptions (in the form of sonnets) of the entertainment provided by a musician called Il Sollazzo during the evenings, at a house party during the Christmas holidays at the fictitious castle of Buongoverno ruled by Pierbaldo. The *novelle* are printed in a modern edition in S. Debenedetti, 'Il "Sollazzo" e il "Saporetto" con altre rime di Simone Prudenzani d'Orvieto', *Giornale storico della letteratura italiana*, suppl.xv (1913). The sonnets alone are published in Debenedetti, *Il 'Solazzo': contributi alla storia della novella, della poesia musicale, e del costume nel trecento* (Turin, 1922), 169–77.

The Faenza Codex is reproduced in facsimile in *Keyboard Music of the Late Middle Ages in Codex Faenza 117*, ed. D. Plamenac, CMM, lvii (1972). For an unconvincing argument that the Faenza Codex was not intended for keyboard, see T. J. McGee, 'Instruments and the Faenza Codex', *EM*, xiv (1986), 480–90.

[31] The easiest way to form an overview of their repertory is through *BrownI*.

[32] Some of these volumes are mentioned in *BrownI*, p.4

[33] On the performance of frottole, see W. F. Prizer, 'Performance Practices in the Frottola', *EM*, iii (1975), 227–35, and Prizer, 'The Frottola and the Unwritten Tradition', *Studi musicali*, xv (1986), 3–37.

[34] See for example H. M. Brown, *Sixteenth-century Instrumentation: the Music of the Florentine Intermedii*, MSD, xxx (1973).

[35] So far as I know, the lutenist Giovanni Antonio Terzi was the first to make explicit the possibility that lute intabulations could be used either as solo pieces or as accompaniments to ensemble music (in the case of his volume, printed in 1593, canzone by Fiorenzo Maschera). The contents of Terzi's volume are listed and described in *BrownI*, 1593[7]. Descriptions of performances make clear, however, that lutenists or keyboard players commonly accompanied ensembles of singers or players. See for example H. M. Brown, 'A Cook's Tour of Ferrara in 1529', *RIM*, x (1975), 216–41, where the principles of scoring madrigals performed at the court of Ferrara are outlined.

[36] On wind bands in the 15th and 16th centuries, see the studies cited in n.41 of the chapter on instruments of the 15th and 16th centuries in this handbook.

[37] On the concept and repertory of English mixed consorts, see W. A. Edwards, 'The Performance of Ensemble Music in Elizabethan England', *PRMA*, xcvii (1970–71), 113ff; Edwards, *The Sources of Elizabethan Consort Music* (diss., Cambridge U., 1974); and Edwards, 'Consort', *Grove6*.

[38] See for example H. M. Brown, 'Embellishment in Early Sixteenth-century Italian Intabulations', *PRMA*, c (1973–4), 49–84; and Brown, 'Accidentals and Ornamentation'.

[39] See H. M. Brown, *Embellishing Sixteenth-century Music*. All the embellishment manuals are listed in E. T. Ferand, 'Didactic Embellishment Literature in the Late Renaissance: a Survey of Sources', in *Aspects of Medieval and Renaissance Music: a Birthday Offering to Gustave Reese* (New York, 1966), 154–72. *Die Improvisation in Beispielen aus neun Jahrhunderten abendländischer Musik*, ed. Ferand (Cologne, 1956) is a useful anthology of examples of written-out embellishment.

[40] N. Bridgman, 'Giovanni Camillo Maffei et sa lettre sur le chant', *RdM*, xxxviii (1956), 3–34.

[41] On the organ tablatures, see W. Apel, *Keyboard Music of the Fourteenth and Fifteenth Centuries*, CEKM, i (1963); and *Das Buxheimer Orgelbuch*, ed. B. Wallner, EDM, xxxvii–xxxix (Kassel, 1958–9). On *giustiniane*, see W. Rubsamen, 'The Justiniane or Viniziane of the 15th Century', *AcM*, xxix (1957), 172–84.

[42] See Brown, *Embellishing Sixteenth-century Music*, 73–6.

[43] The most recent study of this question is D. Bonge, 'Gaffurius on Pulse and Tempo: a Reinterpretation', *MD*, xxxvi (1982), 167–74.

[44] See Chapter VII for a more detailed exposition of the theory and practice of tempo and proportions. A good survey of the problems may also be found in A. Mendel, 'Some Ambiguities of the Mensural System', in *Studies in Music History: Essays for Oliver Strunk* (Princeton, 1968), 137ff.

[45] See Nicola Vicentino, *L'antica musica ridotta alla moderna prattica* (Rome, 1555/R1959). On tempo in Renaissance music, see also C. Dahlhaus, 'Zur Entstehung des modernen Taktsystems im 17. Jahrhundert', *AMw*, xviii (1961), 223ff; C. Jacobs, *Tempo Notation in Renaissance Spain* (Brooklyn, 1964); and J. A. Banks, *Tactus, Tempo and Notation in Mensural Music from the 13th to the 17th Century* (Amsterdam, 1972).

[46] The most detailed study of pitch levels before the 20th century remains A. Mendel, 'Pitch in Western Music since 1500: a Re-examination', *AcM*, l (1978), 1–93, but see also J. J. K. Rhodes and W. R. Thomas, 'Pitch', *Grove6*, xiv, 781–6; and the chapter on pitch by C. Karp in this handbook.

[47] For details, see Chapter VII in vol.ii.

[48] See Bottrigari, *Il desiderio*.

[49] See H. M. Brown, 'Notes (and Transposing Notes) on the Viol in the Early Sixteenth Century', in *Music in Medieval and Early Modern Europe*, ed. I. Fenlon (Cambridge, 1981), 61–78; Brown, 'Notes (and Transposing Notes) on the Transverse Flute in the Early Sixteenth Century', *JAMIS*, xii (1986), 5–39; Brown and K. M. Spencer, 'How Alfonso della Viola Tuned his Viols, and how he Transposed', *EM*, xiv (1986), 520–33; and Brown, 'Bossinensis, Willaert and Verdelot: Pitch and the Conventions of Transcribing Music for Lute and Voice in Italy in the Early Sixteenth Century' (forthcoming).

[50] On the question of transposing keyboards, see the studies cited in Chapter IX n.2.

[51] See for example Girolamo dalla Casa, *Il vero modo di diminuir* (Venice, 1584), vol.ii f.1v, who criticizes wind players who slur *passaggi*; and the brief discussion of this point in Brown, *Embellishing Sixteenth-century Music*, 69–70.

[52] For some suggestions about where to find whatever was written on such subjects in the 16th century, see Brown, *Embellishing Sixteenth-century Music*, 67–71, and D. Fallows, 'Tempo and

expression marks', *Grove6*, xviii, 682–4. For an excellent survey of attitudes towards vibrato on wind instruments, see B. Dickey, 'Untersuchungen zur historischen Auffassung des Vibratos auf Blasinstrumenten', *Basler Jb für historische Musikpraxis*, ii (1978), 77–142.

[53] On François I's musicians and the organization of music at his court, see M. Brenet, 'Deux comptes de la chapelle-musique des rois de France', *SIMG*, vi (1904–5), 1ff; H. Prunières, 'La musique de la chambre et de l'écurie sous le règne de François I', *L'année musicale*, i (1911), 215–51; and P. Kast, 'Remarques sur la musique et les musiciens de la chapelle de François I au Camp du Drap d'Or', *Fêtes et cérémonies au temps de Charles Quint* [*Fêtes de la Renaissance* II]: *CNRS Bruxelles, Anvers, Gand, Liège 1957*, 153ff.

[54] For some notices about instruments regularly employed to play in church, see D. Arnold, 'Instruments in Church: some Facts and Figures', *MMR*, lxxxv (1955), 32–8, and Arnold, 'Brass Instruments in Italian Church Music of the Sixteenth and Early Seventeenth Centuries', *Brass Quarterly*, i (1957), 81–92.

[55] For an overview of the functions of court trumpeters and drummers, with an extensive bibliography, see E. H. Tarr, 'Trumpet', *GroveMI*, iii, especially 641–8. For some specific examples of the functions of a particular court's trumpeters, see for example *Die Münchner Fürstenhochzeit von 1568. Massimo Troiano: Dialoge*, trans. and ed. by H. Leuchtmann (Munich and Salzburg, 1980), and H. M. Brown, 'Orlando di Lasso's Musicians: Massimo Troiano's Account of Munich's Musical Life in 1568' (forthcoming).

[56] Certainly, the instrumentalists at the Bavarian court in Munich in Lassus's time played all genres of music, according to *Die Münchener Fürstenhochzeit*, ed. Leuchtmann, and Brown, 'Lasso's Musicians'. For other examples of the wide-ranging repertory of court minstrels in the 16th century, see Brown, 'Minstrels and their Repertory in Fifteenth-century France' (forthcoming) and the studies cited there.

[57] On the problems of attempting to disentangle the chamber musicians from the other musicians at a Renaissance court, see for example S. Bonime, *Anne de Bretagne (1477–1514) and Music: an Archival Study* (diss., Bryn Mawr College, 1975). The problem is also illustrated in Lockwood, *Music in Renaissance Ferrara*, 314–28; in reporting on the personnel in Ferrara, Lockwood divides the musicians simply between singers and instrumentalists, with little or no attempt to distinguish between chamber musicians and players of loud winds, presumably because the two kinds of performers were not administratively separate in the Ferrarese records.

[58] See Gutierre Diaz de Gamez, *The Unconquered Knight: a Chronicle of the Deeds of Don Pero Niño, Count of Buelna*, trans. and ed. J. Evans (London, 1928), 134–9. On the participation of courtiers with professionals in music-making, see the seminal iconographical study of H. Besseler, 'Umgangsmusik und Darstellungsmusik im 16. Jahrhundert', *AMw*, xvi (1959), 21–43.

[59] The most detailed account of the rules and regulations of a single minstrels' guild remains B. Bernhard, 'Recherches sur l'histoire de la corporation des ménétriers ou joueurs d'instruments de la ville de Paris', *Bibliothèque de l'école des chartes*, iii (1841–2), 377ff; iv (1842–3), 525ff; v (1843–4), 254ff, 339ff. H. W. Schwab, 'Guilds', *Grove6*, includes an excellent bibliography of studies of particular guilds. On freelance French musicians in the 16th century, see F. Lesure, 'Les orchestres populaires à Paris à la fin du seizieme siècle', *RdM*, xxxvi (1954), 39ff.

[60] A number of the volumes listed and described in *BrownI* have such prefaces, or remarks addressed to laymen, beginners or 'those who cannot sing', indicating that they were addressed to an amateur and not to a professional audience.

[61] On the popular poems and songs of France in the late 15th and 16th centuries, for example, see H. M. Brown, *Music in the French Secular Theater: 1400–1550* (Cambridge, Mass., 1963), and B. Jeffery, *Chanson Verse of the Early Renaissance* (London, 1971–5), who publishes in modern edition a number of texts that circulated in simple 'popular' editions in the 16th century.

[62] On the non-liturgical or paraliturgical functions of motets in the late 15th and 16th centuries, see A. M. Cummings, 'Toward an Interpretation of the Sixteenth-century Motet', *JAMS*, xxxiv (1981), 43–59.

[63] On banquets and other venues for the performance of music, see among other studies E. A. Bowles, *Musikleben im 15. Jahrhundert*, Musikgeschichte in Bildern, iii/8 (Leipzig, 1977), and W. Salmen, *Musikleben im 16. Jahrhundert*, Musikgeschichte in Bildern, iii/9 (Leipzig, 1976). The work that offered courtiers a model for behaviour was, of course, Baldessare Castiglione's *Il cortigiano*, the best modern edition of which is that by V. Cian (Florence, rev. 4/1947); English translation by Sir Thomas Hotby as *The Book of the Courtier (1561)* (London, 1928).

[64] For some examples, see Brown, 'Minstrels'.

[65] See for example Bottrigari, *Il desiderio*, and Newcomb, *The Madrigal*.

[66] On Willaert's concerts at the house of Neri Capponi, see Antonfrancesco Doni, *Dialogo della*

Musica, ed. F. Malipiero (Vienna, 1965), and J. Haar, 'Notes on the "Dialogo della Musica" of Antonfrancesco Doni', *ML*, xlvii (1966), 198–224.

[67] See for example *Musique des intermèdes de 'La Pellegrina'*, ed. D. P. Walker (Paris, 1963), and A. C. Minor and B. Mitchell, *A Renaissance Entertainment in 1539* (Columbia, Miss., 1968).

CHAPTER IX

Instruments

HOWARD M. BROWN

Much of what we think we know about musical instruments and their uses during the Middle Ages has necessarily to be conjectural; so little documentation survives that we must rely on secondary sources of information: archival, literary and iconographical. The study of musical instruments in the Renaissance, on the other hand, can to a much greater extent be based on treatises of a more or less technical nature.[1] To be sure, our knowledge of instruments in the 15th century, as for earlier centuries, comes mainly from scattered and fragmentary sources, many of them non-technical in character. Treatises devoted to instruments in general, or to the playing technique of a single instrument, did not begin to be written until after 1500.

As the list of treatises at the end of this handbook shows, however, a few written sources of the 15th century do offer extensive organological information. In accordance with medieval tradition, several writers described contemporary instruments as part of a larger theological or encyclopedic study. Thus Jean de Gerson, chancellor of the University of Paris, explained the instruments of Psalm 150 in contemporary terms in a commentary written about 1430. And Paulus Paulirinus of Prague enumerated and discussed the instruments in common use in eastern Europe about 1460 in the section of his encyclopedia on all the arts that dealt with music.[2]

Other 15th-century studies broke new ground. Ramos de Pareia's *Musica practica* of 1482 was perhaps the first of a number of general music treatises to incorporate a discussion of instruments into the traditional scheme of music theory.[3] Johannes Tinctoris's *De inventione et usu musicae*, presumably printed in the last quarter of the 15th century but lost except for some fragments, is the only treatise from the 15th century to deal with what we would think of today as the reality of musical practice. *De inventione et usu musicae* is important for the valuable insights which one of the most encyclopedic of all 15th-century writers on music provides into the musical uses of instruments. Tinctoris's treatise, and Grocheo's *De musica* of about 1300, are the only two works written before the 16th century that deal extensively with the social uses of music.[4] About 1440, Henri Arnault de Zwolle, physician and astronomer to the court of Burgundy (and later to the French royal court), wrote a treatise devoted to musical instruments (as well as to astronomy and other scientific matters). This gives us the earliest detailed technical specifications we have about the design and construction of the lute, the harp, the organ and various stringed keyboards, among them several types of harpsichord, the clavichord and the somewhat mysterious *dulce melos*.[5]

167

The works by Ramos, Tinctoris and Arnault usher in a new age when practical matters became a fit subject for formal discourse for the first time. Beginning in the first decades of the 16th century, the amount of technical writing about instruments increases enormously, perhaps to meet a growing demand for wider dissemination of cultural matters, especially among the educated classes. A series of didactic works from the 16th century, encyclopedic in a much more specialized and narrowly technical way than any of the medieval compendia, devote all or most of their space to a survey of the instruments in common use, and some of these even include information on the repertory of each instrument and how each was tuned and played. Sebastian Virdung's *Musica getutscht* of 1511 and Martin Agricola's *Musica instrumentalis deudsch* of 1529 (extensively revised in 1545) were presumably intended to instruct schoolchildren. Philibert Jambe de Fer's *Epitome musical*, printed in Lyons in 1556, was more probably meant to tell amateur musicians what they needed to know about the elements of music and about the flute, the recorder, the viol and the violin. Juan Bermudo incorporated extensive information about instruments into his introduction to what we would call the theory and practice of music (*El libro llamado declaracion de instrumentos musicales* of 1555), Lodovico Zacconi's *Prattica di musica* (1592–1622) treats instruments and performance practice as a part of his explanation of the fundamentals of music, and a number of other 16th- and early 17th-century writers on music include some details about instruments in their general musical treatises. To these 16th-century didactic writers we should doubtless also add Michael Praetorius, even though he published his three volumes of the *Syntagma Musicum* between 1614 and 1618, since he made so much use of earlier sources of information and many of his conclusions are more relevant to 16th-century than to 17th-century practice. Moreover, no student of 16th-century instruments can safely ignore the works of Marin Mersenne (1627), Pierre Trichet (*c*1630) and James Talbot (*c*1680), even though they all write about later repertories.[6]

Along with these surveys and summaries of instrumental practice in treatises on music in general, the 16th century also saw the first examples of printed instruction books for particular instruments. Starting with Arnolt Schlick's *Spiegel der Orgelmacher* of 1511, which includes information both about making and playing organs, and his anthology of music for organ and lute of the following year, an enormous number of books about individual instruments began to appear.[7] Many were devoted to the lute, the instrument *par excellence* of amateur and professional alike in the 16th century. Furthermore, a number of anthologies, especially of lute music, begin with introductions, prefaces, dedications and forewords that include some practical information about performance. The earliest of these, Petrucci's rules for those who cannot sing, served as a preface to his first printed anthologies of lute music.[8] Many of these sets of instructions are included in the list of primary sources at the end of the Renaissance section of this handbook. Clearly, by the 16th century, the practice of music was highly valued as a social accomplishment, and widespread enough to elicit a spate of books intended for a public of musically literate amateurs.

Even though there is much left to learn, we know more about the ways musical instruments were used in the Renaissance than in the Middle Ages.

It is far easier, for example, to summarize the inventions and the innovations of the 15th and 16th centuries than those of earlier times. Enough preliminary research has been completed to suggest that we are beginning to understand what was new and different in the period, even though some of the conclusions may well be reversed by further work.

In our present state of knowledge, it would appear that the most significant events in the history of musical instruments during the 15th century included the spread of large organs in cathedrals and churches, and the rise of stringed keyboard instruments: harpsichords, clavichords and virginals. The slide trumpet was invented and then abandoned in favour of the trombone (that is, the sackbut). Both the recorder and the transverse flute may well have been introduced into polite society, perhaps only towards the end of the century, about the same time that the cornett and the crumhorn came into being as instruments to play polyphony in ensemble. The technique of using fingers instead of a plectrum to pluck the strings of the lute developed in the course of the 15th century and enabled performers to play polyphonic music on their instruments, thus making possible the development of the lute as the great virtuoso instrument of the Renaissance. Whereas the fiddle continued to be the most versatile and flexible of all the bowed strings, a distinctive variant, the *lira da braccio* – with a characteristic shape and normally seven strings (two of them off-board drones) – was developed in Italy during the century to accompany the narrative or semi-improvised singing of courtly poet–musicians. By the early decades of the 16th century, the fiddle all but disappeared in upper-class musical circles, except for the specialized role still played by the *lira*. Among the major developments in the history of instruments in the late 15th and early 16th centuries must surely be counted the introduction of the viola da gamba into Italy and the invention of the violin family.

Musicians in the 16th century continued the experimentation, improvement and change that has always characterized the history of instruments in western Europe by inventing new instruments, changing the old, and developing new playing techniques. Although the 16th-century lute, for example, pre-empted all the earlier sorts of plucked strings, music for cittern, guitar, and (in Spain) vihuela constitutes an important repertory, and towards the end of the century a range of new, plucked-string instruments came into existence, such as the chitarrone or theorbo. Among the most important innovations of the 16th century, makers began to build instruments in standardized sizes. Needless to say, this generalization must be qualified, given local variations in pitch levels. We do know, however, that in the 16th century, standard groups of like instruments, that is, unmixed consorts, were regularly played together for the first time. Martin Agricola, Hans Gerle and Michael Praetorius (in the 17th century), among others, discuss consorts of viols, recorders, flutes and other instruments. These pure consorts were modified in the case of the wind bands, in which trombones were combined with shawms for outdoor and gala occasions, and with cornetts to accompany choirs.

By the end of the 15th or the first decades of the 16th century, certain instruments prominent in the medieval instrumentarium had either disappeared or had been transformed into 'folk' instruments associated with the

169

lower classes. Many instruments – notably the hurdy-gurdy, the rebec, the gittern, the citole, the psaltery, the portative organ, the bagpipe and the double recorder – were no longer used regularly for the performance of polyphonic music.[9] Instead, they led a shadowy existence as instruments fit only for beggars, peasants, shepherds and other members of the lower classes.

Indeed, the transformation of the standard instrumentarium between 1400 and 1600 was so radical that it would be tempting to divide the history of instruments not at 1400, as we customarily though perhaps erroneously do for the history of musical style, but rather at 1500. (A similar case could also be made for such a division for the history of musical style.) In many ways, the 15th century looked back to the Middle Ages; musicians then continued to use most of the instruments of the medieval instrumentarium in the traditional manner. The 15th century, however, also looked forward to the 16th; new instruments were invented, new uses were found for traditional instruments, and new playing techniques were introduced. Not all of these developments and inventions have been equally well studied, and not all of them are equally clear to us. We still need to learn about the structure and playing techniques of many instruments, and about the repertories they played and the way that they were used before we can claim to understand the instruments and instrumental practices of the 15th and 16th centuries.

By the early 15th century, large organs began regularly to be installed in cathedrals and churches virtually everywhere in western Europe.[10] In earlier organs, individual ranks of pipes could not be played separately; at most some of them were supplied with a set of Bourdon pipes (or Trompes) operated from a separate keyboard. The greatest technological developments in organ building in the 15th century involved the capacity to build separable stops, enabling players to make use of a much greater range of tone colours and contrasts. This new flexibility also explains why builders began to invent so many new stops (including reeds and stopped pipes) in the 15th and 16th centuries, and why they added more than one manual to many of the larger instruments. Most 15th-century organs seem to have had some sort of pedal board, and most were fully chromatic with five keys for accidentals in every octave, except perhaps the lowest.

Church organists in the 15th century improvised during some liturgical services over cantus firmi drawn from plainchant; a number of instruction books, many of them German, explain the techniques for inventing such semi-improvised polyphony, a central part of organists' expertise for centuries.[11] Many of the countless settings of plainchants in the organ literature from the 15th century onwards reflect the styles and techniques developed in the course of daily services. Church organs also alternated with choirs singing chant or polyphony (so-called *alternatim* performances), as the Faenza Codex and numerous 16th-century collections demonstrate.[12] And some of the preludes, postludes and interludes that organists performed during the liturgy and on other occasions – both free, toccata-like fantasias, and, later in the 16th century, more imitative motet-like compositions – were written down and are preserved. The 15th-century preambles are the earliest surviving examples of what was possibly a widespread practice of improvising such compositions, and they are among the earliest examples of an autonomous instrumerrtal music.[13] In short, it is possible to explain some of the things organists did in church in the 15th and 16th centuries, even if we cannot say with assurance the extent to which they accompanied singers of chant and polyphony. Not until the second half of the 16th century do we have secure evidence in the form of short scores that church organists played while polyphonic choirs sang.[14]

Portative organs can still be seen in 15th-century works of art, and Henri Arnault wrote about them *c*1440.[15] Presumably they still played single lines in ensembles with other instruments or with voices, but they disappear from view – at least they seem not to have been regularly employed in the performance of composed polyphony – by the 16th century. Positive organs are less often seen in pictures than portatives, but other kinds of evidence make clear that they existed and that they were used to play a chamber repertory of sacred and secular music.

Intabulations of polyphonic chansons by Machaut and later French composers, and of ballate and madrigals by Landini and his Italian successors, appear in the Faenza Codex of the early 15th century. The Buxheim Organ Book and the numerous smaller German collections of keyboard music from the mid-15th century are filled with intabulations of vocal pieces by both French and German composers. Numerous 16th-century collections of secular and sacred music were published in France, Italy and Germany, arranged for stringed keyboard instruments or for organs, for no explicit or radical differences of style separated the music for the two kinds of instruments; music by the Spaniards Cabezón and Venegas de Henestrosa even appeared in versions said to be appropriate for keyboards, harp or vihuela, showing the close relationship in musical style for all those kinds of instruments.[16] These sources do not specify whether positive organs or larger fixed instruments were intended for the secular repertory. We can only assume that all of these collections exemplify the standard repertory of the secular organist, whether he played a positive organ or a large church organ.

During the 15th century, stringed keyboard instruments – harpsichords, virginals and clavichords – came into general use.[17] Mechanisms for these instruments were probably invented at the very end of the 14th century and more or less standardized within the next 100 years. The instruments are depicted, albeit infrequently, by 15th-century artists, but the first detailed and technical information we have about harpsichords and clavichords comes from Henri Arnault's treatise of *c*1440. From the beginning of the 16th century onwards various kinds of evidence – iconographical, archival and musical – instruct us about the character and repertory of stringed keyboard instruments, and a number of instruments actually survive from that period. Pictures and extant instruments reveal that various kinds of clavichords and virginals existed in the 16th century, and that there was a fairly standard harpsichord design of Italian manufacture: slender, with a case in which the thin-walled instrument was placed, and with one or two sets of eight-foot strings (or possibly with one eight- and one four-foot set of strings, not always detachable in the earlier part of the 16th century). The characteristic pungent sound of such instruments had a pronounced attack, and some (but not all) had relatively limited sustaining power.

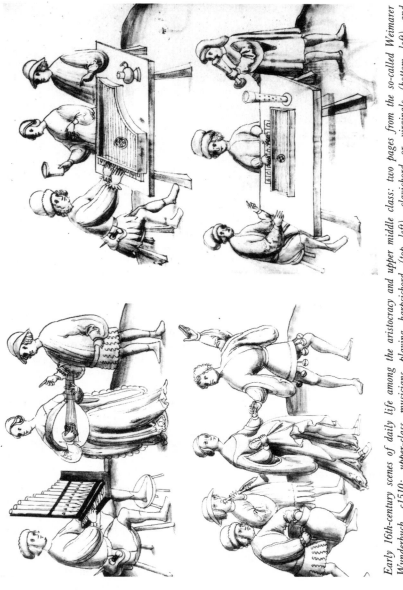

Early 16th-century scenes of daily life among the aristocracy and upper middle class: two pages from the so-called Weimarer Wunderbuch, c1510: upper-class musicians playing harpsichord (top left), clavichord or virginals (bottom left) and portative organ and lute (top right), and a well-born couple dancing while a minstrel plays a shaum (bottom right) (Weimar, Nationale Forschungs- und Gedenkstätten der Klassischen deutschen Literatur, 'Weimarer Ingenieurskunst- und Wunderbuch', f.328)

The earliest collections of music which specifically mention stringed keyboard instruments are the seven volumes of masses, motets, dances, chansons and preludes published by Pierre Attaingnant of Paris in 1531.[18] The title-page of each volume describes the contents as 'reduictes en la tabulature des Orgues Espinettes Manicordions, et telz semblables instrumentz musicaulx', without making any distinction between genre and instrument intended, thus implying that harpsichordists played mass movements as readily as organists played dances (which may or may not be true). Whereas there were not nearly so many volumes of music for stringed keyboard instruments published in the 16th century as collections for solo lute, Attaingnant's anthologies nevertheless strongly suggest that keyboard players performed the same kind of repertory as lutenists, that is to say, music in every genre known from the 16th century. On the other hand, it is not clear to what extent stringed keyboard instruments were used to accompany other instruments or voices during the 16th century. Diego Ortiz's treatise on playing the viola da gamba, published in both Spanish and Italian in 1553, is the earliest volume to call explicitly for a harpsichord accompaniment.[19]

During the 16th century makers experimented a great deal, modifying traditional instruments in various ways. For instance, some harpsichords may have been built to transpose automatically, that is, to sound g, for example, on the lower manual when the key for c' was struck.[20] Transposition down a fourth was evidently seen to be the most useful, and such instruments attest to a widespread convention that enabled musicians to fit music more comfortably to individual voices or make it conform to the limitations of their instruments. Late in the 16th or more probably during the first half of the 17th century, makers in northern Europe began to add a second manual to harpsichords simply for colouristic purposes, to enable players to achieve tonal contrast more easily.[21] Makers also invented new instruments. The earliest extant clavicytherium (a harpsichord with an upright soundboard) dates from c1480. The claviorgan, which combines a stringed keyboard with organ pipes, is mentioned as early as 1539.[22] In the second half of the century, several musicians experimented with keyboards that had complicated enharmonic tunings, some makers combined two separate instruments into a single 'mother-and-child' virginals, and Hans Haiden in Germany even tried to perfect an instrument (the so-called 'Geigenwerk') that involved bowing the strings instead of plucking or striking them.[23]

Throughout the 15th century, the fiddle and just possibly the rebec remained the most widespread and versatile of bowed string instruments.[24] And the *lira da braccio* gradually evolved from the fiddle, especially well adapted to accompany the narrative or semi-improvised singing of a whole class of Italian courtly poet–musicians.[25] It is true that the tromba marina seems to have been invented – or at least widely played for the first time – around the middle of the century, but its musical usefulness seems to have been relatively limited, and its career confined mostly to Flanders and Germany.[26] The late 15th- and early 16th-century developments that had the greatest impact on the sound of music for bowed strings involved the introduction of the viola da gamba into Italy from Spain at the very end of

173

Instruments played by angels attending the Coronation of the Virgin: early 16th-century fresco (detail) by Michele Coltellini showing (left to right) viola da gamba, violin, guitar, rebec and viola da gamba (Pinacoteca Nazionale, Ferrara)

the 15th century, and the invention of the violin family (as instruments especially adapted for loud playing and for dance music) in the first decades of the 16th century.[27] Viols quickly supplanted fiddles everywhere in western Europe as the most versatile and flexible of the bowed strings. Viols in the 16th century differ in many significant ways from more familiar Baroque viols, not least perhaps in that they may not have had sound posts, and thus produced light, silvery sonorities very different from later instruments.[28]

Musicians soon began to experiment with the newly introduced viols, either by modifying the instruments themselves or by playing them in a new way. Silvestro Ganassi in the two volumes of *Regola rubertina*, published in 1542 and 1543, and Diego Ortiz in his treatise of 1553, both describe some of the techniques of the new virtuoso viol players, but we are still not entirely certain whether the chordal playing in the manner of the *lira da braccio* (that is, playing *lira viol*), and playing florid embellishments based on several parts of a vocal model (that is, playing *viola bastarda*) involved special instruments designed for specific tasks, slightly modified versions of the instruments in standard sizes, or merely new techniques of playing.[29] On the other hand, at least one new bowed instrument, the *lirone*, was invented in the 16th century, to serve as a bass version of the *lira da braccio*.[30]

Hardly any written information about the technique of playing the violin comes down to us from the 16th century, for the newly invented instrument seems originally to have been limited to playing dances and other music associated with minstrels. Hence it did not inspire a series of treatises designed for the amateur upper-class musician. Only Philibert Jambe de Fer in his *Epitome musical* of 1556 included instructions for playing the violin, as well as the viol, the transverse flute and the recorder.[31]

At some point in the 15th century lutenists began to pluck the strings of their instruments with their fingers rather than with a plectrum.[32] But even if a finger technique on the lute was not actually invented then, it had certainly supplanted the use of the plectrum by 1500. The new technique enabled performers to play polyphonic music on their instruments, and its success is amply attested by the numerous anthologies of music for one or more lutes, or for lute and voice, published during the 16th century, anthologies that consist mostly of intabulations of every known genre of vocal music – masses, motets and secular music with texts in English, French, German or Italian – as well as dance music and abstract pieces such as fantasias and ricercares conceived specifically for the lute.[33]

The lute, in short, became the characteristic virtuoso instrument of the Renaissance, capable of playing any genre of music, composed or improvised. At the same time, a number of other plucked-string instruments developed. The cittern and the guitar, both radical transformations of earlier instruments, appear to have functioned at least partly as poor men's (or lazy men's) lutes, easier to play than the lute and yet capable of handling more or less the same repertory of polyphony.[34] Citterns traditionally hung in barbers' shops so that clients could while away the waiting time by playing, but there also seem to have been some virtuoso cittern and guitar players in the 16th century, to judge by the surviving anthologies. The vihuela, on the other hand, was a particular variety of guitar used only in Spain, evidently capable of playing pieces as complex as any lute music.[35]

175

Lutes, citterns, guitars and vihuelas were not the only plucked-string instruments of the 15th and 16th centuries. The gittern lived on through the 15th century (but disappeared in the 16th) as the favoured instrument of such Italian virtuosos as Pietrobono of Ferrara.[36] The scattered evidence we have suggests that psalteries began to be struck with beaters in the 15th century as well as being plucked with the fingers or with a plectrum; although the musical consequences of this change of technique are not completely clear, scholarly tradition gives a new name, dulcimer, to the instrument played in this new manner.[37] Musicians continued to seek ways of building a satisfactory fully chromatic harp; the double harp of the 16th century, whose history is still inadequately explored, appears to have been the result.[38] And towards the end of the 16th century, a whole range of new plucked-string instruments came into existence, especially the chitarrone (or theorbo) and the bandora, surely at least partly as a response to the new styles of monodic music.[39]

Probably the most important development in the history of wind instruments in the 15th century was the invention of the slide trumpet and its subsequent abandonment in favour of the trombone or sackbut. This soon became the foundation instrument for loud wind bands in court and city.[40] It was associated with shawms in the performance of semi-improvised dances, and perhaps other kinds of improvised and composed polyphony, including motets and chansons. In the 15th century the standard loud wind band (*alta cappella*) consisted of two shawms and a sackbut, with the larger of the two shawms (the bombarde) playing cantus firmus (at least in the basse danse repertory), while the sackbut and smaller shawm added contrapuntal lines above and below, as Tinctoris relates. In the 16th century the standard wind band seems to have consisted of four or five shawms and sackbuts (in varying combinations) for outdoor or gala performances, and (later in the 16th century) of cornetts and sackbuts for accompanying polyphonic choirs.[41]

The cornetts in such late 16th-century bands seem to have mainly doubled the upper voices, but the cornett also became a virtuoso's instrument in the 16th century.[42] Its history in the 15th century, on the other hand, like the history of the recorder, is somewhat obscure. Pictures of horns as well as whistle flutes with finger-holes can be found in medieval art, and such instruments are mentioned from time to time in works of literature. But there seems little reason to suppose that either instrument took much, if any, part in the performance of composed polyphony or any of the various unwritten repertories heard in court and city before the late 14th or early 15th centuries, at which time the recorder began to be regularly pictured, for example, in the hands of angels.[43] And by the end of the 15th century the cornett had also established itself in western European musical life. Before that time, it seems likely that both the fingered horn and the whistle flute (except for some varieties of pipe and tabor and the double recorders of the 14th century) were mostly the province of shepherds and peasants. But we cannot insist on that conclusion very strongly; the relevant work to support it has simply not yet been done and it is never easy to make a convincing negative argument. In short, the early history of the recorder and the cornett remains to be written.

The transverse flute was used in Germanic lands in the 14th century – it is pictured in association with Minnesänger – and perhaps also in France.[44] It must, therefore, have continued to be played during the 15th century, although precious little information survives about its function and distribution at that time. (In the later part of the 15th and throughout the 16th century it is easy to confuse with the military fife, since both instruments look alike.) Among the earliest depictions of the transverse flute that seem to reflect social reality are the calendar pages from late 15th- and early 16th-century books of hours showing groups of three genteel people in a boat entertaining themselves (presumably with courtly chansons or similar compositions) by singing and playing flute and lute.[45] A similar combination of three ladies can also be seen in the few remaining copies of what was once a widely circulated Flemish picture of the early 16th century.[46] By the 16th century, it seems the transverse flute had become a regular part of the instrumentarium used in polite society.

In 1533 Pierre Attaingnant of Paris published two anthologies of chansons intended either to be sung or to be played on consorts of flutes or recorders, exemplifying one typical way of using wind instruments in the 16th century: in unmixed consorts.[47] Attaingnant's songs must have been played by instruments tuned a fifth apart, with three different sizes (what we would call an alto, two tenors and a bass) distributed among the four voice parts of the music. The organization into like consorts built in standardized sizes may go back as far as the 15th century; at that time shawms seem to have been built in standard sizes a fifth apart. But it was not until the 16th century that such consorts of shawms, recorders and flutes came into general and regular use.

In the course of the 15th and 16th centuries, some wind instruments, notably the bagpipe, lost their previous social status; by 1500, for example, the bagpipe was no longer an instrument commonly heard in court or city, although it doubtless continued to be played for some kinds of dancing, and especially in peasant and rural communities.[48] The pipe and tabor, on the other hand, continued to enjoy a lively existence as a solo instrument for dancing.[49] As always, makers during the Renaissance invented new kinds of wind instruments. The crumhorn seems to have been invented during the second half of the 15th century (and to have died out within 100 years), and various other sorts of wind-capped reeds also make sporadic appearances during the 16th century.[50] Bara Boydell has proposed that the mysterious *dolzaina* (or *douçaine*) should be identified as a 'still shawm', a quiet-sounding shawm with a cup-shaped mouthpiece. The most serious problem with that hypothesis is that shawms with cup-shaped mouthpieces are as often pictured playing with regular shawms as alone. But Boydell may be basically correct in arguing that the *dolzaina* was a kind of shawm (without a wind cap and with a different sort of bore), and it may be that wherever we see shawms playing with soft instruments, we should assume we are looking at a still shawm (that is, a *douçaine*).

We do not know enough about the history of percussion instruments to have a clear picture of the way they developed and changed in the 15th and 16th centuries.[51] Side drums and nakers or larger kettledrums continued to accompany fifes and trumpets or to be played alone for military and ceremonial occasions. We have seen that small tabors were played with pipes for dancing. The encyclopedic writers of the early 16th century mention some folk instruments – the xylophone, for example, and various kinds of friction drum – and they describe triangles, cymbals and tambourines, percussion instruments occasionally depicted in 15th-and 16th-century works of art, but we are far from certain about just what repertory of music such instruments played.

One of the most pressing questions for present-day performers of early music concerns the pitch level at which instruments played in the 15th and 16th centuries. It is not easy to know at what pitch instruments were tuned, not only because reliable information is very difficult to assemble but also because pitch levels almost certainly varied from time to time and from place to place. From a study of surviving 16th-century recorders (among the few instruments with clearly fixed pitches), Bob Marvin has suggested that musicians during the 16th century generally played rather higher than the present-day $a' = 440$.[52] His conclusions are suggestive, but they must be tempered with the realization that we can never be certain about the extent to which the wood of the recorders has changed over the centuries, or, indeed, about what pitches the instruments were said to play at when they were new (so that what we think is a very high a', for example, may in fact have been called bb', b', or some other pitch name in the 16th century).

A whole complex of other questions dealing with pitch also obscures the conventions of performance during the 15th and 16th centuries. How can string instruments have sounded notes below c, for example, given the technology of making strings available to artisans in the Renaissance?[53] What was Ganassi describing when he spoke of viols being played a fourth higher than usual? What did Praetorius mean when he wrote of English consorts of viols tuned a fourth lower than those on the Continent? A part of the answer to these questions may well involve the conventions instrumentalists followed during the 15th and 16th centuries (and possibly even earlier) for transposing the notes they saw in front of them to fit their instruments. For example it may be that they called their lowest string, wherever it sounded, *gamma-ut*, or it may be that they simply moved the compositions they wished to play to a higher pitch. These conventions need to be studied in much more detail than they have been in the past.[54] And our conclusions about transposing conventions need to be correlated with what we know about the instruments that survive from the period, for the difficulty of these questions may arise in part from basic misunderstandings about the standard sizes of some instruments (and especially viols) in the 16th century.

As with medieval music, the most important and difficult questions to answer with regard to the musical uses of instruments in the 15th and 16th centuries have to do with the repertories originally associated with particular instruments. Were some instruments restricted in their use? Were others excluded altogether from certain repertories? Can present-day performers use any instrument known to have existed during the 15th and 16th centuries to perform any music from that period? During the past decade a consensus has emerged that we need to exercise greater caution in answering such questions. Our initial exuberance in discovering the music of the distant past almost certainly led us to tolerate performances that employed too many instruments, some of them inappropriate, and in groupings that were too varied. The time has surely come to retreat from the colourful and heavily orchestrated performances of the 1950s and 1960s.

We need to redouble our efforts to understand the conventions earlier musicians followed in performing the music that interests us. Almost certainly, we shall be compelled to offer highly qualified and limited answers to most of our questions about particular repertories and conventions of performance. Not least of all, we need to take account of national and local styles of performance. We can no longer ask how motets, chansons or madrigals were performed in the 16th century, but rather how they were performed in France, England, Germany, Italy or Spain in a particular decade, city or institution.[55] How, for example, were frottole normally performed during the late 15th and early 16th centuries in Mantua? To what extent can we generalize about the discrepancy between the way they appear in print (that is, in parts like any other polyphonic music) and the fact that we know they were sometimes performed as solo songs accompanied by lute, or sung by three voices – although they appear in Petrucci's volumes with four?[56] To what extent do the descriptions in festival books or in such accounts as that by Cristoforo Messisbugo about the performance of madrigals and other kinds of music in Ferrara reflect common conventions rather than very exceptional circumstances?[57] And to what extent do the arrangements for lute and keyboard of vocal music of all kinds exemplify the standard repertory of all 16th-century instrumentalists rather than merely a handful of virtuosos? Just what is the relationship, in other words, between the written notes and the way music actually sounded in the 15th and 16th centuries?

For the 15th century it is even difficult to secure agreement about what instruments played. Was any 15th-century composed polyphony conceived in the first place for instruments? To what extent did instrumentalists cultivate an improvised repertory that we can never know? Did they make compositions originally composed for voices the central part of their repertory? Or were they excluded altogether from playing composed polyphony, or from doubling or accompanying singers? Whatever the relationship between written and unwritten repertories, some instrumentalists at least were capable of playing composed polyphony – not only the organists for whom the Faenza Codex and the Buxheim Organ Book were compiled, but also the shawm and sackbut players for whom Isabella d'Este's wind band book was prepared – and Heinrich Isaac and his contemporaries in the second half of the 15th century began to write purely instrumental pieces (the so-called 'carmina'), a kind of autonomous instrumental music related neither to the dance nor to the kinds of free improvisatory pieces that keyboard players must originally have improvised and that eventually came to be written down.

Whatever the truth about the nature of instrumental music, we should be cautious about accepting any hard and fast guidelines about the performance of written or unwritten polyphony (or monophony) in the 15th and 16th centuries. Categorical statements about what was or was not done are likely to reveal themselves eventually as mere fanaticism. It is inherently improbable that any one set of conventions governed performance from Sicily to Scandinavia and from 1400 to 1600. And what appears to be clear to us today may well turn out upon closer examination to be a gross oversimplification. Even the scholarly consensus, for example, that has grown up about the complete absence of instruments in performances of sacred music during the 15th or early 16th centuries ought to be regarded with some scepticism. Before we accept that conclusion we need to take full account of those archival documents that record the presence of instruments in some princely chapels; we need to consider the possibility that certain sorts of occasions, such as coronations or weddings, or even some kinds of devotional services at side altars, might exceptionally have called for instruments to play with the choir; and we need to explore the likelihood that particular institutions differed in their arrangements and their performing conventions. Whereas the Sistine Chapel and the cathedral at Cambrai did not even tolerate organ music, some princely chapels may well have accepted instrumental perform-ance into their services, at least on occasion, as early as the 15th century, and there may turn out to be quite different conventions governing northern and southern European churches. Moreover, we need to ask ourselves just when Pisador's arrangements of Josquin's masses for solo vihuela were performed, let alone the countless motets arranged for lute. In sum, we need to know much more before we can claim even to begin to understand the general performing conventions of the Renaissance, let alone the way particular compositions were played and sung.

Notes

[1] For the most recent surveys of musical instruments in the Renaissance, see J. Montagu, *The World of Medieval and Renaissance Musical Instruments* (Newton Abbot, 1976); D. Munrow, *Instruments of the Middle Ages and Renaissance* (London, 1976); and M. Remnant, *Musical Instruments of the West* (London, 1978). On 15th-century instruments, see also E. A. Bowles, 'Instrumente des 15. Jahrhunderts und Ikonographie', *Basler Jb für historische Musikpraxis*, viii (1984), 11–50. *GroveMI* includes entries for all the instruments mentioned in this chapter.

For an attempt to set out guidelines for the performance of medieval and Renaissance music, see T. J. McGee, *Medieval and Renaissance Music: a Performer's Guide* (Toronto, 1985).

[2] For details about the works of Gerson and Paulus Paulirinus, see p.273.

[3] For details about the works of Ramos, see p.273. His remarks on instruments are discussed in N. Meeùs, 'Bartolomeo Ramos de Pareia et la tessiture des instruments à clavier entre 1450 et 1550', *Revue des archéologues et historiens d'art de Louvain*, v (1972), 148–72; M. Lindley, 'Fifteenth-century Evidence for Meantone Temperament', *PRMA*, cii (1975–6), 37–51; and S. Howell, 'Ramos de Pareja's "Brief Discussion of Various Instruments"', *JAMIS*, xi (1985), 14–37.

[4] For details about Grocheo's *De musica*, and the *De inventione et usu musicae* of Tinctoris, see p.273. On Grocheo's work, see also the perceptive remarks in C. Page, *Voices and Instruments of the Middle Ages: Instrumental Practice and Songs in France 1199–1300* (London, 1987), especially 50–54, 66–9, 196–201.

[5] For a modern edition of Arnault's treatise, see p.273. The 1972 reprint of the facsimile edition includes a list of more recent studies based on Arnault's work. See also I. Harwood, 'A Fifteenth-century Lute Design', *LSJ*, ii (1960), 3–8. Arnault's *dulce melos* has been equated, probably erroneously, with the chekker, an instrument whose identity remains somewhat problematic. For conflicting opinions on the nature of the chekker, see E. M. Ripin, 'Towards an Identification of the Chekker', *GSJ*, xxviii (1975), 11–25; C. Page, 'The Myth of the Chekker', *EM*, vii (1979), 482–9; and W. Barry, 'Henri Arnaut de Zwolle's *Clavicordium* and the Origin of the Chekker', *JAMIS*, xi (1985), 5–13.

[6] For details about the treatises mentioned in this paragraph and other treatises from the 16th century, see the Bibliography of Sources, p.273.

[7] For various modern editions of Schlick's *Spiegel der Orgelmacher* and his *Tabulaturen etlicher*

lobgesang und lidlein uff die orgeln und lauten, as well as a list of contents of the latter, see *BrownI*, where they are listed as 1511[2] and 1512[1]. On the temperament proposed by Schlick, see M. Lindley, 'Early 16th-century Keyboard Temperaments', *MD*, xxviii (1974), 134–51.

[8] The books about individual instruments, including the anthologies of lute music, are all listed and described in *BrownI*. The Latin and Italian versions of the rules 'for those who cannot sing', together with an English translation, appear in H. L. Schmidt, *The First Printed Lute Books: Francesco Spinacino's 'Intabulatura de lauto, Libro primo' and 'Libro secondo' (Venice: Petrucci, 1507)* (diss., U. of N. Carolina, 1969), ii, pp.i–iv. On 16th-century treatises on lute playing and the technique of intabulation, see also H. Minamino, *Sixteenth-century Lute Treatises, with Emphasis on Lute Intabulation Technique* (diss., U. of Chicago, 1988).

[9] Like so many of the generalizations in this and the preceding and following paragraphs, the claim that some instruments fell out of use for music of the high culture in the 16th century needs further investigation and, doubtless, considerable qualification. The truth is that the history of musical instruments has seldom been written as a chronicle of innovations and changing functions, connected with surviving (or even with lost) repertories, so my series of summary statements is designed partly as a set of hypothetical conclusions before the evidence has carefully been weighed, intended to stimulate further discussion about the special character of particular times and places.

[10] For the best and most recent introductions to the nature of organs in the 15th century and later, see P. Williams, *The European Organ 1450–1850* (London, 1966), and H. Klotz, *Über die Orgelkunst der Gotik, der Renaissance und des Barock* (Kassel and Basle, 1975), and the studies cited there.

[11] On these instruction books, see W. Apel, *The History of Keyboard Music to 1700*, rev. and trans. H. Tischler (Bloomington and London, 1972), especially 45–55. For examples of *fundamenta*, see *Keyboard Music of the Fourteenth and Fifteenth Centuries*, ed. W. Apel, CEKM, i (1963), and *Das Buxheimer Orgelbuch*, ed. B. A. Wallner, EDM, xxxvii–xxxix (1958–9).

[12] On the surviving 15th- and 16th-century liturgical music for keyboard, see Apel, *History of Keyboard Music*, 34–165. On the duties of an organist in the Renaissance, see among other studies Y. Rokseth, *La musique d'orgue au XVe siècle et au début du XVIe* (Paris, 1930), and B. van Wye, 'Ritual Use of the Organ in France', *JAMS*, xxxiii (1980), 287–325. On manuscripts that contain those chants organists improvised upon and played in alternation with choirs, see O. Gombosi, 'About Organ Playing in the Divine Service, circa 1500', in *Essays on Music in Honor of Archibald Thompson Davison* (Cambridge, Mass., 1957), 51–68, and the studies cited there.

For the argument that the Faenza Codex (*I-FZc* 117, published in a modern edition by D. Plamenac, CMM, lvii, 1972) was not intended for organ, see T. J. McGee, 'Instruments and the Faenza Codex', *EM*, xiv (1986), 480–90. Even granted that there are serious technical difficulties in playing some of the music on a single-manual keyboard instrument, McGee's argument is unconvincing that the collection was intended for two lutes (even though two players of melody instruments would not have needed the sort of score notation found there). McGee's argument is especially unconvincing with regard to the liturgical music in the manuscript, evidently examples of *alternatim* practice. He cites a single instance from the 16th century where a mass was performed by lute (an occasion described by Martin Luther, who was amused by the incident, and clearly contemptuous of the practice). There is no reason to change our view that the organ was the only instrument that normally alternated with singers in the performance of 15th- and 16th-century liturgical music, and that therefore the liturgical music in the Faenza Codex is most likely intended for an organist (who would have needed to prepare just such a score as appears in the manuscript).

[13] On these early preludes, see Apel, *History of Keyboard Music*, 43–5. Most of them are published in modern edition in Apel, *Keyboard Music*, and Wallner, *Buxheimer Orgelbuch*.

[14] On 16th-century organ basses and short scores, see O. Kinkeldey, *Orgel und Klavier in der Musik des 16. Jahrhunderts* (Leipzig, 1910/R1968), 194–215, and *BrownI*, 4, 439–40.

[15] On the portative organ, see H. Hickmann, *Das Portativ* (Kassel, 1936/R1972). On the positive organ, see R. Quoika, *Das Positiv in Geschichte und Gegenwart* (Kassel and Basle, 1957). On the regals, see R. Menger, *Das Regal* (Tutzing, 1973).

[16] The collections are described and their contents listed in *BrownI*, 1557[2] (the volume by Luis Venegas de Henestrosa) and 1578[3] (the volume by Antonio de Cabezón).

[17] F. Hubbard, *Three Centuries of Harpsichord Making* (Cambridge, Mass., 1965), remains the best overview of the history of the harpsichord, but see also the earlier study, R. Russell, *The Harpsichord and Clavichord: an Introductory Study* (London, 1959). D. Boalch, *Makers of the*

Harpsichord and Clavichord 1440–1840 (London, 1956, 2/1974), lists all surviving instruments. E. A. Bowles, 'A Checklist of Fifteenth-century Representations of Stringed Keyboard Instruments', in *Keyboard Instruments: Studies in Keyboard Organology*, ed. E. M. Ripin (Edinburgh, 1971), 11–16, lists most of the known 15th-century depictions of keyboards. For more recent work on the history of stringed keyboard instruments, see especially the essays published in *The Brussels Museum of Musical Instruments Bulletin* and *GSJ*.

[18] For a description of the seven volumes of keyboard music published by Pierre Attaingnant, and a list of their contents, see *BrownI*, 1531[1-7], which includes information about facsimiles and modern editions of each of the volumes. To the bibliography given there should be added the modern edition of the *Quatorze Gaillardes neuf Pavennes, sept Branles et deux Basses Dances* (*BrownI*, 1531[4]), in *Keyboard Dances from the Earlier Sixteenth Century*, ed. D. Heartz, CEKM, viii (1965).

[19] D. Ortiz, *Tratado de glosas sobre clausuas y otros generos de puntos en la musica de violones: Roma 1553*, ed. and trans. M. Schneider (Kassel, 1936).

[20] For the most recent studies on 'transposing harpsichords', some of which raise the question of whether they really existed, see J. Barnes, 'Pitch Variations in Italian Keyboard Instruments', *GSJ*, xviii (1965), 110–16; W. R. Thomas and J. J. K. Rhodes, 'The String Scales of Italian Keyboard Instruments', *GSJ*, xx (1967), 48–62; J. H. van der Meer, 'Harpsichord Making and Metallurgy: Rejoinder ', *GSJ*, xxi (1968), 175–8; J. Barnes, 'Italian String Scales', ibid, 179–83, and Thomas and Rhodes, 'Reply', *GSJ*, xxiii (1970), 168–70; J. Koster, 'A Remarkable Early Flemish Transposing Harpsichord', *GSJ*, xxxv (1982), 45–53; R. T. Shann, 'Flemish Transposing Harpsichords: an Explanation', *GSJ*, xxxvii (1984), 62–71; and G. G. O'Brien, *Ruckers: a Harpsichord and Virginal Building Tradition* (diss., U. of Edinburgh, 1983), chap.4, 'The Stringing and Pitches of Ruckers Instruments'.

[21] See E. M. Ripin, 'The Two-manual Harpsichord in Flanders before 1650', *GSJ*, xxi (1968), 33–9.

[22] On the clavicytherium, see E. M. Ripin, 'Clavicytherium', *GroveMI*. On the claviorgan, see D. H. Boalch and P. Williams, 'Claviorgan', *GroveMI*. On the claviorgan mentioned in 1539, see H. M. Brown, *Sixteenth-century Instrumentation: the Music for the Florentine Intermedii*, MSD, xxx (1973), 22.

[23] On Nicola Vicentino's enharmonic *arcicembalo* and *arciorgano*, see K. Berger, *Theories of Chromatic and Enharmonic Music in late 16th-Century Italy* (Ann Arbor, 1980), 24–5, 37, and the studies cited there. On mother and child instruments, see O'Brien, *Ruckers*, 102–7. On Hans Haiden's *Geigenwerk*, see E. M. Ripin, 'Geigenwerk', *GroveMI*, and the studies cited there.

[24] On the fiddle and rebec, see notes 35–41 in the chapter on medieval instruments in this handbook. Studies of both instruments and their uses in the 15th century are urgently needed. On bowed string instruments in general in the late 15th and 16th centuries, see L. C. Witten, 'Apollo, Orpheus, and David', *JAMIS*, i (1975), 5–55.

[25] On the *lira da braccio* and its functions, see H. M. Brown, 'Lira da braccio', *GroveMI*, and the studies cited there.

[26] On the tromba marina, see C. Adkins and A. Dickinson, 'A Trumpet by any other Name: Toward an Etymology of the Trumpet Marine', *JAMIS*, viii (1982), 5–15; and also Adkins, 'Trumpet marine', *GroveMI*, and the studies cited there.

[27] I. Woodfield, *The Early History of the Viol* (Cambridge, 1984), makes the convincing case that viols were introduced into Italy from Spain at the end of the 15th century.

[28] On the construction and playing techniques of 16th-century viols, see I. Harwood, 'An Introduction to Renaissance Viols', *EM*, ii (1974), 235–46; I. Harwood and M. Edmunds, 'Reconstructing 16th-century Venetian Viols', *EM*, vi (1978), 519–25; I. Woodfield, 'Viol Playing Techniques in the mid-16th Century: a Survey of Ganassi's Fingering Instructions', *EM*, vi (1978), 544–9; and Edmunds, 'Venetian Viols of the Sixteenth Century', *GSJ*, xxxiii (1980), 74–91.

[29] On the *lira viol* (or lyra viol), see F. Traficante, 'Lyra viol', *GroveMI*, and the studies cited there. On the *viola bastarda*, see V. Gutmann, 'Viola bastarda: Instrument oder Diminutions-Praxis?', *AMw*, xxxv (1978), 178–209.

[30] On the *lirone*, see Brown, *Sixteenth-century Instrumentation*, 39–45.

[31] See F. Lesure, 'L'Epitome musical de Philibert Jambe de Fer (1556)', *AnnM*, vi (1958–63), 341–86.

[32] On the lute in the 15th century, see D. Fallows, '15th-century Tablatures for Plucked Instruments: a Summary, a Revision and a Suggestion', *LSJ*, xix (1977), 10–18 (although his suggestion is unconvincing that *Je loe amours* by Binchois was intended for two lutes in its

arrangement in the Buxheim Organ Book where it is marked 'in cytaris vel etiam in organis'; these words probably indicate that it was meant either for harp or for keyboard); and V. Ivanoff, 'Das Lautenduo im 15. Jahrhundert', *Basler Jb für historische Musikpraxis*, viii (1984), 147–62. On the introduction of finger technique in the 15th century, see among other studies Minamino, *Sixteenth-century Lute Treatises*.

On the 16th-century lute and its music, see P. Päffgen, *Laute und Lautenspiel in der ersten Hälfte des 16. Jahrhunderts* (Regensburg, 1978); J.-M. Vaccaro, *La musique de luth en France au XVIe siècle* (Paris, 1981); *Le luth et sa musique*, ed. J. Jacquot (Paris, 1958); *Le luth et sa musique II*, ed. Vaccaro (Paris, 1984); and the essays published in *The Lute: the Journal of the Lute Society* and *Journal of the Lute Society of America*.

[33] These anthologies for one or more lutes are all listed and described in *BrownI*.

[34] On the cittern, see I. Harwood and J. Tyler, 'Cittern', *GroveMI*, and the studies cited there. On the guitar in the Middle Ages and the Renaissance, see J. Tyler, *The Early Guitar: a History and Handbook* (London, 1980), and, most recently, H. Nickel, 'Zur Entwicklungsgeschichte der Gitarre im Mittelalter', *Basler Jb für historische Musikpraxis*, viii (1984), 131–46.

[35] On the vihuela and its repertory, see D. Poulton, 'Vihuela', *GroveMI*; M. Prynne, 'A Surviving Vihuela de Mano', *GSJ*, xvi (1963), 22–7; A. Corona-Alcalde, 'The Viola da Mano and the Vihuela: Evidence and Suggestions about their Construction', *The Lute: the Journal of the Lute Society*, xxiv (1984), 3–32; J. Myers, 'Vihuela Technique', *Journal of the Lute Society of America*, i (1968), 15–18; and M. Weisman, 'The Paris Vihuela Reconstructed', *GSJ*, xxxv (1982), 68–77.

[36] On Pietrobono and the gittern, see n.18 in the introduction to the Renaissance section of this handbook.

[37] On the dulcimer in the Renaissance, see H. Heyde, 'Frühgeschichte des europäischen Hackbretts (14.–16. Jahrhundert)', *DJbM*, xviii (1978), 135–72.

[38] On the harp in the 15th century, see H. Rosenzweig, 'Zur Harfe im 15. Jahrhundert', *Basler Jb für historische Musikpraxis*, viii (1984), 163–82. On the 16th-century harp, see R. Hadaway, 'The Re-creation of an Italian Renaissance Harp', *EM*, viii (1980), 59–62; and C. Bordas, 'The Double Harp in Spain from the 16th to the 18th Centuries', *EM*, xv (1987), 148–63.

[39] On chitarrones, theorbos and archlutes, see R. Spencer, 'Chitarrone, Theorbo and Archlute', *EM*, iv (1976) 407–23; D. A. Smith, 'On the Origin of the Chitarrone', *JAMS*, xxxii (1979), 440–62; and K. B. Mason, *Chitarrone Accompaniment in the Early Italian Baroque (1589–c.1650)* (diss., Washington U., 1987). On the orpharion and bandora, see D. Gill, 'The Orpharion and Bandora', *GSJ*, xiii (1960), 14–25; R. Hadaway, 'An Instrument-maker's Report on the Repair and Restoration of an Orpharion', *GSJ*, xxviii (1975), 37–42; and R. H. Wells, 'The Orpharion', *EM*, x (1982), 427–40. On mandoras and colachons, see D. Gill, 'Mandores and Colachons', *GSJ*, xxxiv (1981), 130–41.

[40] The classic exposition of the invention of the slide trumpet and its subsequent transformation is H. Besseler, 'Die Entstehung der Posaune', *AcM*, xxii (1950), 8–35, to which V. Safowitz, *Trumpet Music and Trumpet Style in the Early Renaissance* (diss., U. of Illinois, 1965), made important additions. The most recent discussion of the instrument – P. Downey, 'The Renaissance Slide Trumpet: Fact or Fiction?', *EM*, xii (1984), 26–33 – denies its existence, but Downey does not take account of the evidence presented by Besseler and Safowitz. Neither H. Heyde, *Trompete und Trompetenblasen im Europäischen Mittelalter* (diss., U. of Leipzig, 1965), nor P. Downey, *The Trumpet and its Role in Music of the Renaissance and Early Baroque* (diss., Queen's U. of Belfast, 1965), has been available to me. On the sackbut, see G. B. Lane, *The Trombone in the Middle Ages and the Renaissance* (Bloomington, 1982), and H. G. Fischer, *The Renaissance Sackbut and its Use Today* (New York, 1984).

[41] On wind bands in the 15th and 16th centuries, see A. Baines, *Woodwind Instruments and their History* (London, 1957, 3/1967); K. Polk, 'Wind Bands of Medieval Flemish Cities', *BWQ*, i (1968), 93ff; Polk, 'Municipal Wind Music in Flanders in the Late Middle Ages', *BWQ*, ii (1969), 1ff; and L. Welker, ' "Alta capella": zur Ensemblepraxis der Blasinstrumente im 15. Jahrhundert', *Basler Jb für historische Musikpraxis*, vii (1983), 119–65. The best overviews of the shawm and its music in the 15th and 16th centuries remain those in A. Baines, *Woodwind Instruments*, 268–72, and Baines, 'Shawm', *GroveMI*.

[42] On the cornett, see the various articles in *Basler Jb für historische Musikpraxis*, v (1981), and the studies cited there.

[43] The best overview of the recorder and its music remains that in E. Hunt, *The Recorder and Its Music* (London, 1962, rev. enlarged 2/1977). A critical study of the role of the recorder before 1500 remains to be written.

[44] On the flute in the Renaissance, see B. Thomas, 'The Renaissance Flute', *EM*, iii (1975), 2–10; A. Smith, 'Die Renaissancequerflöte und ihre Musik: ein Beitrag zur Interpretation der Quellen', *Basler Jb für historische Musikpraxis*, ii (1978), 9–76; and J. Bowers, '*Flaüste traverseinne* and *Flute d'Allemagne*: the Development of Flute Playing in France from the Late Middle Ages up through 1702', *RMFC*, xix (1979), 7–49.

[45] On trios in boats, see H. M. Brown, 'Notes (and Transposing Notes) on the Transverse Flute in the Early Sixteenth Century', *JAMIS*, xii (1986), 7–9.

[46] On trios of musical ladies, see H. C. Slim, 'Paintings of Lady Concerts and the Transmission of "Jouissance vous donneray" ', *Imago musicae*, i (1984), 51–73. On flute players at the banquet for the prodigal son, see Slim, *The Prodigal Son at the Whores': Music, Art and Drama* (Irvine, California, 1976).

[47] Attaingnant's anthologies for flutes or recorders are listed and described, among other places, in *BrownI*, 1533² and 1533³; Smith, 'Renaissancequerflöte', 64–7; and Brown, 'Notes ... on the Transverse Flute', 32–4, where suggestions about the performance of these pieces may be found.

[48] There is, as far as I know, no special study of the bagpipe as it was used in western Europe during the 15th and 16th centuries.

[49] On the pipe and tabor and the fife and drum in the Renaissance, the most recent study is D. Hoffman-Axthelm, 'Zu Ikonographie und Bedeutungsgeschichte von Flöte und Trommel in Mittelalter und Renaissance', *Basler Jb für historische Musikpraxis*, vii (1983), 84–118.

[50] On these various instruments, see B. Boydell, *The Crumhorn and Other Renaissance Windcap Instruments* (Buren, 1982); and K. T. Meyer, *The Crumhorn: its History, Design, Repertory, and Technique* (Ann Arbor, 1983). See also H. W. Myers, 'The *Mary Rose* "Shawm"', *EM*, xi (1983), 358–60, for the ingenious and convincing argument that the instrument brought up from the 16th-century ship, the *Mary Rose*, and described in F. Palmer, 'Musical Instruments from the *Mary Rose*', *EM*, xi (1983), 53–60, is actually the only surviving *dolzaina*.

[51] On percussion instruments, see J. Blades, *Percussion Instruments and their History* (London, 1970, rev. 3/1984), and J. Blades and J. Montagu, *Early Percussion Instruments from the Middle Ages to the Baroque* (London, 1976). For more recent studies of percussion instruments, see A. Tamboer, 'Die Schlaginstrumente im Italien des 14. und 15. Jahrhunderts', *Basler Jb für historische Musikpraxis*, viii (1984), 213–28, and J. Pelrine, 'Die Naqqara: ein Beitrag zur Instrumentenkunde des Mittelalters', *Basler Jb für historische Musikpraxis*, viii (1984), 229–42.

[52] See B. Marvin, 'Recorders and English Flutes in European Collections', *GSJ*, xxv (1972), 30–57. R. Weber, 'Some Researches into Pitch in the 16th Century with Particular Reference to the Instruments in the Accademia Filarmonica of Verona', *GSJ*, xxviii (1975), 7–10, finds that most of the instruments he measured seem to have been tuned to $a' = 450$ Hz, although a few were either slightly higher or at the lower pitch of $a' = 410$ Hz.

[53] On string technology, see among other studies D. Abbott and E. Segerman, 'Strings in the 16th and 17th Centuries', *GSJ*, xxvii (1974), 48–73; and the information about medieval strings found in C. Page, *Voices and Instruments*, 210–42. It should be pointed out, however, that early 16th-century stringed instruments are regularly described as playing down to cello C or even the A below that; therefore, artisans at that time had presumably found ways to make strings appropriate to the task.

[54] On these points, see the studies cited in Chapter VIII n.49.

[55] The quest to make distinctions on the basis of particular times and places relates the subdiscipline of performance practice to the central concerns of many musicologists who are occupied with questions of locality and patterns of local patronage. I think of such recent books as I. Fenlon, *Music and Patronage in Sixteenth-century Mantua* (Cambridge, 1980–82); L. Lockwood, *Music in Renaissance Ferrara 1400–1505* (Oxford, 1984); R. Strohm, *Music in Late Medieval Bruges* (Oxford, 1985); and A. W. Atlas, *Music at the Aragonese Court of Naples* (Cambridge, 1985).

[56] For the most recent discussion of the performance of frottole, see W. F. Prizer, 'The Frottola and the Unwritten Tradition', *Studi musicali*, xv (1986), 3–37.

[57] See among other studies H. M. Brown, 'A Cook's Tour of Ferrara in 1529', *RIM*, x (1975), 216–41.

CHAPTER X

Sacred Polyphony

CHRISTOPHER A. REYNOLDS

Music from the 15th and 16th centuries is uniquely difficult to divide into separate realms of 'sacred' and 'secular'. A broad distinction between religious and profane musical genres is evident in the number of prints and manuscripts that contain either exclusively sacred or secular works. Such collections far outnumber sources with mixed repertories. But our conception of religious music depends too much on the text, and too little on the context of the performance. The problems involved in drawing distinctions between sacred and secular are not so much musical and textual as social and ritualistic. Since the domain of the Church extended well beyond its own doors, and since the influence of worldly styles permeated all levels of the clergy, sacred and secular traits were often not in opposition, but interdependent components of an artistic whole. Performances of motets and madrigals intermingled during banquets, and organists played chansons and madrigals during the Mass. Consequently, the various functions of sacred polyphony are better expressed by contrasts between liturgical and non-liturgical, ceremonial and devotional, or chapel and chamber. Although these are not exclusive categories – motets, for instance, might be performed in any of these contexts – they accurately reflect distinctions that existed in the period. The location of a performance, the importance of the occasion, and even whether or not the work was liturgical, could affect the number of singers involved, the type of instrumental support and the likelihood of improvised rather than written polyphony being performed.[1]

Repertorial distinctions between liturgical and non-liturgical bear directly upon a basic aspect of performance practice that is easily overlooked: the problem of deciding which compositions would have been heard together on any one occasion. For performers today, guidelines about how to assemble a historically appropriate programme are surprisingly hard to find. In order to ascertain what pieces musicians would have performed in Paris in about 1520, or in Mantua 50 years later, a modern performer might begin by determining which composers were fashionable, which were locally employed, and what prints and manuscripts were current. Once that is done, however, several questions will remain. In ecclesiastical contexts, it is no problem to select a hymn for any given feast because the liturgical designations of hymns are reasonably specific; nor is it difficult to match a *Magnificat* antiphon to a modally compatible *Magnificat*, or even to choose settings of psalms and Mass Propers. But we are far from knowing the criteria that musicians used to decide which motets and cyclic masses to perform, especially for masses based on a chanson or a madrigal. The diary of a papal singer in 1568 recommends two works (now found in different Sistine Chapel manuscripts) for the Octave of All Saints', neither of them having any obvious liturgical justification: Loyset Compère's *Missa 'L'homme armé'* and his motet *Ave Maria*. Personal fancy or institutional tradition are equally plausible motives.[2]

That the choir of the Sistine Chapel could perform a mass that Compère had written at least 70 years earlier raises the issue of how long works remained in the active repertory of amateurs and professionals. To modern audiences accustomed to having Bach and Boulez before the interval and Tchaikovsky after it, an evening of Dufay, Josquin and Monteverdi will not seem unduly diffuse. Yet about the time of Dufay's death, Tinctoris made his oft-quoted observation that musicians performed works only from the last 40 years, a time-span roughly comparable to that suggested when Monteverdi traced his own stylistic roots back to the madrigals of Cipriano de Rore, or by the renewed popularity Josquin enjoyed in French prints of the 1550s. Sacred works sung by ecclesiastical choirs undoubtedly stayed in circulation longer than either secular compositions or masses and motets sung away from church. In the 15th century the durability of church polyphony is shown by several sacred manuscripts which present a repertory compiled over three generations, while the new styles and compositions inspired by the Reformation and Counter-Reformation show an even greater tenacity. Lutheran chorales, early Anglican service music and certain compositions of Palestrina have endured not for generations but for centuries. At the other extreme there is the ephemeral popularity of the Elizabethan madrigal. The short life-span of secular music derives as much from changes in poetic styles as from shifts in musical ones.

Secular chansons were employed as the tenors of mass cycles, or as the bases for parody masses, but secular music generally entered the church either in the guise of organ music or in the form of a chanson given a sacred text and performed as a motet. The introduction of textless chansons into a sacred context via the organ is documented in manuscripts for organists which mix secular and sacred works together, by the occasional testimony of proponents (such as the church officials in Bologna who contracted the Burgundian organist Roger Saignand in 1478 to teach a local student six songs in addition to the liturgically sanctioned service music),[3] and perhaps most tellingly, by the condemnation of conservative churchmen. The Florentine Archbishop Antoninus decried the wanton playing of mid-15th-century organists, as had St Bernardino of Siena a generation before him. Regarding vocal music, the wholesale adaptation of chansons to sacred texts is exemplified before the Council of Trent by the contrafacta of several chansons by Josquin, *Plus nulz regretz/Adjura vos* among them (which may also be the basis of Marcantonio Cavazzoni's organ canzona, *Plus ne regres*). Cipriano de Rore's madrigal turned motet *Anchor che col partire/Angelus ad pastorem* is but one instance that occurred after Trent. Since any chanson refitted with a sacred text may have been performed according to the conventions of an ecclesiastical choir (as described below), this type of transformation is not simply a matter of substituting a new text; it entails the probability of a different mode of performance as well.[4]

Modern performances of masses, whether in or out of church, are too often scrupulously complete, as if programming only one or two movements might lay one open to charges of musical turpitude. There are enough manuscripts with partial copies of polyphonic mass cycles to sanction incomplete performances by today's singers; indeed, lute intabulations suggest that in secular surroundings it was permissible not only to perform isolated mass movements, but also to extract single sections: the 'Christe' for instance, or the second half of the Gloria. Medieval practices were thus reversed. Whereas polyphonic cycles of the Mass Ordinary were once assembled from individual movements and mass pairs, singers in the Renaissance on occasion exercised a freedom to dismember cycles into smaller units. In neither instance did the original form of the composition constrain the performers. Our age, on the other hand, values completeness. Masses are esteemed as the Renaissance equivalent of the symphony, and accorded the same full-length presentation. Yet concerts and recitals in the 19th century could include a favourite movement or two of a symphony or sonata. David Munrow showed signs of flexibility by recording a series of individual mass movements by different composers, but even he succumbed to an atavistic impulse to organize them as a complete cycle of five.[5]

While chant had long been sung by substantial numbers of singers, choral performances of polyphony – that is to say, renditions with more than one singer per part – first began to replace performances by soloists in the 15th century. Manfred Bukofzer proposed a date of about 1430 for the advent of the new style, and identified Italy and England as the countries which fostered it.[6] But the recent researches of Reinhard Strohm have revealed occasions when polyphony was sung by at least two to a part in early 15th-century Bruges.[7] Many factors contributed to the rapid spread of choral polyphony, among them the simplification of late medieval notation (making polyphony more accessible to the average singer), the prolonged exposure to the latest musical styles that churchmen from all of Christendom experienced when the upper ranks of the clergy and their musicians gathered at the Council of Constance (1414–18), and the emergence of a class of specialist musician – all of these occurring by the first quarter of the century. Equally important were the cathedral and collegiate choir schools of France, Flanders and England, which educated young boys in grammar, chant, mensural notation and improvised polyphony. These produced skilled musicians in sufficient quantities to supply singers and composers for choirs throughout Europe, but most significantly for the court and church choirs of Italy and Spain. Aside from the choirs of royal chapels, and some of the wealthier ecclesiastical institutions, choral polyphony became a pervasive phenomenon only after about 1460, particularly in the north where endowed church services specified polyphony on a daily basis. The average church choir in Italy, however, probably sang written polyphony only on high feast-days, even in the 16th century. Apparently the performance of chant and improvised polyphony remained the standard practice.[8]

The ensembles capable of singing sacred polyphony were not large, at least initially. For three-voice compositions a total of five or six adult males, or of three adults plus three or four boys, allowed for one tenor, two contras, and the remainder sopranos. In Italy, ecclesiastical choirs varied from four to eight adults and a few boys up until the 1480s, although politics and pestilence often combined to diminish this total for months or even years at a time. For reasons not wholly understood, the last decades of the century witnessed a significant increase in the size of Italian church choirs: Milan Cathedral had an average of seven adults in 1480 and 15 in 1496, while the choir of Florence Cathedral grew from five or six adults in 1480 to 18 in 1493. Some of the impetus may have come from the polyphony itself, with four and five voice parts becoming the normal scoring among composers who followed Dufay; but the sizes of these choirs were not surpassed – or in most Italian churches even equalled – in the 16th century, at a time when compositions often called for six, seven or eight separate voice parts. Another cause of growth was perhaps a competitive emulation of the large choirs found at the major Italian courts. The Aragonese court at Naples maintained one of the most lavish and influential music establishments, supporting 21 (mostly northern and Spanish) singers and two organists, from roughly 1451 until the end of the century. After 1470 choirs of this size existed in Milan, in Ferrara and at the papal court in Rome. Only rarely as at Ferrara when Josquin served there in 1504, and in Rome under Pope Leo X (1513–21) did these groups expand beyond 30 voices. Northern choirs, however, could often muster between 30 and 40 men and boys, notably the Burgundian chapel of Philip the Good (with 30 in 1467), the Chapel Royal in England (37 before 1450), and any of several well-endowed collegiate chapels. Grandest of all was the famous choir Lassus conducted for the Bavarian Hofkapelle in Munich. The total of 62 singers in 1570 included 22 sopranos (16 boys, 6 castratos), 13 male altos, 15 tenors and 12 basses. They were supported by 30 instrumentalists.

It is one thing to know how many singers there were in a choir, but another to establish how many of those singers actually participated in performances of a mass by Josquin or a motet by Palestrina. For all the archival data on the personnel of a choir, detailed accounts of specific performances are comparatively rare and iconographical evidence is often ambiguous. Tastes and practices doubtless varied according to region and according to whether the choir was attached to a church or a court, as indicated by some of the few explicit statements about 15th-century performance forces. A report from the court of Burgundy, dated 1469, prescribes a minimum force for polyphony of six sopranos, two altos, three tenors and as many basses, 14 adults in all, and this at a time when there were 24 singers available.[9] These figures can reasonably be applied to the works of Dufay, who had close associations with Charles the Bold and his court. Yet at Cambrai Cathedral Dufay was content to request a smaller ensemble in his will, instructing nine singers (six of them boys) to perform his own four-voice motet *Ave regina coelorum* at his funeral; and from 1517 to 1521, nearly half a century later, the Dufay Requiem was still sung at Cambrai 'by the master of the choirboys with four or five companions', little more than one to a part despite a cathedral choir which then numbered 34.[10] There were also occasions when every available chorister participated. The 1540 visit of Emperor Charles V was one, bringing together all 34 voices to sing the motet *Preter rerum*, possibly that by Josquin.[11] The more important the ceremony, the greater the likelihood of having the polyphony entrusted to the large ensemble; in other words, the significance of the event, and not necessarily the character of the music, determined the size of church choirs.

Whether comprised of 14 singers or 40, ecclesiastical choirs throughout

Europe employed an abundance of sopranos. The problem of a 'choral balance' did not exist before the 15th century, since medieval choirs only performed chant. However, once polyphony became choral, a sensitivity to the sound of the ensemble resulted in a proportionately greater number of sopranos than found in modern choirs. Only in the latter half of the 16th century did Spanish castratos come to Italy, bringing a new capacity for volume in the upper register, and women, if they sang sacred polyphony in church, rarely did so with men. Church choirs, as Frank D'Accone has observed, depended on expanded sections of boys or male falsettists (or combinations of both) on the top part to match the more powerful voices of adult males on the lower parts. It is not unusual to find soprano sections containing two or three times as many voices as any other part. The Burgundian report cited above recommends this ratio, as did the Flemish singer who promised Lorenzo de' Medici in 1468 that he would recruit an entire ensemble in Rome: a tenor, two altos (one of whom would sing bass in four-voice music), and 'three very high treble singers with good, full and suave voices'.[12] Generations later we find a similar balance at Cambrai in the 1540s – there were six boys, seven male falsettists, four altos, five tenors and six basses – and at Munich in 1568, where Lassus apparently performed the 12 parts of Brumel's *Missa Et ecce terrae motus* with 33 men on the bottom nine parts and 20 boys on the three soprano lines.[13]

Today it is generally agreed that choirs sang sacred music, either alone or with organ accompaniment, while soloists, often with instrumental support, were the norm for secular works; but under certain circumstances soloists continued to perform sacred polyphony throughout the 16th century.[14] Our notion of the conventions specifically appropriate for the performance of sacred music is too restricted and too limited by what happened in ecclesiastical surroundings. There is ample documentation that motets, hymns and the like were sung at banquets and other festivities outside churches and court chapels, yet comparatively little attention to the different conventions that such performances entailed. When motets and chansons were heard together as dinner entertainment, the works we consider sacred would usually have received a performance we would deem secular: one voice per part, possibly even a female on top, an option to double or replace singers with a variety of instruments, and a softer vocal quality than that appropriate in church. For Italian theorists, 'where' musicians performed mattered more than when they performed, or for whom. According to Nicola Vicentino (writing in 1555), 'in churches . . . one will sing with full voices and with a large number of singers', a remark that addresses the disparate qualities of chamber and chapel voices, but also a difference in ensemble size.[15] Subsequently Zarlino (1558) and Ludovico Zacconi (1592) reiterated the distinction between a fulsome *cappella* voice and a 'more submissive and suave' *camera* voice. That the differentiation was not confined to the final decades of the Renaissance is suggested by the apology of a 15th-century Italian, who needed to rest before he could sing in his *voce da camera* because he had just sung in church.[16] Presumably the overly resonant acoustical environments of Gothic and Renaissance churches required large numbers of full-voiced singers to project the intricacies of polyphony, while soloists could manage the less imposing dimensions of court chambers.

The distinction between loud singing in church and soft singing elsewhere also has implications for our understanding of the balance between the individual voice parts. The relationship of the loud *cappella* voice to the ecclesiastical tradition of disproportionately large sections of falsettists and boy sopranos has yet to be fully explored;[17] similarly, there is also more to be learned about the connection between the soft chamber voice and the practice of singing one to a part. Singers may have had two diametrically opposed standards for achieving a musically satisfying balance. When in church, where loud singing was perhaps encouraged if not required by the acoustic, then the volume of the lower voices provided the standard, and enough sopranos were staffed to balance the bottom without excessive forcing.[18] But in private chambers, where acoustical conditions allowed a softer dynamic, the solo voice of a falsettists may have determined the overall volume, and singers on the lower parts restrained their voices sufficiently to balance the top. Undoubtedly other factors than these contributed to the different styles. Instrumental practices, for instance, follow the same path. While singers in private chambers shared the stage with lutes and viols, in church they competed with organs, winds and brass. A thorough study of this issue must also consider Praetorius's early 17th-century description of church choirs singing as much as a minor third lower than chamber pitch, and the conflicting views about pitch differences between *chor-thon* and *cammer-thon* as well. Finally, in order to gain a better idea of how long the opposition of *cappella* and *camera* voices existed, and of how this relates to the balance among soloists and within choirs, studies of Renaissance performing forces need to be extended well into the 17th century. The advent of castratos doubtless changed the possibilities for balance in solo and choral ensembles alike.

As choirs rather than soloists began to sing polyphony, the enlarged ensembles must have struggled with medieval customs for setting text to music. Soloists had only to coordinate their settings with the other voice parts, while two or more musicians attempting to align a single text to the same line encountered myriad opportunities for disarray. It is revealing, then, that the earliest known theoretical discussion of text setting was written in northern Italy during the period of transition to choral polyphony in the mid-1400s. Beginning with an acknowledgement that 'there is no logic in how to adjust words to a melody beyond [that in] the mind of him who has to notate it', the rules are basic: place syllables on strong beats and sing only one per ligature.[19]

A more logical approach to adjusting the words, or at least an attempt to encourage one, arose in the generations after Josquin in the systematic guidelines espoused by Lanfranco (1533), Zarlino (1558) and other theorists.[20] But their commonsense advice to set strong syllables to long notes, sing different syllables to repeated notes and place melismas on the penultimate syllable, clarified the words during performances to a limited extent only. Complaints about garbled texts persisted, and not even the reforms mandated in the 1560s by the Council of Trent solved the problem. Theorists such as Stocker (1570–80), Burmeister (1606) and Cerone (1613) continued to admonish Protestant and Catholic musicians into the 17th century. Textual clarity suffered when singers were forced to use manuscripts with faulty or incomplete texts, to perform compositions with more than one text, to accommodate themselves to instrumental doubling and, perhaps most of all, to cope with the staggered voicing of imitative polyphony.[21] Erasmus also blamed the loud style of singing (he called it 'bellowing') in churches, because 'all sounds are obscured and nothing can be understood'.[22] In the face of these difficulties, the precision that editors and singers strive for today may seldom have been attained, at least by church choirs. It is possible that singers sidestepped one vexatious problem altogether by not setting any text at all to the cantus firmus voices of 15th-century masses and motets, but simply vocalizing the usually untexted ligatures to an open vowel sound. Another alternative is reported from Ferrara (1481), where a mass was sung entirely in solmization syllables, though apparently not in a liturgical service.[23]

Few aspects of performance practice in the Renaissance have been examined from so many different perspectives as the role of organs and other instruments in church. Scholars have gathered archival data on organs, organists and organ builders, scrutinized the available iconographical records of liturgical performances, and analysed repertorial and stylistic evidence in an effort to answer some basic questions about the interaction between voices and instruments during liturgical services.[24] When and where did organs accompany choral polyphony? How did organs participate when they did play with singers? Precedents both for accompanied and *a cappella* performances exist throughout the period, with local traditions very much in evidence. Exclusively *a cappella* traditions are securely documented only for the choirs of the Sistine Chapel and of Cambrai Cathedral, where there was no organ and no record of instrumentalists having accompanied singers. Purely vocal performances are also likely to have taken place in churches with a large organ placed in a gallery far from the singers, as at Notre Dame in Paris (until other instruments began to be included in the 16th century) or at St Peter's in Mantua, since the acoustical difficulties of accompanying choral polyphony from a distant organ seem prohibitive.[25] However, in the more intimate collegiate chapels of England and France, in family chapels, and in any major church with both a large fixed organ and a mobile positive, accompanied polyphony was a viable possibility. For such institutions the hierarchy of 'masses with organ', 'masses without organ' and 'chant masses' Reinhard Strohm has found in 15th-century Bruges is probably representative.[26]

Changes in the duties and skills of church organists rank among the most significant and least understood developments of the period. Organists had to adapt to new musical styles and to the emergence of choral polyphony in the mid-15th century. In succeeding decades they were also required to become proficient with an expanding array of organ stops and registers. There is evidence that playing the organ was not always an activity for specialists during the first half of the 15th century, but was rather one that could sometimes be entrusted (on a short-term basis) to choir members and clergy with rudimentary keyboard skills. After *c*1450 the post of organist apparently required individuals with more specialized talents; this we may surmise from augmented salaries, longer periods of service, and an unaccustomed prominence given at the end of the century to a new breed of virtuosos like Paul Hofhaimer, Isacco Argyropulo and many others. But when choirs first began to sing polyphony, organ music in some churches initially may have diminished in importance, perhaps for lack of organists capable of managing the new style. Roger Bowers has found that salaries for some English organists actually declined for a time, while at St Peter's in Rome the choir managed without any organ at all from 1461 to 1477, just as the number of singers expanded from four to eight and much new polyphony was copied.[27] Exactly how organists' duties changed it is difficult to say. In the 15th century they may have been required to do little more at most services than play simple elaborations of chant intonations or to play the tenor line of a motet or polyphonic mass, although some organists were certainly capable of much more.[28] By the 1500s, however, the ability to improvise polyphony over a chant and to transpose was essential, as was the skill of deriving a fitting accompaniment from the separate voice parts in a polyphonic manuscript.

The practice whereby the organ and choir performed alternate verses of a chant (*alternatim* style) may represent one of the oldest uses of the organ in the church. Organ music for *alternatim* performances of Mass and Office chants survives in the earliest known source of liturgical organ music, the Faenza Codex from the early 1400s. Over a century later the practice was so widespread that it seemed to a music teacher in Verona as if the principal purpose of having an organ in church was to relieve singers rather than to accompany them: 'The organ is allowed in church so that the singers can relax during alternations with the organ and are not exhausted by continuously singing beyond the proper period of time, but are stimulated by it to sing together more alertly'.[29] Chants could be performed according to one of three alternation patterns: a purely choral rendition with chant and polyphony heard on alternate verses, or the organ used in conjunction with either chant or polyphony. The possible musical combinations apparently varied from church to church and from feast to feast, and it is entirely feasible that the different combinations were used on different chants within a single service. At the Cathedral of Constance Heinrich Isaac seems to have composed the numerous *alternatim* settings of his *Choralis constantinus* for performance with organ,[30] and in Rome Palestrina evidently considered an alternation between the organ and choral polyphony to be the normal state of affairs at St Peter's. This is the impression we derive from a letter to the Duke of Mantua who had recently 'purged' several chants of all 'barbarisms and imperfections'. The duke's agent in Rome wrote of Palestrina's wish to use the chants the duke had revised 'instead of the organ on occasions of high solemnity'. This also implies that Palestrina considered a mass sung with chant and polyphony more festive than one that also relied on the organ.[31]

Musicians today who wish to perform *alternatim* compositions with organ and polyphony are hindered less by the meagre selection of organ versets and vocal settings than by the difficulties of making an appropriate combination of the two. Traditionally organists improvised their own versets on those portions of the chant assigned to them; as a result, the versets for organ which have survived in written form give only a small indication of organists' practice from the Middle Ages until the Baroque, and few of these exist with their vocal counterparts. Versets preserved in the Buxheim Organ Book (*c*1470), in two early 16th-century English organ masses, or in publications by Attaingant (1531), are typical of others from Italy, Spain and Poland in their emphasis on settings of chants for the Mass Ordinary and the Office, especially hymns and *Magnificat* settings. Versets for the Proper (as Edward Higginbottom suggests) remained unpublished since those chants were liturgically appropriate only for individual feasts.[32] Similarily for the choir, polyphonic elaborations of alternate verses exist for hymns, *Magnificat* settings, and the Mass Ordinary. *Alternatim* mass cycles – both vocal and for organ – occasionally omit the Credo, particularly after the Counter-Reformation when Pope Clement VIII decided that this text was too important to divide. These *alternatim* cycles without Credo may well provide the appropriate context for performances of the individual polyphonic Credo movements that were first popular in the 15th century. With regard to graduals and other Mass Propers, liturgical settings are infrequent even in fully polyphonic versions before the latter half of the 16th century. The likelihood that the choir as well as the organist improvised on these chants is discussed below.

The norm (as we may term it) of singing polyphony *a cappella* began to decline after 1500 with the vogue for using wind and brass instruments in liturgical services. Civic wind bands had participated in church on festive occasions in previous centuries, playing fanfares at the elevation of the host during Mass, joining with the choir and bells for a ceremonial *Te Deum* and contributing an added majesty to celebrations such as the 1436 dedication of Brunelleschi's dome at Florence Cathedral. According to long-established custom they also took part in liturgical processions through city streets as far as the church door, and there are intriguing reports of choirs employing a single instrumentalist: a chaplain at Savoy who played the 'trompetta' (1450–51), or the *bovensanger*, a singer with a string instrument, at S Janskerk in 's-Hertogenbosch (1482).[33] But references to wind and brass increase in the early 16th century, and not all of them are favourable. In the north Erasmus strenuously objected to the instrumental sounds that brought people 'to church as to a theatre for aural delight';[34] the same complaint was then echoed in Verona by a musician intent on reform who lamented in 1529 that 'the abusive flutes, trumpets, trombones and horns [*tibias, tubas, ductiles, corneasque*] have begun to creep into some sacred places. . . . The lascivious congregations gather here to be entertained by these instruments'.[35] This practice may have developed around the turn of the century at the secular courts of Burgundy and France, as Craig Wright suggests, but already by *c*1480 a French liturgical calendar differentiates between feasts sung by the choir alone and those celebrated with the *banda*, a group of shawms and trumpets, according to Rokseth.[36] 50 years later these 'loud' instruments were fixtures in services everywhere, so much so that churches from Canterbury Cathedral (1532) to St Mark's in Venice (1568) began to retain them on a permanent basis.

Although the presence of instruments may be documented in a church, details about their performances are often sketchy; thus there is much to learn about when and what they performed with singers, with the organ and alone. Accounts revealing that instruments performed with an organ exist from the early 15th century but give no clue about how the forces

Celebration of the Mass in the 16th century, with the singers grouped around a lectern and accompanied by a trombone: from the dedication page of 'Liber primus missarum quinque vocum', f.1v (Antwerp: Tylman Susato, 1546)

collaborated.[37] Instruments playing with the singers would have affected everything from the balance between singers to the conventions for applying *ficta* and ornamentation, and from the audibility of the text to the practicality of transposition. Too few inferences have been drawn from the information that has already been discovered. For instance, rather than simply measuring the capabilities of one organ against another, we might profitably compare innovations in organ building with what we know of instrumental ensembles in church. It is suggestive that organs began to be supplied with wind and brass stops at about the same time as wind bands gained popularity in liturgical contexts, and that strings and string stops make ecclesiastical appearances only at the very end of the century.[38] The increased number of organ stops alone would have transformed the colouristic possibilities and therefore also the listener's expectation of hearing a diversity of sounds. But did the organ lead the expansion of instrumental variety or, more likely, imitate it? If so, the admonition of Francisco Guerrero (1586) to accompany three separate (and alternate?) verses of the *Salve regina* successively with shawms, cornetts and then recorders ('because always hearing the same instrument annoys the listener') ought to apply to organ registrations as well.[39] What does the presence of tremolo mechanisms on organs from the end of the 15th century imply about our predilection for straight, boyish tones from instruments and voices? And what of the 'Voce umana' label given to a stop with an undulating tone?[40] Church choirs – then as now – probably tolerated more vibrato than other ensembles. Even the Sistine Chapel harboured its share of elderly and presumably unfocussed voices, with members that had sung full-voiced for 30, 40 and 50 years. In these circumstances vibrato was not so much an expressive liberty as an occupational hazard.

Singers and instrumentalists probably ornamented written polyphony more often than not, but the conventions varied according to the size of the ensemble.[41] Keyboard players, lutenists and other soloists enjoyed the most liberty; the available evidence suggests that choirs had the least. Beginning in 1535, ten instructional manuals of ornamentation appeared in the 16th century – seven of these in the last two decades – and all were printed in Italy (one of them in Spanish). The concentration of these publications in late Renaissance Italy does not necessarily indicate that Italians were more likely to ornament their music, for there are discussions of ornamentation by Coclico and Finck from Germany in the 1550s and German keyboard treatises survive from throughout the period; nor do the manuals prove that the impulse to ornament was much more prevalent among performers at the end of the century than previously (although the tendency toward unrestrained displays of virtuosity unquestionably grew in the decades before 1600). The manuals may rather relate to a change in the status of musicians educated outside the Church, a change more pronounced in Italy and one that helped foster the stylistic innovations of the early Baroque. The focus of the ornamentation manuals indicates an audience of instrumentalists and secular singers; of the works embellished and printed as didactic examples, the overwhelming majority are madrigals and chansons. Only 20 out of 125 compositions have sacred (primarily non-liturgical) texts, and two of these are contrafacta of madrigals.[42] Singers trained and employed in churches evidently had no need for this sort of instruction, either because they already knew how to embellish written polyphony or because they had fewer opportunities to use this skill. Writing at virtually the same time on opposite sides of the Alps, Zarlino and Finck agree that ornamentation is inappropriate in choral music. According to them, ornaments when there is more than one singer per part only result in confusion, whereas soloists can coordinate the embellishments. However criticisms by theorists are hard to interpret; they often betray the existence of the offending practice.

A survey of the evidence for and against choral ornamentation, much needed, must include the possibility of an accommodation between choral and solo forces that would facilitate some types of diminution. One form of practical compromise may have evolved at St Mark's in Venice, where

Zarlino presumably enforced his bias against choral embellishments during his lengthy tenure as chapelmaster (1565–90). The unusual tradition of performing double chorus music with two groups of unequal size – one larger choir of eight or nine singers and the other of four soloists – would allow for ornamentation by the small ensemble.[43] Charles W. Warren has proposed another type of solution with his suggestion that the series of chords marked with fermatas in Dufay's *Alma redemptoris mater*, and in other works, probably direct soloists to improvise, while other singers sustain the notated pitches.[44] While this theory needs more substantiation, it is analogous to the technique Vicentino prescribed a century later for ensembles intent on embellishing music for four voices. In order to secure the harmonies he recommended having instruments play the parts as written while singers add heterophonic diminutions.[45] Ornaments by many singers on a part could always be performed if the ornaments were composed in advance and learned, as seen in the antiphon *Da pacem* copied in Rome in about 1475 with a separate and fully decorated superius part written out on the facing page.[46] Moreover, it is hard to understand how any choir capable of group improvisation could not also manage some degree of collective embellishment.

In one form or another, choral improvisation on plainchant was a prominent category of liturgical music-making throughout the Renaissance. The three-voice styles of the 15th century (English discant, faburden, and on the continent, fauxbourdon), and the four-voice chordal technique known as *falsobordone* in the 16th century, required singers to improvise one or more parts of simple polyphony. More complex kinds of extemporized polyphony also existed.[47] Zarlino's guidelines of 1573 for improvising invertible counterpoint above a cantus firmus, and even rigorous two-voice canons, presuppose that church singers were capable of creating other, less strict, types of polyphony such as imitation. Indeed, after Vicente Lusitano published a list of rules in 1553 for adding several independent and imitative parts to a chant presented in long notes in the bass, Vicentino quickly derided many of his recommendations as old-fashioned; yet one, that of repeating a single melodic figure as many times as possible, remained popular long enough for G. B. Doni to criticize the Sistine Chapel choir for abusing it in 1647. If this device could be considered out of date in the 1550s, when did singers begin to use it in improvisation? Among composers, Isaac already shows a penchant for repetitive, sequential figures by about 1500. Similarly, Vicentino dismisses imitations of the cantus firmus, another feature of early 16th-century written polyphony, as 'not modern' in ensemble improvisations. It is still impossible to determine whether singers borrowed improvisatory figures from written compositions, or whether composers derived ideas from polyphonic improvisations. Historical precedent might support the latter view, but scholars are now no closer to understanding the relationship between composition and improvisation than today's performers are to extracting a motet from a phrase of chant.[48]

Several questions about choral improvisation bear upon issues discussed above. For instance, were they always (or usually) sung *a cappella*, or did the organ and other instruments play the chant? Although their name suggests some such function, the role of the large 'Teneur' pipes in French organs of the period is not known, nor is the purpose of playing the cantus firmus on the pedals in the 16th century.[49] Did organ improvisations combine with vocal improvisations *alternatim* style? This presents another possibility for *alternatim* performances in addition to alternations between organ and chant or between organ and written polyphony, especially since organists often improvised on many of the same chants that singers used as the basis for extemporized counterpoint: liturgical forms such as introits, graduals, hymns and antiphons. Does the curious practice of painting certain well-known chants on the walls of churches relate to choral improvisations? Rather than helping singers to remember the notes of the *Salve regina*, a chant they had sung frequently since childhood, this visual foundation perhaps made it easier for several singers to make their independent contrapuntal lines agree with the chant and therefore with each other.[50]

Of the issues discussed above, modern editors commonly grapple only with those of text setting, even in so-called practical editions.[51] How different were the scribal (editorial) practices of the Renaissance? The needs of performers shaped many obvious features of Renaissance manuscripts and prints, beginning with size, format and organization. Large choirbook-size folios accommodated choral, as opposed to solo, ensembles; partbooks and parchment rolls with all parts displayed on facing pages offered an alternative to books for occasions when choirbooks were evidently considered inconvenient, and collections of sacred music frequently had their contents arranged by genre, with the genres arranged by mode (as with *Magnificat* settings) or by liturgical criteria (as with hymns). Beyond these very basic conventions, scribes exercised the right to make a variety of decisions that ranged from simple editorial alterations to more extensive compositional changes, all according to the dictates of local performance practices. Thus the scribe of the Ockeghem *Missa 'L'homme armé'* in the manuscript Cappella Sistina 35 rewrote the phrase leading into the 'Et incarnatus est', inserting a cadence to give the pope and other celebrants at papal Masses enough time to kneel, as the liturgy required.[52] In this spirit other scribes adapted complete polyphonic settings of the *Magnificat* to meet the needs of chapels accustomed to *alternatim* performances, omitting the unnecessary verses. No less drastic are the mensural changes made in the Roman copy of Dufay's *Missa 'Ave regina coelorum'*, evidently carried out to simplify the notation for the choir at St Peter's. The quibbles in recent decades about adding barlines to transcriptions seem pedantic in comparison.

The options for editors today are too rigidly split between scholarly and practical considerations. 'Scholarly' means a hardback format with large pages on high quality paper: an expensive production. This type of edition usually includes an appendix of critical notes drawing attention to *ficta*, ligatures and so on. Interpretative cues about tempo, phrasing and dynamics are omitted, as are keyboard reductions. These are left to practical editions, editions too seldom prepared by scholars (with the prominent exception of English music). And because critical editions normally publish the complete works of a single composer, a large body of functional liturgical music, mostly anonymous, remains unavailable to both performers and scholars. In emulation of the practical approaches of Renaissance scribes, there are many steps that editors could take to encourage idiomatic performances (obviously not in a hardback format, but in small collections or even in octavo copies). These might include editions of masses and motets with separate parts for instrumentalists; editions of motets with characteristic ornamentation added from the handbooks of Ganassi, Ortiz and others; or following the advice of Vicentino, ornamented editions for singers with accompanying instrumental parts, and composite editions of *alternatim* works which pair choral verses with surviving organ verses. Each of these steps falls between the two editorial options as they are now defined. They are inappropriate for definitive 'complete-works' publications, yet they require the scholarly expertise of a specialist. Like the contrast between 'secular' and 'sacred', the opposition of 'critical' and 'practical' restricts our appreciation of the intrinsic variety of musical life in the Renaissance. It also abdicates the responsibility for making musical decisions.

Notes

[1] Even psalms could be sung during dinner, as documented by William Prizer in 'Isabella d'Este and Lucrezia Borgia as Patrons of Music: the Frottola at Mantua and Ferrara', *JAMS*, xxxviii (1985), 3. With regard to distinguishing between sacred and secular realms, see H. Hucke, 'Über Herkunft und Abgrenzung des Begriffes "Kirchenmusik"', in *Renaissance-Studien: Helmuth Osthoff zum 80. Geburtstag* (Tutzing, 1979), 103–25; and L. Lockwood, 'Music and Religion in the High Renaissance and the Reformation', in *The Pursuit of Holiness in Late Medieval and Renaissance Religion*, ed. C. Trinkaus and H. A. Oberman (Leiden, 1974), 496–502.

[2] R. Sherr, 'From the Diary of a 16th-century Papal Singer', *CMc*, xxv (1978), 83–98.

[3] Y. Rokseth, 'The Instrumental Music of the Middle Ages and Early Sixteenth Century', in *NOHM*, iii (1960), 447.

[4] In many (if not most) cases contrafacta settings of secular works were made for devotional purposes outside church.

[5] The recording is entitled 'The Art of the Netherlands', EMI SLS 5049/Seraphim SIC–6104.

[6] M. Bukofzer, 'The Beginnings of Choral Polyphony', *Studies in Medieval and Renaissance Music* (London, 1950), 176–89. Howard Mayer Brown surveys many aspects of choral performances in 'Choral Music in the Renaissance', *EM*, vi (1978), 164–9.

[7] *Music in Late Medieval Bruges* (Oxford, 1985), 11.

[8] F. A. D'Accone, 'The Performance of Sacred Music in Italy during Josquin's Time, c. 1475–1525', in *Josquin des Prez: New York 1971*, 610–11. The figures cited below are largely taken from his compilation.

[9] Of several discussions of this report, the most extensive is by David Fallows in 'Specific Information on the Ensembles for Composed Polyphony, 1400–1474', in *Performance Practice: New York 1981*, 109–59.

[10] C. Wright, 'Performance Practices at the Cathedral of Cambrai 1475–1550', *MQ*, lxiv (1978), 303.

[11] ibid, 296.

[12] F. A. D'Accone, 'The Singers of San Giovanni in Florence during the 15th Century', *JAMS*, xiv (1961), 324. For D'Accone's comments on the large soprano sections, see 'The Performance of Sacred Music', 612–14.

[13] C. Wearing, 'Orlandus Lassus (1532–1594) and the Munich Kapelle', *EM*, x (1982), 147–54.

[14] Richard Sherr maintains that solo polyphony may have been the normal practice in the Sistine Chapel through the Renaissance, in 'Performance Practice in the Papal Chapel during the Sixteenth Century', *EM*, xv (1987), 453–62.

[15] Mauro Uberti examines this statement and others like it in 'Vocal Techniques in Italy in the Second Half of the 16th Century', *EM*, ix (1981), 486–95.

[16] See N. Bridgman, *La vie musicale au quattrocento* (Paris, 1964), 197; and Brown, 'Choral Music in the Renaissance', 166.

[17] David Fallows has made a beginning in 'The Performing Ensembles in Josquin's Sacred

Music', *TVNM*, xxxv (1985), 32–64. I am grateful to Dr Fallows for providing me with a copy of his paper before publication.

[18] Conrad von Zabern recommended against forcing in the upper registers in *De modo bene cantandi* (1474); see Joseph Dyer's translation and commentary, *EM*, vi (1978), 207–29. Conrad also advised singers to project low notes in a 'trumpet-like' voice (*grossius sive tubalius*); see ibid, 216–17. Perhaps this relates to occasional records of choirs with larger bass sections.

[19] See D. Harrán, 'In Pursuit of Origins: the Earliest Writing on Text Underlay (c.1440)', *AcM*, l (1978), 217–40.

[20] D. Harrán, 'New Light on the Question of Text Underlay Prior to Zarlino', *AcM*, xlv (1973), 24–56; and also the comments of Edward Lowinsky on the problems of text underlay in the first volume of his edition of *The Medici Codex of 1518*, MRM, iii (1968), 90–107.

[21] A. E. Planchart, 'Parts with Words and without Words: the Evidence for Multiple Texts in Fifteenth-century Masses', in *Performance Practice: New York 1981*, 227–51.

[22] C. A. Miller, 'Erasmus on Music', *MQ*, lii (1963), 340.

[23] This finding of William Prizer is reported by Lewis Lockwood in *Music in Renaissance Ferrara 1400–1505* (Oxford, 1984), 136. On the possibility of vocalizing the cantus firmus voice, see the discussion and bibliography Alejandro Planchart cites in 'Fifteenth-century Masses: Notes on Performance and Chronology', *Studi musicali*, x (1981), 6, n.15; and Fallows, 'Ensembles for Composed Polyphony', 128–31, who argues that all of the lower voices were frequently vocalized. Planchart also proposes that singers may occasionally have repeated a small phrase of text 'as a compromise between singing the full chant text or pure vocalization'; 'Parts with Words and without Words', 250.

[24] James McKinnon evaluates iconographical evidence in 'Representations of the Mass in Medieval and Renaissance Art', *JAMS*, xxxi (1978), 21–52.

[25] C. Wright, 'Voices and Instruments in the Art Music of Northern France during the 15th Century: a Conspectus', in *IMSCR*, xii *Berkeley 1977*, 646; and I. Fenlon, *Music and Patronage in Sixteenth-century Mantua* (Cambridge, 1980), i, 102–3.

[26] R. Strohm, *Music in Late Medieval Bruges*, 46–9. And according to Roger Bowers, a small organ was generally present in the Lady Chapels of British churches from 'the early years' of the 15th century. But he argues 'that the use of the organ actually to accompany voices was an innovation of the later 16th century'; see Bowers, 'The Performing Ensemble for English Church Polyphony, *c*.1320–*c*1390', in *Performance Practice: New York 1981*, 182, 184.

[27] Bowers, *Choral Institutions within the English Church: their Constitution and Development, 1340–1500* (diss., U. of East Anglia, 1975), pp.5100–01; and C. Reynolds, 'Early Renaissance Organs at San Pietro in Vaticano', *Studi musicali*, xv (1986), 39–57.

[28] Planchart identifies several works for which an organ is likely to have played the cantus firmus, in 'Fifteenth-century Masses'. Otto Gombosi's study, 'About Organ Playing in the Divine Service, circa 1500', in *Essays on Music in Honor of Archibald Thompson Davison* (Cambridge, Mass., 1957), 51–68, remains a very useful examination of organ practices in central Europe. Some of his sources are inventoried by Clytus Gottwald in *Die Musikhandschriften der Universitätsbibliothek München* (Wiesbaden, 1968).

[29] Biagio Rosetti, *Libellus de rudimentes musices* (Verona, 1529/R1973). The translation is from A. Preston, *Sacred Polyphony in Renaissance Verona: a Liturgical and Stylistic Study* (diss., U. of Illinois, 1969), 46–7.

[30] W. Mahrt, *The 'Missae ad organum' of Heinrich Isaac* (diss., Stanford U., 1969).

[31] This is recounted most recently in Fenlon, *Music and Patronage*, 91.

[32] E. Higginbottom, 'Organ mass' *Grove6*, xiii, 781.

[33] See R. Rastall, 'Some English Consort-groupings of the Late Middle Ages', *ML*, lv (1974), 179–202; and idem, 'Minstrelsy, Church and Clergy in Medieval England', *PRMA*, xcvii (1971), 83–98. The report of a *bovensanger* is from A. Smijers, *De Illustre Lieve Vrouwe Broederschap te 's-Hertogenbosch, Deel I: Rekeningen van 1330 tot 1500* (Amsterdam, 1932), 175.

[34] C. A. Miller, 'Erasmus on Music', 339.

[35] Biagio Rosetti, *Libellus de rudimentes musices*, trans. A. Preston, *Sacred Polyphony*, 46–7.

[36] Wright, 'Voices and Instruments', 646; and Y. Rokseth, 'Instruments a l'église au XVe siècle', *RdM*, xiv (1933), 206–8. This reference and others to the participation of instruments in church are given in Fallows, 'Specific Information', 127, n.42.

[37] Wilhelm Ehmann quotes several instances in *Tibilustrium* (Kassel, 1950), 40, 156–7. Nanie Bridgman cites one occasion when sackbuts intoned the gradual and sounded the *Deo gratias* and the *Ite missa est*; 'The Age of Ockeghem and Josquin', *NOHM*, iii, 251–2. These are moments often played by the organist.

[38] Barra Boydell has compiled archival references to the appearance of the crumhorn, *cornamusa* and shawm, including the emergence of organ stops with these names, in *The Crumhorn and Other Renaissance Windcap Instruments* (Buren, 1982).

[39] Quoted from R. L. Stevenson, *Spanish Cathedral Music in the Golden Age* (Berkeley and Los Angeles, 1961), 167.

[40] Knud Jeppesen terms tremolo 'sehr beliebt' in late 16th-century Italy, in *Die italienische Orgelmusik am Anfang des Cinquecento* (Copenhagen, 1943), 43, n.52. But by then it had been available for nearly a century on some organs; Peter Williams lists several occurrences of it and the Voce umana stop, in *The European Organ 1450–1850* (London, 1966), 294, 297. And see idem, *A New History of the Organ* (Bloomington and London, 1980), 79, where he comments, 'Tremulants, bird-stops and moving statuary were all known by the end of the fifteenth century'.

[41] For a full treatment of this topic, see H. M. Brown, *Embellishing Sixteenth-century Music* (Oxford, 1976).

[42] These figures are derived from the list of ornamented works Ernest Ferand published in 'Didactic Embellishment Literature in the Late Renaissance: a Survey of Sources', in *Aspects of Medieval and Renaissance Music: a Birthday Offering to Gustave Reese* (New York, 1966), 154–72.

[43] Regarding the double chorus traditions at St Mark's, see J. Moore, 'The *Vespro delli Cinque Laudate* and the Role of the *Salmi Spezzati* at St. Mark's', *JAMS*, xxxiv (1981), 249–78; and D. Bryant, 'The *Cori Spezzati* of St Mark's: Myth and Reality', *EMH*, i (1981), 165–86.

[44] C. W. Warren, 'Punctus Organi and Cantus Coronatus in the Music of Dufay', in *Dufay Conference: Brooklyn NY 1974*, 128–43.

[45] Brown, *Embellishing Sixteenth-century Music*, 57.

[46] This occurs in the manuscript *I-Rvat* S Pietro B 80, ff.233v.

[47] The following examples are from E. Ferand, 'Improvised Vocal Counterpoint in the Late Renaissance and Early Baroque', *AnnM*, iv (1956), 129–74.

[48] Margaret Bent discusses distinctions Tinctoris made between improvisation and composition in '*Resfacta* and *Cantare Super Librum*', *JAMS*, xxxvi (1983), 371–91. In addition to her thorough bibliography of other relevant studies, see K.-J. Sachs, 'Arten improvisierter Mehrstimmigkeit nach Lehrtexten des 14. bis 16. Jahrhunderts', *Basler Jb für historische Musikpraxis*, vii (1983), 166–83.

[49] Peter Williams makes this observation in *A New History of the Organ*, 53.

[50] Craig Wright cites several instances of such wall paintings, in 'Performance Practices at Cambrai', 305.

[51] Another editorial concern is *ficta*, which Karol Berger discusses in this volume. Much remains to be learned about the end of *ficta* conventions. The proliferation of accidentals in 16th-century prints Theodor Kroyer studied in *Die Anfänge der Chromatik im italienischen Madrigal des XVI. Jahrhunderts* (Leipzig, 1902) did not spell the end of *ficta* practices, especially not among church musicians. It should therefore be worthwhile to examine the copies of individual works made in successive centuries for a tradition-bound institution such as the Sistine Chapel. For instance, accidentals present in Palestrina's motet *Jesus iunxit se discipulis* as preserved in *I-Rvat* C.S.29 (from the late 16th century) can be compared with those which appear in the same motet in C.S.97 (from 1687) and C.S.294 (from 1748).

[52] G. Reese, *Music in the Renaissance* (New York, 1959), 125, n.154.

CHAPTER XI

Secular Polyphony in the 15th Century

DAVID FALLOWS

In the years 1975–85 scholars and performers looking at the 15th-century song repertories began to question matters that had seemed entirely settled many years earlier. In doing so they showed how almost any piece of evidence can be interpreted in different ways, how easy it is to inherit assumptions and how strongly one is influenced by aesthetic experience as well as by unconscious aesthetic prejudice. The questioning has covered much of the surviving repertory up to about 1600, and more of it will inevitably follow. But for the moment several issues can be seen especially clearly in the study of 15th-century secular music, in particular: the use of instruments; the limitations of the human voice; the degree to which composers of the 15th century wrote with a particular sound or ensemble in mind; the importance and nature of the fixed forms; and the nature of the musical sources that survive. Related issues that concern all the early repertories include: pitch standards, intonation, articulation, tempo, embellishment and tone quality. Those will be covered only in passing here.

There are various reasons why this questioning has arisen. Perhaps the most important is that a substantial increase in the number of people professionally involved in performance and research of early music during the years 1965–75 has led to a more discriminating awareness of much of the repertory, which in turn begins to prompt questions about value judgments and therefore also questions about whether we are certain that what we are hearing (on the very simplest level) is in any way related to what earlier audiences heard.[1] And without some awareness of at least the broad outlines of a 15th-century sound world it is difficult to address aesthetic or critical issues with any confidence.

That is why the 1990s will almost certainly see more research along those lines. It may lead eventually to some kind of agreement about which components of the answer are clear, which are never to be answered confidently, and which actually matter for a just view of the music. Pending that, a discussion of 15th-century secular music can do no more than outline the main areas of discussion and indicate where things may go from here.

The repertory

For most of the 15th century, secular polyphony means what we call courtly songs, though it is clear that these were performed not only in courts but in many collegiates and, particularly towards the end of the century, in private homes as well as at public gatherings. The main body of that repertory is in

French, in three voices and in rondeau form. Virelais and ballades are rarer, as are pieces in two or four voices. Smaller repertories survive in other languages: Italian, German and Spanish in particular, but also English and Flemish.[2] Most of this material is in some way related to the French tradition which is inevitably the main focus of what follows.

Secular polyphony designed for purely instrumental groups is rare until the last two decades of the century. Before then there is just a small group of pieces that would seem to be conceived for an instrumental ensemble;[3] they are so few that it is difficult to feel at all confident about their aims. But we shall see that the song repertory was quite often performed by instruments alone, and from about 1480 the 'chansonniers' show an increasing proportion of pieces that follow the broad design of the earlier rondeau but are evidently designed as 'songs without words' and probably reflect an increasing interest in instrumental ensemble polyphony.[4]

There is also a repertory of arrangements of polyphony apparently for keyboard. Only three substantial sources of this kind survive from the main body of the 15th century: the Faenza Codex,[5] the *Fundamentum organisandi* of Conrad Paumann[6] and the Buxheimer Orgelbuch.[7] All three sources give their main repertory over to arrangements of secular polyphony with the discantus line heavily embellished. They are presumably to be taken as evidence that courtly songs were occasionally (perhaps often) performed

A young couple in a garden singing from a single sheet of music, which is probably a polyphonic love song: illustration from a 15th-century manuscript (The Hague, Koninklijke Bibliotheek, 76F2, f.Vr)

without words and that in such cases the polyphony was a basis for
something more florid and virtuoso. Certainly the few pieces of early
15th-century polyphony apparently for an instrumental ensemble (that is,
written in parts as opposed to keyboard tablature)[8] show, with only one
exception, the same characteristics of having a florid discantus with a tenor
and contratenor much more in line with the lower voices of the courtly song
repertory. Moreover, starting from the middle years of the century, there are
occasional documents and reports suggesting that lutenists did the same
thing: one player performed the lower voice or voices more or less as they
were written and the 'soloist' displayed his skill in creating a highly
embellished version of the discantus.[9]

Ensembles

Much of the courtly song repertory of the 15th century survives in a uniform
manner: the discantus has one stanza of text underlaid to the music, with the
remaining stanzas at the bottom of the page; on the facing page are the tenor
and contratenor provided with only the first few words of text, apparently for
identification purposes. The tenor tends to be in longer note values and more
heavily ligatured; the contratenor has a more angular line with leaps of an
octave or a fifth. As the century progresses, however, there is an increase of
imitation between the three voices which brings with it an increase in their
similarity of style. Given that no source appears to specify any particular
scoring (for the few cases of a contratenor marked 'trombetta' or something
similar seem likely to suggest the nature of the line rather than its
instrumentation),[10] it has seemed reasonable to conclude (*a*) that the
discantus was vocal but the lower two voices were instrumental and (*b*) that
instrumentation varied according to individual preference and the availability of instruments.

Over the last decade, however, considerable doubt has been cast on these
assumptions, and it may be useful briefly to trace the change of opinion
because it seems likely that much is still to be done in refining and settling
the various disputes concerning the role of instruments in 15th-century
polyphonic song. At the time of writing there is considerable disagreement.
Several scholars have moved from a 'colourful' view of the repertory,
admitting all kinds of instruments, to an approach which suggests that in
many cases only voices took part in the finest performances. The case for
limiting instrumental participation evolved roughly as follows.

First came Edmund Bowles's demonstration that in court culture instruments were firmly divided into two categories, *haut* and *bas* – loud and soft.[11]
Haut were trumpets, shawms, sackbuts and percussion, instruments used for
outdoor ceremonies and on occasions when loud music was required. In
general it seemed that these instruments can have had little to contribute in
the intimate courtly atmosphere of the secular polyphonic song. Their
function was primarily to provide noise and magnificence, not refined
polyphony. *Bas* were lutes, bowed instruments, harp, and certain wind
instruments such as the flute and the *douçaine*. When evidence that
instruments took part in church polyphony begins to emerge, the instruments in question tend to be in the *haut* category: sackbuts, cornetts and

shawms all took part with the singers in several specifically described church ceremonies nearer 1500[12] and throughout the 16th century. To some extent that may be because these instruments are less likely to go out of tune in the course of a long mass in a windy church. But then we also have strong evidence from the 16th century (which can be extrapolated backwards into the 15th) that singing in church was louder than the *voce da camera* of court song.[13] There is also abundant evidence that shawms and sackbuts were used indoors, though normally as an accompaniment to dancing;[14] there is evidence of the polyphonic song repertory being performed out of doors;[15] and it would be wise to remember that the current distinction between sacred and secular tends to be far more rigid than that drawn in the later Middle Ages. It is also plainly true that some ensembles of *haut* instruments were capable of performing composed polyphony,[16] though there is no unambiguous evidence of their having done so together with singers.

And here is perhaps the point. It seems self-evident that the text is part of a song's essence. Even though the music was sometimes (perhaps often) performed without a voice, that can hardly be the best way of reproducing the composer's art. The modern historically informed performer has two possible aims: to do something that is likely to have happened in the 15th century, or to aim at the kind of performance the composer might have had in mind. The latter may seem hopelessly idealistic, but it is obviously true that to perform the music without text is to short-change the original conception. According to that argument it seemed in general wise to avoid the use of the *haut* category of instruments when performing the courtly song repertory.

The next stage came with the recognition that most of the instruments seen in pictures of performances are relatively small: recorders (in any case surprisingly rare in the iconography of the time) never larger than the modern treble recorder, organettos that could scarcely have played lower than middle C, bowed instruments invariably held at the chest and therefore almost certainly incapable (with the string technology of the time as we now understand it)[17] of sounding lower than tenor C but generally of a size that would restrict them to the treble register.

So if a voice is to be used on the discantus line this rather reduces the function of those instruments to doubling, normally at the higher octave. The counterpoint of this repertory is such that the tenor and contratenor must be in the same register and below the discantus, otherwise many second-inversion triads result. Moreover, doubling at the octave has serious side-effects: Dufay, for example, very often designs his songs so that at some point the three voices intertwine and overlap, frequently circulating round a triadic figure;[18] to double any of these lines at the octave would severely impede the textural design implied by the counterpoint. Plainly, these instruments could more easily participate if the discantus was sung by a very high voice; but, as we shall see, it was by then becoming clear that the most common performance range was with a discantus primarily in the octave above middle C.

At that point it also began to seem as though, at least for the discantus, doubling impeded the suppleness and fluidity of line that was the chief glory of so much of this music. (But it is again worth noting that these viewpoints

204

Music at a 15th-century banquet: from 'Le livre du roi Modus', copied in France in the second decade of the 15th century: both haut and bas instruments can be seen in the illustration, which may show the performance of a courtly polyphonic chanson, either arranged for instruments alone, or sung by one or more of the musicians in the gallery accompanied by lute and rebec (Vienna, Österreichische Nationalbibliothek, MS 2577, f.36v)

leave considerable room for disagreement: they are founded largely on subjective judgments that are undeniably rooted in personal musical experience.)

Most recently one further observation has undermined received thinking about 15th-century song. It seems to have begun as a verbal challenge when Peter Holman noted (in 1983) that the secondary literature on the history of instruments and performance practice contained no iconographical evidence whatsoever for bowed instruments with a rounded bridge earlier than about 1475; and he asked for any evidence of rounded bridges existing before that date. In 1986, having received no clear response, he repeated this idea in a published letter.[19] One implication of this question seemed immediately obvious: that flat bridges were suited to drone-based performances of an essentially monophonic and probably semi-improvised repertory and highly inconvenient for participation in polyphony of any sophistication. Many people reluctantly concluded that bowed string instruments had no part in the secular song repertory of the years before about 1475.

At the time of writing, this matter is however very much *sub judice*. The relatively few experts in the iconography of early string instruments appear to have held their fire. Only within the last few months (Summer 1987) they have informally named eight 14th-century pictures that unquestionably depict bowed instruments with a curved bridge.[20] But considerable examination and discussion of these pictures must follow when they have been made available in adequate form. That discussion will concern the size and stringing of the instruments, their iconographic context, and how far they actually offer evidence for believing that certain polyphonic repertories could appropriately be performed with a bowed instrument. This information must also be taken alongside the evidence of Jerome of Moravia (who gives detailed instructions for fingering an extended scale on the *viella*, though without necessarily implying that these notes could be played separately) and Johannes de Grocheo (who states that the *viella* could play all kinds of music, though the context gives grounds for limiting his notion of 'all kinds').[21] It needs also to consider the strong subjective case for preferring a sustained-pitch instrument on the lower voices of, for example, many songs by Dufay and Binchois.

But pending such discussions it remains likely that the role played by bowed instruments was very small.[22] So for all normal purposes it would seem that the only instruments remaining that can confidently be included in the performance of a polyphonic song are the harp and the lute. Additional possible instruments are the *douçaine* (about which virtually nothing was known until recently),[23] the psaltery (though this had probably all but disappeared in the 15th century), and keyboard instruments such as the positive organ or the chekker (though today keyboard players feel distinctly uncomfortable playing just a single line from a polyphonic complex).[24] This is by no means to exclude the likelihood that an ensemble of higher instruments occasionally performed polyphonic songs without a voice and at a higher register than would be acceptable if a voice took part.[25] But the role of instruments in the performance of the 15th-century song repertory now seems considerably smaller than was once assumed.

In retrospect, this should surprise nobody. Minstrels seem never to have written down their music, and it would be fair to suggest that in general they were musically illiterate. Of course the word 'minstrel' covers a wide range of people with strikingly different skills and professional standing; but very few of them are likely to have had reading skills comparable with those of the church musicians. Even the ability to read words was rare in the early 15th century, being something that could be learned (for those without the resources to provide a private tutor) only in church schools: the word 'cleric' meant at the time somebody who could read, and it was more or less synonymous with the word 'churchman'. Nearly all those composers about whom we have any biographical information were churchmen by profession, employed initially as singers in the great church choirs, later in their lives perhaps taking on a lucrative prebend. Minstrels, even in the richest establishments, were in an entirely different category, often passing on their skills from father to son, apparently not using written music, going each Lent to the minstrel meetings where they learned new tunes and new techniques. Small wonder that there should be no evidence suggesting they took part in performances of written polyphony. The known exceptions are harpists: Senleches and Baude Cordier, who composed some of the most intricate music of the late 14th century, were professional harp players (though the identity of Baude Cordier remains hotly disputed); Richard Loqueville, perhaps Dufay's composition teacher in Cambrai, may have been primarily a church musician but there is a document recording a payment to him for having played and taught the harp; later in the century Hayne van Ghizeghem – just one further example among several – seems never to have been part of a church or chapel choir, being employed at the Burgundian court as a *valet de chambre* and singer; that is, as a courtly attendant who excelled in his musical abilities.[26] Moreover it is surely true that courtiers were increasingly able to take part in the performance of polyphonic songs. We can document this for Duke Charles the Bold of Burgundy, for the Prince of Viana and for many lesser men.[27] But the broad pattern began to seem clear: minstrels were musically (and verbally) illiterate; the song repertory was composed and probably performed by church singers.

Two further considerations seemed to support this. First, a search for descriptions of performances that unambiguously concerned polyphonic song before about 1475 soon showed that all such descriptions concerned voices only.[28] The number of such descriptions is extremely small: narrators of the time were not concerned to provide sufficient detail to allow historians 500 years later to reconstruct the performances, and it therefore seems wise to bear in mind the likelihood that the available sample is by no means representative. Yet those descriptions do at least establish that a perform-ance of the polyphonic song repertory using voices alone was relatively common.

Second, researchers began increasingly to focus on the question of pitch and to accept that there is no clear evidence for the concept of a pitch-standard before the 16th century.[29] Until then the situation for polyphony seems to have been the same as for Gregorian chant: the clef merely indicated where the tones and semitones stood within the prevailing modality; apparent lower pitch was merely a function of a different modal organization; and the note middle C was a relationship, not an absolute pitch. Most three-voice polyphony of the years before about 1460 has the same contrapuntal layout: tenor and contratenor in more or less the same range with the discantus occupying a range around a fifth higher. Even though some pieces have the lowest voice going down to bass G or lower whereas others go no lower than tenor F, the relationship of the voices to one another remains the same.

The issue of pitch is discussed elsewhere in this volume in its best context, that of church music. An ecclesiastical musican who was on salary to sing the discantus, for instance, would know where to find his part on the page, would observe the clef with a view to knowing where his semitones lay, and would select his pitch in relation to the highest and lowest notes of his normal range, as represented by the highest and lowest notes on the stave in front of him. This system works extremely well for a purely vocal ensemble, much less well if the group includes string instruments (which can to some extent be retuned according to the pitch selected) and virtually not at all if wind instruments or organ are involved.[30]

These last issues therefore seemed to clinch the case against instrumental participation in the courtly song repertory. But it should be added that most of the information was easily available long before it was widely accepted. Nobody took it particularly seriously until the publication of recordings that virtually dispensed with instruments. At that moment many listeners were astonished by how much more convincing and eloquent the music sounded in a purely vocal performance. It was the musical impact, not the nature of the arguments, that convinced so many musicians that the music can be better without instrumental participation.

Moreover any student of cultural history needs to be suspicious both of sudden reversals of opinion and of rigid, apparently simple answers. In the preceding paragraphs I have been at pains to stress that most of the recent rethinking left room for qualification. In the *haut/bas* distinction it is clear that *haut* was not confined to monophony or to performances out of doors. Concerning the apparent high pitch of most instruments it was a purely subjective judgment to say that doubling was out of the question. Bowed instruments with a flat bridge could surely within certain limitations play a single polyphonic line without a drone; the process may seem clumsy and an adaptation of something designed for another purpose, but such resourceful adaptation is a relatively common phenomenon in cultural history. The argument against curved bridges before the late 1470s seems about to collapse. We do have evidence that at least two professional harpists of the late 14th century could compose music of extraordinary complexity. Besides, it is an often observed characteristic of those brought up in illiterate cultures that they have highly developed memories and can retain the most complex materials with astonishing ease. (Many of us find it difficult to believe how much complicated material the average opera singer can memorize.) The evidence that purely vocal performance happened is scattered, both geographically and chronologically; and it is well to remember that before about 1475 there are numerous descriptions and pictures of musical performances by voices and instruments together which do not indicate whether written polyphony is intended.[31] To say simply that they could all be monophonic performances or semi-improvised polyphony is to focus on just one viewpoint

– a viewpoint that is valid but cannot claim to be exclusive or comprehensive.

Finally, the question of pitch. While it seems more or less certain that a piece apparently written at a lower pitch was intended to sound at more or less the same pitch as one written apparently higher, this does not necessarily mean that there was no concept of a pitch standard. Much research still needs to be done. But it begins to look as though a fairly large proportion of the surviving music from the 15th century was intended to sound at a pitch that happens to approximate more or less to modern concert pitch, and that the relatively few pieces written at a different pitch were thought of even at the time as transposed.[32] It is difficult to conceive of medieval musicians having frequent access to the organ, for example, without having some notion of a fixed pitch. And if the argument for a 'floating pitch-standard' begins to crumble much of the remaining edifice of the 'non-instrument' argument crumbles with it.

It is therefore much too soon for rigid answers. Yet there does seem a case for believing that something important changed after about 1475. At that point we begin to find large numbers of bowed string instruments with a curved bridge, large wind instruments, lute players using tablature, and a considerable repertory of works in the secular manuscripts without text – some of them certainly songs from the earlier *forme fixe* tradition with the texts simply left out, others however plainly never intended to have text.

But even that is by no means a confident judgment. If it were really true that in the years after 1475 instruments became part of the performance tradition for composed, written polyphony for the first time, that would have represented one of the most staggering changes in the entire history of music; and it must be accounted slightly disturbing that none of the many verbose musical theorists writing at the time should have given no more than the most indirect hints of such a change.[33]

Discussion of the scoring therefore points to a delicate issue of historical methodology. Various different pieces of evidence all seem to suggest the same conclusion, one that entirely overturns the generally held views of the last half century; each piece of evidence requires considerable qualification, which could lead to a reinstatement of something approaching the original position; and the conclusions, if accepted, lead to a surprising historical paradox, namely an overwhelming change in the actual sound of composed polyphony without there being any clear acknowledgment of that change in the writings of the time.

Voices and text

If purely vocal performance of this repertory is to be considered so much more common than had been thought, that in its turn raises questions of which voices are to be used and how the untexted lines were sung. It also highlights the simple observation that in the early part of the 15th century secular song was in many ways similar to sacred music. In the works of Dufay, for instance, there are several cases of contrapuntal material being transferred unchanged from one to the other; in the earliest examples of 'parody mass' music the secular chanson parodied is identical in its secular and sacred contexts, and in the last two decades of the century there are many cases of sections from mass settings copied directly into sources primarily of secular music.[34]

It would therefore be reasonable to conclude that there was often no intrinsic difference between the two repertories – sung, surely, by the same people, merely in different contexts. Relevant to that conclusion is the simple if subjective observation that, at the time of writing, most available recordings of the 15th-century song repertory seem too fast. The speeds generally adopted fail to do justice to the intricacy of the polyphony; they tend to contradict the primarily soulful nature of the poetic texts, and they only rarely manage to recreate the atmosphere that seems implied by the music.

Many writers have suggested that sacred music of the early 15th century was for performance by solo singers, sometimes with several voices on the top line[35] – though such doubling must have been considerably rarer in the secular repertory. Given the standard contrapuntal structure of one high voice with two lower voices (tenor and contratenor) a fifth below it – if a fourth voice is added it is usually in the higher register until about the middle of the century – and given the current views on pitch for 15th-century sacred music, it seems likely that most of the polyphonic song repertory was designed for one singer in what we consider the alto register (perhaps normally sung by a man but also demonstrably sung by a woman or a boy) and for the two other lines to be sung in the tenor range.[36] For the reasons already outlined (and discussed elsewhere in this book) pieces written in a higher or lower range must almost certainly have been adapted to this more normal range. It is most unlikely that they were intended for an entirely different kind of ensemble.

For the vast majority of these songs only the discantus is texted. On the face of it that would suggest two alternatives for the lower voices: instrumental performance or vocalization. As we have seen, only the lute, the harp or possibly the *douçaine* seem likely candidates within the instrumentarium of the time. In many cases plucked instruments seem more appropriate to the disjunct lines of the contratenor rather than the ligatured long-note tenors which from their historical position tend to carry the harmonic and structural essence of the counterpoint and need something more sustained to give them sufficient controlling power. Vocalization is a strong alternative. Much of the chant tradition (which was the basis of the training and musical experience of all church singers at the time) is highly melismatic; the idea of singing strings of notes on a single vowel cannot have been as strange to 15th-century singers as it is to singers today, who often find that the lack of syllables and consonants severely constricts their freedom of line, their precision of tuning and their control of saliva. Moreover, since it now seems accepted that sacred polyphony cannot often have tolerated instrumental participation,[37] we must accept that singers were perfectly happy with this arrangement. On the other hand, it is by no means perverse to suggest that the singers on the lower voices often incorporated the text. The argument – which I have laid out at greater length elsewhere[38] – runs as follows.

In the sources the discantus line is normally provided with text for only one stanza: later stanzas must be read from the bottom of the page and adapted to the music. Doing so requires not only musical expertise and a considerable memory but also a strong awareness of the way in which text and music are matched in an often melismatic style. Sometimes, indeed, even the first stanza is underlaid in so approximate a manner as to make it extremely difficult for a singer to perform that stanza intelligently without the exercise of similar skills. To take a simple example: the discantus lines are normally composed so that each line of the poem is set to a phrase of music, beginning and ending with a rest and ending with a firm cadence; but quite often the text scribe does not bother to align text and music even to this degree, and in many cases it would make little sense for the singer simply to pronounce the syllables at the point where they occur below the music: the manuscripts are mostly copied with a view to visual elegance and scribal evenness, not detailed information on underlay.[39] So even for the first stanza intelligent singing requires that the performer know both the text and the music so well that the two can be matched according to the musical sense rather than according to what can be seen in the sources. (Clearly in such cases sight-reading is more or less out of the question, and to talk of sight-reading is to think of 15th-century singers in something of an anachronistic manner: it is to align them with 20th-century musicians who expect to cover within a week's – or even an evening's – work an infinitely wider repertory with an infinitely wider historical and stylistic spread.)

It follows, I believe, that if such skills are needed even for the intelligent singing of the discantus line then there is no particular difficulty in applying precisely the same skills to the singing of the untexted tenor line. Very often the poetic divisions are just as easy to see (or hear) from the tenor line; and it could even be argued that without distractingly misaligned underlay a singer on the lower line would find it somewhat easier to sing his line intelligently with text.

Certain sources do in fact have text to the lower voices: it happens quite often in the Bodleian Library manuscript Can. misc. 213 from the 1430s, in the Chansonnier Cordiforme from the 1470s, in an apparently Burgundian fragment from slightly earlier,[40] and in several chansonniers copied in France during the last decade or so of the century.[41] But in general text is underlaid only to the discantus. It is easy to argue that this latter, more common, pattern was a case of musical shorthand: the text needs to be written once, but no more, given the expertise of the musicians; it might as well be written under the first line to be copied, which was also the most prominent and tuneful line, and there is much to be said for the elegance of the standard layout in these sources, with the discantus line and the poem on the left-hand page and the two equal-range voices, tenor and contratenor, on the facing page.

There is no particular reason to avoid breaking up ligatures or long notes in performance. There are enough cases of concordant sources doing both these things.[42] The more 'held' nature of the tenor lines is such that they were often more conveniently and elegantly notated with ligatures. And, as the preceding pages have attempted to stress, elegance tends to be a hallmark here, not only in the writing of the sources but in the entire ambience of this repertory – as any performance should show.

Plainly this interpretation of the sources and their meaning is not intended to be definitive: there are many cases where one or other of the lower voices has so little relationship with the structure of the poem that texting is not only extremely difficult but musically counter-productive. But it seems important to discourage the attitude that treats a 15th-century manuscript as a literal and complete representation of what happened. It contains the information that was necessary to musicians of the time, but it often needs considerable help if it is to provide enough for the musicians of today. Apart from tablatures, there is only one extant example of a 15th-century song in score.[43] There are no clear surviving compositional manuscripts (though there are one or two cases of pieces apparently rewritten in the surviving manuscript). What we have are homogenized records reduced to their essence: superfluous information is difficult to find in these manuscripts. They can therefore be very misleading for the reader who goes to them expecting information they were not intended to provide; and there is still much work to be done in elucidating precisely what these sources were expected to convey and why.

Forms

This in its turn leads to the issue of forms, which has also recently come under new scrutiny. The vast majority of 15th-century polyphonic song is in rondeau form.[44] From the earlier part of the century there is a small number of ballades; from about 1450 the virelai (or bergerette) came back into fashion, though very much as an offshoot of the rondeau.[45] But there seems to have been a considerable change in fashion from the 14th century: in the works of Machaut and the composers of the generation immediately after him, rondeau, ballade and virelai had more or less equal parts in the secular song repertory; in the 15th century the rondeau held sway.[46] And even when we reach the last years of the 15th century, when people began composing secular music that apparently was never intended to carry text, the outlines of the rondeau form often remain clearly imprinted on the design and balance of the pieces.[47]

This most French and most rarified of all musico-poetic forms had a much more limited career outside the French repertory. There is a small handful of settings of Italian texts in rondeau form, a few German examples without any surviving musical settings, and for England just a little evidence of its cultivation.[48] Outside France in the 15th century song forms tended to be relatively free, with an apparent preponderance of strophic design – though in Italy the ballata to some extent continued from the 14th century, and later in the century the *strambotto* suddenly became extremely popular, perhaps as the first harbinger of the richly varied frottola repertory.[49]

It is in this context that the rondeau's career seems so astonishing, not merely because it was widely cultivated by poets and composers over a period stretching at least from 1280 to after 1520,[50] but also because during the 15th century it accounts for some three-quarters of all lyric poetry in French and for something closer to seven-eighths of the French song repertory.

What was it about the rondeau that gave rise to such a career, both longer and more all-pervasive than that of sonata form? The long answer would

212

involve a fascinating study of poetic changes, courtly mores, musical design and the nature of musical form. The short answer, which must suffice here, includes several simple propositions. The form is almost, but not quite, strophic: the usual representation of its design as *ABaAabAB* (in which capital letters denote a repeat of text and music whereas lower-case letters denote a musical repeat with new text) is perhaps slightly misleading in this respect – *AB aA ab AB* would make it clearer that only the second stanza interrupts the straight strophic design which is therefore fairly easy for the listener to understand but at the same time remarkably sophisticated in its effect. The balance of the two main sections of the stanza is infinitely but subtly variable, each change in length or weight having considerable influence on the broader form. The triple repetition of the first half of the music in the second and third stanzas allows for a building up of tension by the increased expectation of the *b* section of the music, and the momentum generated by the return of the *b* section in the third stanza requires the final refrain stanza to settle it. The complete refrain at the end as well as at the beginning involves a return to the 'essence' of the composition, though often now heard in a new light.[51]

The various ways in which the syntax of the poem establishes internal relationships within the poem also admit of considerable variety. In one of the commonest schemes, the refrain will have its main verb in the second half (*B* section) of the stanza; this means that when the first half of the refrain returns in the second stanza it will have no main verb of its own and will normally therefore join syntactically to the first half of the stanza. In the simplest musical terms this means that performers would be well advised to give a slightly longer pause between the stanzas but to run on the musical repetition within the second stanza, for example, more quickly. On the other hand there are many more ways in which a sophisticated poet can make the various sections interrelate: at the end of the century the theorist Pierre Lefèvre[52] categorizes poems in rondeau form precisely by the way in which the refrains related syntactically to what preceded or followed them.

Yet perhaps the most important clue to the success of the rondeau was surely the feeling that the listener was on familiar ground with this most common of all forms – a matter, like several of the features mentioned above, that makes the later analogy of sonata form by no means useless. At one time modern performers felt that the rondeau needed considerable help to stop it becoming tedious – different instrumentation for each section, the occasional omission of text entirely, curtailment of the form especially for the longer rondeaux of the 1470s which can run to six minutes or more. Recently, many performances and recordings have demonstrated that even the longest rondeau can be wonderfully satisfying without misguided attempts (as they now appear) to enliven them.

As with all the early repertories there is a language problem, and it would be unwise to pretend that this problem does not exist. One solution – which is perhaps preferable for recordings – is to print full texts and translations for the listener to follow. But for live concerts this rarely works and it is perhaps better to follow the practice of some early *puys* in reading out the poem prior to performance and to adapt the practice by reading it in translation.[53] But it is also wise to bear in mind that writers and even poets may not

always have adhered doggedly to the full rondeau form; and this chapter will
end with a brief discussion of some of the formal issues that now urgently
demand further investigation.

Literary syntax is the starting-point. Howard Garey was apparently the
first to tell musicians that there are several cases where it is impossible to
construe or punctuate the rondeau if it has full refrains according to the
received form.[54] The *locus classicus* here is Dufay's *Vostre bruit*[55] where an
ideal form (from a purely syntactical viewpoint) would include only the first
two words of the refrain for each of its returns. And there are many
comparable cases: as an example of a slightly different kind, Dufay's *Ce jour
de l'an*[56] in fact works best as a poem without any refrain repetitions
whatsoever.

That remained, for musicians, merely a puzzling phenomenon until the
discovery of the manuscript Uppsala Universitetsbiblioteket 76A containing
a through-composed rondeau by Agricola which restricts itself to two-word
rentrements rather than full refrains.[57] And it is easy to see, with this evidence
available, that the same is the case in Josquin's *Quant je vous voy*.[58] Neither
example is likely to have been composed earlier than about 1500, at which
stage the musical career of the old *formes fixes* was entirely finished.
Nevertheless they suggest a solution for the syntactical problem of earlier
poems like *Vostre bruit* and suggest the need for further investigation into
apparent ambiguities in the rondeau form earlier in the century. Pending a
full investigation, there are various considerations that could be borne in
mind.

1. Literary scholars seem to agree, largely on the basis of syntactic
evidence, that from the time of Christine de Pizan in the years around 1400
many poets writing in rondeau form sometimes intended no more than a
rentrement.[59]

2. The manuscripts containing the poetry of Charles d'Orléans, for
example, imply returns of a considerable variety of lengths and encourage
attitudes of some flexibility in relation to the form.[60]

3. Several rondeau settings from the 15th century have a fermata (or, more
precisely, a *signum congruentiae*) very early in the stanza, at a point from
which it would be easy to return to the beginning for a second-stanza
rentrement (though rather less easy to conclude the whole piece).[61]

4. There are four cases of 15th-century rondeau settings in which the
source includes a repetition of the words of the first line at the end of the
stanza,[62] here implying that it would be possible to conclude with a
rentrement rather than a full final stanza. (One can also argue that it opens
up ways of singing a curtailed second-stanza refrain.)[63]

5. Particularly in the works of Binchois it is easy to see, as early as the
1420s, a certain impatience with the received forms, evidence of musical
details added to make it possible to curtail the fuller design.

6. While the whole discussion of modality and of tonal unity in the 15th
century is still an extremely uncertain discipline, it remains true that there
are several pieces that end at what seems an unexpected and unprepared
pitch whereas the first cadence seems more central to the entire musical
structure,[64] thereby implying similar short cuts within the form.

Like the issues outlined earlier, this one must surely come in for much discussion in the years to come. It is perhaps difficult to evaluate seriously until some excellent performances have been heard that employ the curtailed *rentrement*. Nobody can deny the Agricola and Josquin cases; but there is considerable aesthetic room for resisting the notion that earlier rondeaux were ever curtailed. After all, the extraordinary history of the form is such that in certain cases musical design can take precedence over syntactical logic; the musico-poetic strength of the form is surely what kept it alive. To accept that composers played fast and loose with the rondeau would make it extremely difficult to understand why they bothered with the form at all.

Once again, the matter of form shows how easy it has been in the past to forget the range of possible implications in the sources, how difficult it can be to imagine how the manuscripts were used, why they were copied as they were, and what the music meant at the time. Moreover, all of the problems discussed in this chapter are ones that compel the severest reflections on the nature, use and evaluation of evidence. And it is far too easy for discussions to become heated when they come so close to the very roots of such a wonderful and richly varied repertory as the 15th-century chanson. It is a subject that still needs much patient, methodical and cool-minded research.

Notes

[1] See for example M. Morrow, 'Musical Performance and Authenticity', *EM*, vi (1978), 233–46.

[2] There is no published handlist of this repertory, though I am currently preparing one. In round figures, the works from the years *c*1420 to *c*1480 comprise: 1000 French songs, 150 Italian songs, 150 German songs, 65 Spanish songs (though there are surely many lost sources and the repertory for the last 20 years of the century is enormously larger), 45 English songs, 20 Flemish songs. The main editions include the following (in approximate chronological order of their repertory): *Early Fifteenth-century Music*, ed. G. Reaney, CMM, xi/1–7 (1955–84); *Die Chansons von Gilles Binchois*, ed. W. Rehm, Musikalische Denkmäler, ii (Mainz, 1957); *Pièces polyphoniques profanes de provenance Liégeoise*, ed. C. van den Borren (Brussels, 1950); *Guillelmi Dufay: Cantiones*, ed. H. Besseler, CMM, i/6 (1964); *Anonymous Pieces in the Chansonnier El Escorial, Biblioteca del Monasterio, Cod. V.III.24*, ed. W. H. Kemp, CMM, lxxvii (1980); *The Mellon Chansonnier*, ed. L. L. Perkins and H. Garey (New Haven, 1979); *Anonymous Pieces in the Ms El Escorial IV.a.24*, ed. E. Southern, CMM, lxxxviii (1981); *The Chansonnier El Escorial IV.a.24*, ed. M. K. Hanen (Henryville, 1983); *Der Kopenhagener Chansonnier*, ed. K. Jeppesen (Leipzig, 1927/*R*1965); *The Musical Manuscript Montecassino 871*, ed. I. Pope and M. Kanazawa (Oxford, 1978); *A Florentine Chansonnier from the Time of Lorenzo the Magnificent (Florence, Biblioteca Nazionale Centrale, MS Banco Rari 229)*, ed. H. M. Brown, MRM, vii (1983); *The Cappella Giulia Chansonnier*, ed. A. Atlas (Brooklyn, 1975–6); *Petrucci: Harmonice musices odhecaton A*, ed. H. Hewitt (Cambridge, Mass., 1942); *Canti B numero cinquanta*, ed. H. Hewitt, MRM, ii (1967); *Das Glogauer Liederbuch: erster Teil*, ed. H. Ringmann and J. Klapper, EDM, iv (1936); *Cancionero musical de la Colombina*, ed. M. Querol, MME, xxxiii (1971).

[3] Most of these pieces are in the manuscript *I-TRmn* 87 and are discussed briefly in C. Hamm, 'A Group of Anonymous English Pieces in Trent 87', *ML*, xli (1960), 211–15; they are all published in the course of two articles by B. Disertori, 'Un primitivo esempio di variazione nei codici musicali tridentini', *Studi trentini di scienze storiche*, xxxv/2 (1956), 1–7; and 'Tyling musico inglese nei codici tridentini', ibid, xxxvi (1957), 10–13. Two further pieces might be included in this category. One, in *D-Mbs* clm 14274, ff.4*v*–5, seems to be unpublished (it is based on the tenor of the English song *Love woll I withoute eny variaunce*, in *GB-Ob* Ashmole 1383, f.68*v*, and is closely related to the settings entitled 'Luffil' and 'Luffile' in the Buxheimer Orgelbuch). The other, in *I–TRmn* 89, ff.402*v*–3*v*, is edited and discussed by Disertori in: 'L'unica composizione sicuramente strumentale nei codici tridentini', *CHM*, ii (1957), 135–45.

[4] For a sensitive discussion of the nature of this repertory see W. Edwards, 'Songs without Words by Josquin and his Contemporaries', in *Music in Medieval and Early Modern Europe: Patronage, Sources and Texts*, ed. I. Fenlon (Cambridge, 1981), 79–92. Further discussions

include L. Litterick, 'On Italian Instrumental Ensemble Music in the Late Fifteenth Century', in Fenlon, op cit, 117–30; and H. M. Brown, *A Florentine Chansonnier*, text vol., especially 71–98.

[5] *I-FZc* 117, containing 48 intabulated pieces copied apparently in the second decade of the 15th century; see the complete edition by D. Plamenac in CMM, lvii (1972).

[6] *D-B* mus.40613, pp.46–92, containing 17 pieces in tablature copied apparently in the late 1450s; see the complete edition by Willi Apel in CEKM, i (1963), 32–51 (this volume contains virtually all surviving keyboard music before *c*1480 apart from the material mentioned in nn.5 and 7 above and below).

[7] *D-Mbs* Mus. Ms.3725, containing 258 pieces in tablature copied apparently in the 1460s; see the complete edition by B. A. Wallner in EDM, xxxvii–xxxix (1958–9).

[8] See n.3 above.

[9] Among recent writings on the 15th-century lute style see P. Danner, 'Before Petrucci: the Lute in the Fifteenth Century', *Journal of the Lute Society of America*, v (1972), 4–17; D. Fallows, '15th-century Tablatures for Plucked Instruments: a Summary, a Revision and a Suggestion', *LSJ*, xix (1977), 7–33; V. Ivanoff, 'Das Lautenduo im 15. Jahrhundert', *Basler Jb für historische Musikpraxis*, viii (1984), 147–62. Concerning the slightly cautious qualification at the opening of this paragraph it should be noted that both Fallows and (independently) Ivanoff reached the conclusion that one piece in the Buxheimer Orgelbuch (no.17) seems likely to have been designated for lute duo with the implication that much more of the music in the manuscript could well be a reflection of what those ensembles played; Timothy J. McGee has reached a similar conclusion about the intabulations in the Faenza codex in 'Instruments and the Faenza Codex', *EM*, xiv (1986), 480–90. Further on the history of the lute and other plucked instruments, see C. Page, 'The 15th-century Lute: New and Neglected Sources', *EM*, ix (1981), 11–21, and H. M. Brown, 'St. Augustine, Lady Music, and the Gittern in Fourteenth-century Italy', *MD*, xxxviii (1984), 25–65.

[10] See J. Höfler, 'Der "trompette de menestrels" und sein Instrument', *TVNM*, xxix/2 (1979), 92–132, especially 114–18; and (apparently independently but reaching the same conclusions by a different route) L. Welker, ' "Alta capella": zur Ensemblepraxis der Blasinstrumente im 15. Jahrhundert', *Basler Jb für historische Musikpraxis*, vii (1983), 119–65, especially 139–41.

[11] E. A. Bowles, 'Haut and Bas: the Grouping of Musical Instruments in the Middle Ages', *MD*, viii (1954), 115–40. For a very strong case against the use of percussion in 16th-century dance part-music, see B. Neumann, '. . . kommt pfeift und trombt . . .: zur Verwendung von Schlaginstrumenten in der Tanzmusik der Renaissance', *Concerto*, iv (Feb 1985), 22–8. Further details about ensembles of wind instruments appear in K. Polk, 'Ensemble Performance in Dufay's Time', in *Dufay Conference: Brooklyn NY 1974*, 61–75.

[12] Early examples are enumerated in D. Fallows, 'The Performing Ensembles in Josquin's Sacred Music', *TVNM*, xxxv (1985), 32–64, especially 33 and notes 7–13.

[13] Some evidence is summarized in Fallows, 'The Performing Ensembles', 64, n.86.

[14] A recent summary of the evidence is in Welker, ' "Alta capella" '.

[15] The most famous case is the song text *La plus grant chiere de jamais* which apparently describes how the composers Robert Morton and Hayne van Ghizeghem astonished the people of Cambrai with their singing which could be heard a great distance away. The text is edited and translated in *Robert Morton: The Collected Works*, ed. A. Atlas (New York, 1981), p.xx.

[16] The clearest cases are the following. (1) At the Council of Constance in 1416, three English players of (presumably) slide trumpets were described as playing together (*prusonettend überainander*) in three parts, in the way that one normally sings; see M. Schuler, 'Die Musik in Konstanz während des Konzils 1414–1418', *AcM*, xxxviii (1966), 165. (2) In 1423, 1426 and 1439 the Burgundian court purchased matched sets of wind instruments, see J. Marix, *Histoire de la musique et des musiciens de la cour de Bourgogne sous le règne de Philippe le Bon* (Strasbourg, 1939), 102–3. (3) Daniel Leech-Wilkinson, 'Il libro di appunti di un sonatore di tromba del quindicesimo secolo', *RIM*, xvi (1981), 16–39, shows that the manuscript *GB-Lbm* Cot. Tit. A.XXVI, of the 1440s, was copied by a wind player aboard ship for his own use; but most of the songs contained in it appear there in drastically simplified versions. (4) The manuscript *I-Rc* 2856 apparently contains the repertory used by the Ferrarese court *piffari* in the 1480s; see most recently L. Lockwood, *Music in Renaissance Ferrara* (Oxford, 1984), 269–77. But this information needs to be treated with caution since the court accounts make it clear that at this stage the *piffari* included lute and harp players; see D. Fallows, review of Lockwood, *Music in Renaissance Ferrara*, in *EMH*, vi (1986), 279–303, especially 300. Further details appear in H. Fitzpatrick, 'The Medieval Recorder', *EM*, iii (1975), 361–4; K. Polk, 'Ensemble Instrumental Music in

Flanders, 1450–1550', *Journal of Band Research*, xi (1975), 12–27; Polk, 'Civic Patronage and Instrumental Ensembles in Renaissance Florence', *Augsburger Jb für Musikwissenschaft*, iii (1986), 51–68; Polk, 'Instrumental Music in the Urban Centres of Renaissance Germany', *EMH*, vii (1987), 159–86.

[17] D. Abbott and E. Segerman, 'Strings in the 16th and 17th Centuries', *GSJ*, xxvii (1974), 48–73; Abbott and Segerman, 'Historical Background to the Strings used by Catgut-scrapers', *FoMRHI Quarterly*, iii (1976), 42–7; Segerman, 'The Interaction between Gut String Technology and Instrument Ranges and Sizes up to the 18th Century', *FoMRHI Quarterly*, x (1978), 41–2.

[18] See for example *Guillelmi Dufay: Cantiones*, ed. H. Besseler, CMM, i/6 (1964), no.3, bars 29–31, no.6, bars 13–17, no.7, bars 20–22, no.8, bars 5–7, and *passim*.

[19] P. Holman, letter to the editor, 'Viols and Bridges', *MT*, cxxvi (1985), 452. See also the following correspondence from C. Harris, *MT*, cxxvi (1985), 649, and from C. Page, *MT*, cxxvii (1986), 11. This correspondence arose from a review of a book that contains much important information on 15th-century bowed instruments, I. Woodfield, *The Early History of the Viol* (Cambridge, 1984); see especially 9–79.

[20] Two appear in M. Remnant, *English Bowed Instruments from Anglo-Saxon to Tudor Times* (Oxford, 1986), plates 39 and 99; six more are promised for publication by Howard Mayer Brown in *EM*, xvii (1989), which includes the important point that with most medieval pictures it is impossible to tell the shape of the bridge. Of course bridge-shape can have several possible meanings. E. Segerman and D. Abbott, 'Some Speculations on Medieval Fiddle Technique', *FoMRHI Quarterly*, vi (1977), 36–7, offer the possibility that a flat bridge could be made to work effectively as if it were a rounded bridge by careful gradation of the notches for the strings, though it is perhaps too easy to add that this is technically no easier than making a rounded bridge and that if the *viella* was intended to take a single part in a polyphonic context it would have been – as we know it – singularly ill-equipped to do so. B. Ravanel, 'Rebec und Fiedel: Ikonographie und Spielweise', *Basler Jb für historische Musikpraxis*, viii (1984), 105–30, points out, pp.124–7, that several pictures show a *viella* with a bridge in the form of a comb, that is, with projections to carry the strings – in which case it would of course be easy to bring down any unneeded string from its projection to make the playing of a single line easier. A sane evaluation of the available evidence is in Segerman, 'Flat Bridges I: Focus on the Lira da Braccio', *FoMRHI Quarterly*, xliii (1986), 105–7. On definitions of flatness, see Segerman, 'Round Bridges: the Geometry of Clearance Angles', *FoMRHI Quarterly*, xliii (1986), 101–4.

As this essay was going to press, I was able to see a typscript of Howard Mayer Brown's article 'The Trecento Fiddle and its Bridges' (forthcoming in *EM*) which shows five examples of curved bridges and lists eight more. Brown also notes that fiddles with a curved bridge tend to show a relatively short string-length, no more than that of the modern violin. Given the state of string technology at the time, as we now understand it, these instruments would therefore have some difficulty in sounding much below middle C and could hardly be appropriate for the lower lines on which they seem so desirable. It should be noted, however, that this restriction does not apply to the fiddle illustrated in Remnant, *English Bowed Instruments*, plate 99.

[21] On Jerome of Moravia, see the careful discussion, transcription and translation of the passage in C. Page, 'Jerome of Moravia on the *Rubeba* and *Viella*', *GSJ*, xxxii (1979), 77–98. On both Jerome and Grocheo, see Page, *Voices and Instruments of the Middle Ages* (London, 1987), 61–76, 126–33, 196–201.

[22] The nearest to evidence is in Simone Prudenzani's sonnet sequence *Il Saporetto*, written in the early 15th century, edited in S. Debenedetti, 'Il "Sollazzo" e il "Saporetto" con altre rime di Simone Prudenzani d'Orvieto', *Giornale storico della letteratura italiana*, suppl.xv (1913), 91–188, and discussed at length, with republication of the musical sonnets, in Debenedetti, *Il "Sollazzo": Contributi alla storia della novella, della poesia musicale e del costume del trecento* (Turin, 1922). On some possible qualifications of Prudenzani's evidence, see D. Fallows, 'Specific Information on the Ensembles for Composed Polyphony, 1400–1474', in *Performance Practice: New York 1981*, 140–41. But one further point, irrelevant to my earlier discussion, lies in his use of the word 'vivola'. On this instrument Sollazzo plays (Debenedetti, 1913, p.110; Debenedetti, 1922, p.175) several works whose names correspond with those of pieces known from the polyphonic repertory, including works by Landini, Ciconia, Zacara and Bartolino da Padova. It seems possible that in this context 'vivola' was a plucked instrument, as it definitely is in several sources from the years 1450–1536, and as it seems to be in its etymological origins. This stanza follows a stanza in which he quite definitely plays bowed instruments: 'L'altra sera puoi venner suon d'archeto, / Rubebe, rubechette et rubecone' (loc cit); but the important

difference is that the works played on these instruments do not correspond with anything now known from the polyphonic repertory. Just as the pieces that Sollazzo plays on the harp and the organ are known polyphonic pieces, it seems likely that 'vivola' was a plucked, lute-like instrument. It is of course possible that 'vivola' was a bowed instrument; but then even the most elaborate bowed instrument with a curved bridge would be a singularly poor medium for polyphony of this complexity. The most cautious possible conclusion is that the *Liber Saporecti* cannot be used as evidence for bowed instruments playing polyphony; a more audacious conclusion would be that it is evidence for precisely the reverse.

[23] To the good article on the *douçaine* by Barra Boydell in *GroveMI*, three relevant details on its later history can now be added. Herbert W. Myers has offered a convincing identification of a surviving 16th-century example in 'The *Mary Rose* "Shawm"', *EM*, xi (1983), 358–60. R. Strohm, *Music in Late Medieval Bruges* (Oxford, 1985), 80–83, recounts a description of a state entry into Bruges in 1440 at which, among the groups of instruments playing, one of harp, lute and *douçaine* is mentioned several times (in which Strohm perhaps misleadingly translates the original Flemish 'doulcheyne' as 'dulcian'; see my discussion in *EMH*, vi (1986), 283–4). Finally, in his poem *Le champion des dames* (*c*1442), Martin le Franc concludes with a section describing how each of the Muses celebrates the Champion's victory playing a particular instrument: Melpomene plays the 'douchaine'; and the beautiful manuscript painting illustrating that passage in *F-Pn* f. fr.12476, f.109v (copied at Arras in 1451) shows her playing an instrument remarkably like the instrument from the Mary Rose discussed by Myers.

[24] This is of course the difficulty with attempts to argue that even the sacred music of the early 15th century was performed with an organ on the lower voices. The layout of the parts in the surviving sources is such that – in, for example, much of the four-voice music of the Old Hall Manuscript – it is extremely difficult to imagine how a player would be able to read the two lower voices simultaneously, filled as they are with complicated ligatures; and it is even more difficult to imagine anyone ever thinking that this was a sensible way of laying out music intended for performance on an organ. Despite some excellent recent writing on the early history of the organ and its use, there is still much to be done on defining its role in the church service; and it seems increasingly likely that the organ was kept well apart from polyphonic vocal performances – improbable though this may initially seem. The only clear exception is in the extensive evidence for *alternatim* performance; but what we know about this suggests that the organ normally alternated with monophonic chant, not polyphony.

[25] See n.16 above.

[26] See the articles on these composers in *Grove6* and the considerations of the cases of Cordier and Loqueville in *JAMS*, xxxiv (1981), 550–52, and of Cordier in *MD*, xxxviii (1984), 89–92.

[27] On Charles the Bold as a musician, see D. Fallows, *Robert Morton's Songs: a Study of Styles in the Mid-fifteenth Century* (diss., U. of California, Berkeley, 1979), 300–324; for the description of performances by Don Juan, prince of Viana, see Fallows, 'Specific Information', 137.

[28] Fallows, 'Specific Information', 132–9. Further material on this matter appears in C. Page, 'Machaut's "Pupil" Deschamps on the Performance of Music', *EM*, v (1977), 484–91; Page, 'The Performance of Songs in Late Medieval France', *EM*, x (1982), 441–50. One possible piece of early evidence for voice together with instruments appears in the 14th century in Bartolomeo de' Bartoli da Bologna, *Canzone delle virtù e delle scienze* (*F-CH* 599 (1426)), transcribed in Brown, 'St. Augustine', 33–4: 'Chomè per simphonia/ In son di boccha per organo e corda/ Appare quand'ella acorda/ Ciaschuna insemme a la nostra memoria', which Brown translates 'as appears in the concord of voice with organ and stringed instrument when she tunes each one together in our memory'. On singing technique see A. von Ramm, 'Singing Early Music', *EM*, iv (1976), 12–15; J. Dyer, 'Singing with Proper Refinement from *De modo bene cantandi* (1474) by Conrad von Zabern', *EM* vi (1978), 207–27; R. Stewart, 'Voice Types in Josquin's Music', *TVNM*, xxxv (1985), 97–193; F. Lesure, 'Propos sur la voix de la renaissance', in *Arts du spectacle et histoire des idées: Recueil offert en hommage à Jean Jacquot* (Tours, 1985), 204–12.

[29] The following lines owe much to the important articles by Roger Bowers: 'The Performing Pitch of English 15th-century Church Polyphony', *EM*, viii (1980), 21–8; 'Further Thoughts on Early Tudor Pitch', *EM*, viii (1980), 368–75; 'The Performing Ensemble for English Church Polyphony', in *Performance Practice: New York 1981*, 161–92; 'The Vocal Scoring, Choral Balance and Performing Pitch of Latin Church Polyphony in England, *c*.1500–58', *JRMA*, cxii (1987), 38–76. Further thoughts related to this matter are in M. Bent, 'Diatonic *ficta*', *EMH*, iv (1984), 1–48, and in Fallows, 'The Performing Ensembles', 47–53.

[30] This accepts the view that organs were tuned to something approaching a Pythagorean scale,

though it is of course clear that by the middle of the 15th century other temperaments were known, see in particular the discussions by Mark Lindley in, Chapter 00, vol.ii.

[31] For access to the most important of these materials there are three studies that will be needed by anyone at all interested in the subject: H. M. Brown, 'Instruments and Voices in the Fifteenth-century Chanson', in *Current Thought in Musicology*, ed. J. W. Grubbs (Austin, 1976), 88–137; E. A. Bowles, *Musikleben im 15. Jahrhundert*, Musikgeschichte in Bildern, iii/8 (Leipzig, 1977); Bowles, *La pratique musicale au moyen âge/ Musical Performance in the Late Middle Ages* (Geneva, 1983). Further important materials are discussed in H. M. Brown, 'On the Performance of Fifteenth-century Chansons', *EM*, i (1973), 3–10. English documentation is described in R. Rastall, 'Some English Consort Groupings of the Late Middle Ages', *ML*, lv (1974), 179–202. Italian information is assembled in V. Ravizza, *Das instrumentale Ensemble von 1400–1550 in Italien* (Berne and Stuttgart, 1970). A broad, recent survey is T. J. McGee, *Medieval and Renaissance Music: a Performer's Guide* (Toronto, 1985).

[32] For an extreme case (perhaps a test case) see the discussion of *Absalon, fili mi* (normally accepted as by Josquin but currently being reconsidered) in Fallows, 'The Performing Ensembles', 52–3. For a contrary view, see K. Kreitner, 'Very Low Ranges in the Sacred Music of Ockeghem and Tinctoris', *EM*, xiv (1986), 467–79.

[33] Indeed Tinctoris, writing in the mid-1470s, describes the greatest changes as having taken place some 30 years earlier.

[34] For Dufay see D. Fallows, *Dufay* (London, 1982), 88–9; for the earliest parody mass movements see the editions by Gilbert Reaney in CMM, xi/5–6 (1975–7); on the last two decades of the century see Edwards, 'Songs without Words'.

[35] The classic study is M. F. Bukofzer, 'The Beginnings of Choral Polyphony', *Studies in Medieval and Renaissance Music* (New York, 1950), 176–89. For some subsequent material see Bowers, 'The Performing Ensemble', 175–8; Fallows, 'Specific Information', 120–26; Fallows, 'The Performing Ensembles', 38–43.

[36] There is still a widely held (but, I think, unjustifiable) view that neither falsettists, nor boys, nor women were normally involved and that the usual singing pitch was therefore for a tenor and two basses. On women and boys, see Fallows, 'Specific Information', 133–40; on pitch, op cit, 117–26.

[37] See F. A. D'Accone, 'The Performance of Sacred Music in Italy during Josquin's Time, *c.*1475–1525', in *Josquin des Prez: New York 1971*, 601–18; and C. M. Wright, 'Performance Practices at the Cathedral of Cambrai 1475–1550', *MQ*, lxiv (1978), 295–328.

[38] *Le chansonnier de Jean de Montchenu*, ed. G. Thibault, J. Porcher and D. Fallows (Paris, forthcoming), section on 'Placement des paroles'.

[39] This fact makes all the more valuable those few manuscripts (or more particularly sections of manuscripts) in which the text was written before the music. While the main available discussions of texting in the 15th-century chanson draw largely on theoretical writings of the 16th century, there is still much to do in drawing conclusions from details of the texting in, for instance, *I-Bc* Q15, *GB-Ob* Can. misc. 213, *D-Mbs* Cod. gall. 902 and the final section of *F-Pn* n. a. fr.6771. To the literature itemized in G. Reese and G. M. Jones, 'Textunterlegung', *MGG*, xvi (1979), cols.1843–52, add: A. Atlas, 'Paolo Luchini's *Della Musica*: a Little-known Source for Text Underlay from the Late Sixteenth Century', *JM*, ii (1983), 62–80; *A Florentine Chansonnier*, ed. Brown, text vol., 168–80; D. Harrán, *Word–Tone Relations in Musical Thought* (Stuttgart, 1986).

[40] *D-Mbs* Mus. Ms.9659.

[41] L. Litterick, 'Performing Franco-Netherlandish Secular Music of the Late 15th Century: Texted and Untexted Parts in the Sources', *EM*, viii (1980), 474–85.

[42] Most discussions in the published literature concern sacred music; for the secular repertories, see H. Schoop, *Entstehung und Verwendung der Handschrift Oxford Bodleian Library, Canonici misc.213* (Berne, 1971), 76, 82; L. L. Perkins, 'Toward a Rational Approach to Text Placement in the Secular Music of Dufay's Time', in *Dufay Conference: Brooklyn NY 1974*, 103–14, especially 103–4.

[43] *A-Wn* 5094, f.148*v*; see facsimile in H. Besseler and P. Gülke, *Schriftbild der mehrstimmigen Musik*, Musikgeschichte in Bildern, iii/5 (Leipzig, 1973), 155.

[44] See, in addition to the more obvious sources of reference, F. Reckow, 'Rondellus/rondeau, rota', *HMT*.

[45] While it is by no means easy to see any consistent 15th-century usage that distinguishes 'virelai' from 'bergerette', it is possible to say that there is absolutely no basis to the theory that late 14th-century settings had three stanzas and must therefore be virelais whereas the late

15th-century settings had only one and are therefore bergerettes. The full three-stanza form scarcely ever appears in France except in the mainly monophonic settings of Machaut; but there is at least one late Dufay setting which has two stanzas. For further questions about the meaning of the world 'bergerette' as concerns musical form see R. W. Linker and G. S. McPeek, 'The Bergerette Form in the Laborde Chansonnier', *JAMS*, vii (1954), 161–78. See also M. Françon, 'On the Nature of the Virelai', *Symposium*, ix (1955), 348–52.

[46] The best summary of this evolution is in the book that is the fundamental literary study of the French lyric genres in the 14th and 15th centuries, D. Poirion, *Le poète et le prince: l'évolution du lyrisme courtois de Guillaume de Machaut à Charles d'Orléans* (Grenoble, 1965), 311–60.

[47] See n.4 above.

[48] The known Italian rondeau settings are Bruolo's *O celestial lume*, Bartolomeo da Bologna's *Mersi chiamando*, Dufay's *Dona gentile* and the anonymous *Biancha nel bruno* in *GB-Ob* Can. misc.213, though there are several more that look as though they are Italian rondeau settings but lack the proof of subsequent stanzas. On German poetry in rondeau form, see C. Petzsch, 'Ostschwäbische Rondeaux vor 1400', *Beiträge zur Geschichte der deutschen Sprache*, xcviii (1974), 384–94. On the rondeau in England see D. Fallows, 'English Song Repertories of the Mid-fifteenth Century', *PRMA*, ciii (1976–7), 61–79, especially 70–75, and Fallows, review in *JRMA*, cxii (1987), 133–6.

[49] On fluidity of form in the Italian song of the 15th century see N. Pirrotta, 'On Text Forms from Ciconia to Dufay', in *Aspects of Medieval and Renaissance Music: a Birthday Offering to Gustave Reese* (New York, 1966), 673–82. On the performance of later Italian forms, see W. F. Prizer, 'Performance Practices in the Frottola', *EM*, iii (1975), 227–35.

[50] For the later history of the form, see in particular the 600 rondeaux in the manuscript *F-Lm* 402, edited by M. Françon in *Poèmes de transition* (Paris, 1938), the 544 rondeaux in the closely related MS Jean de Saxe now in Dresden, Moritzburg, Schlossbibliothek, and the 330 rondeaux in Oxford, Taylor Institution, Ms 8°F3, edited by K. Chesney in *More 'Poèmes de transition': Notes on the Rondeaux of a Taylorian Manuscript* (Oxford, 1965).

[51] See Poirion, *Le poète et le prince*, especially 319–20.

[52] *Le grand et vrai art de pleine rhétorique de Pierre Fabri*, ed. A. Héron (Rouen, 1889–90), ii, 62–7.

[53] It goes – or should go – without saying that translations used for such purposes must be done with considerable care, ideally by a professional writer, and that the reading should itself be no more amateur than the performance.

[54] H. M. Garey, 'The Fifteenth Century Rondeau as Aleatory Polytext', *Le moyen français*, v (1980), 193–236; Garey, 'Can a Rondeau with a One-line Refrain be Sung?', *Ars lyrica*, ii (1983), 9–21.

[55] Ed. CMM, i/6 (1964), no.83; also in *The Mellon Chansonnier*, ed. Perkins and Garey, with further extended discussion of the poem.

[56] Ed. CMM, i/6 (1964), no.38.

[57] *A Florentine Chansonnier*, ed. Brown, text vol., 57–61; see Garey, 'Can a Rondeau?'.

[58] *Werken van Josquin des Prés*, ed. A. Smijers et al, afl.54, Wereldlijke werken, bundel 5 (Amsterdam, 1968), p.41, no.65; see H. M. Brown, 'Josquin and the Fifteenth-century Chanson', *Proceedings of the British Academy*, lxxi (1985), 119–58.

[59] N. Wilkins, *One Hundred Ballades, Rondeaux and Virelais from the Late Middle Ages* (Cambridge, 1969), 4, 137. See also Wilkins, 'The Structure of Ballades, Rondeaux and Virelais in Froissart and Christine de Pisan', *French Studies*, xxiii (1969), 337–48.

[60] Those in the manuscript of English translations, *GB-Lbm* Harley 682, are accurately reproduced in *The English Poems of Charles of Orléans*, ed. R. Steele and M. Day (London, 1941–6). For a somewhat rigid evaluation of whether a full refrain or merely a *rentrement* is appropriate in Charles's French poetry, see G. Defaux, 'Charles d'Orléans et la poésie du secret: à propos du Rondeau XXXIII de l'édition Champion', *Romania*, xciii (1972), 194–243. Further on rondeau refrains and *rentrements*, see M. Françon, 'Les refrains des rondeaux de Charles d'Orléans', *Modern Philology*, xxxix (1941–2), 259–63; and Françon, 'Sur la structure du rondeau', *Romance Notes*, x (1968–9), 147–9.

[61] See for example the rondeau *Ay mi lasse* in *I-TRmn* 87, f.92v, text in *GB-Lbm* Harley 7333, f.36v, where it is ascribed (probably incorrectly) to Charles d'Orléans. I have published a reconstruction of the song, together with a consideration of its authorship, in *JRMA*, cxii (1987), 134–6. Later examples are particularly common in the Pixérécourt chansonnier (*F-Pn* f. fr.15123).

[62] *L'aultre d'antan* by Ockeghem, as it appears in the Mellon Chansonnier (*US-NH* 91),

discussed in Garey, 'Can a Rondeau?', and in H. M. Brown, 'A Rondeau with a One-line Refrain Can Be Sung', *Ars lyrica*, iii (1986), 23–35. The other three examples are all in the manuscript *GB-Ob* Can. misc.213: Vide's *Vit encore ce Faux Dangier*, and Malbecque's *Dieu vous doinst bon jour et demy* and *Ouvrés vostre huys*. In none of these cases does any detail of the stucture or meaning of the poem help to offer a cogent reason for any possible curtailment implied.

[63] See the suggestions in Garey, 'Can a Rondeau?', and Brown, 'A Rondeau'; whatever the virtues of their solutions, both authors here make important points towards understanding the nature of the sources in an appropriate manner.

[64] Brown, 'A Rondeau'.

CHAPTER XII

Secular Polyphony in the 16th Century

ANTHONY NEWCOMB

Given the importance of 16th-century secular music, and especially of the Italian madrigal, in our view of this and subsequent periods, it is surprising how little specific information concerning the context of its performance has so far been assembled. On the performance of secular music in France almost no work has been done. While recent scholarship has brought us careful and well-documented studies of ornamentation and of large-scale princely festivities in Italy, we still know relatively little about many other matters. How were pieces integrated into more common contexts, such as an evening's entertainment in an upper-class *salone*? What were the methods of voice production used in the period and what were the prevailing ideals of virtuosity, both instrumental and vocal? What variety of instrumental and vocal arrangements might be acceptable for a given piece – that is, what variety of uses and users might have been served by those non-committal printed partbooks in which most secular polyphony of the 16th century survives?

Contemporary documents normally deal with such matters only obliquely, and there are few publications whose stated subject is performance practice. Most of these are treatises on ornamentation or descriptions of exceptional festivities organized by ruling families, which explains why ornamentation and large public festivities are the best-documented areas of the field to date. Information concerning other areas tends to be widely scattered – in diplomatic dispatches, in personal letters, in fictional vignettes, in paintings and so on[1] – and it is just as likely to be brought to light by chance as by a systematic investigation. As scholars in all areas of 16th-century studies become more aware of the important questions still unanswered in the area of performance practice, we can hope that they will become more likely to recognize significant details in the midst of the wide range of documents that they look through, probably for other purposes.

Our picture may thus become richer in detail; it will also probably become still more heterogeneous. Details will accumulate, but they will not always agree. We may expect that questions will be illuminated, but not that they will be unequivocally answered. There was for Renaissance secular music (just as there is for modern popular music) no single way to proceed from the written text to a performance of it. But there are artistic decorums of a general kind, and it was possible to flout them entirely: it would, for example, be anachronistic to perform an intimate and sophisticated madrigal designed to be heard in a small room in a large public space and with several musicians to a part. In this matter of establishing the limits within which a

222

stylish performance might take place modern research has much work still to do.

In order to understand these limits, it is well to divide up what we know about the performance of 16th-century polyphony in various ways, ways that overlap and interlock rather than being mutually exclusive. Of the three categorizations proposed below – kinds of performance contexts, kinds of styles of pieces and kinds of performing groups – the first may be the most important in re-creating a stylistically appropriate and successful perform-ance of a 16th-century piece. The goal is not to re-create these contexts detail for detail but to understand how they might have coloured a given performance and then to find a modern analogue – especially important in the case of pieces that seem, because of their text, texture, tessitura or whatever, to be bound closely to a certain performance context.

Performing contexts

Secular music of the 16th century was performed both outdoors and indoors. Spaces and occasions varied considerably even for outdoor performances. Music (especially wind music) adorned processions on important civic occasions. It might also be played on a moving *carro* or boat, or from a balcony above the town square on festive occasions. The most intimate occasion for outdoor music was the private summer party on a small terrace or in a secluded bower. Ferrarese chroniclers of the 1580s reveal that solo singers who normally sang madrigals in small indoor rooms might also sing them in a summer garden while some members of the audience played cards and others followed the texts being sung in separate booklets.[2]

Indoor performing contexts covered a similar range from large to small – from the welcoming ceremony for an important visiting dignitary, held in the largest public rooms of the state thrown open to a numerous public, to the private concert (*musica reservata*) held for a select audience of less than ten in a small room (one can still see the rooms used for this purpose in the Mantuan and Ferrarese ducal palaces), and even to private lute playing in one's own *studiolo*.

The presence of an audience is a significant issue in 16th-century secular music. There is reason to believe that when madrigals or *villanesche* were performed in urban academies throughout the century the audience was made up of people who might also become performers in the next piece, and that the music was therefore largely designed for the entertainment of the music-makers themselves.[3] It may well be that, in many of the performing contexts in which secular polyphony was heard, the idea of a separate audience did not become common until the rise of the virtuoso ensemble in the last quarter of the century. This is one of the many questions on which the relevant information remains to be assembled and analysed.[4]

Explicitly dramatic performances are a case apart, for dramatic represen-tation affects the space and the occasion in which the performance occurs. The place of musical performance in the semi-improvised productions of the *commedia dell'arte* can be documented from the very beginnings of this kind of theatre.[5] The *Dialoghi* of Massimo Troiano (1569) and the various madrigal comedies by Orazio Vecchi and Adriano Banchieri convey an impression of

Music at an outdoor party: detail from the painting 'Spring Landscape' (1587) by Lucas von Valckenborch, in the Kunsthistorisches Museum, Vienna: young men and women sit on the ground around a cloth laid with food and sing from partbooks; soft ('bas') string and wind instruments are piled to one side, and an ensemble of professional musicians playing three shawms and sackbut accompany a couple who dance

the place that various kinds of music could assume during the later 16th century. Nino Pirrotta also discusses the place of music in other kinds of theatrical performances (classical theatre and learned comedy) during the 16th century: an occasional song or dance in the main action, as well as increasingly developed *intermedi* between acts.[6] Colin Slim identifies and prints several early madrigals that were composed for such theatrical occasions.[7]

Related to such explicitly theatrical occasions are those instances in which a singer or singers, usually professionals, sang to a separate audience with the intent of projecting the affective content of an emotionally charged text. No explicit description of the singing of a printed polyphonic madrigal in this spirit in mid-century is known to me, but expressive declamatory pieces such as Rore's setting of Della Casa's sonnet *O sonno* suggest such performance, and these ideals are reflected in a passage in Galilei's *Dialogo della musica antica e della moderna*.[8] This attitude towards the expressive projection of a serious text to a separate audience can be seen as having led to the declamatory settings of passages from Tasso's *Gerusalemme liberata* and Guarini's *Pastor fido* by such composers as Wert, Marenzio and Monteverdi from the late 1570s until the early years of the next century.[9]

With the idea of the projection to a separate audience of a text set to music came the idea of expressive musical declamation as an imitation of the delivery of a practised actor or orator.[10] This declamatory model is particularly important for the ideal of flexibility of tempo and dynamic that it brought with it, an ideal which seems to have gained momentum across the second half of the century and which became firmly associated with the 'modern madrigal' by the beginning of the 1600s.[11] It also brings with it an implication that pieces appealing to this model should be taken at a tempo such that their texts as set can be spoken naturally and effectively.[12] The same criteria for choice of tempo are not as clearly implied for a piece designed with a different aesthetic model in mind – say, a Gombert chanson.

Given the importance of the projection of the sung text with a 'spoken' clarity and effectiveness, it is unfortunate that we still have little information on the pronunciation of 16th-century Italian at various times and places. Standard histories of the Italian language simply assert that pronunciation, like spelling, varied from region to region at a given time, and that particular spellings are accurate phonetic representations of the pronunciations implied.[13] There is as yet no well-developed position on how to handle the variety of spellings in the contemporary sources. We are better provided when it comes to the intrinsically more difficult matter of French and English pronunciation at the time.[14]

Pieces

It is usually difficult to link particular surviving pieces with specific occasions. For example, pictures show musicians as part of important civic processions, but we have no firm information as to what they might have been playing.[15] It would seem that trumpeters on such occasions played simple fanfares, much like the one that begins Monteverdi's *Orfeo* and Vespers.[16] A more elaborate style of music for one outdoor civic occasion

225

may survive. In his early 20th-century history of music in Bologna, Francesco Vatielli quotes a late 16th-century account of the popular tune *Girometta* 'arranged as polyphony for trombones, cornettes, and dulcians', played from the balcony of the city hall by excellent players 'in alcuni tempi festevoli'.[17] The Bologna manuscript Q38 preserves a textless arrangement for two four-voice choirs of *La Girometta*, ascribed to Costanzo Porta (who was closely connected with Bologna) and which is perfectly suited to the reported group of players.

Andrea Gabrieli's six-voice madrigal *Nel bel giardin/ Ma pria odorate* from the *Concerti* of 1587 offers an example of outdoor music for a more intimate occasion.[18] Its text indicates that the piece was designed as a prelude to a convivial summer meal among friends (as opposed to a large, formal banquet) on a terrace or in a garden bower.

Numerous examples of specific pieces connected with official ceremonies in large public rooms are provided by the various printed Florentine *intermedi*. Regular madrigal books are full of pieces for similar occasions, although the occasions can rarely be determined with any certainty. I have proposed, for example, that Alessandro Striggio's Fourth Book for five voices contains three madrigals designed for particular occasions connected with the arrival of the family of Bianca Cappello in Florence in 1579.[19] Here we are lucky enough to have an independent verbal description of one of these occasions with some particulars about the music. Most often, however, reports of a particular occasion do not mention music in any detail. One must judge from the text and the musical style of the individual piece what kind of performing context it was created for. Howard Brown describes the large ceremonial piece in the 1520s as characteristically 'written in fairly simple textures, predominantly chordal or in lightly animated homophony alternating with clear points of imitation'.[20] A similar formulation would describe such pieces as they were at the end of the century: texturally simple so as to sound well in a large resonant room; largely homorhythmic with hints of animation inserted through rhythmic imitation of dotted motifs that do not disturb the clear harmonic foundation.

At the opposite end of the spectrum stands the texturally and rhythmically intricate piece for small spaces and highly cultivated audiences – what musicians, of the latter half of the century at least, seem to have called 'musica reservata'. Slim's work on Verdelot gives us particular pieces from the early part of the century to connect with such occasions, as does Doni's *Dialogo* (1544) for the 1540s.[21] One could speculate that the expressive declamatory settings of serious lyric poetry such as mentioned above – for example the madrigals from Willaert's *Musica nova*, Rore's *Vergini* or *O sonno* and Palestrina's *Voi mi poneste in foco*, all from about 1550 – may also have been designed for this performing context, although we have no specific description of any performance of these pieces. For similar pieces later in the century – the *Gerusalemme liberata* settings of Wert and Monteverdi, Marenzio's *Giovane donna* or *Crudele acerba inesorabil morte* for example – we have only the dedications of the printed sources to connect the pieces with certain courts or cities, after which we can turn to general descriptions of madrigal performances in those centres. These descriptions support the idea of performance in small rooms to a select audience.

Title-page of Willaert's 'Musica nova' (Venice: Antonio Gardane, 1559), with a dedication to Alfonso II d'Este, Duke of Ferrara

By no means all pieces were specifically applicable to only one kind of space. Pieces of simpler texture appropriate to large spaces are often reported as having been performed in small rooms, as in the performance for a bride *in camera* of a Lasso *moresca*, recorded in Troiano's *Discorsi* of 1569.[22] Indeed, these 'lighter forms' (to use Alfred Einstein's phrase), with their simple, homorhythmic textures, chiselled motives and clear repetition schemes, were among the most versatile of 16th-century pieces. They could appear as ensemble pieces played by instruments; they might be sung on open-air *carri* and in theatrical or quasi-theatrical settings such the *commedia dell'arte* or a *mascherata* for a banquet; singers, both professional and amateur, might perform them as solo songs in small rooms to the accompaniment of a chordal instrument.[23]

In summary, we should use the few pieces that we can link to specific occasions to gain an idea of what music for such occasions was like. These ideas can then be used in considering the proper performing context and style for other, similar pieces. Above all, it is clear that the dichotomy between a performance in a large space and one in a small room is an important one. It is one on which 16th-century sources insist repeatedly. The two situations are often said to call forth different kinds of pieces and to require different kinds of performers. Even a particular composer may be seen as specializing in one or the other (this is how I interpret the reference to the young Monte in a letter of 22 September 1555).[24] The small-room piece and its attendant performance style pose clear difficulties for concert presentation in the modern age. It may have found its ideal modern medium in the sound recording or the video tape.

Performing groups

Here, as in so many aspects of Renaissance music, if there is a cardinal rule, then that rule is variety.[25] In attempting to organize this variety it may be convenient to begin from the most intimate of the performing contexts outlined above. Such evidence as we have is in agreement that it was normal to have only one singer to a part when performing secular music with voices alone in small or medium-size rooms. The detailed descriptions of banquets in Ferrara in 1529,[26] of Venetian *ridotti* around 1540,[27] of Ferrarese chamber concerts in the 1580s,[28] and many more could be cited on this point. Even in the large-scale Florentine *intermedi* only the finales used some doubling of the vocal parts.[29]

In large rooms and on more public and festive occasions, when musicians performed pieces whose music and texts were less closely worked, doubling became more usual. (In the Florentine *intermedi* again, only two pieces out of some 100 were performed by an ensemble of vocal soloists alone.) This doubling usually involved additional instrumentalists rather than more singers.

As a way of augmenting the sound – not only in volume, but especially in richness and variety – melodic instruments might double a vocal part.[30] It was necessary only that the range of the instrument be adequate and that it be appropriate for the particular performing space. (Trumpets and shawms, for example, were not considered appropriate for small rooms in the 16th century; conversely, muted cornetts made little effect from a balcony over a town square the size of Bologna's *Piazza maggiore*.) Brown analyses the several descriptions of Florentine *intermedi* in the 16th century to extract information on the various instrumental combinations,[31] some with symbolic connotations, used on such occasions. Several writers remark that the lowest voice in particular needs doubling when a louder sound is needed; trombones or viols were most often used. Contemporary chronicles also report the use of cornetts and violins to double the upper voices. All the evidence suggests that the outer voices were the most likely to be doubled. Several writers say that strings are appropriate for doubling voices in the middle range where more reinforcement was required. Some chronicles report that flutes or recorders were used to double middle voices at the upper octave.

Some writers (for example, Galilei, 1581) express the opinion that violins, normal cornetts and trombones are too strident for private rooms, yet a chronicler at the Ferrarese court in 1583 reports that an intimate group 'went to dine as usual with music by trombones, cornetts and other instruments'. Violins and cornetts especially were domesticated in the course of the century, perhaps as techniques were evolved that permitted the requisite gentleness and flexibility of tone (see 'Voice types' below). A chronicle of 1590 mentions 'music for harps, for violins and for other delightful instruments' in the private rooms of Lucrezia d'Este at Ferrara.[32] And two of the most famous private musicians of the age (one of the Pelizzari sisters and Luigi Zenobi) were cornett players.[33] Bottrigari (1594) remarks on the use of cornetts and trombones in the chamber concerts of the nuns of S Vito in Ferrara, but adds that they are 'the most difficult of instruments' (he seems to mean that they do not lend themselves to such surroundings).

A melodic instrument might also replace some of the vocal parts. Again, this was a practice that predates the 16th century, and one for which a quantity of evidence exists.[34] Such experiments with mixtures of instruments and voices need only separate the instrumental parts in function and idiom to arrive at the concerted style of the early 17th century. It seems likely that such experiments were performed by composer-performers in late 16th-century courts, although musical sources do not survive.[35]

An even more convenient and more frequent doubling or replacement for some of the vocal parts was a chordal instrument such as lute, harpsichord or harp.[36] Some harpsichords or lutenists transcribed the music from the standard partbooks into instrumental tablature for these purposes.[37] Some improvised a reduction directly from the bass part.[38] In this last case, we do not yet know how false chords or rests in the bass part were handled – perhaps only by trial and error. A study of the originals intabulated by Willaert in the 1530s, or by Verovio at the end of the century will give an idea of the style of piece thought appropriate for this sort of performance: its texture is largely chordal; its text is complete in a single voice and its melodic activity is well represented by that same voice.[39]

Contemporary documents make it clear that in performances by solo voice and chordal instrument (whether played by the singer or by another), value was placed on singing by memory, with some (tasteful) ornamentation, and even with some bodily reflection of the content of the text.[40] In the context of performance by solo voice and chordal instrument (as well as in the context

An Elizabethan masque in performance: detail of the 'Memorial Portrait of Sir Henry Unton' (c1596) in the National Portrait Gallery, London: Mercury and Diana lead the entry of masquers and torch-bearers who process round a broken consort (a consort of viols can be seen in the upper left-hand room)

of purely instrumental chamber music), it is well to stress the importance of the harp. Some of the most famous singers of the century, men and women alike, accompanied themselves on the harp, and some of its most famous instrumentalists were harpists.[41] This large part of 16th-century practice has not yet been revived. Unfortunately little of the instrumental music written explicitly and idiomatically for the harp seems to survive.[42]

Likewise, the use of members of the bowed string family to play chordal accompaniment to solo singing, especially of the *lira da braccio* to accompany the singing of recitational stanzas, was widespread, at least in humanistically inclined centres of the 16th century, but this has yet to be revived in modern performances.[43]

Finally, melodic instruments may replace all the parts in what is (or may have been) a piece of vocal music. Here again it seems best to talk first of kinds of groups, then of kinds of pieces. Vocal polyphony seems to have been played on courtly occasions in the late 15th century by the shawm band, often with a trombone on the bottom part.[44] By the early part of the 16th century these instruments were gradually being replaced, at least in smaller chambers, by gentler sounds in which cornetts, viols, even flutes replaced the shawms.[45]

As to the kinds of pieces played, very little of the polyphonic repertory until the middle of the century seems to have been explicitly designed for instruments alone. On the other hand, it is clear that motets and mass movements, French chansons, even Italian secular pieces were often played by instruments alone. The question as to what kind of piece was considered particularly appropriate for performance by instruments alone, especially in the early years of the century, is one that is still much discussed.[46] The contents of the manuscript Rome Biblioteca Casanatense 2856 gives an idea of what a wind band played at court in the 1480s.[47] The manuscript Bologna Q18 may do the same for a wind band in an Italian city-state (Bologna) in the early 16th century.[48] The manuscript Copenhagen 1872 seems to preserve the repertory of the Danish royal instrumentalists around 1550.[49] All of these collections indicate that the division between vocal and instrumental music (like that between sacred and secular) was by no means clearly drawn, a situation which seems to have continued even as the century drew to a close. The Gardane edition of Gombert's First Book of Motets for four voices (1541) is advertised on the title page as for 'Lyris maioribus, ac Tibiis imparibus accomodata' (suitable for viols and consort of winds). In his dedication to his Fifteenth Book of Madrigals (1592) Monte mentions that the dedicatee was familiar with them through having heard them played by viols. On the other hand, even textless ricercars (printed from the 1540s onwards) and textless canzonas (from the 1570s onwards), which one would assume were primarily for instruments, are advertised on the title pages as 'for singing and playing'. And instrument-specific tablatures for lute and keyboard (the latter much rarer) mainly contain intabulations or arrangements of vocal pieces. Decisions as to the appropriateness of a piece for performance by instruments alone would seem to have rested less on firm rules than on flexible, contextual criteria, such as whether the piece lay well for the instruments available and appropriate for the kind of setting in which one wanted to perform, whether it was strongly linked either to declamation or expression of the text, and whether the style of the piece itself was appropriate for the kind of room and occasion in which it was to appear.

Programmes

How various kinds of pieces and ensembles were put together as part of a social event (presumably in a single kind of space) is again a matter on which relatively little information has been assembled and analysed. One thing appears clear: in the exceptional formal festivities of courtly society – the type of occasion about which we have most information – variety in both types of pieces and combinations of sounds was a consistent ideal. Most occasions, of course, were not of this nature. The circumstances described by Doni (1544) are probably closest to those of a typical upper-class salon or academy, where the available variety of sound was considerably smaller than in the exceptional courtly festivity. Even here, and in such intimate gatherings of connoisseurs as might be found daily at a music-loving court such as the one at Ferrara, the smaller group of instruments and voices available seems still to have been exploited for maximum variety.[50]

The actual pieces played are rarely specified in descriptions of these more everyday occasions. Repertory doubtless varied with the availability of music, and with the tastes of the patrons and the performers. Several sources suggest that a balance was struck between prepared performances of favourites (often memorized and ornamented) and the reading through of new music from partbooks.[51] Madrigal prints preserve examples of madrigals that end with a plea to sing a famous older madrigal often used for solo singing, suggesting that the newer piece was sung by an ensemble of soloists as a prelude to a performance of the older favourite by a single singer with chordal accompaniment.[52] Bottrigari stresses the positive value placed on finding and performing new pieces, adding (with characteristic sourness) 'even in our corrupt time, after the singing of a new *cantilena*, it is repeated immediately'. Doni, too, remarks that, when a new piece was found interesting, one often decided to try it again. Such repetition of unfamiliar pieces – even of early music – might serve modern performers and audiences well.

Most social events of which music formed part were not restricted to music alone. Music often accompanied meals (and the conversation that went with them). Castiglione's idealized courtiers played games, played and sang music, and held learned disputes. Doni's performers punctuated their performances with discussion of numerous other subjects. The Ferrarese courtiers played cards and talked as they listened. The modern concert situation, where a functionally separate audience is intent solely on the music, sometimes existed even in intimate secular surroundings in the Reanissance, but it was not the normal situation – a fact which contributed further to the ideal of variety.

Voice types

Throughout the literature of the second half of the century at least, writers dwell on the pronounced difference between the techniques used for singing in small rooms and those used for singing in larger spaces, such as major churches.[53] The famous falsettist Giovanni Luca Conforto is reported as singing alto when he sang *a voce piena*, and soprano when he sang in small rooms (*in camera e in oratorii*).[54] A great deal of other evidence could be advanced to support this sharp difference of voice production in the two situations. Many singers were thought to be good for only one or the other kind of singing.

It is unlikely that we shall ever have firm knowledge on specific techniques of either kind of voice production in the 16th century.[55] The most detailed description found so far comes from a letter written in 1562 (Maffei 1562). Its author was Neapolitan, however, and it is clear from various sources that singing techniques varied greatly from one local style to another.[56] Thus Maffei's detailed observations may have only limited validity.

On one thing all descriptions of 16th-century voice production agree. Even when singing *a voce piena* one should not sing loudly. Finck, Vicentino, Morley, Maffei, Ferrarese chroniclers of the 1580s and many others are unanimous that a light, flexible voice was the ideal. One should sing 'very easily', and produce a 'pleasing and soft' sound, said Maffei. One admirer of the young Ferrarese soprano Livia d'Arco in 1582 seems to parallel modern critical vocabulary when he praises her for her 'very white voice' (*voce candidissima*).

Beyond this constant requirement, it may be well to distinguish between singing in the normal polyphonic ensemble and solo singing to a chordal instrument. In the polyphonic ensemble, Finck says that imitations should be delivered in a 'clearer, more distinct voice than is usual', while Vicentino warns that the bass must be particularly careful to tune his octaves with others, for this is the source of perfect harmony – advice that seems refreshingly pragmatic.

In the music printed in partbooks – and presumably designed with the normal polyphonic ensemble in mind – we note the increasing prominence of parts for high voices as the century moves on. Parts in the soprano and mezzo-soprano clefs were doubtless sometimes taken by male falsettists (Conforto can again serve as a famous example), especially in sacred music, but even in secular chamber music and at the end of the century. And Richard Sherr shows that another option was available: there were castratos from at least the 1560s onwards in France, Spain and Italy, and they sometimes sang secular chamber music.[57]

The female soprano, however, was doubtless by far the most frequent choice for parts in the treble to mezzo-soprano clefs. Female singers were after all in good supply. On the amateur level, 16th-century society placed a premium on a woman's ability to sing as a social grace. Beyond this, there had been a small number of professional women singers from the very beginning of the century (and even in the 15th century).[58] By the end of the century, the female madrigal singer was a figure of tremendous prominence in many courts, as she doubtless was in the lower social levels that imitated courtly life. Although many of these female singers probably sang alone to the accompaniment of a chordal instrument, their increasing importance is reflected in the printed repertory of ensemble music as well. It is not uncommon to find madrigals with two or three of their five parts in mezzo-soprano, soprano or treble clefs.[59] The change of the standard madrigal scoring from the low, male-dominated (probably often all-male) ensemble of the Rore generation, to the bright, female-dominated one of the last quarter of the century is a striking one.[60]

To judge from printed partbooks, the range expected from the normal singer of madrigals in a polyphonic ensemble was roughly the range of the standard staff – a tenth or an eleventh. (Basses might be asked for a little more – perhaps a twelfth or thirteenth.) Here, as elsewhere, the expectations from a solo singer were quite different, especially for the two dominant types of the 16th century, the soprano and the bass. (The solo tenor, though an important figure, seems not to have attained the stardom of the sopranos and basses.) Musical documents that attempt to capture in notation a perform-ance by such a solo singer do not survive before the very beginning of the 17th century (for example Luzzaschi's *Madrigali* of 1601, Caccini's *Nuove musiche* of 1602 and 1614, and Puliaschi's *Gemma musicale/Musiche varie* of 1618).

A number of descriptions, however, mention the ideals of virtuosity which singers might be expected to meet. One set of instructions for testing a bass in 1589 is particularly specific: 'Find out if he has a good voice, if his voices [*sic*] are soft (*dolci*), if he sings discreetly and flexibly, how he produces his high notes, and how far down he goes, expressing this last by means of a flute...'.[61] Giustiniani remarks that from about 1575 onwards the style of singing of Neapolitan and Roman basses was particularly admired – basses who covered a range of three octaves and sang graceful diminutions.[62] Maffei (1562) suggests that the style was older than Giustiniani knew or remembered, for he requires of the ideal bass the ability to sing with ease and flexibility in ranges from bass to alto, and feels that the bass voice is the perfect solo instrument.[63] One document of 1584, describing a Roman bass who is being considered for employment, makes clear the general require-ments placed on solo singers of this type:

> He ... displays lovely fantasy (*capricci*) in the singing of *napolitane* and in making up words and tunes of great attractiveness. By profession, he sings bass voice to the accompaniment of the lute, and he has a very sweet (*dolce*) voice. I do not know how he succeeds in ensemble singing, never having heard him perform so. For the rest, he has an alert mind and makes agreeable conversation.[64]

Documents concerning the recruitment of the falsettist Conforto for Mantua in the 1580s paint a similar picture.[65]

Although women solo singers in court may not have been asked to be quite such versatile entertainers, it is clear that the musical requirements placed on them were roughly the same. The range required in some of Luzzaschi's madrigals for one, two and three sopranos (1601) is well over two octaves, while the diminutions are remarkable.

Ornamentation

It seems clear that the ability to negotiate, and even to invent, ornamentation of some complexity was a requirement for all professional soloists, instru-mentalists and vocalists alike. That it may not have been as basic a requirement for ensemble singers is suggested by Mantuan agents recruiting castratos in France in 1582–3. A young castrato of 17 years was judged inappropriate for chamber music because he 'cannot sing softly, cannot ornament, and (like one accustomed to singing in a chorus), knows no songs by heart'.[66]

Our information on ornamentation in 16th-century performance practice is summarized and analysed by Howard Brown.[67] A number of instruction books, printed from 1535 onwards, but becoming common only as the end of the century approaches, give an idea of the graces and divisions applied by contemporary performers. These instruction books (most of them by instrumentalists), together with published arrangements by lutenists, can give some idea of the kind of ornamentation employed by famous instrumental soloists. The collections of Luzzaschi, Caccini and Puliaschi mentioned above can do the same for highly trained solo singers at court. One should remember that these are the extreme examples of the style. Although less exalted soloists doubtless ornamented a good deal more simply, contemporary documents are full of warnings against excess in this matter.[68] One should also remember that all our documentation on vocal ornamentation comes from the second half of the century, most of it from the last two decades.

The extent to which ornamentation was applied in ensemble singing is difficult to assess. Whereas the famous soloist might often pass from decoration to arrangement or even transformation in the ornamentation of a piece, the ensemble singer was not expected to do so. Indeed, ornamentation as a whole may not have been as widespread in ensemble singing as we tend to surmise, easily influenced as we are by the surviving verbal documents (in this case the ornamentation treatises). Ornamentation may have been primarily the province of the expensive professional soloist. Conforto (1593) remarks that vocal ornamentation could be heard only in big cities and princely courts. Maffei (1562) indicates that the role of ornamentation was open to considerable argument at that time, even in an advanced centre such as Naples (the source of the most famous solo singers of mid-century). He reports that at one musical party those present argued vigorously as to whether they should perform the music with or without ornamentation (and with or without instrumental doubling).

Still Maffei gives some general advice for ensemble ornamentation,[69] which advice is generally confirmed by other 16th-century writers. Ensemble ornamentation should be simpler than soloistic and primarily restricted to (important?) cadences. It should be done on the penultimate syllable of a word (or at least on an accented syllable) and by only one voice at a time.[70] Maffei goes beyond most in advising against ornamentation on the vowels 'i' and 'u', and recommending 'a' as particularly appropriate. He recommends that only four or five moments in a piece be ornamented. Zacconi (1592) recommends that ornamented passages should not all be concentrated in one or two sections of the piece and that the complexity of the ornamentation itself should increase as the piece moves towards its end.[71]

Most authors (for example Zacconi) stress that the tempo of the piece should be maintained in ornamented passages (with a possible slight stretching at the final cadence). Some sources make clear that melodic material in imitation need not always be ornamented the same way, and that ornamentation should be avoided on the distinctive opening part of an imitative subject. Some say that the top voice is the most appropriate for ornamentation; others say the outer voices. On the other hand, some (Coclico, 1552 and Bottrigari, 1594) explicitly oppose ornamentations for the bass in ensembles, and Zacconi (1592) prints a set of simpler ornaments specially designed for the bass when it functions as sole harmonic support. A similar concern that the harmony remain well defined informs Vicentino's opinion (1555) that ornamentation is better reserved for pieces for five or more voices, so that the harmony can be preserved complete, and that ornamentation is better applied when instruments double the voices in an ensemble, since the instruments can then play the lines as written to ensure that the 'harmony is kept complete'.[72] The spicy heterophony that would sometimes result from such a practice seems to have delighted rather than offended the 16th-century ear.[73]

If we compare the statements of the theorists with the surviving examples of music having written-out ornamentation, or even if we compare the theorists' statements amongst themselves, contradictions are easily found. Here, as in so many other areas of Renaissance performance practice, it was doubtless easy to transgress the boundaries of stylistic propriety, but there seems to have been no general agreement on the one correct way to proceed.

Notes

[1] Note that Maffei (1562) was originally published as part of a collection of letters: *Delle lettere del Signor Gio. Camillo Maffei da Solofra, libri due, dove … v'è un discorso della voce e del modo d'apparare di cantar di garganta* (Naples, 1562).

[2] See A. Newcomb, *The Madrigal at Ferrara 1579–1597* (Princeton, 1980), i, 27, 263.

[3] See for example Antonfranceso Doni, *Dialogo della musica (1544)*, ed. F. Malipiero (Vienna, 1965).

[4] H. Besseler, 'Umgangsmusik und Darbietungsmusik im 16. Jahrhundert', *AMw*, xvi (1959), 21–43, begins this project, and gives an idea of its interest and importance.

[5] See N. Pirrotta, *Music and Theatre from Poliziano to Monteverdi* (Cambridge, 1982), chap.3, 'Realistic use of music in comedy'.

[6] Pirrotta, *Music and Theatre*.

[7] H. C. Slim, *A Gift of Madrigals and Motets* (Chicago, 1972).

[8] Translated in O. Strunk, *Source Readings in Music History* (New York, 1950), 310–19.

[9] These pieces, although they are polyphonic and do not make musical sense as solos with chordal accompaniment, are the answer in high art to the solo-voice *arie per cantar sonetti* of the early and mid-century (on these last, see for example H. M. Brown, 'The Geography of Florentine Monody', *EM*, ix (1981), 147–68). Since vocal polyphony was still the normal way to set a serious text in the high style, there was no crippling contradiction in a realistically mimetic five-voice setting of a dramatic monologue. Each of the five singers acts as part of a single entity that is impersonating the impassioned declamation of the protagonist.

[10] See Vicentino (1555) as quoted in *Readings in the History of Music in Performance*, ed. C. MacClintock (Bloomington, 1979); the above-cited passage by Galilei; and especially F. Razzi, 'Polyphony of the *Seconda Prattica*: Performance Practice in Italian Vocal Music of the Mannerist Era', *EM*, viii (1980), 298–311, where other relevant documents are cited.

[11] See the preface to Frescobaldi's First Book of Toccatas (1615), quoted, among other places, in MacClintock, *Readings*, 133.

[12] See Razzi, 'Polyphony of the *Seconda Prattica*'.

[13] See for example B. Migliorini, *Storia della lingua italiana* (Florence, 1960).

[14] For a guide to the pronunciation of French see J. Alton and B. Jeffrey, *Bele buche e bele parleure: a Guide to the Pronunciation of Medieval and Renaissance French for Singers and Others* (London, 1976). See also the guide by Alan Robson to the pronunciation of Renaissance French

in Thomas Crecquillon, *Twelve chansons*, ed. B. Thomas (London, 1976). (Other volumes in this series provide similar guides.) A number of 16th-century guides to French pronunciation are mentioned in R. Stewart, 'Voice Types in Josquin's Music', *TVNM*, xxxv (1985), 188, n.29; see also E. Green, 'La prononciation du français dans les chansons de Josquin des Prez', *TVNM*, xxxvi (1986), 52–65. For a guide to the pronunciation of English see E. J. Dobson, *English Pronunciation 1500–1700* (Oxford, 1957, 2/1968).

[15] For speculations on this subject, see H. M. Brown, 'On Gentile Bellini's *Processione in San Marco*', in *IMSCR*, xii *Berkeley 1977*, 649–58.

[16] See H. M. Brown, *Sixteenth-century Instrumentation: the Music for the Florentine Intermedii*, MSD, xxx (1973), 58–9. A Ferrarese chronicler in 1582 reported as follows an occasion on which the Duke and Duchess of Ferrara went with about 100 of their entourage on a ceremonial barge (*bucintoro*) to meet the Prince and Princess of Mantua, who were proceeding with their own retinue down the Po toward Ferrara on a similar barge: 'Upon encountering the visitors, one fired an artillery salute from accompanying boats. Then the trumpets of the Duke on the *bucintoro* played a fanfare [*fecero una sonata*]. When this was finished, there was music with trombones and cornetts until one arrived [at Ferrara].' The implication is that, as the visitors' boat drew closer, one progressed from less to more subtle noise – from artillery salute to trumpet fanfare to music, presumably polyphony, for cornetts and trombones.

[17] *Arte e vita musicale a Bologna* (Bologna, 1927), i, 45. Vatielli cites the dialogue *Il Bottrigaro* by Ciro Spontone, which I have been unable to trace.

[18] *Andrea Gabrieli: Complete Madrigals 9–10*, ed. A. T. Merritt, RRMR, xlix–1 (Madison, Wisc., 1983).

[19] See Newcomb, *The Madrigal*, i, 33.

[20] H. M. Brown, 'A Cook's Tour of Ferrara in 1529', *RIM*, x (1975), 229.

[21] Slim, *A Gift of Madrigals and Motets*. For Doni see n.3 above.

[22] M. Troiano, *Discorsi delli triomfi* (1569), 146.

[23] For this last, see W. F. Prizer, 'Performance Practices in the Frottola', *EM*, iii (1975), 227–35, and D. G. Cardamone, Preface to *Adrian Willaert and his Circle, Canzoni Villanesche alla Napolitana and Villotte*, RRMR, xxx (Madison, Wisc., 1978).

[24] Quoted, among other places, in C. V. Palisca, 'A Clarification of "Musica Reservata"', *AcM*, xxxi (1959), 148.

[25] For an idea of the dizzying variety of performing groups assembled in the 16th century, see the pictorial evidence assembled in W. Salmen, *Musikleben im 16. Jahrhundert*, Musikgeschichte in Bildern, iii/9 (Leipzig, 1976).

[26] Brown, 'A Cook's Tour', 232.

[27] Doni, *Dialogo*, ed. Malipiero.

[28] Newcomb, *The Madrigal*, i, chap.3.

[29] Brown, *Sixteenth-century Instrumentation*, 74. Practical performance experience suggests the same thing: the ideal of flexible, oratorical declamation of the text becomes radically harder to achieve with more than one singer to a part.

[30] See for example E. Elsner, *Untersuchung der Instrumentalen Besetzungspraxis der weltlichen Musik im 16. Jahrhundert in Italien* (Berlin, 1935), 53ff.

[31] Brown, *Sixteenth-century Instrumentation*.

[32] Newcomb, *The Madrigal*, i, 102.

[33] ibid, 100, 181–3. It is not yet clear to what degree the documented instances of the combination of voices and melodic instruments in a polyphonic ensemble represent a widespread practice or an exceptional solution to the problem of performing secular music, adopted only on particular occasions. Maffei (1562) expresses reservations about the desirability of the practice in any case (see 'Ornamentation' below). See David Fallows's careful analysis of the evidence as regards sacred music around 1500, 'The Performing Ensembles in Josquin's Sacred Music', *TVNM*, xxxv (1985), 32–8. No such study exists as yet for 16th-century secular music.

[34] See Prizer, 'Performance Practices', and 'Isabella d'Este and Lucrezia Borgia as Patrons of Music', *JAMS*, xxxviii (1985), 1–33; Brown, 'A Cook's Tour', and *Sixteenth-century Instrumentation*; Newcomb, *The Madrigal*.

[35] Newcomb, *The Madrigal*, i, 58–67.

[36] A replacement of this sort is a prototype of the later basso continuo, although the watershed in the evolution of the continuo comes when the bass part is explicitly and exclusively designed for this function.

[37] *I-V Eaf* Cod.223 and Willaert's intabulations of Verdelot madrigals (*BrownI*, 1536[8]) are such lute tablatures from the middle of the century.

[38] See Newcomb, *The Madrigal*, i, 55, 270, concerning Caccini in the 1580s.

[39] *BrownI*, 1596[8] and 1589[8].

[40] For example Vicentino (1555), as cited in MacClintock, *Readings*, 76–9; R. Sherr, 'Guglielmo Gonzaga and the Castrati', *RQ*, xxxiii (1980), 33–56; Newcomb, *The Madrigal*, i, 270.

[41] For example, Giovanni Leonardo dall'Arpa (E. Durante and A. Martellotti, *L'Arpa di Laura*, Florence 1982, 41–4) in Naples and Rome from the 1540s into the 1590s; Laura Peverara, the most famous member of the Ferrarese *concerto di donne* in the 1580s and 1590s (Newcomb, *The Madrigal*, i, 187–90). Documentation on the instrument and its players in the 16th and early 17th centuries is assembled in Durante and Martellotti, *L'Arpa*.

[42] What little does survive comes from Spain or Spanish-dominated Naples. A fantasia in Mudarra (1546, for vihuela) imitates a famous harpist. Both Henestrosa's *Libro de cifra nueva* (1557) and the posthumous *Obras de musica* of Antonio de Cabezón (1578) are designated on their title-pages as 'for keyboard, harp and vihuela', although no pieces therein are specifically or idiomatically written for harp. A few pieces using idiomatic harp writing appear in the first part of the Neapolitan collection *GB-Lbm* Add.30491, apparently from around 1600. A few more appear in the Second Books of Mayone (1609) and Trabaci (1615). In spite of the regional concentration of this evidence, the harp was clearly well known and valued in Rome and Ferrara by the 1580s (Newcomb, *The Madrigal*, i, 102, 126).

[43] The *lira da braccio* was the Renaissance replacement for the classical lyre. The Orphic echoes that it brought with it for a Renaissance public will probably never resound for a modern one.

[44] L. Lockwood, *Music in Renaissance Ferrara 1400–1505* (Oxford, 1984), 266ff.

[45] I. Woodfield, *The Early History of the Viol* (Cambridge, 1984), documents the adoption and adaptation of the viol by the Italian courts around 1500 and its subsequent spread throughout Europe. Prizer, 'Isabella d'Este', gives examples of more lightly instrumented chamber groups from around 1500 and suggests that viols, lutes and keyboard instruments were by then the instruments considered appropriate for a woman's chambers; Brown, 'A Cook's Tour', 233–5, gives a wealth of purely instrumental combinations played at a courtly banquet of 1529, combinations that included a homogeneous consort of viols and one of transverse flutes, as well as various more heterogeneous consorts.

[46] See D. Kämper, 'Kriterien der Identifizierung instrumentalen Sätze in italienischen Chansonniers des frühen 16. Jahrhunderts', in *Formen und Probleme der überlieferung mehrstimmiger Musik im Zeitalter Josquins Desprez: Wolfenbüttel 1976*, 143–66; Kämper, 'Studien zur instrumentalen Ensemblemusik des 16. Jahrhunderts in Italien', *AnMc*, x (1970); and H. M. Brown, *A Florentine Chansonnier from the Time of Lorenzo the Magnificent (Florence, Biblioteca Nazionale Centrale, MS Banco Rari 229)*, MRM, vii (1983), ii, especially 138–42.

[47] Lockwood, *Music in Renaissance Ferrara*, 269–72.

[48] S. F. Weiss, 'Bologna Q18: some Reflections on Content and Context', *JAMS*, xli (1988), 63–101.

[49] Modern edition in *Music from the Time of Christian III*, ed. H. Glahn.

[50] E. Elsner, *Untersuchung*, gives documentation to this effect drawn from sources of various kinds throughout the century, and Brown, 'A Cook's Tour', about a single courtly banquet in 1529. Brown, *Sixteenth-century Instrumentation*, analyses Florentine court *intermedi* from 1539 to 1589; Troiano (1569) describes various festivities surrounding a court wedding of 1568. Doni (1544) and Newcomb, *The Madrigal*, give information on more intimate occasions from the 1540s (presumably) and the 1580s respectively.

[51] Doni, *Dialogo*; Bottrigari, *Il desiderio overo de' concerti di varij strumenti musicali* (Venice, 1594), ed. and trans. C. MacClintock, MSD, ix (1962); Newcomb, *The Madrigal*, i, 20–46.

[52] Newcomb, *The Madrigal*, i, 270, gives a pair of examples.

[53] ibid, i, appx.V, docs.8, 9, 52; Sherr, 'Guglielmo Gonzaga'; I. Fenlon, *Music and Patronage in Sixteenth-century Mantua* (Cambridge, 1980), i, docs.56–9. That the same was true in the 15th century is implied by the document quoted in N. Bridgman, *La vie musicale au quattrocento et jusqu'à la naissance du madrigal (1400–1530)* (Paris, 1964), 197.

[54] Fenlon, *Music and Patronage*, i, 110.

[55] M. Uberti, 'Vocal Technique in Italy in the Second Half of the Sixteenth Century', *EM*, ix (1981), 486–95, though stimulating, remains speculative.

[56] Conforto, for example, was reported by a Mantuan recruiting agent to 'sing gracefully, but according to the local style [of Rome], which has little of the Neapolitan. I do not know how this will agree with the style of Lombardy' (Fenlon, *Music and Patronage*, i, 110–11). The most extensive documentation on the practices of singing in the late 15th and early 16th centuries, including information on vocal ranges and local voice types, is presented in Stewart, 'Vocal Types', 97–134.

[57] Sherr, 'Guglielmo Gonzaga'.

[58] See H. M. Brown, 'Women Singers and Women's Songs in Fifteenth-century Italy', in *Women Making Music: the Western Art Tradition 1150–1950*, ed. J. Bowers and J. Tick (Urbana, 1986), 61–89.

[59] See Newcomb, *The Madrigal*, i, 67–89.

[60] In this regard one might note that vocal parts – usually printed in alto or tenor partbooks – written in the alto clef seem designed for men singing in the light head voice suitable for the small room. I know of no instances of parts written in the alto clef that are specifically for a female voice, while there are a number of such parts that are specifically for men. (See for example the part of Tirsi Nunzio in Gagliano's *Dafne*.) It would seem that modern editions should most appropriately print these parts in the transposing *g* clef, and that they should be sung by men in modern ensembles.

[61] Newcomb, *The Madrigal*, i, 170.

[62] L. Giustiniani, *Discorso sopra la musica* (1628), ed. and trans. C. MacClintock, MSD, ix (1962), 69.

[63] Translated in MacClintock, *Readings*, 43.

[64] Newcomb, *The Madrigal*, i, 47, 269. Giustiniani adds that Pitio was also a *Buffone nobile* (a first-class comedian), bringing up the frequent connection between solo singers in the 16th century and the nascent *commedia dell'arte*.

[65] Fenlon, *Music and Patronage*, i, 110–11.

[66] Sherr, 'Guglielmo Gonzaga', 38–9. Fenlon, *Music and Patronage*, i, 110–11, summarizes the requirements of the recruiting agents of Duke Guglielmo Gonzaga of Mantua when looking for a musician: he should be able to sing in both small and large spaces (*in camera* and *in cappella*) and to play at least one instrument; he should be able to sing from memory, read securely and improvise ornamentation.

[67] Brown, *Embellishing Sixteenth-century Music*.

[68] For example Giustiniani, *Discorso*, ed. MacClintock, 69 (concerning Conforto).

[69] MacClintock, *Readings*, 52–3; summarized in Brown, *Embellishing Sixteenth-century Music*, 54.

[70] Maffei does not seem to admit the kind of pre-arranged coordination of simultaneous ornamentation in several voices that clearly happened in the *concerto di donne* at the Ferrarese court in the 1580s – see Newcomb, *The Madrigal*, i, appx.V, doc.57 – where we are clearly no longer in the realm of 'improvised' ornamentation.

[71] Translated in MacClintock, *Readings*, 70–71.

[72] Brown, *Sixteenth-century Instrumentation*, 55, describes the opposite effect in a Florentine *intermedio* of 1565. There instruments add ornaments over simpler sung lines.

[73] Brown, *Embellishing Sixteenth-century Music*, 57.

CHAPTER XIII

Monophony and the Unwritten Tradition

JAMES HAAR

Monophony: chant and Latin song

The history of plainchant, despite the timeless stability and changeless authority attributed to the music by medieval and Renaissance writers, is one of change. Styles, forms and even genres foreign to the oldest identifiable repertory were added, with the composition of new chants (or at least the recomposition of old ones) continuing, if with decreasing frequency, until the 16th century. In spite of Carolingian efforts to supply and then to enforce the performance of a standardized musical liturgy, the pre-Tridentine Church was always marked by some diversity of rite, at first chiefly monastic in origin and later differing by region. The regions might be large, as in the case of the Sarum rite which, in the 15th century, was observed not only in much of England but also in parts of the Continent, or they might be small: a diocese or even a single privileged church. Scholars have become increasingly aware of the need to take these differences into account, for their own sake and for the study of polyphony related not to plainchant in general but to the forms it took in particular places.[1]

Early chant notation, long thought to be a single-minded effort to fix patterns of pitch, is in the opinion of some recent scholars more a series of cues indicating the manner or style of performance: tempo, accent, kinds of vocalization, in short, as Helmut Hucke states, 'products of a performance practice'.[2] It is unfortunate that these elements receded and finally disappeared as chant notation matured, becoming a written language – almost a kind of dead language – rather than a set of reminders about how to sing a repertory known through oral transmission.

Thus if we use chant books of the 14th, 15th and 16th centuries we may get the 'right' notes (though not the same ones in every source) but they do not come with directions or even hints about how to sing them. Most performers of early music have followed the 'Solesmes method', more or less loosely. The work of the Solesmes scholars has produced an evolving set of theories and the evolution is far from finished.[3] A 'correct' performance of chant according to Solesmes will not be the same in the 1980s as it was in the 1950s. Nonetheless, the original aim of the Solesmes scholars has remained constant: to recapture the chant as it was written in its earliest extant redaction and to reconstruct the mode or modes of performance used in the 10th and 11th centuries.

This in itself is laudable; but what is its application to modern performances of Renaissance music? If chant is sung in a programme of sacred polyphony from the 15th and 16th centuries, there is really very little sense in

240

trying to sing it – the chant – as it would have been done in the 10th century. Could one try to perform chant as Ockeghem might have heard it, or as it was sung in the papal chapel in the 16th century? This would invite some guesswork, but the effort might be worth making. To take an example, suppose a programme of *Veni sancte spiritus* compositions were planned. The index to Gustave Reese's *Music in the Renaissance* lists settings by Dufay, Josquin, Willaert, Palestrina and Victoria (there are of course many others).[4] The chant, a Pentecost sequence which survived the Tridentine reform, is a very well-known melody; but it was not identical at all times and places, as ex.1 shows. Details of melody (and often, though not in this

Ex. 1*a* *Graduale Sacrosanctae Romanae Ecclesiae* (Tournai, 1932)

b Graduale Sacrosancte Romanae Ecclesie.... Iuxta ritum Missalis novi ex decreto Sacrosancti Concilii Tridentini restituti (Venice, 1580)

c *Graduale Romanum Iuxta Missale Ex decreto Sacrosancti Concilii Tridentini resti-tutum* (Antwerp, 1620)

example, text placement) differ; and from ex.1c we see that the chant was rhythmicized, in this case producing a rocking triple rhythmic pattern, one that must often have been used for hymns as well and which is seen in the *lauda* of the 14th and 15th centuries. Ex.2 shows an inclination towards the triple rhythm used in the 'Medicean' chant version in all the polyphonic settings (ex.1c). This rhythmicized kind of chant, closely associated with Roman practice in the late 16th century, may have been older and more widespread than we know. It would in any case seem to be the most appropriate form of the chant for performance in *alternatim* settings like that of Dufay. Ex.2d and e show that Palestrina and Victoria knew a form of the

Ex.2
(a) Dufay: *Veni Sancte Spiritus*

Et e - mit - te cae - li - tus

Et e - mit - te cae - li - tus

Lu - cis tu - ae ra - di - um.

Lu - cis tu - ae ra - di - um.

(b) Josquin des Prez: *Veni Sancte Spiritus*

Superius

Ve - ni, sanc - te Spi - ri-

Altus

Ve - ni, sanc -

Quinta Vox

Ve - ni, sanc - te Spi - ri - tus,

Tenor

Ve - ni, sanc - te Spi - ri -

Sexta Vox

Bassus

Ve - ni, sanc - te Spi - ri - tus,

243

(c) Willaert: *Veni Sancte Spiritus*

(d) Palestrina: *Veni Sancte Spiritus*

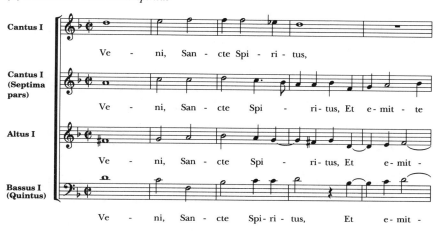

(e) Victoria: *Veni Sancte Spiritus*

melody beginning on D, the modal final. This was doubtless a 'reformed' version of the melody.[5] It is interesting that Dufay, writing more than a century earlier, also uses a D opening.[6]

We assume that in the late Middle Ages chant was normally sung in unmeasured, largely equal values. Was a portion of it, at least, habitually sung in rhythmicized fashion? There is evidence that at some period it was. Prosdocimus de Beldemandis, writing in the early 15th century, tells us:

> people of former times had a certain way of singing plainchant which they called the 'modus organicus' because they had derived it from the playing of the organ. The method consisted in not performing all the notes of the plainchant in the same rhythm, but lengthening some and shortening others according to the different groupings of the notes and according to the difference in the ligatures, some having stems and others not.[7]

The post-Tridentine chant reform resulted in the publication of graduals and antiphonals with melodies showing reduced melismas, with initial notes and cadential points modally regularized, and with 'barbarisms' of text accent removed, all in an effort to return the chant to a presumed state of antique purity.[8] A less sympathetic view of the reform is taken by Mary Berry, who describes the new editions as containing melodies 'truncated, distorted, semi-mensural, and with the underlay of the text following the principles of Renaissance grammarians rather than those of tenth-century cantors'.[9] She points out that the 'Ratisbon' editions of Pustet, possessing canonical authority in the late 19th century, descend directly from the early 17th-century reform books. For chant as it was sung in the late Renaissance, these editions, normally ignored by performers of early music, are paradoxically better texts than those of Solesmes.[10]

If not sung in regular rhythmic patterns, chant may have been strongly accentual in performance, the patterns differing in accordance with local pronunciation of Latin. To this day Latin pronunciation is (or can be) strongly influenced by the vernacular; and in the Renaissance it must have been even more so.[11] Ornithoparchus tells us that accent varies 'according to the manner and custom of country and place'; he is speaking of the reading of priests, but his remarks might well apply to the singing of choirs.[12] Thus a performance of chant influenced by Italian or French accentual patterns might be appropriate in certain contexts, where chant and a localized polyphonic repertory appear together.

There is no reason to think that chant was always sung unaccompanied. By the 15th century the growing popularity of *alternatim* practice, with the organ performing hymn or sequence verses or Mass sections in alternation with plainchant, put that instrument in close proximity to chant.[13] That the two came together is demonstrated by Adriano Banchieri's *L'organo suonarino* (1605), for example, which gives organ basses for chant melodies, describing a practice that can hardly have been new.[14] In a period when *falsobordone* vocal accompaniment of psalmodic chant was common, organ accompaniment would have represented little more novelty than a change of sonority.

The performance of chant in the later Middle Ages and Renaissance has not yet been the object of sustained study.[15] Whether or not it becomes so, we should remember that in this period the singing of chant not only reflected local usages but was generally the product of centuries of practice without any theorizing about stylistic propriety. Chant influenced the composition and performance of polyphony, that we know; perhaps the reverse was true as well. In any event modern singers of chant should try for a mode of performance that reflects the various periods in which it was sung, not just the earliest and hence, by real misuse of an historicist approach, the most nearly correct.

Cultivation of Latin song within or outside the liturgy took various forms in the later Middle Ages, among which the *cantio*, a strophic song with links both to chant and to popular song, was prominent.[16] Here accentual properties are of prime importance, and the regularity of construction of many of the melodies invites a rhythmicized performance even where the notation gives no hint of it. It is tempting to assume that performers of these devotional songs used a strongly accentual mode of performance for chant as well, at least for hymns, sequences and other more song-like forms.

Monophony with vernacular text

Accentual patterns were important in Renaissance vernacular song, sacred or secular, whether or not the melodies were mensurally notated. In songs given a coating of ornament of the kind used in polyphonic compositions this feature could be disguised to some extent, but projection of text must always have been important in solo song.[17] This means that performance of song should always begin with close study of the sound as well as the meaning of the text.

It is not easy to describe or define the repertory of vernacular monophonic song in the 15th and 16th centuries. In Italy the devotional *lauda* and its secular cousin the ballata were, to judge from surviving examples, turning into polyphonic genres.[18] (The trecento madrigal had apparently been polyphonic from its origin; it was in any event much less cultivated in the 15th century, and its 16th-century revival, in much altered form, is known to us only in polyphonic dress.) Local song types such as the *giustiniane* of the

Veneto and the *strambotto* of the south and of Tuscany were doubtless melodies or melodic formulas, not polyphonic complexes, though they must have been sung to some kind of accompaniment if contemporary verbal and pictorial comment on them is any guide. Cicco Simonetta's request for *giustiniane* and other Venetian poems to be sent from Venice to Milan, together with the music (*canto*) of several of them, as examples of the *aere venetiano* suggests that a repertory of basic tunes was in existence and that it was on occasion transmitted in written form.[19] It is tempting to think of *O rosa bella*, in the setting attributed to Dunstable or Bedyngham, as containing references to such an *aere* or *aria*.[20] Whether the music Simonetta asked for would in performance have exemplified an art now totally lost, or perhaps have drawn on the melodic and rhythmic vocabulary of polyphonic music, is a question that cannot be answered.[21]

Arie were also used as the basis for the art of the *improvvisatori*, who sang, or at any rate declaimed, epic and lyric poetry to their own accompaniment or, on occasion, to that of a *tenorista* (on this see below, 'The unwritten tradition'). This practice had its roots in medieval minstrelsy of indeterminate but surely venerable age. Such musical narrators, often indeed called *cantastorie* in Italy, must at varying times have been a part of every European musical culture. For the 15th and 16th centuries we are best informed about their vogue in Italy; there is little to suggest their presence in any number elsewhere in Europe. As will be seen, there is some 16th-century evidence for

Singer declaiming a narrative poem, accompanying himself on the lira da braccio: woodcut from the epic 'Morgante maggiore' by Luigi Pulci, printed in Florence, c1500 (Österreichische Nationalbibliothek, Vienna, Sign.Ink.5.G.9)

248

what the melodies used by *improvvisatori* were like. It is hard to determine what the life-span of an *aria* of this sort may have been, but melodic types subject to much variation of detail may have lasted a good deal longer than, say, a popular tune circulated in relatively stable form.

A small number of Italian popular tunes survive, embedded in the quodlibets of the turn of the 16th century, in the four-voice *villotta* popular in the Veneto *c*1520–35, and in scattered earlier and later sacred works, an example being the *La verginella non è bella* found in a Dufay Credo.[22]

The existence of several chansonniers containing a number of monophonic pieces is testimony to the currency of solo song in French-speaking lands; these pieces are decidedly popular in tone and character.[23] A *chanson rustique* as opposed to a *chanson musicale* does not necessarily mean the contrast of monophony to polyphony; the difference is rather one of poetic theme and language.[24] Still it is reasonable to suppose that a popular or popularesque text found its first musical expression in a simple tune. The survival of *chansons rustiques* as tenors in polyphonic chansons shows one use of such tunes. To see this phenomenon as nothing other than a Renaissance version of the 'Trianon set' playing pastoral games may be short-sighted. Polyphonic arrangements may instead have been formalized versions of what performers had been doing with such tunes, written down for amateurs with the same purpose that motivates 20th-century publication in sheet music form of second-hand jazz tunes. And as with Italian secular forms, French polyphonic chansons may have been performed in versions worked out by performers with no more than casual reference to a written text, with sufficient emphasis on the melodic line to make them qualify as accompanied solo song. Unless the presence of a score is noted by an observer, or artist, of the time we cannot assume that the presence of several performers means that a piece was being performed *as written* or even that the texture was polyphonic in any strict sense of that term.

Like the *lauda* in Italy, the English carol of the 15th century is extant mostly in polyphonic form. A few monophonic pieces survive, however, and there are references to tunes by name. Unison passages in polyphonic carols may also indicate the style of, perhaps even the survival of melodies from, a monophonic tradition.[25] Once again it might be said that the existence of this repertory in polyphonic form does not preclude its having been performed in a monophonic fashion.

The Meistergesang of Nuremberg and other German cities is perhaps a unique example of the deliberate and exclusive cultivation of monophonic art song, in this case unaccompanied, in the 15th and 16th centuries. Much of this repertory survives. It is hard to determine what connections Meisterlieder may have had with popular song and popular hymnody, and thus the extent to which Meistergesang, which by definition held itself aloof as a genre, can be said to be characteristic of solo song in German lands.[26]

In all of Europe, monophonic tunes circulated widely, their popularly known text incipits serving as cues for their use in secular and sacred contrafacta (see below). In some cases these tunes were written out to accompany their new texts, making the musical archeologist's dig an easy one; in others only the incipits are known to survive, so that an occasional lucky find makes musicological news.[27] It is dangerous to assume that what sounds 'popular' to us in Renaissance music is a direct reference to an otherwise lost tune; on the other hand it is timid to assume that no such references exist. We can only hope that more instances of persuasively argued connections between artistic polyphony and popular melody will be made in future.

What survives of the monophonic repertory is notated in various ways, often though not exclusively mensural. We would like to know how freely it was sung rhythmically, how much and what sort of ornamentation may have been used, and above all whether some kind of accompaniment was added. The notation merely fixes in writing a basic form of the music; singers may have known songs in versions that departed from this recorded form, and without the need to mesh with other voices in a predetermined contrapuntal texture they would have been free to sing as they wished, adding personal touches of melodic and rhythmic independence to their performances.

The ability to add ornament at will was a prized feature of the solo singer's art. We do not know precisely how it was done, at least in earlier periods; the nature of the *gringotage* spoken of as an ornament of French singing in the 15th century remains unclear.[28] There is however no reason why the kinds of ornaments used in polyphonic voices should not serve as a guide, especially if we postulate an improvised accompaniment against which suspensions and syncopations could have sounded. In the 16th century, singers regularly added ornament to voices of polyphonic compositions, and it would be far-fetched to suggest that ornament for monophonic music was of a totally different character. Thus the improvisation manuals of the 16th century may serve as a general guide to the art of ornamentation as it was practised throughout the Renaissance.[29] Changing fashions in ornament are reflected in the written repertory; observation of these can help prevent stylistic anomalies in the use of unwritten ornament. Instrumentalists may on occasion have played solo, single melodic lines for informal dancing or similar diversions; they would surely have applied ornament heavily. A few 14th-century dance pieces for solo instruments give evidence of how this was done.[30] The kind of ornament applied by instrumental performers to intabulations of vocal polyphony, revealed in sources such as the Faenza Codex of the early quattrocento and the German keyboard sources of the later 15th century, may be a guide to the ornamentation of monophonic music as well.[31]

The trecento repertory of madrigals and ballate shows, in the considerable variety of melodic and rhythmic ornament found in different sources for the same music, that performers enjoyed a good deal of latitude when singing unaccompanied or with a relatively simple supporting part.[32] Walter Rubsamen's discovery that the heavily ornamented superius lines of several three-voice pieces in Petrucci's sixth book of *Frottole* (1505) – pieces that are evidently the *giustiniane* referred to in the volume's title and which are older than most of Petrucci's repertory – are elaborated versions of simpler 'originals' is evidence of a mid-15th-century practice of vocal ornamentation that may to some degree have been typical of the period.[33] For the 15th century, examples drawn from the repertory are of particular importance since no ornamentation manuals for vocal practice are extant.

For all its simplicity and naturalness unaccompanied solo singing before an audience is a practice that to many of us may seem strange, so great is our dependence on harmonic context and polyphonic depth as necessary elements in artistically satisfying music. There is a kind of *horror vacui* here: a feeling that unaccompanied melody is somehow lacking in substance. (True folksingers, as opposed to the commercially minded ones, have never had this feeling.) The beauty of unaccompanied solo singing in the soloistic portions of plainchant, for example, is a surprise to our harmonically conditioned ears. Unaccompanied secular song, such as the monophonic ballata of the trecento, can be similarly fresh and strong in its impact when performed imaginatively.[34] Pieces such as these ballate may, of course, have been performed with an improvised accompaniment played by a plucked or a bowed string instrument. For some of the solo vocal repertory of the Renaissance instrumental or vocal accompaniment was not thought necessary, as in songs used in the theatre.[35] In some instances, indeed, it was expressly ruled out; this appears to have been the case with the Meistergesang.[36] If instrumental participation was not necessarily called for in performance of polyphonic song in the 15th century it may not always, or even often, have been present in the solo song of the period.[37]

Let us assume, however, that instrumental accompaniment was added on occasion to solo songs of the Renaissance. What form did the accompaniments take? The answer to this question is of course dependent on the choice of instrument. A *lira da braccio* is best used to produce arpeggiated chords, as are the guitar (which rose to prominence in something like its modern form in the 16th century) and other 'strumming' plucked instruments; the *lira* can also of course play a melodic line.[38] The viol, the fiddle, various kinds of harps and (in the 15th century) the lute could be used for single-line accompaniments, whether conceived as a full second voice or as a simpler line of sustained or repeated drone-like notes coupled with cadential formulas. A second performer, like the *tenorista* used by an *improvvisatore*, might play the accompaniment if the singer chose not to do so. As for the style of this accompaniment, bass lines such as those used for the *villancico* and the simpler forms of the frottola might serve as models. Any competent musician of the period was expected to be able to devise, without writing it down, a counterpoint against a melodic line; why not an accompaniment to a song? Looked at in this way, even a partly chordal accompaniment such as might be played on a *lira da braccio* would be a counterpoint to the melody, and a monophonic song with ad libitum accompaniment would not be radically different from a two-voice discant structure. Part of the mystery associated with improvisation is surely of our making, the result of what must be a false assumption that improvised music was very different from what has survived in written form.[39]

The unwritten tradition

The question of how unwritten music was performed, be it played and sung from memory or in varying degrees improvised, may seem a fruitless one to ask. If we do not know what the music itself was like, what good are speculations as to how it was performed? Hard evidence on the nature of orally transmitted music and on the technique and style of improvisers can come only from fragments of actual music that were for some reason written down. A number of these have been identified and discussed by scholars active in the study of 15th- and 16th-century music.[40] Nino Pirrotta, one of whose lifelong concerns has been to stress the importance of the unwritten tradition, has added to our knowledge of notated references to this tradition while at the same time emphasizing the distance between written notes and the lost art of individual styles and schools of improvised art.[41] More recently Reinhard Strohm has advanced a series of new hypotheses about the relationship of unwritten to written music in 15th-century Italy.[42] In his view the distinction was not an important one to patrons and listeners who enjoyed and occasionally described performances without knowing or indeed caring whether the music was the performers' invention or an artfully handled version of a written-down piece by someone like Dufay. Strohm further suggests that much of the unwritten repertory might have taken notated music as its point of departure and that we might therefore possess – admittedly without the individual touches that made an *improvvisatore* like Pietrobono of Ferrara so famous – more of the unwritten tradition than we know.[43] A consequence of this view is that the unwritten tradition may have been closer to notated music in a general way than a pessimistic view of the subject would have it. One should of course remember that in possessing a corpus of 15th-century polyphony in written form we do not have as a consequence any very precise information about how this music sounded in performance. Still, it seems useful and not unduly optimistic to postulate that written and unwritten music, at the level of the professional performer, may not have been two very different things.[44]

ARIE One of the most important genres in the unwritten tradition during the Renaissance was the use of melodic formulas for singing epic and lyric poetry *all'improvviso*. In Italy this was the much-praised art of the courtly *improvvisatore* and of the humbler *cantastorie* or *cantimbanco* who entertained crowds in the piazzas of cities and towns through the peninsula.[45] (Its currency elsewhere in Europe is not well documented and remains unexplored.) The music consisted of melodies, if such a precise term for them may be ventured, known as *aere* or *arie*. They differed not only from singer to singer but by locale. Much pleasure was taken in hearing not only familiar styles of singing but those said to be from different, sometimes remote places; the vogue of the *canzona alla napolitana* in northern Italy in the 16th century had ample 15th-century precedent. *Aria* might mean, as Pirrotta has often argued, a whole mode of performance including vocal production, style of accompaniment, virtuoso freedom and variety of declamation, even mimetic gesture.[46] It did, however, mean simply 'tune' or 'air' as well. If a performer came in person from afar one could learn his whole style through listening and watching; short of this one could at least try to grasp the melodic patterns he used.

The letter mentioned above from Cicco Simonetta, writing from Milan to Venice to ask for poems by Giustiniani along with music ('le note del canto') for several of them, so that *l'aere venetiano* could be learned, suggests that *arie* were indeed tunes. The letter also asks for a boy who is a trained singer; but it appears that the music itself, however bare as a sketch for actual performance, would provide a basis for an audibly Venetian mode of singing.[47] If the music was sent it was doubtless notated mensurally, perhaps even in two or three parts; this would then have been memorized and used freely in performances that would be heard and applauded as *all'improvviso*.

It would be a mistake to think that *arie* must have been so simple and so stereotyped that they lacked individuality and consisted of little more than a few basic melody types. Pietrobono was praised not only for his skill as a performer but for the music he sang; and whatever may have been the source of his music, in his hands it became an improvisatory art.[48] On the other hand, Serafino dall' Aquila was known above all for the matchless style of his delivery; the material he based it on may have been unremarkable in itself.[49] This is suggested by some surviving musical settings of Serafino's verse, possibly from his circle if not of his own composition.[50]

Amateur poets and musicians, not content with passive admiration of the art of the *improvvisatori*, wanted to imitate them, to sing Petrarch or classical Latin verse or their own poetry and that of their friends. Surely it was to satisfy this demand that Petrucci included *aere* and *modi di cantar sonetti*, *capitoli* and *versi latini* in his frottola books. These formulaic pieces, scattered through the ten surviving frottola prints, are sometimes accompanied by a text, meant simply as an example of how to underlay the music, and sometimes textless. Curiously, the *barzelletta*, most common of frottola forms, and the *strambotto*, closest in form to the *ottava rima* stanzas beloved of the improvisers, are not included among these patterns; but it would not be hard to substitute other texts in those forms for many of the pieces Petrucci published.

Anyone who wanted to sing a sonnet *all'improvviso* could do so by committing to memory the top line of a piece such as ex.3. Use of the internal repeat would take care of the quatrains; singing straight through would serve for the tercets. The whole piece would be sung through four times (only the first quatrain of the sample text is given here) to complete a sonnet, a procedure similar to that used in Petrucci's volumes for the eight-line *strambotto*, which normally consists of two phrases, the whole sung four times. Each of the phrases in ex.3 has 12 text-bearing notes (counting the

Ex.3 Anon, Per sonetti: *Piu volte me son messo a contemplarte*

Per   ve - der s'in   te   fus - se al - cun   di - fe   -   cto
Ma   per che l'o- chio a - vess' di - vin   ob - je   -   cto

Mi - rar non po   co - me cie - cho si   par   -   te.

two-semiminim group in the first phrase as one unit); this would allow for a melisma to give a leisurely finish to phrases one and two (bars 4 and 8), while the two minims before the end of the third phrase could be sung as such or fused into a semibreve. If the piece were read from Petrucci's print or a copy of it, this would be about the limit of flexibility possible. Four performers could read it, and in this instance, unlike many frottola settings, the text could be easily accommodated to all the parts and thus be performed by four singers.

This mode of performance would be possible though dull; but it is surely not what Petrucci had in mind. The text is given as an instance of *a* sonnet sung to this music, but the indication 'per sonetti' means that *any* sonnet one wished to sing would fit the notes. A singer would therefore commit the melodic line to memory, then use it ad libitum. The three lower lines, written out in polyphonic form in the print, could be adapted for whatever instrumental accompaniment was desired; for keyboard, using all of Petrucci's material; for *lira da braccio*, using the tenor line plus some arpeggiated chords at the beginning and end; for lute, omitting the alto and rearranging the tenor and bass as needed or desired; for viol, using a kind of *solus tenor*, a combination of bass and tenor parts. Once the piece was learned the singer could take all sorts of liberties (a flexible response on the part of the instrumentalist, if different from the singer, is here assumed), such as repeating the opening notes of phrases one and two as often as desired and then converting what follows into melismas; ornamenting and perhaps extending the cadential bars; lengthening or shortening note values; singing the tenor instead of the superius by exchange with the accompaniment. The possibilities are many, once we free ourselves from the notion that the music must be performed as written.[51] In the hands of an intelligent and enterprising singer – not necessarily a virtuoso performer – this schematic little piece could be the basis for a varied and effective act of improvisatory singing.

Arie appear from time to time in printed collections, individually in madrigal prints, and in sources such as the manuscript songbook of Cosimo Bottegari, a lutenist–singer at the Medici court in Florence in the late 16th century.[52] The genre changes less than one might expect since *arie* tend to avoid extremes in melody, rhythm and harmony. Tunes must have come and gone, had moments of popularity and then vanished; the basic approach remained fairly constant. Bottegari's songs have been called 'some of the earliest known monodies';[53] but the line between *aria* and monody is a thin one if it exists at all. Any accompanied solo song is after all a form of monody.

The celebrated *arie* called passamezzo, romanesca, ruggiero etc, found without their names in the *Trattado de glosas* of Diego Ortiz (1553) and common in the music of the late 16th and early 17th centuries, appear from their regularity of construction and sturdiness of harmonic design to be instrumental in concept, patterns learned on their own rather than as accompaniment to a singer's art, but nonetheless susceptible to alteration and embellishment when put to practical use. Melodies of related but not identical character were indeed sung over them, and this makes them *arie*; but the concept is one in which the priorities appear to have been reversed; the singer (or player) improvises, or elaborates upon, a melodic *cursus* dictated by the bass rather than singing a tune under which some sort of accompaniment is furnished. The two approaches may overlap, and something of the bass *aria* may always have been in the vocabulary of *improvvisatori*; the distinction is nonetheless one that seems worth emphasizing.[54]

Zarlino speaks of 'these *modi* on which we now sing the sonnets and canzoni of Petrarch or the *rime* of Ariosto'.[55] The stanzas of *Orlando Furioso* were popular with madrigalists; they also gave a new repertory of chivalric lore to the *cantastorie*, material vibrant in imagery and written in clear, refinedly Petrarchistic language that was of great appeal to courtly improvisers and their patrons.[56] Although madrigals on texts from *Orlando Furioso* were written in a variety of styles, a favoured idiom was a declamatory, chordal structure emphasizing the textual rhythms of Ariosto's endecasyllabic verse. Many of these pieces are polyphonic equivalents to *arie*; some of them use melodies, or melodic types, that recur often enough to suggest that well-known tunes are being cited. This is an unmistakable feature of Jacquet Berchem's *Capriccio*, a set of four-voice madrigals based on about 90 stanzas from Ariosto's poem.[57] Berchem's collection, dedicated to a member of the Este family, patrons of Ariosto, is clearly designed as a composer's version of the art of the *improvvisatore*. The chosen texts form a selective, carefully arranged narrative drawn from the epic, concentrating on Orlando's love for Angelica, his madness and its magical cure. Each piece has a running heading of text explaining its narrative role, a most unusual feature in madrigal prints.[58] And the music, which varies in texture from chordal declamation to fairly intricate polyphonic writing, includes a number of melodic patterns that find repeated use. Some of these, drawn from a number of pieces within the *Capriccio*, are given in ex.4.

Of these tunes the last two are of special interest because they can be found in the music of a number of madrigalists, often (but by no means always) in the setting of Ariostan texts.[59] Melodic resemblances can of course be a matter of coincidence, so that not every appearance of a line approaching that of ex.4c need be claimed as deliberate use of a pre-existent tune. Berchem's emphasis on the melody of ex.4c is convincing evidence, as is its use by both him and Arcadelt in a madrigal cycle; the idea here is not merely one of melodic economy and coherence but also of the kind of linkage between stanzas that an *improvvisatore* would provide.

Ex.4d is used primarily for settings of stanzas from *Orlando Furioso*.[60] Its

Ex.4 Melodic patterns found in Berchem's *Capriccio* (1561)

(a) I, 25: *Queste non son più lachrime che fuore* (Canto)

(b) I, 27: *Non son io quel che paio in viso* (Canto)

or I, 3: *O gran bontà de Cavalier antiqui* (Canto)

(c) I, 14: *C'haver puo donna al mondo più di buono* (Canto)

(d) I, 4: *Ricordati Pagan quand' uccidesti* (Altus)

resemblance (close but not perfect) to the ruggiero bass pattern, its connection with the stanza beginning 'Ruggier, qual sempre fui tal esser voglio', and its rhetorical character, easily perceivable as the basis for decisive, even heroic declamation – all of these factors make ex.4d a strong candidate for a melody actually sung by improvisers reciting epic verse.

The use of this melody by madrigalists would therefore constitute an allusion to the unwritten art of the *cantastorie*. Its sound, in a polyphonic context, would not be much closer to improvised declamation than a 15th-century secular-tune cantus firmus is to its popular source, except that it never appears in long-held notes. If we wish to speculate how melodies such as this were used in their 'live', pre-written state, the madrigal literature is of limited help; only the declamatory chordal rhythmic patterns prominent in some of them suggest the delivery of an *improvvisatore*. The closest approximation to an improvisatory style among settings of ex.4*d*, the ruggiero theme, is that for voice and vihuela by Valderrábano, given here as ex.5.[61] In

Ex.5 Valderrábano: *Soneto* v

the index to the print containing this work the piece is indicated as 'en primero grado', the easiest technical level, and indeed it seems easily playable; more than that, its barely figural chordal support is of a kind that a lute or any strumming instrument could effectively manage. The vocal melody is a third lower than the form of the tune known in Italy. The melody could be sung starting either on the third or fifth degree of its scale; perhaps it was known in both forms, or the lower one might have been a counterpoint to the upper one in a version seen or heard by Valderrábano.[62]

CONTRAFACTA Another kind of music-making dependent at least in part on memory rather than on written notation involves the use of melodies, or of whole polyphonic pieces, for texts other than those for which they were originally intended. *Laude* were made from madrigals and ballate in the trecento; 15th-century chansons appeared with German and Italian texts; secular tunes were used for Flemish psalm settings; chansons and madrigals were 'spiritualized' through substitution of pious for amatory texts; motets written for specific occasions were reused with partially or totally new texts; noëls used *timbres*, chanson tunes well enough known so that citation of their opening words sufficed to remind singers of their melodies. These are only some of the textual substitutions used in the Renaissance. There is no particular reason to dwell on these in a discussion of performance practice, but the existence of such a large and varied number of contrafacta is part of a general attitude toward music that does have ramifications for performance.

In the Renaissance musical compositions were of course enjoyed for their own sake, and their popularity was not always as brief as we have come to think in our idealization of a past when creativity and liking for the new was all-important. Works by Dufay and Josquin at one end of the spectrum, some popular tunes at the other, are examples of music that remained in the active repertory for more than a few years. Music was also regarded as in itself a source for further musical activity, in ways and to a degree that are different from the modern or post-Romantic view of artistic creativity. Thus a chanson could be put to new use, its original text – whether platonizing or frankly erotic – being no hindrance to its aptness as a bearer of a devotional message. An *improvvisatore* could make something fresh and individual out of a composition originally designed for quite different purposes. Here some musical adjustments and a good deal of individual style in performance would essentially re-create a piece, not just use it as a contrafactum. What seems to have been regarded as unusual was to compose *ex nihilo* and invent everything – what Zarlino called composing 'di fantasia'.[63]

IMPROVISED POLYPHONY The technique of musical parody, already evident in the 15th century and of great importance in 16th-century music, belongs to the history of written polyphony. But the simple citation of a known melody in a new context could occur within either a written or an oral tradition; so could the use of a *cantus prius factus*, whether of plainchant or of secular origin. When we think of cantus firmus it is the genres of mass and motet that come to mind. To a Renaissance musician there would have been another important category, that of 'counterpoint', the improvised or at any rate unwritten embellishment of a chant by one or more singers employed at what was called *cantare super librum*, singing 'upon the book'.

Polyphonic embellishment of chant is, in the form of parallel and near-parallel organum, of considerable antiquity. It is not known when the practice started (the organum treatises of the 9th, 10th and 11th centuries are concerned with precise measurement of intervals and with avoidance of the tritone rather than with description of a new phenomenon), nor indeed when it came to an end. The development of artistically refined polyphony in the 12th century did not mean the end of a simpler practice but rather its relegation to increasingly peripheral locations. As late as the 15th century a kind of note-against-note, unmeasured combination of chant and a second voice was in existence. A few written examples survive; the practice must on the whole, however, have been one that did not require notation.[64] This does not mean that it did not require skill; it was not restricted to parallel motion, and Prosdocimus de Beldemandis, who calls the procedure a 'modus cantandi cantum planum binatim', says that the practice was ancient but that a 'few skilled moderns' excelled in it. The skill it took to keep together in unmeasured counterpoint is also noted by Tinctoris.[65]

Cantus planus binatim could be performed 'from the book' with one or more singers reading the chant, another singing counterpoint in a process that we call, for want of a better word, improvisation. There could be a third added voice as well; written examples of such pieces have been found in Italian sources in recent years.[66] The English practice of singing counterpoint 'upon the book' through a system of sights, known to us from a group of 15th-century treatises, belongs to this same general tradition.[67] Singers at some of the greatest musical institutions of the time, such as Cambrai Cathedral, were given instruction in the art of *cantare super librum*.[68]

The art of singing counterpoint, not necessarily restricted to note-against-note movement or to a two-voice structure, 'upon the book' is described by Tinctoris, who notes that its one firm requirement is that all added voices be consonant with the tenor.[69] *Cantare super librum* means that the added counterpoint is 'in the mind', not written; but in the same chapter counterpoint is said by Tinctoris to be 'scripto vel mente', that is, 'in writing or in the mind'. Margaret Bent has argued forcefully that counterpoint, whether written or sung with the notes 'in the mind', is not the same thing as improvisation as that term is now commonly understood.[70] She disputes the notion that several singers improvised at once, letting the discordant chips fall where they might, and questions the whole theory that counterpoint was ever sung without careful preparation (not necessarily involving a process of writing).

Counterpoint, it should be noted, is distinguished from 'composition' by Tinctoris. His distinction is a technical one; but for later theorists the study and practice of counterpoint was in part preparatory exercise for would-be composers, in part musical education like the study of counterpoint today, except for one vital difference: its intimate connection with performance.[71] Thus all Renaissance musicians, whether or not they had the compositional gift that in the 18th century was to be called 'goût', were expected to be able to make, that is, make up, music at the level of counterpoint.

Counterpoint could be made not only upon a plainchant tenor but upon the tenor or possibly another voice of a polyphonic composition. The *si placet* added voices that one finds in some copies of late 15th- and early 16th-century sacred and secular pieces are written-down examples of contrapuntal improvisation of a careful and well-established kind.[72] As the vogue for parody – which really involves simultaneous consideration of all voices and hence demands a written score or set of partbooks as model – increased, the practice of adding parts through almost purely linear 'contrapuntizing' decreased; but it never completely disappeared.[73]

In a description of *contrapunctus floridus* the early 17th-century theorist Joachim Thuringus says that it consists of voices in a mixture of note values and rhythmic patterns added to a chant tenor 'ad imitationem sortisationis', 'in the manner of improvised counterpoint'.[74] As an example he cites Josquin's *Stabat mater*, a five-voice motet based on a slow, equal-note tenor. By the time of Thuringus a work by Josquin could have had little more than didactic interest. But if one considers Josquin's piece as Thuringus might have looked at it, it is indeed a series of rather distinct, even unconnected sections of counterpoint, mainly for two or three voices, against tenor segments, and many of the musical ideas are commonplaces of the style of Josquin and his contemporaries.

Ernst Ferand, commenting on Thuringus's remark, says that if one believes it 'one has to conclude that composers of Josquin's generation, in compositions of the *contrapunctus fractus* type, aimed at catching the spirit of improvisation, and that of improvised counterpoint in particular, composi-tions we are accustomed to consider, in the terminology of Tinctoris, *res factae*'.[75] Among such pieces, or sections of pieces, by Josquin that could be singled out are the Kyrie I and the Benedictus duos of the *Missa Hercules Dux Ferrariae* (ex.6) This music is usually regarded as rather rigid, even archaic in its repetition of formulaic patterns. If one regarded it as written 'counterpoint' meant to resemble what singers could do *super librum*, an element of the improvisatory, even of the playful (not of course in a frivolous sense) is introduced – rightly, I believe – into its make-up. That this would

Ex.6 Josquin des Prez: *Missa Hercules Dux Ferrariae*, Kyrie 1

affect the way the piece is performed (it is usually done in a solemn and rather brassy way) seems self-evident.

'Improvisation' may not, at least with regard to counterpoint, have been a completely impromptu matter, and it was regarded as a serious activity. Among Renaissance theorists only Morley appears to have taken a dim view of the results as musically chaotic.[76] Most writers praise the art of *cantare super librum* as excellent when done well, and exhort students to master it as an indispensable part of their training.[77] More and more explicit advice and detailed examples were given as the 16th century proceeded until the art of 'improvised' counterpoint became as schematically ordered as that of creating melodic diminutions and *passaggi*. Composers are known to have written out counterpoints; Costanzo Festa in applying for a licence to print his entire *oeuvre* listed 'contraponti' (these do not survive) as a genre of works.[78]

A volume of four-voice settings of the Mass Proper, using the chant as a cantus firmus, was published in Lyons in 1528 under the title *Contrapunctus seu figurata musica super plano canto missarum solennium totius anni*.[79] Although the music in this collection does not always follow Tinctoris's definition of counterpoint (there are places where a voice is consonant with the bass, or the whole concentus, while forming a fourth with the tenor), it has the air of being counterpoint rather than 'composition'; there is comparatively little imitation, and what there is often consists of use of short motives in several voices over a repeated-note cantus firmus – just the kind that would be easy to work out in an 'improvised' setting.[80] These pieces are an excellent written guide to the kind and possible level of counterpoint that, the theorists tell us, was practised 'upon the book' without being written down.

For later 16th-century practice the numerous examples given by Zacconi could well serve as model.[81] Students of modal counterpoint would do well to sing these, not merely study them silently; even better would be inclusion of *cantare super librum* in counterpoint courses, with controlled improvisation a requirement and with counterpoint sung and heard before or even instead of being written. And if present-day singers can perform from 16th-century partbooks should they not go on to master the art of *cantare super librum* and

261

to demonstrate their mastery to an audience provided with the plainsong on which they are making counterpoint?

Notes

[1] For an example of an effort to identify chant sources for the work of one Renaissance polyphonist see W. Elders, 'Plainchant in the Motets, Hymns, and Magnificat of Josquin des Prez', in *Josquin des Prez: New York 1971*, 523–42. Some of the difficulties in this kind of investigation are outlined in J. A. Mattfeld, 'An Unsolved Riddle: the Apparent Absence of Ambrosian Melodies in the Works of Josquin des Prez', *Josquin des Prez: New York 1971*, 360–66. See especially p.362: 'Some of us . . . have assumed that a choir singer . . . if commissioned to write for a particular occasion or to set a specific text, would have turned . . . to the chant versions prescribed in the ritual books used in the church or diocese to which the choir or chapel was attached. We do not in fact *know* that this was so, however, either categorically or for particular individuals'.

A few composers can be shown to have drawn on local versions of chant. One example is Francisco de Peñalosa, a member of Ferdinand of Aragon's chapel at the turn of the 16th century. See J. M. Hardie, *The Motets of Francisco de Peñalosa and their Manuscript Sources* (diss., U. of Michigan, 1983), chaps. 2 and 5.

[2] H. Hucke, 'Towards a New Historical View of Gregorian Chant', *JAMS*, xxxiii (1980), 464. For a similar view of the character of early chant notation see L. Treitler, 'Reading and Singing: on the Genesis of Occidental Music-writing', *EMH*, iv (1984), 135–208, and the relevant bibliography cited therein.

[3] See P. Combe, *Histoire de la restauration du chant grégorien* (Solesmes, 1968). On some earlier and some more recent 20th-century trends in chant performance see M. Berry, 'The Restoration of the Chant and Seventy-five Years of Recording', *EM*, vii (1979), 197–217. L. Brunner, 'The Performance of Plainchant', *EM*, x (1983), 317–38 deals with a few late medieval aspects of chant performance.

[4] G. Reese, *Music in the Renaissance* (New York, 1954), 1018.

[5] The 'reformed' chant books were not yet published in the lifetime of these composers. But a 16th-century observer of the papal choir remarked that they sang the chant quite differently from the way it appeared in the books, indicating that 'reform' elements were being practised before the publication of the Medicean Gradual. See B. Meier, 'Choralreform und Chorallehre im 16. Jahrhundert', *Geschichte der katholischen Kirchenmusik*, ed. K. G. Fellerer (Kassel, 1972–6), ii, 49.

[6] The chant given by Besseler for *alternatim* use in Dufay's setting is taken from a modern (Solesmes) Gradual.

[7] *Tractatus practice cantus mensurabilis ad modum ytalicorum*; for the unique copy containing this passage see W. Dalglish, 'The Origin of the Hocket', *JAMS*, xxxi (1978), 12, n.35, where the Latin text is given. Dalglish lists in this same footnote some references to rather little-known older studies on *cantus fractus*, as this rhythmicized version of chant has been called.

[8] Meier, 'Choralreform und Chorallehre', 45–53.

[9] Berry, 'The Restoration of the Chant', 99.

[10] loc. cit.

[11] See J. Marouzeau, *La prononciation du latin: histoire, théorie, pratique* (Paris, 1931, 2/1938), 9, where it is said that in the late Middle Ages and early Renaissance 'on prononce le latin bonnement à la française. On écrit, donc on dit: *per santan crusan redemisti mondon* (per sanctam crucem redemisti mundum) . . . Dans *requiescant in pace* on entend: *qui est-ce? Quantin? Passez!*'. F. W. Westaway, *Quantity and Accent in Latin* (Cambridge, 1913, 2/1930), p.ix, tells of Scaliger hearing, at Leyden in 1608, a long speech in Latin delivered by an Englishman, at the conclusion of which the distinguished listener apologized for understanding so little of the speech owing to his faulty command of English.

Italian pronunciation of Latin (today called 'Church Latin') had wide currency, and was thought by many to be closest to what the ancients had sounded like. Humanistic efforts such as those of Erasmus and Ramus at restoring ancient pronunciation apparently had little effect, and were in any event based on too little knowledge.

A survey of English, French, German, Italian and Spanish idiosyncrasies in Latin pronunciation, derived from a reading of contemporary treatments of the subject such as those of Beze,

Erasmus, Estienne, Lipsius and Tory, is given in R. W. Duffin, 'National Pronunciations of Latin, ca.1490–1600', *JM*, iv (1985–6), 217–26.

[12] Andreas Ornithoparchus, *Musice active micrologus* (Leipzig, 1517/R1977), cited from p.69 of Dowland's translation (1609) in Treitler, 'Reading and Singing', 192. On p.75 of the Dowland version there is mention of different quantities given Latin syllables in different places; on pp.79–80 some German mispronunciations of Latin vowels are singled out. The following remarks of Ornithoparchus (p.88), while instructive, should not perhaps be taken as a guide to modern singers: '. . . diverse Nations have divers fashions, and differ in habite, diet, studies, speech, and song. Hence is it, that the English doe carroll; the French sing; the Spaniards weepe, the Italians, which dwell about the Coasts of *Ianua* caper with their Voyces; the others barke: but the Germans (which I am ashamed to utter) doe howle like wolves'.

[13] See E. Higginbottom, 'Alternatim', 'Organ mass', *Grove6*.

[14] A. Banchieri, *L'organo suonarino* (Venice, 1605); there is a facsimile of this, together with the revised edition of 1611, and an *Appendice* of 1638, with an introduction by Giulio Cattin (Amsterdam, 1969). See especially the *quarto registro*, where basses (for singers and organ) and vocal sopranos are given for the *Magnificat* tones in mensural paraphrase. In the *primo registro* (p.17) there is an *alternatim* setting of *Veni sancte spiritus* with the organ bass in □ ◇ rhythms.

[15] See J. W. McKinnon, 'Performing Practice §2(i)', *Grove6*, xiv, 373. Speaking of chant in the later Middle Ages McKinnon says, 'Considering that *cantus planus* was altogether more diligently fostered than was polyphony, that it persisted for centuries, and that it survives in a vast number of carefully notated manuscripts . . . the neglect by scholars of what might be called the *seconda prattica* of plainchant is to be regretted'.

[16] On the *cantio* see K. H. Schlager, 'Cantiones', *Geschichte der katholischen Kirchenmusik*, i, 286–93. A list of cantionals (manuscript collections of *cantiones*) is given in the article 'Plainchant' in *Grove6*, xiv, 818–19.

[17] For a new view of 15th-century attitudes toward text and music see D. M. Randel, 'Dufay the Reader', *Studies in the History of Music*, i: *Music and Language* (New York, 1983), 38–78.

[18] Or perhaps the notated repertory was a polyphonic one, monophonic tunes being easily transmittable orally. For this repertory as for that of the chanson, pieces with a strongly profiled discant melody might have been sung as tunes with improvised accompaniment. In this view the 'oral' tradition might consist in part of music we know in formal polyphonic dress, performed in more informal guise. The whole question of 'popular polyphony' as a link between the monophonic and polyphonic song is one that needs more emphasis than it has until recently had.
I am here echoing the arguments of Reinhard Strohm, given in an unpublished paper, 'Towards a Reappraisal of Musical Culture in Fifteenth-century Italy', which was discussed at a symposium on 15th-century music at Princeton University in April 1985. I am grateful to Professor Strohm for allowing me to refer to his paper; I hope his views may soon pass from the 'unwritten tradition' into published form.

[19] E. Motta, 'Musici alla corte degli Sforza', *Archivio storico lombardo*, xiv (1887/R1977), 554.

[20] On this piece see N. Pirrotta, '*Ricercare* and Variations on *O Rosa Bella*' (1972), republished in his *Music and Culture in Italy from the Middle Ages to the Baroque* (Cambridge, Mass., 1984), 144–58.

[21] For some *giustiniane* present, in heavily ornamented form, in a Petrucci frottola book see below and n.33.

[22] *Guillaume Dufay: Opera omnia*, ed. H. Besseler, CMM, i/4 (1962), no.4. The 'Amen' of the related Gloria has a French chanson tune similarly embedded in the texture.

[23] G. Reese and T. Karp, 'Monophony in a Group of Renaissance Chansonniers', *JAMS*, v (1952), 4–15.

[24] H. M. Brown, 'The *Chanson rustique*: Popular Elements in the 15th- and 16th-century Chanson', *JAMS*, xii (1959), 16–26.

[25] J. Stevens, 'Carol', *Grove6*, iii, 804, and the nine monophonic pieces in the appendix of *Mediaeval Carols*, transcribed and ed. by Stevens, MB, iv (1952).

[26] See H. Brunner, 'Meistergesang', *Grove6*, xii, 73–9, an article which contains a description of sources and a list of modern editions of the repertory.

[27] An interesting study of a long-lived and internationally known tune is that of J. Wendland, ' "Madre non mi far Monaca": the Biography of a Renaissance Folksong', *AcM*, xlviii (1976), 185–204.

[28] H. M. Brown, *Music in the French Secular Theater: 1400–1550* (Cambridge, Mass., 1963), 101–5. The term refers not only to vocal ornament but to singing 'upon the book', improvising counterpoint against a chanson (?) tenor.

263

[29] For a survey of these manuals see H. M. Brown, *Embellishing Sixteenth-century Music* (Oxford, 1976).

[30] See J. Wolf, 'Die Tänze des Mittelalters: eine Untersuchung des Wesens der ältesten Instrumentalmusik', *AMw*, i (1918), 10–42, especially the *stampite* from *GB-Lbm* Add.29987 given on pp.24ff. There has been some criticism of Wolf's transcriptions; see H. Wagenaar-Nolthenius, 'Estampie / Stantipes / Stampita,' *L'ars nova italiana del trecento II: Certaldo 1969*, 399–409. The London manuscript has been published in fascimile, MSD, xiii (1965). See also G. Reaney, 'The Manuscript London, British Museum Additional 29987 (*Lo*)', *MD*, xii (1958), 67–91.

[31] A list of 15th-century sources containing keyboard music, several of them with pieces based on vocal models, is given in 'Sources of Keyboard Music to 1660', *Grove6*, xvii, 717–33. Most of the ornament in the Faenza Codex is applied to the upper voice, to which the lower part or parts are very subsidiary in the intabulator's mind. For the view that many of these 15th-century intabulations are meant for lute and harp as well as the keyboard see T. J. McGee, 'Instruments and the Faenza Codex', *EM*, xiv (1986), 480–90.

[32] Among madrigals *Appress' un fiume chiaro* and *Nascoso el bel viso* might be cited. See *The Music of Fourteenth-century Italy*, ed. N. Pirrotta, CMM, viii/1 (1954), 8, 20 (Pirrotta prints two versions of the first, three of the second piece, making their considerable variety visually clear). The monophonic ballate are found in only one source; but the variety of ornamental melisma within these pieces suggests a comparable latitude of choice on the singer's part.

[33] W. Rubsamen, 'The *Justiniane* or *Viniziane* of the Fifteenth Century', *AcM*, xxix (1957), 172–84. Rubsamen actually found a simpler version of only one of these pieces, *Aime sospiri* (in *E-E* iv.a.24); but his generalizations seem well taken. The elaboration is more constant and fussy, almost like that of an organist, than most singers would have done.

[34] Examples may be heard in Esther Lamadier's recording, *Ballate monodiques de l'Ars Nova Florentine* (Astrée AS 56). The pieces for which the singer does not supply an accompaniment of her own devising are to my ear more satisfying than those presented with instrumental support.

[35] See Brown, *Music in the French Secular Theater*, 98.

[36] See W. Salmen, 'European Song (1300–1530)', *NOHM*, iii (1960), 362–3: 'The singing was strictly monophonic, without instrumental accompaniment; in fact instrumental music of any kind was considered in bad taste, since ... *"Was thöne gont nü vs eim ror, / gar offenbor, / das achtent wise meister nit ein hor / wann gütten sang, den hörn si gern ..."* (Wise masters pay no heed to sounds from a pipe, but they gladly listen to good singing)'.

Five lieder by Hans Sachs may be heard sung unaccompanied on ARC 73222, Early Renaissance Series B: *From Oswald von Wolkenstein up to the Lochheimer Liederbuch*.

[37] On this now somewhat vexed question see C. Page, 'Machaut's "Pupil" Deschamps on the Performance of Music: Voices or Instruments in the 14th-century Chanson?', *EM*, v (1977), 484–92; R. Bowers, 'The Performing Pitch of English 15th-century Church Polyphony', *EM*, viii (1980), 21–8; and especially D. Fallows, 'Specific Information on the Ensembles for Composed Polyphony, 1410–1474', in *Performance Practice: New York 1981*, 109–59. On p.132 Fallows generalizes that 'there appears to be very little conclusive evidence for polyphonic songs having been sung as we would now expect – that is, with instruments on the untexted lower voices'; and on the same page he adds the remark that 'the central theme of this whole enquiry is the difficulty of knowing whether a particular item of evidence concerns monophonic music, perhaps with improvised accompaniment, or whether it concerns composed polyphony'.

[38] See H. M. Brown, 'Lira da braccio', *GroveMI*.

[39] On this see below, and n.44.

[40] Interest in this subject is not new. See for example R. von Liliencron, *Deutsches Leben im Volkslied um 1530* (Stuttgart, 1884); T. Gérold, *Chansons populaires des xve et xvie siècles avec leurs mélodies* (Strasbourg, 1913). Scholars in the 20th century have tended to be more cautious, identifying single pieces here and there rather than asserting confidently the existence of large amounts of Renaissance popular music. But for more general discussions and citations of Italian popular music see K. Jeppesen, 'Venetian Folk Songs of the Renaissance', *PAMS 1939*, 62–75; F. Torrefranca, *Il segreto del quattrocento* (Turin, 1939), a work full of references to pre-existent bits of poetry and music embedded in the *villotta*.

[41] See for example 'New Glimpses of an Unwritten Tradition' (1972) and 'The Oral and Written Traditions of Music' (1970), both republished in *Music and Culture*. The theme is one that runs through nearly all of Pirrotta's work on early music.

[42] See n.18 above.

[43] On Pietrobono see L. Lockwood, 'Pietrobono and the Instrumental Tradition at Ferrara in the Fifteenth Century', *RIM*, x (1975), 115–33; Lockwood, *Music in Renaissance Ferrara 1400–1505* (Oxford, 1984), chap.10, 'Pietrobono and the Improvisatory Tradition'; see especially pp.107–8, where some of Pietrobono's teaching repertory, including pieces known in polyphonic settings, is mentioned and discussed. A new treatment of the subject is that of W. F. Prizer, 'The Frottola and the Unwritten Tradition', *Studi musicali*, xv (1986), 3–37.

[44] Cf the view of M. Bent, '*Resfacta* and *Cantare super librum*', *JAMS*, xxxvi (1983), 371–91, especially 377ff. Bent is speaking of unwritten counterpoint, not the oral tradition in general, but her argument is none the less of relevance here.

[45] There is a fairly large but mostly scattered and in general rather old literature on this subject. A useful article is that of E. Haraszti, 'La technique des improvisateurs de langue vulgaire et de latin au quattrocento', *RBM*, ix (1955), 12–31. For a study of a single figure see Lockwood, 'Pietrobono'. A more general approach may be seen in J. Haar, *Essays on Italian Poetry and Music 1350–1600* (Berkeley, 1986), chap.4, '*Improvvisatori* and their Relationship to 16th-century Music'.

[46] See his '*Ricercare* and Variations on *O Rosa Bella*' (1972), republished in *Music and Culture*, 144–58, especially 146–8.

[47] See n.19 above.

[48] Antonio Cornazano's enthusiastic account of Pietrobono's music, contained in Canto VIII of his *Sforziade* (1459), is cited and commented on by Pirrotta, 'Music and Cultural Tendencies in 15th-century Italy' (1966), reprinted in *Music and Culture*, 80–112; see especially 89–91, 93–6.

[49] See Haraszti, 'La technique', 28, quoting Serafino's contemporary biographer Vincenzo Calmeta, who says that the musician modelled his efforts on those of other performers, 'vedendo molti sonatori e cantori che la forza del recitare più che del comporre li haveva dato fame'.

[50] C. Gallico, *Un libro di poesia per musica dell'epoca d'Isabella d'Este* (Mantua, 1961), especially 14–15, and musical examples 1, 4–7.

[51] Much of the secular repertory printed by Petrucci might be treated with a certain amount of freedom in performance, although the books themselves must on occasion have been read from and hence their contents performed fairly literally. The intabulations for voice and lute of Petrucci frottole made by Francesco Bossinensis are quite literal arrangements; but their function may have been in part to provide a framework for more flexible use.

[52] *The Bottegari Lutebook*, ed. C. MacClintock, WE, viii (1965). The *aria di sonetti* (no.62, f.24*v*) in Bottegari's book could be treated in much the same way as ex.3 above. H. M. Brown, 'The Geography of Florentine Monody: Caccini at Home and Abroad', *EM*, ix (1981), 147–68, gives a discussion of a Neapolitan print assembled by Rocco Rodi, *Aeri racolti ... dove si cantano Sonetti, Stanze & Terze Rime* (1577). Brown's article also contains a useful discussion of the formulaic nature of *arie* and of the kind of ornament that performers routinely added to them.

[53] MacClintock, 'Bottegari, Cosimo', *Grove6*.

[54] See the articles on 'Folia', 'Passamezzo', 'Romanesca' and 'Ruggiero' by Richard Hudson in *Grove6*, as well as those by John Ward in *MGG*. The notion that at least some of these patterns were considered soprano tunes is indicated by titles such as Sigismondo d'India's setting of a Rinuccini text 'Sopra il basso della romanesca', *Musiche di Sigismondo d'India* (Milan, 1609), 26.

[55] G. Zarlino, *Le istitutioni harmoniche* (Venice, 1558/R1965), bk3, chap.79: 'un certo Modo, overo Aria, che lo vogliamo dire, di cantare; si come sono quelli modi di cantare, sopra i quali cantiamo al presente li Sonetti, o Canzoni del Petrarca, overamente le Rime dell' Ariosto'.

[56] See J. Haar, 'Arie per cantar stanze ariostesche', *L'Ariosto: la musica, i musicisti*, ed. M. A. Balsano (Florence, 1981), 31–46, and the list of 16th-century settings of stanzas from *Orlando Furioso* by Haar and Balsano in the same volume, pp.47–78.

[57] Two stanzas, 'Se christianissimi esser voi volete' and 'Ma tu gran padre' (pp.64–5 in the print) are Ariostan in theme but not found in the poem itself; they may represent earlier or alternate versions of material recast by the poet. The last madrigal, *O s'io potessi donna*, is not an Ariostan text. It was included, says the print, 'A requisitione d'uno amico'.

[58] These are not included in Emil Vogel's entry for the print (*Bibliothek der gedruckten weltlichen Vocalmusik Italiens aus den Jahren 1500–1700*, Berlin, 1892/R1962, i, 86); nor do they appear in *Il Nuovo Vogel*, ed. F. Lesure and C. Sartori (Pomezia, 1977), i, 201–3. The information about texts contained in n.51 above is not given in the *Nuovo Vogel*.

[59] For examples see Haar, 'Arie per cantar', and *Essays on Italian Poetry and Music*, chap.4, exx.24–34; these are only a sampling of what may be found in the repertory of the madrigal up to about 1560.

[60] For example, in the first 15 madrigals in Berchem's *Capriccio*, the melody of ex.4*d* is clearly

cited in four pieces in the cantus part alone. Ex.4c, of which Berchem was particularly fond, appears eight times; ex.4b is cited six times, ex.4a three or possibly four times. For other citations of ex.4d see Haar, 'Arie per cantar'.

[61] Enríquez de Valderrábano, *Libro de música de vihuela, intitulado Silva de sirenas* (Valladolid, 1547), ed. E. Pujol, MME, xxi (1965), 28 (music section). The piece is called 'soneto'; on the meaning of the term in this context see Pujol on p.28 (text section) of the volume cited above.

[62] The 'Rugier glosado de Antonio' in Venegas de Henestrosa's *Libro de cifra nueva* (Alcatá de Henares, 1557), ed. H. Anglés, MME, ii (1944), 190, is given at the usual pitch, starting on the fifth degree of the melody's scale.

[63] Zarlino, *Le istitutioni harmoniche*, bk3, chap.26.

[64] For examples see *Italian Sacred Music*, ed. K. von Fischer, PMFC, xii (1976), nos.2, 10, 11, 21, 45.

[65] F. A. Gallo, ' "Cantus planus binatim": polifonia primitiva in fonti tardive', *Quadrivium*, vii (1966), 79–89. The citations from Prosdocimus and Tinctoris are on pp.79–80.

[66] R. Strohm, 'Neue Quellen zur liturgischen Mehrstimmigkeit des Mittelalters in Italien', *RIM*, i (1966), 77–87. On 'primitive' polyphony in Germany during the late Middle Ages and Renaissance see A. Geering, *Die Organa und mehrstimmigen Conductus in den Handschriften des deutschen Sprachgebietes von 13. bis 16. Jahrhundert* (Berne, 1952).

[67] See B. Trowell, 'Sight, sighting', *Grove6*; Trowell, 'Faburden and Fauxbourdon', *MD*, xiii (1959), 43–78. The vexed question of interpretation of the English theorists cannot be gone into here.

[68] C. Wright, 'Performance Practices at the Cathedral of Cambrai, 1475–1550', *MQ*, lxiv (1978), 295–328, especially 313ff.

[69] J. Tinctoris, *Liber de arte contrapuncti* (1477), bk2, p.xx.

[70] Bent, '*Resfacta* and *Cantare super librum*', *passim*.

[71] Lodovico Zacconi, *Prattica di musica, seconda parte* (Venice, 1622/R1967), iii, chap.35, p.163; cited in E. Ferand, 'Improvised Vocal Counterpoint in the Late Renaissance and Early Baroque', *AnnM*, iv (1956), 165.

[72] Bent, '*Resfacta* and *Cantare super librum*', 389–90; the author also suggests that families of pieces such as multiple versions of well-known chansons may have their origin in this practice.

[73] For example, Palestrina added a fourth voice to a three-voice hymn setting by Festa. See L. Feininger, 'The Music Manuscripts in the Vatican', *Notes*, 2nd ser., iii (1946), 394.

[74] J. Thuringus, *Opusculum bipartitum de primordiis musicis* (Berlin, 1624, 2/1625), 18; cited in Ferand, 'Improvised Vocal Counterpoint', 134–5 and also in the same author's *Die Improvisation in Beispielen aus neun Jahrhunderten abendländischer Musik* (Cologne, 1956), 9. On *sortisatio* see Howard Mayer Brown's article in *Grove6*, and the bibliography cited there.

[75] 'Improvised Vocal Counterpoint', 135.

[76] T. Morley, *A Plaine and Easie Introduction to Practicall Musicke* (1597), ed. R. A. Harman (London, 1952), 206.

[77] A long list of treatises in which the subject is at least mentioned is given in Ferand, 'Improvised Vocal Counterpoint', 143–4.

[78] J. Haar, 'The "Libro Primo" of Costanzo Festa', *AcM*, lii (1980), 153n.

[79] *The Lyons Contrapunctus (1528)*, ed. D. A. Sutherland (Madison, Wisc., 1976). See vol.i, p.xiv, for references to other volumes (manuscript) of the same nature.

[80] Corteccia's cycle of Mass Propers is noticeably less imitative, more a series of counterpoints to chant, than is his normal style. See Sutherland, *The Lyons Contrapunctus*, vol.i, pp.xiv–xv.

[81] Zacconi, *Prattica di musica, seconda parte*, nearly all devoted to *contraponto alla mente*.

Bibliography of Sources to 1600

*Treatises from before 1500
that include information about performance practice*

Information about performance practice in the Middle Ages is apt to appear in a wide variety of scattered sources, archival, literary and iconographical, as well as theoretical. Many general musical treatises, for example, include at least one or two passing remarks that illuminate some aspect of performance. The following list, organized chronologically, cites only those treatises that deal extensively with matters of performance, and especially with musical instruments. The number of books written about instruments and other matters of performance increased enormously shortly after 1500, a date that therefore stands as a natural dividing line in our knowledge of the performing conventions of the Middle Ages and the Renaissance.

This list omits certain categories of books. It does not include, for example, treatises on the measurements of organ pipes, bells, monochords or *organistra*, since in the Middle Ages these tended to be theoretical studies of tuning systems rather than practical manuals of instruction. Lists of those treatises can be found in the following works:

J. Smits van Waesberghe, *Cymbala: Bells in the Middle Ages*, MSD, i (1951)
J. Smits van Waesberghe, *De musico-paedagogico et theoretico Guidone Aretino eiusque vita et moribus* (Florence, 1953)
K.-J. Sachs, *Mensura fistularum: die Mensurierung der Orgelpfeifen im Mittelalter* (Stuttgart, 1970–80)
J. Smits van Waesberghe, 'Organistrum, Symphonia, Drehleier', *HMT*

Many medieval biblical commentaries and the works of the Church Fathers include information about musical instruments, albeit much of it without relevance to contemporary practices. For a survey of this material, see J. W. McKinnon, *The Church Fathers and Musical Instruments* (diss., Columbia U., 1965), and two articles derived from his dissertation, 'The Meaning of Patristic Polemic against Musical Instruments', *CMc*, i (1965), 69–82, and 'Musical Instruments in Medieval Psalm Commentaries and Psalters', *JAMS*, xxi (1968), 3–30. The useful list of references to medieval stringed instruments in C. Page, *Voices and Instruments of the Middle Ages* (London, 1987), 160–209, includes verse narratives, lyric poetry, treatises on the vices and virtues, and various other kinds of prose works, as well as musical theorists. Excerpts from various kinds of documents relevant to the study of performance practice are given in English translation in C. MacClintock, *Readings in the History of Music in Performance* (Bloomington, 1979).

Pseudo-Jerome, *De diversis generibus musicorum* (Epistle to Dardanus) (9th century). For the text and commentary, see R. Hammerstein, 'Instrumenta Hieronymi', *AMw*, xvi (1959), 117–34; for the text, and a translation into German, see H. Avenary, 'Hieronymus' Epistel über die Musikinstrumente und ihre altöstlichen Quellen', *AnM*, xvi (1961), 55–80

267

Bartholomeus Anglicus, *De proprietatibus rerum* (*c*1250). For the section on instruments, see H. Müller, 'Der Musiktraktat in dem Werke des Bartholomaeus Anglicus De Proprietatibus Rerum', in *Riemann-Festschrift* (Leipzig, 1909), 241–55

Egidius de Zamora, *Ars musica* (*c*1270), ed. and Fr. trans. R. Tissot, CSM, xx (1974)

Elias Salomo, *Scientia artis musicae* (1274), in *GS*, iii, 16–64

Jerome of Moravia, *Tractatus de musica* (*c*1300), ed. S. M. Cserba (Regensburg, 1935). The section on instruments is translated into Italian in A. Puccianti, 'La descrizione della *Viella* e della *Rubeba* in Girolamo di Moravia', *CHM*, iv (1966), 227–37, and into English in C. Page, 'Jerome of Moravia on the *Rubeba* and *Viella*', *GSJ*, xxxii (1979), 77–98. An excerpt is also given in English translation in MacClintock, *Readings*, 3–7

Johannes de Grocheo, [*De musica*] (1300), ed. and Ger. trans. E. Rohloff, *Der Musiktraktat des Johannes de Grocheo* (Leipzig, 1943), and, with facsimiles of the two principal sources, in E. Rohloff, *Die Quellenhandschriften zum Musiktraktat des Johannes de Grocheio im Faksimile herausgegeben nebst Übertragung des Textes und Übersetzung ins Deutsche, dazu Bericht, Literaturschau, Tabellen und Indices* (Leipzig, 1967); Eng. trans. A. Seay (Colorado Springs, 1967, 2/1973)

Berkeley, University of California Music Library, MS 744 (*olim* Phillipps 4450) (*c*1375), ed. and trans. O. B. Ellsworth, *The Berkeley Manuscript* (Lincoln, Nebraska, and London, 1984). The section on instruments has also been translated into English in C. Page, 'Fourteenth-century Instruments and Tunings: a Treatise by Jean Vaillant? (Berkeley, MS 744)', *GSJ*, xxxiii (1980), 17–35

Eustache Deschamps, *Art de dictier et de fere chançons* (1392), in *Oeuvres complètes d'Eustache Deschamps*, ed. Le Marquis de Queux de Saint-Hilaire and G. Raynaud (Paris, 1878–1903), vii, 266–92

Jean de Gerson, *Tractatus de canticis* (*c*1430). The section on instruments is reproduced and translated in C. Page, 'Early 15th-century Instruments in Jean de Gerson's "Tractatus de Canticis"', *ÉM*, vi (1978), 339–49

Henri Arnault de Zwolle, [*Treatises on musical instruments*] (*c*1450), facs. edn. with transcription and commentary in G. le Cerf and E. R. Labande, *Les traités d'Henri-Arnaut de Zwolle et de divers anonymes (Paris: Bibliothèque nationale, ms. Latin 7295)* (Paris, 1932; repr. with an afterword by F. Lesure, Kassel and Basle, 1972)

Paulirinus of Prague, *Liber viginti artium* (*c*1460). The section on instruments is ed. in J. Reiss, 'Pauli Paulirini de Praga Tractatus de Musica (etwa 1460)', *ZMw*, vii (1925), 259–64. For an English translation and commentary, see S. Howell, 'Paulirinus of Prague on Musical Instruments', *JAMIS*, v–vi (1979–80), 9–36

Conrad von Zabern, *De modo bene cantandi choralem cantum* (1474). Ed. K.-W. Gümpel, *Die Musiktraktate Conrads von Zabern* (Mainz, 1956). For a partial English translation and commentary, see J. Dyer, 'Singing with Proper Refinement', *ÉM*, vi (1978), 207–27. An excerpt in English translation is also given in MacClintock, *Readings*, 12–16

Cambridge, Trinity College, MS 0.2.13, [Rules] To sette a lute (*c*1493–1509). This brief note is reproduced in J. Handschin, 'Aus der alten Musiktheorie: V. Zur Instrumentenkunde', *AcM*, xvi–xvii (1944–5), 3, and in C. Page, 'The 15th-century Lute: New and Neglected Sources', *ÉM*, ix (1981), 13–14

Johannes Tinctoris, *De inventione et usu musicae*, in *Johannes Tinctoris und sein unbekannter Traktat*, ed. K. Weinmann (Tutzing, 1961); partial English translation in A. Baines, 'Fifteenth-century Instruments in Tinctoris' *De inventione et usu musicae*', *GSJ*, iii (1950), 19–26. On newly discovered fragments of the treatise, see R. Woodley, 'The Printing and Scope of Tinctoris's Fragmentary Treatise *De inventione et usu musicae*', *EMH*, v (1985), 239–68

Bartholomeo Ramos de Pereia, *Musica practica* (1482), ed. J. Wolf (Leipzig, 1901/R1968). For a translation of the passage on instruments, see S. Howell, 'Ramos de Pareja's "Brief Discourse of Various Instruments"', *JAMIS*, xi (1985), 14–37

Sixteenth-century treatises that include information about performance practice

Writers of theoretical treatises in the 15th and 16th centuries, like those of earlier centuries, are apt to make passing remarks about contemporary practice. The following list includes only the most important works that deal extensively with performance. Much useful information about the techniques of particular instruments can be gained from prefaces and introductions to the various instruction books and anthologies published during the 16th century. Further information can be found about them in *BrownI*. These volumes (identified by their numbers in *BrownI*) give information about the following instruments:

Bandora: Barley (1596[6])
Cittern: Le Roy (1564[5], 1565[3]); Vreedman (1568[6]); Phalèse (1570[3]); Kargel (1575[3], 1578[4])
Guitar: Le Roy (1551[3]); Phalèse (1570[4])
Harp: Cabezon (1578[2]); Henestrosa (1557[2]); Mudarra (1546[14])
Keyboard (both harpsichord and organ): Schlick (1511/12); Santa María (1565); Ammerbach (1571[1], 1575[1]); Valente (1576[3]); Schmid (1577[6]); Cabezón (1578[3]); Diruta (1593)
Lute: Petrucci 1507; Judenkünig (151?[1], 1523[2]); Attaingnant Tres breve (1529[3]); Oronce Finé (1530[2]); Gerle (1532[2], 1552[1]); Newsidler (1536[6]; 1540[1], 1544[1], 1547[4], 1549[6]); Barberiis (1546[2]); Francesco da Milano and Pietro Paolo Borrono (1546[8], 1547[3], 1548[3]); Giovanni Maria Crema (1546[11]); Pierre Phalèse (1547[7] and 1547[8]); Wyssenbach (1550[4], 1563[10]); Albert de Rippe (1553[9]); Lieto (1559[5]); Paladin (1560[3]); Wolff Heckel (1562[3] and 1562[4]); Galilei (1568[2]); Le Roy (1568[3]); Jobin (1572[1]); Le Roy (1574[2]); Carrara (1585[5]); Adriansen (1592[6]); Waissel (1592[12]); Barley (1596)
Orpharion: Barley (1596[5])
Recorder: Ganassi (1535)
Vihuela: Luis Milan (1536[5]); Narváez (1538[1]); Mudarra (and harp) (1546[14]); Valderrábano (1547[5]); Pisador (1552[7]); Fuenllana (1554[3]); Daza (1576[1])
Viola da gamba: Ganassi (1542 and 1543); Ortiz (1552[3] and 1553[6])

Sebastian Virdung, *Musica getutscht und aussgezogen* (Basle, 1511). Facs. and ed. by L. Schrade (Kassel, 1931), by K. W. Niemöller (Kassel and Basle, 1970), and in PÄMw, ed. R. Eitner, vol.xi (1894). The treatise was translated into French as *Livre plaisant et tresutile pour apprendre a faire & ordonner toutes tabulatures hors le discant* (Antwerp, 1529), into Latin as Ottomar Luscinius, *Musurgia seu praxis Musicae* (Strasbourg, 1536), and into Flemish as Jan van Ghelen, *Dit is een zeer schoon Boecxken om te leeren maken alderhande tabulatueren wten Discante* (n.p., 1554/R1568)
Johannes Cochlaeus, *Tetrachordum musices* (Nuremberg, 1511). Eng. trans., C. A. Miller, MSD, xxiii (1970)
Zurich, Zentralbibliothek, MS 284: Hans Buchner, [*Fundamentbuch*] (c1520). Ed. C. Paesler, 'Fundamentbuch von Hans von Constanz', VMw, v (1889), 1–192
Martin Agricola, *Musica instrumentalis deudsch* (1529, rev. 2/1545). Modern edition in quasi-facsimile in PÄMw, ed. R. Eitner, vol.xx (1896). Partial English translation in W. E. Hettrick, 'Martin Agricola's Poetic Discussion of the Recorder and Other Woodwind Instruments', *The American Recorder*, xxi (1980), 103–13, and xxiv (1983), 51–60
Hans Gerle, *Musica teusch, auf die Instrument der grossen und kleinen Geygen, auch Lautten, welcher massen die mit grundt und art irer Composicion auss dem gesang in die Tabulatur zu ordnen und zu setzen ist* (Nuremberg, 1532), rev. and enlarged as *Musica und Tabulatur auff die Instrument der kleinen und grossen Geygen auch Lautten* (Nuremberg, 1546/R1977)

Bibliography of Sources to 1600

Giovanni Lanfranco, *Scintille di musica* (Brescia, 1533/*R*1969). Eng. trans., B. Lee, *Giovanni Maria Lanfranco's 'Scintille di Musica' and its Relation to 16th-century Music Theory* (diss., Cornell U., 1961)

Silvestro di Ganassi, *Opera intitulata Fontegara* (Venice, 1535/*R*1934, 1970). Ger. trans. H. Peter (Berlin-Lichterfelde, 1956). Eng. trans. H. Peter and D. Swainson (Berlin-Lichterfelde, 1959)

Silvestro di Ganassi, *Regola rubertina* (Venice, 1542–3/*R*1970). Ger. trans. H. Peter (Berlin-Lichterfelde, 1972), and also by W. Eggers (Kassel and Basle, 1974). Eng. trans. H. Peter and D. and S. Silvester (Berlin-Lichterfelde, 1977), and also by R. D. Bodig in *Journal of the Viola da Gamba Society of America*, xviii (1981), 13–66 and xix (1982), 99–163

Jerome Cardan, *De musica* (*c*1546), and other works. Eng. trans. in Cardan, *Writings on Music*, ed. and trans. C. A. Miller, MSD, xxxii (1973)

Heinrich Glareanus, *Dodecachordon* (Basle, 1547/*R*1969). Eng. trans. C. A. Miller, MSD, vi (1965)

Diego Ortiz, *Tratado de glosas sobre clausulas* (Rome, 1553). Ed. and Ger. trans. M. Schneider (Kassel, 1936; 3/1961). Eng. trans. P. Farrell in *Journal of the Viola da Gamba Society*, iv (1967), 5–9

Juan Bermudo, *El libro llamado declaracion de instrumentos musicales* (Ossuna, 1555/*R*1957)

Hermann Finck, *Practica musica* (Wittenberg, 1556/*R*1972). The chapter on singing is published in a German translation in R. Schlecht, 'Hermann Finck über die Kunst des Singens, 1556', *MMg*, xi (1879), 129–33, 135–41

Philibert Jambe de Fer, *Epitome musical des tons, sons et accords, es voix humaines, fleustes d'alleman, Fleustes a neuf trous, Violes, & Violons* (Lyons, 1556). Facs. ed. in F. Lesure, 'L'Epitome musical de Philibert Jambe de Fer (1556)', *AnnM*, vi (1958–63), 341–86

Discours non plus melancoliques que divers, de choses mesmement qui appartiennent a nostre France, et a la fin la maniere de bien et justement entoucher les lucs et guiternes (Poitiers, 1557)

Giovanni Camillo Maffei, *Delle lettere ... libri due* (Naples, 1562). The letter on singing is pubd. in N. Bridgman, 'Giovanni Camillo Maffei et sa lettre sur le chant', *RdM*, xxxviii (1956), 3–34

Claudio Sebastiani, *Bellum musicale inter plani et mensuralis cantus reges* (Strasbourg, 1563)

Tomás de Santa María, *Libro llamado arte de tañer fantasia* (Valladolid, 1565/*R*1972). Partial German translation by E. Harich-Schneider and R. Boadella (Lippstadt, 2/1962)

Adrian le Roy, *Les instructions pour le luth (1574)*, ed. J. Jacquot, P.-Y. Sordes and J.-M. Vaccaro (Paris, 1977)

Girolamo dalla Casa, *Il vero modo di diminuir* (Venice, 1584/*R*1970)

Vincenzo Galilei, *Fronimo ... sopra l'arte di bene intavolare* (Venice, 2/1584, *R*1978). Eng. trans. C. MacClintock, MSD, xxxix (1985)

Giovanni Bassano, *Ricercare, passaggi et cadentie* (Venice, 1585)

Thoinot Arbeau, *Orchésographie, et traicté en forme de dialogue, par lequel toutes personnes peuvent facilement apprendre et practiquer l'honneste exercice des danses* (Lengres, 1589, 2/1596). Ed. L. Fonta (Paris, 1888). Eng. trans. C. W. Beaumont (London, 1925) and M. S. Evans (New York, 1948)

Samuel Mareschall, *Porta musices, das ist Eynführung zu der edlen Kunst Musica, mit einem kurtzen Bericht und Anleitung zu den Violen, auch wie ein jeder Gesang leichtlich anzustimmen seye* (Basle, 1589)

Giovanni Bassano, *Motetti, madrigali et canzoni francese ... diminuiti* (Venice, 1591). The lost printed volume and a surviving manuscript copy are described in E. T. Ferand, 'Die Motetti, Madrigali, et Canzoni Francese ... Diminuiti ... des Giovanni Bassano (1591)', in *Festschrift Helmuth Osthoff zum 65. Geburtstage* (Tutzing, 1961), 75–101

Ricardo Rognono, *Passaggi per potersi essercitare nel diminuire* (Venice, 1592)

Lodovico Zacconi, *Prattica di musica* (Venice, 1592–1622/*R*1967)

Giovanni Luca Conforto, *Breve et facile maniera d'essercitarsi ad ogni scolaro ... a far passaggi* (Rome, 1593 or 1603?/*R*1922)

Girolamo Diruta, *Il Transilvano* (Venice, 1593–1609/*R*1979, 1983)

Ercole Bottrigari, *Il desiderio* (Venice, 1594/*R*1924, 1979). Eng. trans. C. MacClintock, MSD, ix (1962)

Giovanni Battista Bovicelli, *Regole, passaggi di musica, madrigali e motetti passeggiati* (Venice, 1594/*R*1957)

Aurelio Virgiliano, *Il dolcimelo* (*c*1600). Facs. of the manuscript in Bologna, Civico museo bibliografico musicale by M. Castellani (Florence, 1979)

Scipione Cerreto, *Della prattica musica vocale et strumentale* (Naples, 1601, 2/1611, *R*1979)

Pietro Cerone, *El melopeo y maestro* (Naples, 1613/*R*1979)

Michael Praetorius, *Syntagma musicum* (Wolfenbüttel, 1614–18/*R*1958–9). Part of vol.ii is translated into English by H. Blumenfeld (New York, 2/1962) and D. Z. Crookes (Oxford, 1986). Eng. trans. of vol.iii by H. Lampl (diss., U. of Southern California, 1957)

Marin Mersenne, *Harmonie universelle* (Paris, 1636–7/*R*1963 with introduction by F. Lesure). Eng. trans. of the books on instruments by R. E. Chapman (The Hague, 1957)

Pierre Trichet, [*Traité des instruments de musique*] (*c*1630–40). Large excerpts appear in F. Lesure, 'Le traité des instruments de musique de Pierre Trichet', *AnnM*, iii (1955), 283–7, and iv (1956), 175–248, and *GSJ*, xv (1962), 70–81, and xvi (1963), 73–84

Oxford, Christ Church Library, MS 1187: James Talbot's manuscript (*c*1680). Sections transcribed and explained in *GSJ*, i (1948), 9–26; iii (1950), 27–45; v (1952), 44–7; xiv (1961), 52–68; xv (1962), 60–69; and xvi (1963), 63–72

Index

Index

Burmeister, Joachim, 190
Busnois, Antoine, 139
Byrd, William, 140

Cabezón, Antonio de, 171; *Obras de musica*, 238 n.42
caccia, 98
Caccini, Giulio (*Nuove musiche*), 234, 235
cadences: addition of *ficta* to, 116–18, 124 n.65; tuning at, 80, 81–2
Calmeta, Vincenzo, 265 n.49
Cambrai, Cathedral, 148, 157, 180, 188, 189, 191, 207, 259
cammer-thon, 190; *see also* pitch
Can Grande della Scala, court of, 32 n.5
canon, 118–19, 196
canso, 69
cantare super librum, 50, 258–62
cantastorie, 248–9, 252, 255, 256
Canterbury, Cathedral, 193
Cantigas de Santa Maria, 17, 27, 56
cantimbanco, 252
cantio, 247
cantiones, 128
cantus, 94
cantus coronatus, 128–9
cantus firmus: improvising over, 50, 152, 196, 258; performance of, 29, 151, 158, 191, 199 n.23, 199 n.28
cantus fractus, 128
cantus planus, 48, 128, 130, 141 n.1 6
cantus planus binatim, 258
cantus prius factus, 258
canzona, 186, 231
canzona alla napolitana, 252
Cappello, Bianco, 226
Carmina burana, 55
carol (English), 249
caroles, 5, 103 n.61
Castiglione, Baldassare, 232
castrato, 188, 189, 190, 233, 235
causa necessitatis, 114
causa pulchritudinis, 116
Cavazzoni, Marcantonio, *Plus ne regres*, 186
cent, 80, 81, 83
Cerone, Pietro, 190
ceterare, 23
chanson de geste, 90, 99
chanson musicale, 249
chanson rustique, 249
chant books, 38, 49, 50, 51, 52, 262 n.5
Chapel Royal, 188
Charles V, 188
Charles the Bold, 188, 207
Charles d'Orléans, 214, 220 n.61
chekker, 180 n.5, 206
chitarre, 23
chitarrone, 169, 176
choirboys: instruction of, 149, 157, 187; use of, 150, 157, 187–90, 210, 219 n.36

chor-thon, 190; *see also* pitch
Christine de Pizan, 214
Ciconia, Johannes, 217 n.22
Cistercians, 49
cithara, 23, 25
citole, 17, 27, 31, 170
cittern, 156, 169, 175
civic music, 159–60, 225–6
clausula, 87, 90, 130, 142 n.28
clavichord, 18, 28, 31, 167, 169, 171
clavicytherium, 173
claviorgan, 173
Coclico, Adrianus Petit, 123 n.51, 195, 236
Cologne, 46
coloration, 139
commedia dell'arte, 223–5, 228, 239 n.64
Commemoratio brevis, 44, 45–6, 128
communion, 129
Compère, Loyset, *Ave Maria* 186; *Missa 'L'homme armé'*, 186
concerto di donne, 238 n.41, 239 n.70
conductus: monophonic, 49, 128–9; polyphonic, 84–92 *passim*, 101 n.17, 128, 130, 142 n.28
Conforto, Giovanni Luca, 233, 234, 235, 238 n.56
consort, 25, 154, 156, 169, 177
Constance: Cathedral, 192; Council of, 187, 216 n.16
contrafacta, 186, 195, 198 n.4, 249, 257–8
contrapunctus, 73
contrapunctus fractus, 259–60
Contrapunctus seu figurata musica super plano canto missarum solennium totius anni, 261
contratenor (part-name), 94, 97–8, 99, 203, 204, 208, 210
contratenor (voice), 187
copula, 86, 87, 130, 141 n.23
Cordier, Baude, 99, 207
cornett, 151, 154, 158, 169, 176, 195, 203–4, 226, 229, 231, 237 n.16
Corteccia, Francesco, Mass Propers, 266 n.80
counterpoint, improvised, 50, 196, 259–62; addition of *ficta* to, 113–16
court musicians, 157–9
Credo, 49, 129, 249
cross relations, 115–16
crowd, 25
crwth, *see* crowd
crumhorn, 169, 177
currentes, 130
cymbala, 102 n.50
cymbals, 178

Da laudis homo, nova cantica, 66
dance: during the liturgy, 40, 53 n.4; instruments accompanying, 29, 31, 154, 158, 175, 176, 177, 204; music, 5, 56, 73, 74–5, 90, 93, 225, 250

273

Index

Index

Solesmes method, 38, 50–51, 54 n.33, 240, 246
solmization, 191
solus tenor, 254
song repertory, 201–3, 206–7
sonnet, 253–5
soprano (voice), 187, 188, 189, 190, 233–4
Spataro, Giovanni, 121 n.13, 121 n.18, 139
Sponsus, 41–2
Spruche, 56, 67
stantipes, 129
Stocker, Gaspar, 149, 190
strambotto, 212, 248, 253
Striggio, Alessandro, Fourth Book of Madrigals, 226
string technology, 178, 184 n.53
Summa musicae, 100 n.11
superius, 250
syntax, 213, 214

tablature, 154, 209, 212, 229, 231, 237 n.37
tabor, 31
tabourineur, 158
tactus, 87, 127, 133, 134–5, 142 n.54, 155
Talbot, James, 168
tambourine, 31, 178
Tasso, Torquato, *Gerusalemme liberata*, 225, 226
Te Deum, 193
temperament, *see* tuning
tempo, 44, 49, 86, 88, 126–34, 155, 210, 225, 235
tempus: 131–40 *passim*, 141 n.4; *tempus diminutum*, 134–8 *passim*, 142 n.54
tenor (voice), 187, 188, 189, 234
tenor (part-name), 27, 86–7, 88, 92, 98, 122 n.32, 130, 186, 192, 203, 204, 208, 210, 249, 254
tenorista, 248, 251
Terzi, Giovanni, Antonio, 164 n.35
text and text setting: 65–7, 98, 147–9, 190–91, 197, 204, 209–12, 219 n.39, 225; *see also* singers and singing, vocalization
theatre, 223–5
theorbo, 169, 176
Thuringus, Joachim, 259
timbre, 257
time, 132–3
Tinctoris, Johannes, 25, 115, 122 n.32, 135, 138, 139, 140, 167–8, 176, 186, 219 n.33, 258–61; *De inventione et usu musicae*, 35 n.42, 167; *Liber de arte contrapuncti*, 123 n.47; *Liber de natura*, 122 n.23
Trabaci, Giovanni Maria, 238 n.42
Tractatus de contrapuncto (Berkeley treatise), 8
transposition, 111–12, 122 n.26, 156, 173, 178, 192
Trent, council of, 49, 186, 190
Trez dolz et loyauls amis, 93

triangle, 178
Trichet, Pierre, 168
Tridentine reforms, 241, 246, 262 n.5
triplum, 86, 94
Troiano, Massimo: *Dialoghi*, 223–5; *Discorsi delli triumphi*, 228
tromba marina, 173
trombetta, 203
trombone, 151, 169, 176, 226, 229, 231, 237 n.16
troubadour and trouvère chanson, 3, 5, 21, 55–75 *passim*, 90
trumpet, 17, 29, 31, 151, 157, 158, 169, 176, 177, 193, 203, 216 n.16, 225, 228–9, 237 n.16
tuning, 7–8, 24, 25, 33 n.19, 44, 79–84, 155–6, 219 n.30; *see also* Pythagorean intonation

Ugolino of Orvieto (*Declaratio musicae disciplinae*), 121 n.20, 122 n.26

Valderrábano, Enrique de, 257
valets de chambre, 158, 207
Vanneo, Staphano, *Recanetum de musica aurea*, 120 n.8
Vecchi, Orazio, 223–5
Veni sancte spiritus, 48, 241–6
Venice, 149, 150, 161, 193, 195–6, 228, 248, 252–3
Verdelot, Philippe, 150, 226, 237 n.37
Verona, 192, 193
Verovio, Simone, 229
verse-drama, 41–2
vers, 56, 58, 69, 73
versus, 48–9
vibrato, 44, 84, 88, 195
Vicentino, 189, 196, 198, 233, 236
Victoria, Tomas Luis de, *Veni sancte spiritus*, 241–6
Vide, *Vit encore ce Faux Dangier*, 221 n.62
viella, 23, 206, 217 n.20
vihuela, 140, 169, 171, 175, 180, 238 n.42, 257
villancico, 251
villanesca, 223
Villani, Filippo, 15
villota, 249
viol, 153, 154, 156, 168, 169, 175, 178, 190, 229, 231, 238 n.45, 251, 254
viola bastarda, 175
viola da gamba, 156, 169, 173–5
violin, 157, 158, 168, 169, 173–5, 229
Virdung, Sebastian, *Musica getutscht*, 168
virelai, 58, 83, 93, 202, 212, 219–20 n.45
virginal, 18, 28, 31, 169, 171, 173
Visitatio sepulchri, 41
vivola, 217–18 n.22
vocalization, 39, 98, 191, 199 n.23, 210
Vocem iocunditatis, 47

280

Index

Walter of Odington (*Summa de speculatione musicae*), 83
Wert, Giaches de, 225, 226
Willaert, Adriano, 115, 149, 150, 161, 229, 237 n.37; *Musica nova*, 226; *Quid non ebrietas*, 110; *Veni sancte spiritus*, 241–2, 243
whistle flute, 23, 29, 176
wind band, 151, 158, 159, 160, 169, 176, 179, 193, 194, 223, 231
Wolkenstein, Oswald von. 58
women, 150, 151, 159, 177, 189, 210, 219 n.36, 231, 233

xylophone, 178

Zabern, Conrad von (*De modo bene cantandi*), 44, 199 n.18
Zacara, 217 n.22
Zacconi, Lodovico (*Prattica di musica*), 168, 189, 235–6, 261
Zarlino, Gioseffo (*Le istitutione harmoniche*), 115, 119, 149, 162 n.9, 189, 190, 195–6, 255, 258
Zenobi, Luigi, 229
Zwolle, Henri Arnaut de, 167–8, 171, 180 n.5

281